PLAYED OUT

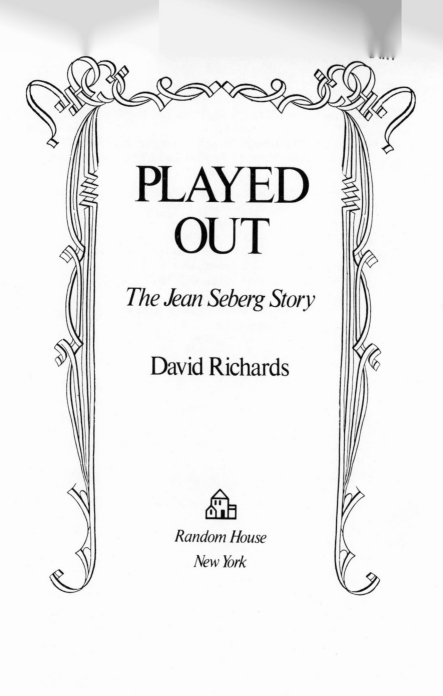

PLAYED OUT

OUT

The Jean Seberg Story

David Richards

Random House
New York

Published in the United States by Random House, Inc., New York,
and simultaneously in Canada by Random House of Canada Limited,
Toronto.

Library of Congress Cataloging in Publication Data
Richards, David, 1940–
Played out.
Includes index.
1. Seberg, Jean.   2. Moving-picture actors and
actresses—United States—Biography.   I. Title.
PN2287.S343R5   791.43'028'0924 [B]   80-5303
ISBN 0-394-51132-8
Manufactured in the United States of America
2 4 6 8 9 7 5 3
First Edition

For Elizabeth Richards Crabb

Acknowledgments

So many helped. Especially David Beacom, who got the ball rolling and kept it rolling; Kathleen Stabile, whose willingness to research the odd fact at the odd hour was inexhaustible; William L. Thomas, who gave me a home each time I went to Los Angeles; Adeline Lesot, who did the same in Paris; Milton Goldman, who offered introductions to everyone he knows, which, it turns out, is most of the world; Steven Martindale, who was a friend long before he became my lawyer; Michel Amengual, who is one reason I have always found Paris to be a welcoming city; Jerome and Minouche Canlorbe, who took my mind off work with dinners and trips; Betty Desouches, whose unflagging good humor was a lesson in itself; Paton Price, who trusted and opened up his heart; Dennis Berry, who always spoke with candor and feeling and gave me a big lift the day he said, "Jean would have liked you"; Hannah Heyle, who was the first of Jean's friends to become my friend; Warren Robeson, who opened the door to Marshalltown; Dawn Murray Quinn and Lynda Haupert, who shared their memories unstintingly; Roger L. Stevens, who put me in touch with many crucial sources; Murray Gart, my editor at the Washington *Star*, who let me go for a year; Kitty Kelley, who listened; Don Freed and Patty Ezor, who were warm and encouraging to a perfect stranger; Nora Cortese, whose Italian is much better than mine; Emily Sieger, who was helpful in locating many of Jean's films; Charlotte Mayerson, my editor at Random House, who patiently took a lot of my crazy calls; Andrée Veron, who, a long time ago, taught a timid young American how to speak French; plus the dozens I tried to thank along the way.

I'm grateful.

D.R.

Prologue

The car went unnoticed for ten days.

It went unnoticed because the Paris street on which it sat, the Rue du Général Appert, is scarcely two blocks long. Not many pedestrians use the narrow byway on summer days, when the city is all but abandoned by vacationing Parisians. Fewer use it at night, when it is lit by only two street lamps.

Then, too, the Rue du Général Appert is in the 16th arrondissement of Paris, a prosperous neighborhood of turn-of-the-century apartment buildings that reflect the upstanding lives of their inhabitants. There is something stolid about the architecture, like a plump banker who has just pushed himself away from a five-course meal. The concierges are evermindful of keeping the sidewalks clean. Even the ivy on the wrought-iron fences knows its place. No one expects the unseemly here.

So when the alert went out for a white Renault bearing the license plate 334 APK 75, the police looked for it elsewhere. The embarrassed explanations came later: perhaps if the cars had been parked less closely together; perhaps if a layer of dust and dead leaves hadn't settled over the nondescript vehicle, making it even more inconsequential; perhaps if it hadn't been right under their noses, only a block and a half from the nearest *commissariat de police,* it might have been spotted sooner. But the search took ten days.

Then at dusk on the tenth day, September 8, 1979, two policemen on motorbikes turned into the Rue du Général Appert. One of them pulled up beside the car and looked in. It was empty except for a bulky object wrapped in a blue blanket and wedged between the front and the back seat.

When he opened the unlocked door, the pestilential odor of decaying flesh, so thick it might have been a viscous liquid, spilled from the car. Fighting off nausea, the officer tugged at the blanket. There lay the frail body of Jean Seberg, decomposed almost beyond the point of recognition. At her side was a tube of barbiturates and an empty bottle of mineral water.

"It wasn't a pretty sight," said one of the first journalists to arrive on the scene. "The car doors were the sort that close hermetically, so the body had literally baked in the sun for ten days. The odor was unimaginably foul. It just seemed to hang in the warm summer air for hours."

Only when the body had been wrapped in a rubber sheet and transported to the morgue did officials discover the note Jean Seberg clutched in her hand. Written in French and addressed to her son, Diego, it read simply:

> Forgive me. I can no longer live with my nerves. Understand me. I know that you can and you know that I love you.
> Be strong.
>
> > Your loving mother,
> > Jean

The Renault was towed away, and two young sanitation workers, visibly upset with the assignment, were summoned to hose down the street and disinfect the gutters.

It was a macabre ending to a destiny that at one point appeared to have been charted by the fan magazines. At seventeen, Jean Seberg had been plucked from the heartland of the United States, an untutored actress and a virtual unknown, to play the lead in *St. Joan*. For a brief moment her future had seemed extraordinarily bright—a miraculous incarnation of the American Dream. Overnight, she became the idol for a generation of American girls bored with the placidity of life in the 1950s and the moral rigidity on which it rested. *St. Joan* failed, but Jean went on to defy the odds a second time by becoming a star in France. And the myth took on new resonance. The French welcomed her as *"la charmante petite Américaine,"* whose blond beauty embodied the perverse innocence of the new world, while her homeland proudly viewed her as the quintessential American Abroad and secretly envied her Continental ways. She dressed in the latest high fashion, lunched with Charles de Gaulle and corresponded regularly with novelist André Malraux. Whenever she appeared in public, normally blasé Parisians craned to get a glimpse. Jean Seberg was always more complex than any of her thirty-seven films indicated, however. Only one, *Lilith*, truly plumbed the contradictions that eventually overwhelmed her. The drama of her own life far eclipsed any she was called upon to play on the screen.

A year before her suicide, she remarked to her mother-in-law, Gladys Berry, "I used to be a little princess. They'd come and get me in black limousines. They don't come anymore." But her silvery smile banished any self-pity. More than anyone else, Jean Seberg appreciated the ironies of her life.

Then, ten weeks before her forty-first birthday, wan and despairing, she had apparently driven herself to her own death. In the investigation that followed, the Paris police grappled with the unresolved details of a life that had turned crazed and sordid. Jean's friends tried to face up to the larger, more troubling question of Why?—the inevitable legacy of a suicide.

"At her innermost being, Jean was an incredibly good person," reflected one of them. "But over the years she had strayed so far from her true nature. I believe that in an awful moment of lucidity, she foresaw the utter impossibility of ever getting back to the person she had once been. And so . . ."

Her father, Ed Seberg, had a different interpretation. After a memorial service for Jean in Marshalltown, he issued a typewritten statement to the press:

> Jean attempted all of her life to be of help and comfort to any who were in need. The dogs and cats she would bring home when she was a child, saying, "They followed me." The Indians, the Blacks, the friends, the relatives and others, any who thought she would help them. And she did. She lived her convictions until the people in our world showed they did not understand her convictions. Then she gave up.

PLAYED OUT

1

"A girl in a million."

—PUBLICITY RELEASE

The early publicity about Jean Seberg invariably focused on the fact that she was born and raised in Marshalltown, Iowa. It wasn't that Marshalltown seemed distinctive in the publicists' eyes. If anything, the town was just another notch in the Bible Belt and, as a result, not an especially lucrative market for the movie industry.

But what was there to say? The details simply weren't that exotic. With no great imagination, however, the town could at least be depicted as an unlikely stepping stone to fame. Making a virtue of necessity, the publicists emphasized the prosaic aspects of her background.

They were right.

Marshalltown loomed large in the life of Jean Seberg. Her attitudes toward her birthplace were ambivalent, but they were constant. She once described the town as "the same as always, full of grim, kind, dried-up people who are afraid to open up." At the height of her fame, though, she maintained with a certain pride that "I am just a country girl at heart" and believed it. Early on, she flouted the strict morality that hugged the populace like a binding suit of clothes. But she never entirely forsook a corn-fed innocence that is as much a part of that landscape as the sunflowers.

However hypocritical she found Marshalltown, part of her

always remained accountable to its ideals—which is probably what one older resident meant when he observed, "Jean Seberg left when she was a young girl. After a while we didn't see much of her around here. But I don't think she ever really got away. You don't get away from a place like Marshalltown."

Her visits home did, in fact, grow less frequent over the years. Then they stopped altogether. In the last year of her life, by which time she had become a virtual expatriate, an impoverished Jean Seberg felt compelled to abjure the United States forever. She did so by writing a letter to the editor of the *Times-Republican,* Marshalltown's daily newspaper.

When Jean was born on November 13, 1938, Marshalltown counted 18,000 inhabitants, most of them of Scandinavian stock, Protestant faith and Republican politics. Rising like an island in a vast sea of loam that was black as coal and eighteen feet deep in spots, the town was part of a community which drew not only prosperity from the land but also an unspoken conviction in the basic goodness of life. "A lot of people have a pretty optimistic view of things, probably because we don't know what the rest of the world is doing," observes the current editor of the *Times-Republican,* only half jokingly.

A certain amount of isolationism was consistent with the town's belief in self-reliance, industry and probity, values that are reflected in the tallest building, the stolid Marshalltown County Courthouse. Dwarfing even the Tallcorn Hotel on Main Street, it sits like a humorless judge at the center of the community. Majestic elms once shaded the courthouse square and the World War I veterans who wandered down from the Iowa Soldiers Home to play shuffleboard on courts now gone. But photographs show that even before the trees were struck down by Dutch elm disease, the foliage didn't entirely relieve the stern demeanor of the edifice.

In 1938 Marshalltown, or at least the best part of it, fit snugly between the Iowa River to the north and the railroad tracks to the south. Its streets were pleasantly treelined and boasted the kind of trim, modest houses that once served to illustrate grade school readers.

The shops on either side of Main Street were pretty much those of any Midwestern county seat: several clothing stores, a Kresge's, the *Times-Republican* office, Lillie Mae's candy store, three savings banks, the Orpheum movie house and a jeweler whose sign, a huge mirror-plated diamond ring, asserted a tradition "since 1914." In short, Marshalltown was one of those towns of which it is said, partially by way of apology for the lack of excitement, that it is a good place to raise a family.

Jean's roots in the area went back several generations. Her paternal grandparents were Swedish immigrants. When he arrived in the United States in 1882, Edward Carlson changed his name to Edward Seberg because "there were already too many Carlsons in the New World." Seberg, reuniting sea and mountains, provided a pleasant reminder of his homeland. Ed Seberg, Sr., worked in a clothing factory in Marshalltown and then in the railroad yards, before finishing his life as the janitor of the Trinity Lutheran Church. His devotion to the latter job earned him a promotion to "custodian," and while the title entailed no increment in pay, relatives say that he walked a little taller afterward.

Jean's maternal grandparents, Ernest and Frances Benson, tilled the soil near La Moille, ten miles west of Marshalltown, and traced their ancestry back to John Hart, the thirteenth signer of the Declaration of Independence. Feisty and self-sufficient, Frances Benson also had a reflective nature. Widowed at seventy-three, she liked to write poetry, and in carefully stylized printing she recorded the events of her life in a diary, which was kept locked away in a bank vault. At the time of her death it ran to more than six thousand ledger pages.

Through diligence and education, Jean's parents had both improved on the humble lot that seemed mapped out for them. An attractive, gentle woman, Dorothy Arline Benson left the farm to attend Iowa State Teachers College and taught primary school for several years. Ed Seberg, Jr.'s ambition was to be a doctor. The studies proved too costly, however, and he had to settle for second best. Working part-time as a bottle washer, he put himself through the State University of Iowa School of Pharmacy. When the druggist married the schoolteacher, he was earning only $15 a week, but produce from the Benson spread helped make ends meet.

Two years after Jean's birth, Ed opened his own store, Seberg's Pharmacy, thirteen blocks west of the town square. Given the dimensions of Marshalltown then, the pharmacy's slogan—"the Suburban Store with the Downtown Service"—was not overly exaggerated.

Seberg's Pharmacy contained a post office substation and a soda fountain, but its main appeal was the integrity of the pharmacist, a principled man who put in long hours behind the counter, listened attentively to the ailments of his customers and found his escape in occasional fishing expeditions. Some of his customers—elderly women from the old folks home or illiterate farmers—would bring in prescriptions they themselves had written on the backs of envelopes or on scraps of paper. Pushing their requests over the counter, they would wait patiently while the druggist rustled up a remedy for "body lies" or "roomatizum" or, sometimes, certain sexual dysfunctions not openly acknowledged in Marshalltown. It pleased Ed Seberg no end that he could decipher their childish scrawlings. The more impenetrable the request, the greater his satisfaction in honoring it. Over the years, he would save the curious bits of paper in a cigar box and drag them out now and then to show to friends—almost by way of proof that he was, in fact, part psychologist and part doctor, too. Ed Seberg rarely raised his voice, and his laughter, when he laughed, never amounted to more than a dry chuckle. Not that he was dour, he just preferred to hide his deepest feelings. In the Seberg house, his word was law. The mere hint of displeasure on his face carried the authority of a birch rod.

Warm and slightly subservient, his wife seemed content to stay at home and keep their two-story stucco house on 6th Street tidy and their four children well-fed and decently dressed. Jean was her second child. A daughter, Mary Ann, had been born three years before, and two sons came later—Kurt three years after Jean, and David eight years after him.

"I always had nice feelings about the Sebergs," says one of Jean's childhood companions. "Of all my friends' families, Jean's was the happy one. Ed Seberg was the traditional father figure, solid and dependable. Dorothy was usually bustling about the kitchen, baking bread and cookies. I don't think I ever saw her without an apron. Their house always smelled good, and I liked going by. At Christmastime Dorothy would prepare glögg, a hot, spicy Swedish punch, and we children were allowed to taste it. Probably because there was quite a bit of alcohol in it, we were given only a sip."

By all accounts, the Sebergs represented good Midwestern people who subscribed unquestioningly to the mores of small-town America eager, after the war, to settle down and build a life. Ed Seberg strongly believed in the work ethic—on the day of his own wedding he left the reception early because he was expected to be on the job until nightfall—and his children were encouraged to follow suit. Making something of themselves, as he had done, was the goal. Application was the key. If they tried hard enough, they'd succeed. The first complete sentence Jean pronounced, Dorothy Seberg liked to tell people, was "I can do it by my 'lone."

The family's belief in the value of work was buttressed by a deep religious faith. The Sebergs went to church every Sunday, without fail; at home, grace preceded each meal. Whatever the hardships of life, they were accepted as the will of God, to be endured patiently and preferably in silence.

If the Sebergs were counted as solid citizens, there was, seemingly, nothing unusual about the family, typical of many in Marshalltown. Now and again, however, neighbors thought they caught Ed Seberg gazing at Jean with a quizzical look in his eyes, as if he wondered just where she'd sprung from.

"That family was a placid stream," says Harry Druker, her Marshalltown attorney. "And Jean was full of rapids."

2

"I am a sunflower rising from the sod."

—JEAN SEBERG

Almost from the time she had feelings about herself, Jean Seberg knew she was different and secretly prided herself on it. Her upbringing varied little from that of most middle-class girls in Marshalltown, striving at their parents' behest to "be normal," although Marshalltown had a restricted view of what normal was. Mostly it boiled down to fitting in, being a good sport and, in a girl's case, eventually settling down to home and family.

When the townsfolk began noticing Jean Seberg, however, it was because she didn't quite fit in. Their perceptions vary from the disdainful ("She was on stage all the time") to the downright romantic ("There was a quiet about her, as if she were instilling herself with the fighting spirit for the battles ahead"). Hindsight colors most of their reactions.

The one thing everybody agreed upon was that she took after her grandmother, Frances Benson, who often said that she had yearned to run away as a child to be a bareback rider in a circus. Mrs. Benson had a "wild streak," and the eccentricity that was deemed improper in the young was regarded affectionately in the independent old lady.

Jean was enrolled at five in Rogers Elementary School and went through a typical tomboy stage, galloping about like a horse and rider when she wasn't scrambling up trees. "She was always picking up stray cats and dogs and bringing them home," says Dorothy Seberg. "When I'd ask her where they came from, she'd just shrug, 'Oh, they followed me.'" A child's interest in animals is not unusual but Jean seemed to show a heightened concern over their fate. She begged her mother to shoo bugs out the kitchen door instead of taking after them with a fly swatter. Sometimes, in fact, the animals she brought home were dead, and she would bury them in the yard and conduct religious services over their graves.

In fourth grade she wrote and produced her first play, *Be Kind to Animals*. It won top honors in the Animal Rescue League's contest, but Jean refused to collect her reward, a puppy, for fear of hurting the feelings of Rusty, the family dog.

To counteract her tomboy tendencies, her parents signed her up for dancing lessons. Every Saturday for several years Jean received the across-the-board training—tap, acrobatic, ballet —that is characteristic of small-town dance academies. She was not a particularly graceful student, but it is easy to pick her out of recital photos. Her hair is in bangs, she has a gentle, unselfconscious smile, and the perfect arch of her brows sets off her luminous eyes. She is also usually in the center.

In the final year of her life Jean was interviewed in Paris for a book on child rearing called *How to Educate Our Parents*. She was asked which one of her parents she preferred, as a child of six.

"Oh, Papa," she replied without hesitating.

"And twelve?" asked the interviewer.

"Papa."

"Sixteen?"

"It was always Papa until very recently."

According to several accounts, most of her youthful energy was directed at winning the approval of the taciturn druggist. She felt a rivalry with her older sister, Mary Ann, although like most emotions in the Seberg household, it was rarely allowed to break the tranquil surface of daily routine. Mary Ann, an honor student who later graduated Phi Beta Kappa from the State University of Iowa, was frequently held up as the example. "Mary Ann was the conventional daughter," says one Marshalltown neighbor. "She was serious and well-behaved.

She applied herself and got good grades, and Jean was expected to do the same. In those early years I guess we just naturally thought of Jean as Mary Ann's little sister." Later in life, Jean would tell friends that Mary Ann had always been the favored daughter.

There was nothing more than imagination at play the day Jean announced her decision to be a toreador and assiduously set about practicing with a dishtowel in the backyard. But her subsequent change of mind was calculated to win the heart of her father. She knew how much Ed Seberg had wanted to be a doctor. Going his ambition one better, she announced that she would become a celebrated brain surgeon.

This momentous decision was greeted less enthusiastically than she had anticipated. Like most youthful aspirations it did not last long, even though Jean went so far as to borrow a textbook from a neighborhood doctor and to dissect the heart of a cow with a knife and toothpick. When Jean went into psychoanalysis in the mid-seventies, she dredged up painful memories of what seemed to outsiders an unexceptional childhood. She once recounted to Gladys Berry, her mother-in-law, that she had gone from door to door with a paper bag, begging for food. Mrs. Berry knew that the Sebergs had always been comfortable, if not rich, and interpreted Jean's recollection as a manifestation of the rejection—real or imaginary—she felt at the time.

"She certainly loved her parents," says Hannah Heyle, a close childhood friend, "but she didn't feel they spoke her language."

Jean escaped from the close and strict family atmosphere by retreating into a fantasy world. She read omnivorously, and encouraged by her grandmother's example, started writing dreamy idealistic verse.

"She liked Edna St. Vincent Millay a lot," recalls Heyle, "but her favorite poem was Emily Dickinson's 'I'm Nobody. Who are you?' Afternoons, we would go down to the banks of the Iowa River behind the Soldiers Home. Jean knew a place where she said there were Indian graves. We'd sit there and read Emily Dickinson by the hour. Jean was supersensitive, and she enjoyed the poetry, but I think she enjoyed the *idea* of reading it even more. It was the sort of thing no one in Marshalltown did."

One of Jean's earliest poems betrays the Emily Dickinson influence, as well as the adolescent alienation she experienced at twelve.

> They laugh
> And say I'm too naïve,
> But really—
> I just prefer to believe.

For most of Marshalltown's youth, movies were the Saturday afternoon pastime. The fare at Marshalltown's four cinemas usually ran to Roy Rogers Westerns, Betty Grable musicals, and Abbott and Costello comedies. One particular Saturday, however, Jean paid her fifteen-cent admission and settled into the dark to watch *The Men,* in which Marlon Brando made a low-keyed film debut as a paraplegic GI having trouble adjusting to life after the war. "Maybe the combination of medicine and acting had something to do with it," she later recollected, "but I was really very deeply impressed, and I left the movie feeling strangely shaken. For some reason the film made me aware of the power in acting, although Marlon Brando was certainly not my conception at the time of a typical movie star."

Forgoing the usual cherry Coke at Lillie Mae's, she dashed to the public library and requested some books on acting. The librarian gave her Stanislavski's *An Actor Prepares,* holy writ for the Method school, then in full vogue. She pored over it that night, but understood little of the Russian director's introspective theories, which were rooted in sense memories and the "inner truth" of the subconscious. Unenlightened but undiscouraged, she returned the book the next day. The movie magazines on the rack in her father's drugstore were more accessible.

"For a while Jean carried around all the fan magazines with Marlon Brando on the cover," says Heyle. "I can still see her in my mother's kitchen, the sun glinting off her hair, which was very blond in those days. She'd clutch the magazines to her breast and announce dramatically, 'I'm going to be a very famous actress, you know.' 'Famous' was a word she used a lot."

Brando's performance also inspired her first fan letter. "Dear Mr. Brando," she wrote. "I know you must get tired of all those reporters and photographers annoying you, so if you would like to, you are very welcome to come and stay with me and my family as long as you want." The letter went unanswered, but years later, when she met Brando in Paris and told him of her girlish proposal, he quipped, "Try me now."

Jean's childhood religious training had a similarly powerful effect. Certain of Marshalltown's twenty-two churches were known as "society churches," but the brick-and-clapboard Trinity Lutheran Church was not one of them. It was strict and somber, and its view of man as a fallen creature brooked no compromise. The minister, unbending in his faith, thundered at his congregation and occasionally, Jean thought, foamed at the mouth. The constant harping on original sin frightened the young girl, while the notion of eternal damnation gave her nightmares. She resolved to live as piously as possible and took to practicing hymns on the family piano.

In June 1952 Jean was confirmed in the church. While her faith lessened as she grew older, many of the harsher strictures imposed on her in catechism class stayed with her. Some of her friends believe that this severe religious instruction left her with profound feelings of unworthiness, which she tried to combat all her life. "I was a believer for a long time," she said. "I lived for the return of Jesus on earth." In fact, Lutheranism exacerbated the sensitivities of an already sensitive child.

In psychoanalysis, Jean traced some of her adult anxieties to the funeral of her grandfather, Ernest Benson. As she related the incident, the farmer had been laid out in an open coffin. When the family filed past the body, Dorothy Seberg whispered, "Kiss your grandfather good-bye." Jean recoiled, but her mother insisted. "I could see it meant so much to her that I forced myself to obey," Jean said. "The body was cold to the touch."

Although she was actually sixteen at the time, Jean invariably placed the event earlier in her life and alternately told people she was ten or twelve when the funeral occurred. It may have been the result of a faulty memory, by then blurred with drugs and alcohol. On the other hand, she may simply have felt it was more dramatic that way. In either case, the memory haunted her long after. As an actress, she would rely on it whenever she was obliged to cry in a film. "All I have to do is touch something cold," she explained. "It can be an ice cube or a stone or a damp wall—St. Joan's dungeon, for example. The cold brings back the memory of that funeral, and the tears flow automatically."

The Sebergs usually spent their summers in Marshalltown. One year Jean worked as a counselor in Riverside Park and met several of the black children who lived down by the viaduct. "I tried to write a book about a white girl and a Negro boy," she admitted afterward. "I couldn't. I didn't know anything about it."

Nevertheless, at fourteen she applied by mail for membership in the Des Moines chapter of the NAACP. The act startled her parents and her friends, who wondered where she'd gotten "that crazy idea." The black community in Marshalltown was all but invisible. Most of the town's fifty or so families were clustered by the tracks and kept to themselves. One winter an abandoned black infant was found frozen in a snow drift. When doctors brought the baby back to life, the miraculous news merited headlines in the *Times-Republican.* For the most part, however, the white community closed its eyes and went about its business, convinced that an integrated school system made the community enlightened enough for all practical purposes.

"No one had a sense of racial discrimination in those days," says one former resident. "It just wasn't something anyone thought about. By the same token, no one had a sense of racial mixing, either. There were just these two separate worlds."

At the height of the civil rights movement in the 1960s, Jean looked back and tried to explain her early concern. "I really don't know why I did it," she told *Cosmopolitan* reporter Joan Barthel. "There was a black athlete at our high school who fascinated me. There would always be aftergame parties at which he'd dance with the white girls. He could hold them as aggressively close as he wanted to, which he sometimes did with a vengeance. But when the dance was over, the Iron Curtain fell and that was it. One night he asked to walk a girl home, and he had the bejesus beaten out of him.

"I can think of a thousand reasons for my joining the NAACP that make me sound terrific, but the only valid reason I can think of is a kind of alienation. I was raised in a rather strict atmosphere, and I thought that other people who were alienated in other ways must feel much more deeply."

"Jean was always riding a white charger, even back then," Harry Druker recalls. "She was an angel who didn't believe that evil could exist in the world."

Hannah Heyle has a similar explanation. "Jean had a very strong idealistic streak. Joining the NAACP was just another instance of her being different. She probably didn't understand the philosophy behind it, but she certainly loved every little living creature."

Her burst of conscience was not appreciated by Ed Seberg. In a draft of the memoirs she was composing at the time of her death, Jean reported their conversation:

"'Jean, people will say you're a Communist,' he said to me.

"'Papa,' I replied, 'I don't care what people think.'"

She did care, of course. Jean's adolescence seems to have been guided by two contradictory impulses. She wanted to join in and prove herself in all the traditional activities, like her sister. Simultaneously, she retreated into visions of a singular destiny and took solace from the fact that she was not like everyone else. Perhaps that is simply the dialectic of growing up, but it governed Jean with a particular acuteness. It also explains why there are those who saw her as "a boiling pot" and others who described her as a "deep, still pond." All of them are right.

By the time she entered Marshalltown High School in the fall of 1953, people were noticing Jean Seberg for another reason as well. She had flowered into a striking young woman. Lithe and gamine-like, she stood five feet four inches. Her gray-green eyes lent a special animation to her face, but her beauty also suggested a golden sensuality beyond her years. Townsfolk remember that pedestrians sometimes stopped on Main Street to watch her go by.

3

"I have just one big ambition in life—to make you proud of me and glad you helped me as you did."

—JEAN SEBERG TO HER HIGH
SCHOOL DRAMA COACH

If few people in Marshalltown took Jean's aspirations to be an actress seriously, Carol Hollingsworth did. She was the speech instructor at Marshalltown High School and single-handedly pushed for theater in a community whose natural enthusiasm was reserved for the Bobcats, the championship basketball team. "Carol was probably only a fair-to-middling actress herself," says one of her former students, "but she was the closest thing we had in Marshalltown to a star. She was flamboyant and vital, and she played up her eccentricities. She always had lots of stories to tell. She introduced us to *Theatre Arts* magazine and the Broadway theater, and made it all sound terribly alive."

Married late in life, Carol Hollingsworth was rumored to have a "tragic past"—a possessive mother who had rejected all her daughter's suitors, a fiancé who had been killed in an automobile accident—and that only enhanced her aura in the eyes of her students.

"We identified with her a lot," says Hannah Heyle. "We thought of ourselves as her children. We were sure she understood us when our own parents didn't."

During school hours, Carol was called "Coach." Away from

the two-story red-brick building, she was "Ma." When the energetic teacher married Ralph Dodd, the kindly man became "Pa" and seemed to take as keen an interest as his wife did in the drama students who congregated at their house for cast parties. They all played charades—using play titles only—and to Jean and her friends, it was wildly sophisticated, especially when one of them had to act out *'Tis Pity She's a Whore.*

"I remember one night during her first year in high school, Jean dropped by the house at about ten-thirty," says Hollingsworth. "I had her in one of my speech classes, but she hadn't acted for me yet. She wanted to know if I thought she had what it took to be a good actress. She was so serious about it—I guess all the girls were—but she told me she had to have an answer right then. That was Jean—so full of go. She wouldn't take on a job unless she thought she could do it well."

Hollingsworth gave her what she called her DDT lecture: acting required drive, determination and talent. Jean drank it in avidly. From then on, her course was set. Gazing into a crystal ball, *The Pebbles* (the high school newspaper) made this "twenty-years-from-now" prediction: "Jean Seberg has become a second Helen Hayes and in her spare time she's a soda jerk at Seberg's."

"Jean had a self-assurance the rest of us didn't," says Martha McCallister, another high school friend. "She just knew where she wanted her life to go. She realized who could help her, she cultivated the right people and pulled the right strings. It was all part of being more aware, I suppose. It's unusual, coming from that normal middle-class background—fireplace and everything—to be tuned into things so young. But she was. She was writing poetry before most of us knew what it was. She read all the time and put me on to *Forever Amber,* which was pretty advanced for Marshalltown."

Carol Hollingsworth taught her students the basic principles of acting—how to build a character, make an entrance and project the voice—and kept after them to improve their diction. After her first year of classes, Jean boasted that she could "hang *pictures* in *February*" (not "pitchers" in "Febooary") to her teacher's satisfaction.

"Jean would have been about perfect for every play we

did," recalls Hollingsworth, "but I tried to be fair and distribute the good roles among the students." Consequently, Jean's first stage assignment in her junior year was as an understudy in *Ladies of the Jury*. With little to do, she threw herself into backstage chores and carried out her duties as "assistant to the director" with special seriousness.

Before long, under Hollingsworth's guidance, Jean was entering the various oratorical contests and one-act play competitions that were held regularly throughout Iowa every spring. Her performance in Thornton Wilder's *The Happy Journey to Trenton and Camden* won her her first citation. "She was the best Beulah I have ever seen," concluded one of the judges, who apparently had seen a few.

Jean's activities in high school covered a broad spectrum. Being "well-rounded" was a goal propounded by Ed Seberg. She played the glockenspiel in the band and sang with the mixed chorus (enhancing it more with her looks, one friend joked, than with her voice, which tended to waver). She participated in the extramural girls' basketball league, which fell under the sponsorship of the Marshalltown churches and required no great athletic ability as a prerequisite—only regular attendance at Sunday school. She was also a member of GY (Girls Y), the YWCA social club and a magnet for Marshalltown teen-agers. "I don't know what we kids would have done without the Y," recalls Marlene Turner, one of Jean's companions. "We'd all gather there after school and on weekends and dance in our stocking feet for hours to the latest 45s. Sometimes we'd sneak off to Lillie Mae's after a dance or a game. But our parents usually didn't approve. That place was known as the greasers' hangout."

At one of the Saturday night dances at the Y, Jean was approached by a good-looking young man neither she nor her girl friends had seen in town before. As the dance was about to end, Jean cornered her classmate Bob Norris and whispered urgently to him, "Look, this guy has asked to walk me home. Would you *please* follow us and make sure that nothing happens to me."

Gallantly, Norris told her not to worry. When Jean and her conquest of the moment left the Y, he slipped out after them, darting from bush to tree at a proper distance so as to remain undetected. As he got closer to 6th Street, he noticed that several others were engaged in the same clandestine activity. By the time he reached the Sebergs' front lawn, he realized that he was part of the ten-man body guard Jean had mobilized that night. The stranger never paid a return call.

Carol Hollingsworth rapidly became the dominant influence during Jean's high school years. The teacher's indefatigable emphasis on self-expression and the need to be true to oneself helped counter the fierce pressures to conform. "I must be an individual, you know," Jean echoed in one of her papers for speech class. Acting allowed her to shine. It was also something she did better than Mary Ann, who had been unexceptional in high school plays.

"I imagine we were pretty insufferable then," says Hannah Heyle, "but we thought we were special. And what did Marshalltown know? There was nothing remotely intellectual about the place. The basketball team won the state championship in February, and the town celebrated until June. High school was cliquey. If you weren't a cheerleader or a member of the pep club, you were suspect. We, of course, were going to be serious actresses. When we did *Our Town* in our junior year, we went around for a week dressed in black."

Not all Jean's acting was reserved for the stage. "She had my mother in absolute tears once with this long, tragic story about her unrequited love for a neighborhood boy," Marlene Turner remembers. "It was all made up, but my mother believed every word."

One afternoon Jean returned home to discover that Dorothy Seberg had invited guests over for tea. "Run upstairs and clean up for company," her mother instructed. Several minutes later Jean came back downstairs, dressed in a purple formal gown. Then she politely made the rounds, shaking hands with all her mother's friends as if nothing were amiss. "I should have known then," Dorothy Seberg said, laughing, "that she was going to be an actress."

James Dean's death threw the teen-ager into despondency. She had seen *East of Eden* seven times on a single ticket by flirting with the theater manager. "I'm going to die young," she announced frequently to her friends after that. "I won't live past forty." Feeling hopelessly romantic and misunderstood, she informed her parents that she'd probably put a gun to her head someday. Such fatalistic declarations would color her conversations throughout her life.

Jean later sent a letter of condolence to James Dean's aunt and enclosed $5 for flowers to be put on his grave in commemoration of his birthday. She received a warm note in return, but showed it only to two of her friends—Dawn Murray Quinn and Lynda Haupert. The others, she feared, would make fun of her.

"You never knew what to expect next with Jean," says Lynda, now an attractive free-lance artist. "She could be awfully mischievous and she loved to shock people. She took me aside one day and said that she was going to tell her boyfriend she was pregnant. I must have looked shocked, because she quickly added, 'Oh, just to see what his reaction is.'"

In that small puritanical community, sex was rarely discussed. Premarital sex was taboo. Occasionally the back-fence gossip hummed with the news of a girl who had dropped out of school because she was pregnant. It was a shame, of course, but the compassionate clucking didn't entirely mask the sentiment that shame was fair retribution. Jean had heard the stories. At slumber parties the late-night chatter would work its way around to those who, in the lingo of the day, had gone "not far enough," "too far" or "all the way." In a chapter of her unfinished memoirs, Jean confessed that she went "all the way" in a drive-in one night during high school. A month later, the Merck medical manual that Ed Seberg kept in the house confirmed all her worst fears. She confided in her grandmother, who by then was living with the Sebergs. Wasting no time, Mrs. Benson secretly took her to the doctor for a rabbit test. The results were negative, but Jean, stricken with guilt, insisted on a second test. "Several days later," she wrote, "I had my period. I don't think anyone thanked God as fervently as I did that day."

Jean's taste in boyfriends ran to what she called "bohemian types," those who seemed to dwell, as she felt she did, on the fringes of the rigid community. "I never liked gentlemen," she once commented. "Jean was gorgeous and she was never without a couple of boyfriends," says Lynda Haupert. "Sometimes Mary Ann would bring guys home from the university, and Jean would steal them out from under her nose."

For a while she dated Paul Richer, a burly instructor who had been fired from the staff of the junior high school in tiny Riceville, Iowa, for what local officials considered his controversial teaching methods. (As *Time* magazine reported then, he had taught a two-and-a-half week unit on Communism and read his students passages from *Of Mice and Men*. For a theme topic, he once assigned a line from *The Green Pastures*: "Even bein' God ain't no bed of roses." To the consternation of the town elders, the students followed him like the Pied Piper.) "Paul was certainly Jean's most dramatic romance," says Hannah Heyle. "It caused a lot of gossip in Marshalltown. Paul had a liberal cause and therefore was forbidden. Jean talked endlessly about whether or not she should marry him. If she did, she would simply have to run away, she said, because her parents would never understand."

In fact, Ed Seberg actively disapproved of the romance and was relieved when Richer was called up for his military service. Jean took partial consolation in the theater, which, she was discovering, could be an outlet for sensitivities that were misunderstood or mocked elsewhere. In a self-evaluating essay written for Carol Hollingsworth at the end of her junior year, she observed: "I would still like to lower my voice pitch and develop a wider range . . . I want to, and should, know more about acting and not over-act or drop lines. My participation in the oratorical contests has practically abolished my fear of audiences (though I'm still a little nervous before plays). Probably what I consider most valuable was the reading of plays. It opened a whole new field of interest to me. I loathe work—I hate dusting, cooking, clerking and waitressing. This year I've found a kind of work that requires thought and preparation and use of every part of a person, and I've really enjoyed it. I'd like to continue, as it's my favorite class. P.S. Thank you for being so patient with me."

The summer between her junior and senior year, Jean was chosen to represent Marshalltown High School at Girls' State, a youth forum sponsored by local auxiliaries of the American Legion. In a mock election in Cedar Rapids, she was voted lieutenant governor, which qualified her to go to Washington, D.C., for Girls' Nation, where the process was repeated on a national scale. Jean's politics, to the extent that she had any, were largely those of her parents, staunch Eisenhower supporters. The family conservatism was hardly apt to be challenged by the speakers at Girls' Nation, who took a somewhat narrow view of women's place in a society that was then under the thrall of McCarthyism. Mrs. Percy Lainson, national president of the American Legion Auxiliary, told the hundred delegates, "You must help your husband advance socially and make business contacts that will send him forward on his business or professional career. As a part of safeguarding your home, you must know about civil defense, so that if we are attacked you are prepared to fight for freedom on these shores. When you are co-heads of a family, there is much you can do to combat juvenile delinquency—by taking your families to church, by having daily prayers in the home and by seeing that the children all sit around the table with the adult members of the family at least one meal a day."

The girls held their own presidential election and Jean was nominated the vice-presidential candidate of the Nationalist Party. She campaigned vigorously and though the Federalists carried the day, Jean's congeniality impressed her peers, who voted her "All-Round Girls' Stater."

The honors continued in her senior year of high school. In December 1955 the governor of Iowa named her the first teen-age chairman of the Iowa March of Dimes campaign, and her picture appeared in the paper. Jean's civic-mindedness won the quiet approval of her parents. At Marshalltown High School, though, there was growing resentment among the student body. It was said that Jean was stuck on herself, an impression she fostered by the heightened effervescence she displayed in public and her "phony" way of articulating. "Jean certainly had her popular side," says Hannah Heyle. "She went to all the dances, had dates and belonged to the right clubs. She did everything you were supposed to do. But I never thought she had too strong a grip on reality. There was an elusiveness, a dreaminess about her as well. You always felt there was a side to her you couldn't really know. Fewer people trusted that side. Frankly, Jean was too much for Marshalltown, whatever the town says now. It was mean to her and there was a lot of petty jealousy just below the surface. Jean pretended it didn't matter. At graduation we talked about how much we'd miss the place, but she was relieved to get out."

Jean braved the criticism, but according to Dawn Murray Quinn, it stung her. "She would tell people that she was going to meet Marlon Brando someday, or that she would visit James Dean's grave, or that she was going to be a big movie star. They'd just laugh at her and say she was imagining things. Nobody believed in her talent. At one point she even received some anonymous phone calls and unsigned letters running her down and asking her who she thought she was. When she told me about them, she broke into tears. 'Dawn,' she said, 'I'd trade all my honors and talent for some true friends and a boy who really loves me.'

"Jean was far more sensitive than anyone thought. Oh, like most teen-agers, we'd 'slam' one another and crack one another up by trading insults. But Jean was never caustic and she wouldn't hurt a soul. She'd even go out of her way to befriend kids no one else would—unpopular kids you weren't supposed to be interested in. She certainly saved my life. My parents had moved to Marshalltown in my senior year from an even smaller town in Missouri and I was frightened and alone. Our backyard touched the Sebergs' and one day she wandered over and said, 'Hi, I'm Jean.' We became fast friends immediately. Her parents sometimes called her Jeana, pronouncing the *J* like a *Y*, the way her Swedish grandfather had. She was 'Jeana' to me all her life."

"Jean was different from all the rest of them," agrees Rose Druker, Harry's wife. "She was the most poised teen-ager I ever knew. There was an elderly lady—old Mrs. Blackburn—who lived next door to me and who used to help me take care of my children. Whenever Jean came by, she'd always make a special effort to sit down and talk with Mrs. Blackburn. She had time for the lonely and the old. I don't know how she'd thought it out. Intuition, maybe."

Carol Hollingsworth also recognized that poise and felt it made Jean the best choice for the lead in *Sabrina Fair,* the school production of January 1956. Somewhat prophetically, she cast Jean as a chauffeur's daughter who acquires polish and sophistication in Paris, and then returns to Long Island to enchant the sons of her father's employer. "She knew all her lines the first day of rehearsal," says Hollingsworth. "And she was lovely in the part."

The production played before a thousand spectators, packed into the hardwood chairs of the Marshalltown High auditorium. Jean's vivacity, which appeared exaggerated elsewhere, was appealing and natural on the stage. "The applause was tremendous," says Hannah Heyle, who acted in the production too. "Our parents sent us each a dozen red roses for the curtain call. Actually, it was Jean's idea. But we feigned surprise and stood there, cradling the roses in our arms, convinced we were in this rarefied atmosphere. But there's little doubt that it was Jean's big triumph. I think people looked at her a little differently afterward."

Jean read her first rave several days later in the *Times-Republican,* which praised her "outstanding talent, perfect enunciation" and, not least of all, her fluent French. Since Marshalltown High School offered only Latin and Spanish courses, her skill with French was deemed especially meritorious.

"Most of us knew then," says Stephen Melvin, her high school music teacher, "that if she really wanted to pursue an acting career, she could make it." A repeat performance was arranged a month later for the benefit of the Community Hospital. Jean spearheaded the door-to-door ticket sales. *"Sabrina Fair,"* she wrote Carol Hollingsworth afterward, "was absolutely the greatest moment of my life."

With renewed zest she entered various drama competitions that spring, performing a twelve-minute cutting of Maxwell Anderson's *Joan of Lorraine,* another prophetic choice. She played Joan, Cauchon and several saints as well. High marks from the judges spurred her desire to attend a drama school in the East that fall.

That was not her parents' idea of higher education, however. They expected her to follow in Mary Ann's footsteps at the State University of Iowa and they were uneasy about the growing importance theater was assuming in her life. Jean's visions of a career on the stage were usually checked with a prudent "Yes, but first . . ."

"Theater just wasn't the kind of activity the Sebergs understood," says one neighbor. "It wasn't *serious*. I think they always looked upon it as a den of iniquity that attracted show-offs, deadbeats and for some mysterious reason their daughter."

Their apprehension increased when Jean announced that Carol Hollingsworth had arranged for a scholarship enabling her to apprentice that summer at a theater on Cape Cod. Jean pointed out that her room and board would be free and that the Norrises, close family friends, were driving east that summer. She could ride along with them. Reluctantly, the Sebergs agreed.

In June 1956 Jean graduated from high school, eleventh out of the 197 students in her class. Her yearbook, *The Post Script,* lists nine lines of her various activities. A caricature shows her pursuing a helmeted motorcyclist and calling out "Marlon, Marlon." The caption reads: "Same Old Chase." The class poll named her "Most Likely to Succeed," "Most Sophisticated" and "Best Dancer," but, oddly enough, not "Best-Looking."

The comments she scribbled in the yearbooks of her two closest friends are telling. For Dawn Murray Quinn she wrote: "I think you are one of the most Christ-like persons I know and this has quite a different denotation than 'Christian.' . . . The new neighbor who was once a stranger has become beautiful to me, because of the depth of her understanding, her trustworthiness, her terrific sense of humor and her loyalty to her ideals. . . . I thank you for helping make 'of the timber of my body, not a tavern, but a temple,' for this is the true meaning of friendship."

In Hannah Heyle's yearbook: "As far as true friends go, this past year has been one of the best of my life and I consider you one of the truest. Wasn't *Sabrina Fair* fun? I die of jealousy at your comedy touch and sense of timing. I truly hope we can visit the Great White Way as a duo this summer. But at any rate, we'll make it sometime."

There, in embryonic form, were the two faces of Jean Seberg—the actress and the idealist. Over the next two decades they blended together so closely that it was often difficult to tell where one left off and the other began. Acting itself was an ideal, and Jean would try to duplicate in real life the heightened sense of the moment that she experienced on the stage. By the same token, her idealism was intrinsically theatrical and would permit her to play the most dramatic of all roles— the sacrificing of oneself on the barricades.

That June, however, Jean seemed to be merely one of those bright, nervous teen-agers that small towns sometimes produce in defiance of the molds. Nothing about her really indicated an extraordinary destiny. Promising her parents that she would be back for college in the fall, she rode east with the Norrises to try her hand at summer stock.

In an interview in 1974 Jean described the path that seemed to lay ahead back then. Her future looked fairly predictable. "Because of all the sexual repression of my Midwestern upbringing," she reflected, "I would have quickly gotten involved with some guy at the university. And because of my upbringing, I would have married him. It would have been a disaster, and we would have broken up. I would have gone to New York to try to fulfill my ambition to be an actress and probably married a second time, an actor or a director. And that would have been about it."

4

"Her most outstanding quality was an inner serenity that was remarkable in a seventeen-year-old girl . . . You had a feeling that Jean possessed an inner core that nobody and nothing could disturb."

—RICHARD SHEPPARD, A FELLOW ACTOR

The bare bulb threw a harsh light over the stage. Jean walked hesitantly to the center and announced that she would be performing a selection from Maxwell Anderson's *Joan of Lorraine.*

"Oh, God!" murmured one of the five directors out front. "Not 'Light your fires' again!"

That chilly June morning the staff of the Priscilla Beach Theater was scrutinizing forty young actors and actresses who had made their way to the weather-beaten barn on a bluff just outside Plymouth, Massachusetts. For the next eight weeks they would paint sets, take tickets, gather props, sew costumes, and if their audition went well, act. To Jean, at seventeen the youngest, it was an exciting prospect.

"'King of Heaven, I come to fulfill a vow,'" she began, the eloquent words contrasting curiously with the sweater and black toreador pants she was wearing.

"That audition speech was so overused," recalls Jeanne Cassidy, one of the PBT staff. "But you noticed Jean. Her delicacy was what struck you first. As you got to know her, however, you sensed this incredible eagerness to learn. Despite her fragile appearance, she was a real trouper. The combination made her immensely appealing."

The directors agreed instantly to cast her in *Picnic* as Madge, the local beauty queen who is dying of boredom in William Inge's back-porch drama about a drab Kansas hamlet. Physically, she was the logical choice for the role, and her accent and small-town sincerity clinched it.

Mornings at PBT were devoted to classes. There Jean received grounding in the Stanislavski system of acting, which had eluded her years before. Rehearsals began after lunch and often continued until midnight. Jeanne Cassidy still remembers one rehearsal incident vividly: "There's a moment in *Picnic* where the daily train passes by in the distance. The whistle throws a spell over the characters, who stop and listen to it wistfully. Most of the kids in the company were from large cities in the East and the meaning of that moment escaped them entirely. 'A train whistle? What's the big deal?' they asked."

One day Jean lost her patience. "I'll tell you what that train whistle means," she exploded. "It's your connection with the outside world. Every time it goes by, you listen with all your heart because it means there's a way out. Somehow, you feel, if you're lucky you might get out too. That whistle is like a faraway promise."

Normally soft-spoken, Jean surprised the company with the force of her explanation.

"Her passion went right to the heart of the play," says Cassidy. "I've thought a lot about it since. She didn't know what her fortunes as an actress would be, but inside this lovely, quiet person, there was a huge amount of determination. It obviously meant everything to her to get out into the world."

Jean was cast opposite John Maddox, a lanky, curly-haired actor from Fort Worth, Texas, who during his college days had been known to climb on the roof of the men's dormitory and hurl Shakespearean sonnets at the stars. As Hal, the strapping heartthrob who turns the heads of Inge's women, he was seemingly every bit as typecast as Jean. Before long, the two had fallen in love.

"I think it was Jean's first serious affair," recalls Barbara

Saturnine, a member of the company. "It certainly was the big romance of the summer. They were a beautiful couple. And the theater by the seaside—well, they couldn't have had a more idyllic setting."

Free from the constraints of Marshalltown, Jean's relationship with John flowered sexually.

"John was devastatingly handsome. He worked out a lot. He had great power over people, women especially, and he could never divorce himself from it," says one of Maddox's closest friends, Ed Rooney. "He was obsessed with success and people who had wonderful careers. Many years after Jean became famous, he told me that they used to drive out into the fields at night in an old pickup truck he had and make love under the stars. He could never completely forget her."

At rehearsals, Jean and John brought an intensity to their love scenes that mirrored their growing involvement with each other and promised to help make *Picnic* a hit.

Jean reveled in the community of actors, knit together by the bad food (PBT, they decided, really stood for Peanut Butter Theater), bonfires on the beach, and late-night talk sessions. The first day, the company had dubbed her "Grace Kelly" because of the dreamy innocence she projected. The nickname stuck.

"We gave Jean credit for knowing that the stork is just a bird," says Richard Sheppard, who went on to a career in show-business journalism. "But her knowledge stopped right there. The more worldly among us would twit her unmercifully. When things theatened to get out of hand . . . she'd train those green-gray eyes on whoever was talking and punctuate his story with frequent comments—'Really? Is that so?'—all the while looking as if she were accepting every word as gospel truth. She got so good at it that a few people actually believed her sexual education was a complete blank."

To general surprise, Jean had a low estimation of her looks, especially her body. She thought her calves too thick, and her thighs "too short." "It's different with girls who are beautiful . . ." she would sigh.

During one rehearsal break she took Sheppard aside and confided disconsolately about her bosom, "My kid sister in the play is bigger than I am." When Sheppard told her the five-and-dime store in Plymouth sold certain "appliances" that would remedy the deficiency, Jean blushed and changed the subject. On opening night several of the actors gathered at the back of the auditorium. As Jean made her entrance they let out a collective gasp and then a burst of approving laughter that baffled the paying customers. For her debut, she had conquered her scruples: she looked as amply endowed as Jane Russell.

At the opening-night party held in a nearby nightspot, the band was asked to play "Moonglow and the Theme from *Picnic*," then popular on the airwaves. John invited Jean to dance, and the others cleared the floor.

"It sounds corny now," Barbara Saturnine admits. "But you felt you were watching something special. I never saw Jean so luminous. It's strange. So many members of that company have since died or committed suicide. But for a short time, we were all terribly close and alive."

The Priscilla Beach Theater was the hub of an operation that Dr. Franklin Trask, a theater buff and regular Yankee trader, had set up in southern New England and New Jersey. Every spring he canvassed schools and colleges for their best drama students. In a form letter he congratulated them for their recent performance in _____ and invited them to spend the summer at PBT. The fine print spelled out the fees to be paid. From the actors who gathered at Priscilla Beach, Trask then formed smaller companies that were packed off by station wagon to his other theaters.

After *Picnic,* Jean worked the rest of the summer at the Cape May Playhouse in New Jersey, where she earned the first salary of her career—$15 a week. The money went for her board in a Victorian rooming house and the communal food supply—hot dogs, American cheese and pizza being the staples. She played roles in *The Last of Mrs. Carroll, The Late Christopher Bean* and *Claudia.*

"I took my first single curtain call last night in *Claudia*—a real thrill," she wrote a friend. The season concluded with Noël Coward's *Hay Fever,* which the cast members found far more amusing than the meager audiences did. Still, it was the kind of hectic, liberating summer that fostered dreams. Jean had hers. In the fall she and John would go to New York, rent a small apartment in the Village and make the rounds together. She was uncertain how to break the news to her parents. The prospect of following in the footsteps of her sister at the state university enchanted her less and less.

One night she accompanied several of her friends to the Cape May movie house, where they saw a trailer announcing that film director Otto Preminger would undertake a world-wide talent hunt for an unknown actress to play the lead in *St. Joan.* Aspiring candidates between the ages of sixteen and twenty-two were urged to fill out application forms available in the theater lobby.

With the superior attitude of a member of the legitimate theater, Jean dismissed the contest as a gimmick. She was not alone in her skepticism. Much of the motion picture industry believed that Preminger was looking for publicity, not an actress. Once he had canvassed the major cities in the United States, Canada and Great Britain, reaping headlines and raising false hopes, he would produce the starlet he'd had in mind all along. And that would be that.

"Besides," one of Jean's friends pointed out, "Shaw described Joan as a big girl. You're too small."

In Marshalltown, however, a man named J. William Fisher was of a different mind. A folksy, eccentric millionaire, he headed Fisher Controls, the town's major industry. Out of valves and locks for pipelines his family had built a considerable fortune that allowed him to subsidize operas at the Met and to amass an imposing collection of French Impressionist paintings. Despite his wealth, he insisted that the townsfolk call him Bill and he remained an inveterate hometown booster.

Right after he read about Preminger's contest in the *Times-Republican,* he telephoned Carol Hollingsworth. "I'm going to submit that girl who presented me with the gold cuff links in the ceremony at the YWCA last year. What was her name?"

"You mean Jean Seberg?"

"That's the one. I'm going to write a letter of recommendation today, and I think you should, too. Two letters are bound to be better than one."

Carol Hollingsworth forwarded the application form to Jean, who vacillated before filling it out. John Maddox had misgivings. "Don't worry," she reassured him. "I won't win."

Nonetheless, she reasoned, if Preminger were to drop an encouraging word or two, she could use his approval as leverage with her parents. Maybe then they would take her acting career more seriously and allow her to move to New York. It was worth a try.

Looking back on that summer and the girl he knew then, Richard Sheppard later remarked, "It was like putting fresh, clean putty in Otto's hands."

5

"I have no specific image or character in mind. I only know there are certain qualities necessary to portray this part, which I hope to recognize when I meet the girl."

—OTTO PREMINGER

Whether or not Preminger would find his St. Joan that fall was an open question, but no one doubted he would get the newspaper coverage he was after. With prodding from the publicists, the *St. Joan* competition was touted as the biggest talent hunt since David Selznick had scoured the country for an actress to play Scarlett O'Hara in *Gone With the Wind.* More than 18,000 entries flooded Preminger's Hollywood offices—a figure that would have gone higher, according to one press agent, had Preminger not vetoed a proposal to paper Asia and Latin America with application forms. If she could do nothing else, his St. Joan would have to speak English.

Hot from *The Man with the Golden Arm,* Preminger had always been good copy, but for reporters after a hometown angle the contest was a natural, too. A few jaundiced onlookers relished the thought of the autocratic director subjected to an endless parade of virginal and semivirginal actresses mangling Shaw. It was, they thought, a torment he richly deserved.

At the end of the summer when Jean returned to Marshalltown, she found a form letter waiting for her. Her picture and application had survived the initial screening, and she could count herself among the 3,000 finalists Preminger would personally audition in the weeks to come. She was instructed to learn two designated speeches from the play and to report to the Sherman Hotel in Chicago at 10 A.M. on September 15, 1956. As expected, her parents were cool to the idea; to them, her education came first. Jean argued passionately that auditioning for a director of Preminger's stature could only stand her in good stead. Finally Ed Seberg consented to drive his daughter to Chicago on one condition: beforehand, she would have to enroll at the State University of Iowa. Dutifully she repaired to the Iowa City campus, declared herself a drama major, met her roommate and pledged her sister's sorority, Kappa Alpha Theta.

As the audition approached, Jean downplayed her natural excitement. "What bothers me most," she told a friend, "is that I'm going to have to miss the big Woody Herman concert." In her absence, she was positive that Woody was going to hit the highest note of his career on the clarinet. And where would she be when musical history was being made? In Chicago! More precisely, in the Bal Tabarin of the Sherman Hotel, where Preminger had installed his headquarters, rather like a visiting general in occupied territory. Three hundred actresses, some in a state of near-hysteria, milled about the faded room that Saturday morning, disregarding the attempts of Preminger's harried staff to impose a semblance of alphabetical order.

"Most of the girls were dressed in black skirts and black turtlenecks and wore their hair pulled back austerely," says Dyanne Earley (then the aspiring actress Dyanne Teasdale), who fell just behind Jean in the line-up. "A startling percentage of them had silver crosses around their necks. Coming from a small town as I did, it seemed like an awfully artsy crowd to me and I'm sure it did to Jean, too."

Preminger and his assistants had installed themselves in an adjoining room, furnished with a raised platform and with two bright spotlights which made it difficult to see the director. There was no mistaking the accented voice, however, that crisply ordered each actress to begin.

"It was a real cattle call," says Earley. "It took all morning and most of the afternoon. Little by little, the line inched toward the door. Just before going in, almost every girl would slip off her shoes, ask the person behind her to mind her purse and then disappear. A minute later she'd come out, looking pretty despondent."

When Jean's turn came she entrusted her handbag and shoes to Earley. "But she didn't come out for fifteen minutes or so. The longer she stayed in there, the more excited and nervous everyone became. Then the door opened and Jean floated right past us in a daze and headed for the elevator. She'd completely forgotten about her bag and shoes."

Preminger later admitted that "something clicked" as soon as he saw the fresh-scrubbed candidate from Marshalltown. In her audition she had revealed a blend of the innocence and strength he sought. But it was in conversation that she most impressed him.

"She was a vital young woman and she had great personality," he observed. "And she was very anxious to play the part."

One of the questions he asked her was why she hadn't worn a cross.

"My family is too poor to afford one," Jean replied, bowing her head. When Preminger threw her a doubtful look, Jean laughed.

"Because I knew all the other girls would be wearing them," she admitted sheepishly.

Preminger met later that day with the Sebergs and informed them that he would like Jean to come to New York in a month for the final round of auditions. Under the circumstances, he advised, it would not be imprudent to postpone Jean's studies. "You have a very talented daughter," he said in conclusion.

Momentarily tongue-tied, Ed Seberg finally replied, "Yes, well, she's our baby."

With her mother cueing her between kitchen chores, Jean immediately set about learning Shaw's play by heart. She did not have to wait the full month. Preminger wanted her in New York two weeks early to read through the text with him in preparation for the screen test that constituted the final audition. A publicist met her at the airport and accompanied her to the Ambassador Hotel.

The following day in his suite at the same hotel, Preminger displayed the first signs of his formidable temper. What had happened, he raged, to the fresh reading Jean had given in Chicago? She had obviously been studying with someone, and it hadn't helped one bit. The outburst caught Jean off-guard. She *had* asked for a little outside advice, she confessed, but only in the hope of improving her performance.

Preminger's anger bore a double edge. On the one hand, he genuinely appreciated her untutored freshness, a quality he was determined to preserve on film, and he was distressed to see it endangered. On the other hand, his ego was at stake. The actress he chose for *St. Joan* would be his creation, and his alone. Meddling was forbidden.

Jean remained in New York for several days and bucked up her spirits by seeing plays and friends from summer stock. When she checked out of the hotel she thought it only fit, given Preminger's disappointment, to pay for her meals and phone calls herself. Her scrupulousness failed to impress him. "If she gets the part," he remarked to one of his associates, "wait a year and see what happens."

Chastened and disheartened, Jean flew home, no longer knowing what she could do to prepare herself for the all-important audition. She was back in New York in mid-October, by which time the pressure had mounted drastically. Preminger had reduced the field to three: Kelli Blaine, a New Yorker who had studied at the Actors Studio; Doreen Denning, a Swedish actress who had come from Stockholm to audition; and Jean.

To record the event, Preminger had hired Bob Willoughby, a jovial young still photographer who was between movie assignments. Willoughby remembers arriving shortly before noon at Preminger's office, where he was introduced to Jean.

"Her hair was long, and she had tiny moles on her face. I'm afraid I found her rather plain," he says. "I began snapping away, and before long I realized that just Jean and I were left in the office. Nobody had bothered to ask her to lunch."

Feeling protective, Willoughby took her to La Potinière, a small midtown French restaurant, contemplated the menu and asked her if she'd like to begin with the artichokes.

"When they came," he says, "I sat there, waiting for her to

start, smiling and talking and waiting. And then it dawned on me: My God, she's never eaten an artichoke before! 'Do you want me to show you how?' I asked her. She blushed and said yes. From that moment on, we had a nice feeling toward each other."

That night Willoughby escorted her to a Martha Graham performance on a pair of freebies he'd wangled from *Dance Magazine*. "She was really terrified of the screen test," he reports. "She clung to me all evening." After the performance he bought her a bouquet of violets from a woman on a street corner, wished her good luck and dropped her at her hotel.

Jean brought the violets with her to the Fox Movie-Tone studios the next morning and Willoughby, a romantic Irishman at heart, viewed it as a sign that he was to shepherd her through the ordeal. Already, most insiders thought that Preminger favored the teen-ager from Marshalltown. Their suspicions were confirmed early in the day when he asked her, after her initial scenes, if she would be willing to cut her hair for the rest of the test. Jean eagerly agreed. As the hairdresser chopped off her blond hair, her features were thrown into sharp relief. Her lips appeared fuller, her cheekbones more prominent, and her eyes acquired even greater radiance. At the same time, the closely cropped haircut gave her a distinctly androgynous look, not inimical to Shaw's conception of St. Joan.

Preminger drove Jean mercilessly throughout the day, forcing her to repeat difficult scenes over and over again. The harder she tried, the more biting his criticisms. "Well," he sneered after one take, "you did that almost as well as Rita Hayworth."

The grinding routine and hot lights took their toll. Jean slumped to the floor.

"What's the matter? Don't you have the guts to go on?" Preminger asked sarcastically.

Jean flared up. "I'll rehearse until you drop dead," she retorted, surprising herself as much as Preminger. Although she did not realize it at the time, the goading was one of Preminger's directorial tricks. If other directors preferred to coax emotions from a performer, Preminger jabbed for them. He later admitted he was secretly pleased with Jean's spunk.

Nerves frayed, she resumed the scene. Soon one of her arms was trembling so badly that she had to take hold of her leg to steady it. Finally she broke into hysterical sobs.

Preminger the tyrant immediately became Preminger the comforter. Encircling her with his arms, he lifted her off the floor and reassured her that the screen test had gone wonderfully.

"There was no question," says Willoughby, who witnessed the performances of all three candidates, "that Jean was the winner. The others were more polished, but Jean had the sincerity Otto was after. Unfortunately, he would stamp it entirely into the ground. I saw him the next day as he came out of the screening room and told him that in my mind there was no choice—Jean was the best. He just smiled, but I could see in that smile that he agreed with me." Preminger informed Jean of his decision that night and swore her to secrecy.

The publicity campaign had been carefully charted in advance. Preminger would announce the winner at a special press conference at noon on Sunday, October 21, and then introduce his find to the nation that evening on *The Ed Sullivan Show*. When publicist Mike Beck called the Sebergs on Friday evening, he could tell them only that Jean's screen test had gone well. Could they possibly fly to New York for the weekend on the chance that Jean might be chosen?

Ed Seberg hedged. It would mean leaving the drugstore and finding a neighbor to look after Kurt and David. Already, Jean's career was impinging on the family routine, and Ed Seberg appreciated order in his household. Beck managed to convince him. Unbeknownst to Jean, her parents were put up at the St. Moritz Hotel, to be produced miraculously at the opportune moment.

As it turned out, they hardly got to see their daughter in the crush of reporters and photographers who gathered in the executive offices of United Artists, which would release the film. Everyone munched on lox and bagels while a projectionist showed Jean's test. Oozing charm, Preminger then introduced Richard Widmark, who had earlier been cast, against type, to play the weak-willed Dauphin.

However, the director reserved his most effusive introduction for Jean, who was nervously waiting in a nearby office. A few hours before, she had called Carol Hollingsworth with the good news. It was one of her last independent actions: as she stepped into the room where the press and her parents waited, she officially became Preminger's chattel. Henceforth he would control her experience, and press agents would mold her image.

A reporter cornered Mrs. Seberg and asked if she had any reservations about her daughter's new life. "She's in good hands. We won't worry about her," replied the druggist's wife, tears streaming down her face.

That evening Ed Sullivan described Jean as "the girl who caught lightning in a bottle." Preminger beamed and Jean re-enacted her audition scene before sixty million viewers. The program also included comic Jack Paar, singer Marion Marlowe and, not inappropriately, a teeterboard act and the boxing Scimpini chimps.

Later that week Jean was whisked away by limousine to Boston. Demanding perfection, Preminger had arranged to have the moles removed from her face and throat. The procedure was simple and of no consequence, but Preminger insisted that it be done in secret. When Jean wrote a friend back home, she limited herself to saying: "I'm [here] storing up a little reserve for the festivities I hear they're preparing for me in Marshalltown."

In the succeeding months, oceans of ink would be spilled on Jean Seberg, who gamely repeated her humble stories of growing up in a small town and grappled with questions about a craft in which she had little experience. If the resultant newspaper features seem extraordinarily bland today, they do attest to the country's voracious appetite for a Cinderella story. Jean's adventure was a throwback to the Old Hollywood that tapped the good and the lovely for overnight stardom. Didn't her heritage, like Lana Turner's, include a soda fountain?

The studio system was dying, but the myths it spawned were more resistant. That Jean came from the Midwest only enhanced her appeal. America in the 1950s had outgrown its small towns, but not its small-town values. Virtue may no longer have been its own reward, but many Americans were reassured to know that it could still get you a film contract.

Jean's discovery, right down to the Sunday night consecration by Ed Sullivan, was the quintessential fairy story for the Eisenhower years.

In that sense, Jean's return to Marshalltown early in November proved to be more than just a big welcome home. It was a celebration of beliefs, an improbable mix of Chamber of Commerce boosterism, hometown pride and Hollywood flack.

"The town hadn't seen so much fanfare in quite some time," says Barbara Gates McIver, whose election as Marshalltown High School homecoming queen was eclipsed by the festivities. "Everybody's adrenaline was pumping."

Jean was met at the Des Moines airport by her family and friends, a clutch of photographers and a sizable crowd of onlookers, all shivering in the chilly fall air. Exchanging her gray cloth coat for a borrowed mink, she perched on the back of a Cadillac convertible for a ride to City Hall. There she received an orchid corsage, a key to the city and a small gold-plated ear of corn, by which the Chamber of Commerce meant to remind her of the region's productivity, not the pitfalls of her new profession. A police escort then accompanied her and her parents during the fifty-mile drive northeast to Marshalltown.

"Remember old Mr. Mendenhall?" Ed Seberg asked on the way. "He came into the store after *The Ed Sullivan Show* and every time he tried to tell me something, he'd burst out crying. 'Oh, Ed,' he'd say. 'She can do so much good!' And then, 'Boohoo!'"

The ancedote amused Jean. "I guess I'll marry Elvis Presley and reform him," she quipped. Her Lutheran father had intended the story to be instructive, however.

Preceded by the Marshalltown High School band, the convertible inched down Main Street, passed under a banner reading MARSHALLTOWN SALUTES YOU, and pulled up in front of the Community Y. An eight-foot portrait of Jean fluttered from a second-story window.

As the mayor gave her her second key to the city that day, and other town officials made congratulatory speeches, she hopped up and down to keep warm and waved at her friends.

"First of all, I want to know if this key will open any

banks," she said with a girlish giggle when it was her turn at the microphone. Then, with the gravity her audience expected, she continued, "It'll be a big help to know that you are all encouraging me. I hope I can make this role come to life. I'll do my best."

Preminger's office had sent along footage from Jean's screen test. To climax the homecoming, as much of Marshalltown as could fit crowded into the Orpheum Theater to watch the thirteen-minute clip. On admittedly premature evidence, the *Times-Republican* wrote: "Her portrayal of St. Joan brought a lump to the throat and a tear to the eye. Viewers came away certain that stardom was assured."

"It was like a huge pep rally," recalls Nick Nichols, then a first-year drama student at Marshalltown High School. "Jean had done the work, but it was as if we had all won. Maybe she wasn't as talented as we all thought she was, but the town never blamed her for that. Whatever happened afterward— well, it just wasn't her fault. Jean's success, after all, was our success."

Jean's friend Dawn Murray Quinn has another view: "That town had been so mean to her in the past. All of a sudden, everyone was fawning all over her. She was still the same girl, though. It was terribly hypocritical. By the end of the day, Jean was exhausted and close to hysterics."

Reporter Helen Eustis, there to do a feature for *McCall's,* also had reason to doubt the general euphoria. "I've never felt as if I belonged here," Jean told her later in the day in the privacy of her bedroom. "I know my parents love me—I don't mean it that way and I know this is silly—but I always felt as if I didn't fit in.

"I'd look at all the people in this town who just get up in the morning and go to work and go home to bed and I'd think, If that's all there is to life, I don't want it. I was always pretending I wasn't afraid, and I blustered and bluffed my way to all kinds of prizes and things. But I've never really been a very happy person.

"I used to have a dream where I was being chased through backyards by somebody who was going to stab me in the back. I always thought I'd die young."

The *McCall's* piece, which didn't appear for several months, stands out in the early spate of articles, probably because no one else—not even Jean herself—imagined that there could possibly be a dark side to the destiny that lay ahead.

During her week at home, Marshalltown High School held a special assembly in Jean's honor. It was announced that Masque and Dagger, the drama society, was inaugurating an annual Jean Seberg Award. Each year the most promising drama student would have his name inscribed under hers on a plaque in the school. (Thereafter, Jean also provided a $25 prize.) Then she answered questions from the students.

After *St. Joan,* she said, she hoped to do "something in Technicolor." She described Preminger as "a shrewd and kindly man." She had to decline a request to re-enact her audition scene, however. Her seven-year contract with Preminger, she said, prevented it.

That contract assured her of $250 a week the first year, money that was free and clear, since Preminger would take care of all her living expenses. The second year her salary escalated to $400 a week for forty weeks. By the seventh year she would be earning $2,500 a week. The figures were astronomical by Marshalltown standards. Ed Seberg re-established a sense of proportion by decreeing that the money would go into a bank account. Jean's weekly allowance would be $25.

On November 13, her eighteenth birthday, the movie star who had yet to make a movie boarded a plane for New York on her way to London, where *St. Joan* would be filmed. She took with her a Bible bound in white calf leather which Dawn Murray Quinn had given her, photographs of her parents, the golden ear of corn, and a satin mouse that Francis Benson thought might bring her granddaughter luck.

Three years later Nick Nichols also left Marshalltown to become an actor, an ambition he eventually abandoned. "We were raised in innocence in that town," he says now. "Marshalltown instilled in us the belief that if we did the right things, the honorable things, we would be a success. Our generation had what they used to call values, but we got into trouble with them. We discovered that the rest of the world wasn't playing by the same rules. No matter what surface sophistication we achieved, a lot of us held on to our adolescence. We never grew up, I guess."

In words that could just as easily apply to Jean, he adds, "We were all restless and we desperately wanted to get out. Now we all desperately want that security back again. It's hard to describe. I mean, we all grew up knowing, for example, that Riverside Cemetery is one of the ten most beautiful cemeteries in the country."

6

"I took my acting lessons before the largest audience in the world."

—JEAN SEBERG

Many years after *St. Joan* had been relegated to what Jean ruefully called "international flopdom," Otto Preminger dropped into a New York cinema one afternoon to catch a revival of the film. Viewing it with a cold eye, he claimed to understand what had gone awry.

"I made the mistake of taking a young, inexperienced girl and wanted her to be St. Joan, which, of course, she wasn't," he explained. "I didn't help her to understand and act the part. Indeed, I deliberately prevented her, because I was determined that she should be completely unspoiled. I think the instinct . . . was right, but now I would work with her for perhaps two years until she understood the part right through. Well, that was a big mistake, and I have nobody to blame but myself."

In December 1956, however, Preminger was operating on a more manipulative premise: despite herself, Jean could be *made* to play Joan of Arc. It sufficed to exploit her natural qualities. There would be nothing collaborative about the effort. He would provoke the desired performance. If the character was distraught, Jean could be rendered distraught. Preminger had not discovered an actress; he had engaged a puppet.

As soon as Jean's plane touched down in London, she en-

43

tered a world entirely of Preminger's making, a world both intensely lonely and painfully public. Preminger sequestered her in a suite at the elegant Dorchester Hotel and repeatedly advised her to concentrate on the task ahead. Yet, he was fully aware of the wealth of publicity she represented which, ideally, could accrue to his film.

On the slightest pretext he would summon journalists, and with the acumen of a carnival pitchman, pitch Jean their way. He wanted to keep her unspoiled, but he also wanted the world to know how unspoiled she was. When Jean was not being subjected to the glare of the international spotlight, she was facing the more calculating glare of her mentor. Preminger mistook her malleability for consent.

To much of the press, his dictatorial manner passed for a kind of stern paternalism. Following Jean to London, a reporter from the Des Moines *Register* wrote back that "the protective cordon they have thrown up around her is the most heart-warming element of the whole storybook situation." Jean, however, later likened it to being in prison. "Otto wanted nothing less than total control," says Bob Willoughby, who by then had been engaged as a still photographer on the set and became Jean's closest confidant during the three months of shooting.

Her introduction to the British press was more in the nature of a debutante's coming out. The reporters sat on gilt chairs, Jean wore white gloves and the champagne flowed. "She was entirely too sweet and naïve for the English reporters," Willoughby recalls. "They'd ask her how she liked her short haircut, and she'd reply, 'I like it a lot because now I can slip down low in the bathtub.' It sounds charming, but it wasn't something you said to the British."

When she let it out that one of her high school friends had nicknamed her Dowdy Mouse, the London *Sketch* gleefully branded her Little Miss Dowdy Mouse in a two-part series devoted to her unlikely leap to fame. If the "storybook situation" continued to intrigue the British, they also felt dutybound to express reservations that an Iowa maid could actually portray a French saint as viewed by an Irish dramatist.

The molding process soon began in earnest. Preminger had

lined up a French teacher for his charge, an elocution master to shape her flat Iowa accent into more acceptable "mid-Atlantic" speech, and a grizzled historical adviser to teach her how to draw a broadsword. In the unseasonably warm December weather, she donned tweeds and cantered hesitatingly along Hyde Park's fashionable Rotten Row on a steed named Monster. "I'm so tired and busy," she cabled Dawn Murray Quinn. "Nine hours on a horse yesterday. All goes well."

There was a round of theatergoing—with Preminger picking both the plays and the escorts. After a performance of Noël Coward's *Nude with Violin,* she went backstage to meet John Gielgud. A photographer captured Jean's slack-jawed admiration of the star, who would play the Earl of Warwick opposite her in the film. (Preminger's first choice had been Richard Burton, but negotiations had fallen through.)

On December 17 the *St. Joan* cast met at Alexander Korda's town house for the first read-through of Graham Greene's screenplay. Along with Gielgud, Preminger had hired some of the finest talents of the English theater: Richard Todd, Finlay Currie, Felix Aylmer, Anton Walbrook and Margot Grahame.

The omnipresent photographers were joined this time by an entire documentary-film crew. "Jean and Margot Grahame were the only two women there, so it was rather like a board meeting," says Gielgud. "I felt awfully sorry for her having to go through the ordeal. It was enough to make an experienced actor terribly nervous." Photographs taken that day, however, show her reciting her lines with a vivacity that Preminger would progressively eliminate from her performance.

"I really think Otto wanted Jean to feel overwhelmed," says Lionel Larner, then one of Preminger's casting agents. "He saw Joan of Arc as this birdlike creature, surrounded by the massive pillars of church and state. One of the ways he tried to achieve that was by surrounding Jean with all these hugely talented British repertory players. But it didn't work out."

Despite the ceaseless activity, Jean underwent serious bouts of loneliness, compounded by the absence of news from John Maddox. "You're the only one of the NY gang that's written," she admitted in a letter to Richard Sheppard. "I must confess it makes me feel pretty disappointed. I've just posted my fourth letter to John without a reply." Dejected by the abrupt change in their fortunes, John Maddox had, in fact, resolved to break off his relationship with Jean.

"It hurt him a lot," says Barbara Saturnine, "but his male ego was at stake. Jean was going to be a big star and he wasn't. But he also didn't want to be a burden to her. When he got the news that Jean had been selected by Preminger, he knew it was all over.

"He wouldn't talk to her on the phone or answer her letters. He was stubborn and when he made up his mind, he made up his mind. He went through a couple of marriages after that. Neither worked out too well. Jean was always in the back of his head. I know that he kept two mice statuettes she had given him for a long, long time."*

With Christmas approaching, Preminger magnanimously offered his star a four-day trip to France, during which she would visit the habitats of Joan of Arc. The pilgrimage would provide her with a change of pace and first-hand knowledge that could only benefit her performance. And the fact that several American magazines were interested in a spread about Jean in Joan of Arc country certainly weighed in the decision.

Otto and Jean were accompanied by Willoughby and also by Tom Ryan, a rotund American journalist who would join Preminger's staff as a script reader. If Preminger was Jean's surrogate father, Willoughby and Ryan were becoming her surrogate brothers. In Paris they strolled up and down the Champs Elysées, explored the Left Bank night life and generally played tourist. Four years later Jean's closely cropped hair would be as identifiable as Maurice Chevalier's straw hat. This time, it attracted surprised looks from the Parisians, some of whom wondered audibly what sex she was.

At Dior's, Preminger treated Jean to a black satin evening dress and a hooded evening coat. The saleslady solicitously suggested that Mademoiselle might want to wear a wig with the

---

* Years later Maddox became seriously manic-depressive. In one of his manic states, he chartered a sailboat for a voyage down the Atlantic coast. None of his friends is sure what happened next. The boat left the inland waterway along the Virginia coast, headed out to sea and presumably disappeared in the Bermuda Triangle.

outfit. The next evening Jean watched a performance of *Tea and Sympathy* and visited with its star, Ingrid Bergman, in her dressing room. "With each generation, Joan's hair gets shorter and shorter," remarked Bergman, who had played the role in the 1948 film.

Preminger stayed on in Paris while Jean, Ryan and Willoughby went on their pilgrimage. On Christmas Day she attended mass in the village of Domremy, where Joan was born and first heard her voices. "Home at last," Jean scribbled on a postcard to her parents. The trio moved on to the cathedral at Rheims, to Vaucouleurs and to Rouen, where Joan had been burned in the marketplace and her ashes scattered over the river. The Iowa girl later said it was the rolling countryside, not Paris, that inspired her love affair with France.

Willoughby snapped pictures every step of the way. "One day," he remembers, "it began to snow. Jean was freezing, but she wanted to push on. All of a sudden I realized she was blue with cold. Oh my God, I thought, we're responsible for Preminger's star and she's going to catch pneumonia and die. So we dashed into a nearby café and started pouring brandies down her throat. Well, she wasn't much of a drinker and before long she was looped. By this time I could picture the headlines: 'Joan of Arc Is a Drunk!' We tried madly to sober her up on the way back to Paris, but Jean was happy as a clam.

"We had a great time during that trip. We were all young and spoke the same language. Jean really had no defenses against Otto, and I think even he realized we were a good thing for her. We could jolly her out of her states."

Jean was moved by her pilgrimage, but on her return to London she allowed that "I didn't really get a new conception of Joan, because I have always believed in her. I'm trying to make her simple, faithful and honest. She has always been real to me . . . another girl."

That reality faded when shooting began in the drafty Shepperton studios early in January 1957. The night before, jittery and scared, she had telephoned her parents for advice. "Go to sleep," replied Ed Seberg.

A flood of telegrams awaited her at the studio, including one from her sister, Mary Ann, and another from Ingrid Bergman, wishing her luck in "the best of any roles an actress can play." Once again, Preminger had convoked the press. When it came time for Jean's first scene, Joan's arrival at the court of the Dauphin, she looked helplessly at the assembled reporters and mumbled, "I have to go now."

For the next eight weeks the "protective cordon" grew tighter and tighter. She was awakened at five-thirty with breakfast on a tray. An hour later a limousine picked her up in front of the Dorchester for the forty-five-minute drive to Shepperton Studios, usually with Preminger and Willoughby. At seven-thirty she reported for make-up and costumes and was locked into her twenty-eight-pound suit of armor. Occasionally her hair had to be trimmed shorter, a ritual she grew to dislike.

During lulls in the shooting, Preminger would discourage any fraternization with the cast and counsel her to return to her dressing room to study her script. One day, behind his back she regaled the crew with a quick, unsteady tap dance in her armor.

"I really think Jean worked her heart out to please Otto," says Willoughby. "She was very frightened and insecure, but she was determined to do a good job. Otto was a tyrant on the set, though. Nothing had an effect on him. He kept her on a constant emotional pitch, which isn't a professional way of acting. Often at the end of the day's shooting, she would be sobbing hysterically. The crew would call 'Break,' and Jean would be broken."

After watching rushes, Jean was driven back to the Dorchester for a solitary dinner in her suite and, exhausted, would fall into bed by nine. Several weeks into this routine, Willoughby proposed that Jean have her dinners with him and Max Weiss, an American record executive who was sharing his suite at the Royal Court Hotel.

"Jean jumped at the idea," he says. "For a while the limousine dropped her off at our place and then came and sped her back to the Dorchester after dinner. None of us had any night life at the time, but I think the camaraderie helped relieve the pressure for her. Max was a bit eccentric, and he and Jean invented a strange language they spoke together. He called her 'Thelma,' for a reason that now escapes me. We were all going through it together, and we cried on one another's shoulders. But Jean never complained, no matter how brutal things got. She knew the movie was a great opportunity."

One evening they slipped away to a nearby restaurant that featured American steaks and live guitar music. Jean spotted a starry-eyed couple among the diners and concluded they were in love. Back at her hotel, she stayed up until two in the morning trying to draft a short story about them. "Otto wouldn't like that, would he!" she confided to a friend.

On the set Preminger continued to bear down hard. "That was as cold as a cucumber," he ranted one day. "You're not thinking the part. *You're not thinking the part!*" What she was supposed to be thinking was increasingly mysterious to her. Forced to repeat some takes ten or twenty times, she felt the spontaneity draining from her. Her face froze and her body stiffened.

In the edited film, the strongest impression she would make was that of a helplessly bewildered girl struggling valiantly to get things right. Yet her fortitude won her the admiration of the crew and her fellow actors, who tried to temper Preminger's fury with gifts or gentle words of encouragement.

"You couldn't not like her," says Kenneth Haigh, who played the compassionate Brother Martin. "She was like someone who had just been born. There wasn't an unkind bone in her body. And she was so unimaginably fresh!"

Gielgud was particularly generous, and Jean described him as "the light of my life." On one occasion, sensing that she was near the breaking point, he remained on the set, silently lending support, even though his own work was done. Not long after, he brought her a cup and saucer that had belonged to his illustrious great-aunt, the actress Ellen Terry.

"She didn't know much about phrasing, climax, all the things the part needed," says Gielgud. "Even in bits on the screen, it was a tremendous role to attempt to do. Jean was childishly and sweetly grateful to me because I showed some interest in her and tried to help. For a couple of years after we'd done that film, she'd ring me up whenever she was in London and tell me that she thought of me with great affection. It touched me."

Occasionally, even Preminger relented after hours. He

would assuage his charge with presents—a typewriter, a phonograph on which she played her Frank Sinatra and Ella Fitzgerald records, and a framed print of Picasso's "Child with White Dove," her favorite artwork. He would run his hand through her short hair, hug her affectionately and call her "baby."

The rare social events he permitted dazzled the young actress. Hardly six months out of high school, she found herself keeping dinner company, albeit rather silently, with Vivien Leigh, Sir Laurence Olivier and Peggy Ashcroft. Weighing both the pros and cons of her situation, she wrote her parents: "I am very happy in this work. It is intensely difficult and exhausting and sometimes infuriating, but it is what I wanted." As if Preminger were dictating, she added: "Any time away from the part gives me a guilty conscience."

Not all her youthful spirits were extinguished by the rigors of shooting. She enjoyed a moment of playful revenge when Harry Belafonte passed through London. Belafonte had recently starred for Preminger in *Carmen Jones,* and a dinner party was promptly set up at the Brompton Grill.

"Jean, Max Weiss and I thought we'd give Otto the big elbow," relates Willoughby. "So we arranged to have the restaurant staff roll out the red carpet. Only, we told them to refer to Otto as Mr. Hitchcock. The waiters were superb. 'How are you, Mr. Hitchcock?' 'Nice to see you, Mr. Hitchcock.' The first few times, he let it pass. But by the end of the evening he was pounding the table with his fist and screaming, 'That is not my name! I am Otto Preminger!' It may be the only time Otto was had."

Preminger had saved the biggest scene, Joan's burning at the stake, for the final week of shooting. In what was turning out to be mostly a static, talky film, this was the one chance to pull out all the stops. Several hundred extras, more than had ever been assembled on an English sound stage, jammed into Roger Furse's replica of the Rouen marketplace.

It was another natural for publicity, so a herd of reporters from Fleet Street swelled the crowd at Preminger's invitation. As Jean was dragged through the marketplace and manacled to the stake, the extras jeered raucously. "There was something absolutely petrifying about the hordes shouting, 'Burn her, burn her!'" says Lionel Larner, who watched from the sidelines.

Jean cast her eyes heavenward, and the hooded executioners strode forward to light the pyre, which was fed by seven gas cylinders concealed under a mound of faggots. Only five of the seven ignited. Suddenly the gas from the other two erupted in a whoosh of smoke and flame, enveloping Jean.

"I'm burning!" she howled. Instinctively she tugged her arms free of the chains and covered her face as a ball of fire swept upward over her knees, her stomach and the backs of her hands. Her costume was burning as well.

Panic ran through the studio. One of the executioners leaped up onto the pyre, wrenched the chains away from Jean's neck, and studio firemen attacked the blaze with extinguishers.

"I was transfixed," said Willoughby. "It happened so fast."

Jean was carried to her dressing room and a doctor treated her for minor burns. "I smell like a singed chicken," she joked bravely, before volunteering to continue with the scene. But Preminger canceled the rest of the afternoon's shooting.

Predictably, the accident made all the London newspapers and several magazines. *Life* devoted a page of pictures to the near-immolation. Preminger was accused by some cynics of pulling off the greatest publicity stunt ever. It wasn't true, of course. Perched on a crane above the tumult, Preminger had experienced a moment of stark terror. Later, however, he noted phlegmatically, "We got all of it on film. The camera took four hundred extra feet. The crowd reaction was fantastic. I'll probably use some of it." He did.

Jean reassured her parents that night by telephone that she was all right. "What I really want," she whimpered, "is to be home for two weeks without a reporter within a hundred miles."

Her hand bandaged, she joined Preminger, Willoughby and Ryan in the limousine the following morning. En route to the studio, the vehicle hit a patch of ice, skidded out of control, spun around twice and careened into a lamppost. Cushioned by the portly Ryan, Jean suffered only a nosebleed, but Preminger fractured his wrist and Willoughby's cameras were smashed. Preminger wondered what else could possibly happen. Jean managed a note of levity: "I could fall into a pond with my twenty-eight pounds of armor."

That afternoon, still badly shaken, she watched the rushes from the previous day's shooting. Seeing herself in flames, she fell to pieces. Jean never remounted the pyre. Subsequent shots were done with mirrors and a dummy.

"That film was supposed to be the trial of St. Joan, but it really turned into the trial of Jean," Willoughby reflected a long time afterward. "When it was over, she was a different girl . . . liberated in a way. It was like getting out of school or prison. But she'd done it. She was battered, but she was a survivor." As a result, Jean's suicide twenty-two years later mystified him. "The girl I knew just wasn't a loser," he said.

Preminger had also developed a grudging admiration for Jean's strength under duress. Riding back to the Dorchester one night, he informed her that he had acquired the rights to Françoise Sagan's best-selling novel of adolescent ennui, *Bonjour Tristesse.* He was releasing the information to Ed Sullivan that he had settled on a star: Jean Seberg.

Jean's gratitude was immense.

The scars which the fire had left on her stomach would never go away, however.

7

"Her future could not look brighter."

—MARSHALLTOWN *Times-Republican*

Some neighbors in Marshalltown thought that Dorothy Seberg, despite her calm exterior, secretly relished the hubbub over her daughter. Ed Seberg was less enthusiastic about the disruptions it imposed on their life. When asked what he thought about Jean's career, he usually replied, "Ask me again in ten years."

Nevertheless, at the end of February 1957, the Sebergs were cajoled into taking part in the CBS television program *Stand Up and Be Counted.* During the daily show, the studio audience and home viewers were requested to supply their views on less than pressing questions of the moment.

"Will you continue to live in Marshalltown or move where your daughter goes?" the Sebergs were asked. The studio audience was of the firm opinion that they should remain in Marshalltown. Unwittingly, Mrs. Seberg underscored the nonsense by responding, "We hadn't planned to do anything else." They were, in fact, contemplating the purchase of a ranch house several blocks west of the stucco house on 6th Street and were worried that the move, which seemed to coincide with Jean's stardom, might be perceived by the townsfolk as "putting on airs."

Under strict instructions from Preminger to rest, Jean returned home for three weeks and a welcome-back dinner (conscientiously reported by the *Times-Republican*) of fried chicken, Bing cherry salad and meringue pie.

The *McCall's* article about Jean's homecoming the previous November had since hit the newsstands. Local feathers were ruffled and there were grumblings that Jean Seberg was getting too big for her britches. The Sebergs were upset and Jean hastened to mend fences with a public apology. "I always wanted to act," she explained to the Des Moines *Register,* "and I wanted to go where I could act. There is more opportunity elsewhere. But that doesn't mean I don't love Marshalltown. I hope the people won't be mad at me. It was a wonderful place to grow up."

Afterward she was quick to tell her friends, "Don't believe what you read about me in the papers." But the spite she had always sensed in the homely town bothered her.

In preparation for her upcoming role in *Bonjour Tristesse,* to be filmed on the Riviera, that summer, Jean boned up on her French and took swimming lessons at the Y. She caught up on friendships, although the incessant talk of marriages and basketball games now struck her as foreign. As if to underscore the fact that Jean remained a hometown girl, however, the *Times-Republican* published a full page of pictures showing her going about her daily routine.

In mid-April she departed for New York, where she had the first intimations that *St. Joan* might be less than a triumph. At a sneak preview at the Astor Theater, the afternoon audience was largely inattentive; a number of patrons stalked out before the end. Clutching the arm of a publicist, Jean watched herself half in tears, half in panic. "It was the longest picture I ever saw," she confessed afterward. The experience so unnerved her that she required sedation before going to bed that night. It also seemed to her that Preminger's scorn had acquired a sharper edge. "I don't like the way you talk, walk or dress," he barked at her several nights later.

Still, she tried to rationalize that *St. Joan* was an "intellectual" movie. The test would come in Paris on May 12, when it would have its world premiere in the ornate Opera House.

Preminger's sights were no longer fixed exclusively on *St. Joan.* Before seventy-five photographers, he arranged for Jean to meet Françoise Sagan. The young author had sold the rights to *Bonjour Tristesse* as an unpublished manuscript for the risible sum of $10,000. Now it was being hailed as a literary phenomenon. Preminger had to ante up considerably more than $10,000, but the difference was not going into Sagan's pocket. She looked sullen and uncooperative.

The world-weariness that had made her renowned at eighteen contrasted sharply with Jean's American wholesomeness. Sagan resented being corralled into a public encounter, and she gazed like a hawk at the actress who would soon be incarnating Cécile, her disillusioned heroine. Privately, Sagan wondered how.

The *St. Joan* premiere momentarily eclipsed the annual Cannes Film Festival, then in full swing, and received lavish coverage in the Paris newspapers. Ticket prices from $100 to $1,000 benefited the Polio Foundation. The auditorium crawled with such celebrities as Maurice Chevalier, Salvador Dali, Yul Brynner, Gérard Philipe, Arletty, Eddie Constantine, François Mitterand, Olivia de Havilland, and Anita Ekberg, fancifully described in one report as "luminous and immense like the Archangel Michael."

Jean wore an aqua Givenchy evening dress, a gift from Preminger, and her hair, which had begun to grow out, was styled in soft waves. "She has the eyes of a dove and an expression of infinite peace," rhapsodized a Paris daily, which also interpreted her stage fright as "a bit of the inspired insolence of the Maid before her judges." Jean took only partial reassurance from her parents' opening-night telegram. "We don't care whether it fails or not," they had cabled. "You're still our star."

The glittery audience was warmed up by Bob Hope and French comic Fernandel, who improvised a short sketch about a naïve American tourist and the crafty waiter who relieves him of his billfold. The film, however, promptly cooled everyone off. As the lights came up, applause was polite at best. Most of the celebrities made perfunctory appearances at the party afterward at Maxim's. Several failed to show at all.

"I knew how hard I had worked. I was so excited about it," Jean later told Mike Wallace. "Everybody came up to me and said, 'You were wonderful.' I was so gullible. I thought the film was a huge success."

Harry Belafonte took her out on a date several nights later. Jean breathlessly recounted to her friends that they had gone for a stroll and the singer had crooned "My Funny Valentine" to her by a Paris fountain. It was as if she were living a page from the fan magazines.

The *St. Joan* reviews quickly corrected that impression. A couple of the French critics perceived in Jean a tantalizing mixture of innocence and eroticism, and while that didn't accord at all with their views of their national heroine, it did, at least, augur well for *Bonjour Tristesse*. The film itself was dismissed as "a heavy error" that "is moving at no moment." It did negligible business during its first-run engagement on the Champs Elysées.

In the face of what loomed as a disaster, Preminger's tactic was simply to throw the publicity machine into high gear. Jean was trundled off on a twenty-seven-day tour of twelve cities in the United States and Canada. By one estimate, she tallied 105 radio interviews, 18 photo sessions, 16 press conferences, 30 newspaper interviews and 22 "special events," which meant anything from hyping a department store to dispensing greetings on the steps of city hall. Hollywood settled for a cocktail party in her honor.

Shortly after her return to the United States, Jean had met Paul Desmond, the thirty-two-year-old saxophonist with the Dave Brubeck Quartet. With typical abandon, she threw herself headlong into the relationship. "He is much too old, much too complex and much too wonderful for me," she confided to Lynda Haupert, her Marshalltown friend. "He isn't attractive at all. He's just beautiful." The two saw each other again briefly during her publicity stopover in San Francisco. Jean left convinced that it was true romance.

Throughout the tour, she impressed interviewers with her poise and modesty. "I've learned you can go anywhere and get along with anyone if you're honest," she told herself. Inwardly, however, the doubts were beginning to pile up rapidly.

Flying back across the Atlantic for the London premiere,

Jean tried to crystallize her feelings in verse. In the margin of her newspaper she scribbled:

> I run too fast,
> I fly so high
> I hit so hard
> Too wide my eye
> Too full my heart
> Too deep my pain
> So short the kiss . . .

She struck out the last line and was unable during the remainder of the flight to find a suitable conclusion.

Clutching the newspaper and a copy of *The Catcher in the Rye* in her arms, she posed for cameramen on the steps of the airplane at London airport. The London *Daily Mail* craftily enlarged the photo, discovered the poem and splashed it across its pages. Readers were promised £5 for the best final line. Jean was embarrassed. "That poem was just for me and about me," she complained.

The London reviews of *St. Joan* followed the Paris pattern, only this time the movie was assailed for tinkering with a Shavian masterpiece. Preminger saw no further point in flogging a dead saint. He let Jean escape to the South of France to nurse her wounds.

By now, what was billed as the Western Hemisphere Premiere—at the Orpheum Theater in Marshalltown on June 25—had been reduced to an empty formality. "Jean, of course, will be absent," wrote publicist George Thomas to Marshalltown authorities. "Possibly, the eight-foot painting of her for last fall's homecoming could be installed for the affair."

Jean's absence in no way dampened the zeal of seventy Marshalltown merchants, who bought a full-page ad in the *Times-Republican* for an "Open Letter to Jean Seberg." "While we are immensely proud of your original selection from thousands of young women to play the title role of *St. Joan*," the letter went, "we have been even prouder of your modest acceptance of the honors and the public adulation that have come your way in the meteoric rise from a 'home town girl' to a star of international recognition. Too, we are most grateful for the worldwide publicity you have given Marshall-town . . . basking in the limelight of your activities."

Exactly 914 Iowans, a sell-out crowd, packed the newly painted movie house draped with bunting for the 8 P.M. premiere. "I hope you enjoyed the movie as much as I enjoyed making it," Jean wished them in a tape-recorded message not intentionally ironic. Thomas had warned the Sebergs beforehand that the reviews for their daughter's performance were apt to be "mixed." While seven-year-old David slept through most of the film, snoring audibly at times, they watched attentively, trying to restrain their pride.

In a front-page review the following afternoon, the *Times-Republican* attempted to wax enthusiastic. "Those of us who have known Jean from childhood may have difficulty separating the Jean Seberg we know from the Maid of Orleans she plays," it said before concluding, somewhat ambiguously, "Her performance was more than her home-town fans had a right to expect."

The American reviews were not "mixed." They were vitriolic. Preminger's relentless publicity campaign seemed to have triggered a backlash among the critics, and Jean was the principal beneficiary of their hostility.

The *coup de grâce* was delivered by *Time* magazine, which wrote:

> Actress Seberg, with the advantage of youth and the disadvantage of inexperience, is drastically miscast. Shaw's Joan is a chunk of hard bread, dipped in the red wine of battle and devoured by the ravenous angels. Actress Seberg, by physique and disposition, is the sort of honey bun that drugstore desperadoes like to nibble with their milkshakes.

A year later the movie's world-wide grosses had amounted to less than $400,000.

"What good are successes," quipped Preminger, "if you can't have a failure once in a while?"

8

"Otto Preminger is the world's most charming dinner guest and the world's most sadistic director."

—JEAN SEBERG

Jean said that after the disastrous *St. Joan* premiere, she had fled to Nice because it was the only town in France whose name she could pronounce correctly. Actually, she was badly run-down, and Preminger felt that the warm climate might help restore her health and spirits. Since much of *Bonjour Tristesse* would be filmed in the nearby village of Le Lavandou, Preminger also thought that soaking up some of the hedonistic atmosphere of the Riviera wouldn't hurt.

Having played a saint, Jean would now be trying her luck as a sinner—albeit an unconscious one. Cécile, her character, is an indolent teen-ager, living a life of freewheeling pleasure with her dashing father (to be played by David Niven). Following Sagan's book, Arthur Laurents' screenplay details the events of one summer on the Riviera, when the loose bond between father and daughter is jeopardized by the arrival of Anne, an attractive widow (Deborah Kerr). To preserve her facile existence, Cécile indirectly causes Anne's death and comes to experience the "sadness" of the title. Jean's winsomeness was in direct opposition to the velvet amorality of Sagan's book, but Jean described the role as "easier than Joan, definitely, in the sense that Cécile is a young, extremely modern girl who enjoys life."

In June of 1957 Jean also viewed herself in those terms. "I am alternating between such mad heights of happiness and depression I think I'll die," she wrote Lynda Haupert before the six-week filming began.

The depression was rooted in the scathing reviews of *St. Joan,* which had been sent to her in a neat bundle, the least insulting on top. They had caused a deep wound, but they also brought into question the Seberg family credo that application pays off. "It is always difficult to believe that if everyone has worked so hard on something, it can be anything but a success," she wrote home. "When it isn't, you doubt yourself." But, she reasoned, "If it had been a success, I probably would have become unbearable."

The dizzying heights of happiness stemmed from her infatuation with Paul Desmond. Jean had been, no doubt, a passing fancy in the musician's life. But with an ocean between them, she imagined herself in a full-blown affair. "I am, in my usual, awful impetuous way, sending flowers and gifts and calling from Nice," she confided to Haupert. "My father will flip because I'm not that rich. But I can't help it."

Jean had rented a tiny studio apartment with kitchenette on the Rue Andreoli in Nice, and according to her letters, tried to perk it up with a yellow tablecloth and orange gladioli. On her record player, the Dave Brubeck Quartet played nonstop.

Most mornings she went to the pebble-lined beach, spread out her books and writing materials in the sun and let her health mend. Three times each week, a doctor gave her a shot for her anemia. Afternoons she would stop in a café on her way back from the beach and drink a couple of pastis, an alcoholic, licorice-flavored apéritif, especially popular in the South of France. Jean thought it was a fruit drink, savored its strange flavor and sometimes wondered why she was so drowsy afterward. She tried to cook for herself at night, although on several occasions the cupboard was empty and she had to cable Ed Seberg to send some of the money he was keeping for her.

French starlet Mylene Demongeot, who lived in Nice and had been cast as Niven's mistress in the film, remembers meeting her at this time: "One day this adorable American arrived, brimming with gaiety and ambition. She had her typewriter and her 'library' with her and said she secretly wanted to be a writer. We laughed about that because her complete library then consisted of *The Portable Hemingway, The Portable Proust* and *The Portable Faulkner.* She was so full of life and totally unselfconscious. She would walk around her apartment without a stitch on."

For transportation, Jean had acquired a Quatre Chevaux, a tinny little Citroën with a motor that hiccuped a lot, and she scooted in and out of the Nice traffic, "honking my bleeting baby horn and feeling every inch Françoise Sagan's much poorer Iowa cousin."

A policeman approached her one day for a minor parking infraction. Unable to talk her way out of the ticket, Jean tried tears. The policeman demanded to see her papers, recognized her as the actress who had played Joan of Arc, and sniffed, "Joan of Arc would not cry."

Although Jean was taking French lessons, her command of the language was still hesitant. "My French is so bad, I can't understand unless I concentrate," she wrote Haupert. "When 'I vant to be alone,' I just let my mind wander and bango, they (the French) are shut out as deftly as if I'd turned off a hearing aid."

Being a foreigner in an unfamiliar city, she cultivated her solitary side. When Richard Sheppard, her summer-stock pal who by then was working for *Photoplay* magazine, contacted her regarding a possible article, she urged him to respect her past confidences regarding John Maddox. "What you know above and beyond my respect for Otto Preminger is quite personal, too," she wrote. "The only important thing is that I do want to be an actress some day and that I know I have a lot to learn, that right now everything is secondary to work . . . I have tried to take stock of whither I goest and hope I can maintain a steady line through life. I am discovering it isn't easy, nor is it easy to be alone, but as G.B.S.'s S.J. said, one can find a strength in loneliness, too. Anyway, I am proud to have managed to survive and even eat in a strange place on the romantic Riviera alone."

She closed the letter: "Take care, work hard, love life and living—it is amazingly, silvery beautiful. And most of all, be gentle." It was the philosophy Jean Seberg tried to live by all her life.

In July she returned to Paris for costume fittings with Givenchy—who would also reinstate her *St. Joan* crew cut—and the first scenes of her new movie. Preminger had decided to film the present-day sequences in and around Paris in black-and-white. They would frame the events of the preceding summer, which would be shot on the Riviera in color.

The director had changed neither his manner nor his methods, but there was one small improvement. Jean was no longer carrying the full burden of the film, as she had in *St. Joan.* Both Niven and Kerr, mature, experienced stars, deflected some of Preminger's unpleasantness on the set. "It's going to be you up there—your face, your expression and your way of reading the lines, not the director's," Kerr reminded her when Preminger got difficult. For her part, Jean admired the handsome red-headed actress, who seemingly had combined a successful career and personal life.

Preminger had arranged to film the Riviera sequences in the three-story villa of Pierre Lazareff, a French publishing magnate. Overlooking the Mediterranean, the house enjoyed a superb setting. The red rocks, turquoise water and baby pines were made for Technicolor. After the drafty Shepperton studios, Jean responded to the beauty and warmth of the surroundings. Not that Preminger had become any less intractable. He was, some observers suspected, fully disenchanted with Jean by this time, and his insistence on using her in *Bonjour Tristesse* had less to do with her burgeoning talents than his own desire for vindication.

His rages resumed on an almost daily basis. Accounts of one day's shooting are characteristic. The script called for Jean to emerge from the sea and to run, dripping wet, toward the camera with a broad smile on her face. According to Demongeot, Jean had informed Preminger of the time of the month when she would be better off staying away from the water. Either by coincidence or calculation, Preminger scheduled the scene for one of those days.

Jean was doused with a bucket of water, the film rolled, and she gamboled girlishly toward the camera and smiled. Preminger was not pleased and called for an additional dousing. Each time he found something else to criticize. Shivering less from the chill than from the verbal abuse, Jean carried on until she was near the point of fainting. By the end of the day, some of the crew thought she looked ill.

As Gielgud had done on *St. Joan,* Niven tried to allay her nervousness and keep things in perspective. "It's only a movie," he whispered in her ear one day. "They'll pay seventy-five cents. Then they'll leave the theater and say, 'Who the heck was that guy with the mustache?'"

Jean's growing friendship with Kerr helped, too. In their scenes together, she managed to appear relatively relaxed and natural. Kerr regretted that their paths split after *Bonjour Tristesse.* "I formed a very deep respect for the quiet strength with which she put up with all the extravagant publicity that had been forced on her by her discovery and the lashing she took from the critics. This strength was also apparent in her coping with Otto, who as a friend and social companion is a charming and witty person, but who turns into a demon when directing. At least he did on *Bonjour Tristesse* as far as Jean was concerned. I think any other woman would have collapsed in tears or just walked out. But she calmly took all the berating and achieved a very interesting and true Sagan-type heroine."

Much of that strength was a façade, however. Preminger's lashings sometimes drove the hypersensitive girl to bleak thoughts of suicide. When the company moved down the coast to film at the Carlton Hotel in Cannes, Jean hit bottom.

"She threatened suicide a couple of times," confirms Aki Lehman, a friend of both Jean's and Preminger's. "But it was like a bribe with her. She did it when she felt unloved or unappreciated. She probably had read that Brigitte Bardot had tried to slit her wrists. Jean was very unhappy during much of that filming. She admired Otto as a father figure, and at the same time she hated his guts."

Three years later Jean attended the Cannes Film Festival, escorted by Sidney Poitier. She was by then an elegant, accomplished star. At a banquet at the Carlton she sat next to director Daniel Petrie and in the course of conversation laughed at how strange it was to find herself back at the hotel under such altered circumstances. "Do you know that during the filming of *Bonjour Tristesse* I stood on a balcony of this very hotel and seriously considered throwing myself off the edge?" she said to him. "Part of me refused to give Otto Preminger the satisfaction, though." Jean was so composed and seemed so well-adjusted at the time that Petrie discounted her remarks. Not until he himself directed her in *Mousey* in 1973 would he realize the extent of the damage that Preminger had wrought.

Despite Preminger's invective, *Bonjour Tristesse* was not a repeat performance of *St. Joan.* Bob Willoughby, who joined the company midway through the filming, sensed a transformation in Jean. "She was no longer the dependent girl I'd known in London," he said. "She'd emerged from her cocoon. There's something liberating about the sun. I think she had come to some sort of sexual revolution in her life. She was very aware of herself as a woman and she knew that men found her very desirable. Before, she had been like a puppy. Now she was a movie star. I didn't like her as well in her new guise, but maybe it's just because she didn't need me as much."

Preminger no longer controlled her behavior off the set quite as rigidly as he had in London. The summer season was at its peak on the Riviera. He and his stars were besieged with dinner and cocktail-party invitations. Jean's delectable beauty and the reams of publicity surrounding her career made her a curiosity for the vacationing socialites.

One of the centers of Riviera social life was the palatial villa of armaments millionaire Commandant Paul Louis Weiller. At La Reine Jeanne, his St. Tropez estate, Weiller entertained such international celebrities as Greta Garbo, Douglas Fairbanks Jr. and Merle Oberon, assorted dukes and duchesses, and those anonymous hangers-on who, by virtue of their charm or looks, were allowed to flesh out the cast. Yachts anchored regularly offshore.

One Saturday, Niven, Kerr and Jean were invited for lunch. Although Charlie Chaplin was present, Jean was captivated by one of Weiller's less famous houseguests—François Moreuil, a twenty-three-year-old lawyer whose considerable charm, some felt, masked considerable ambition. He was staying at the villa for the summer, and that afternoon he showed her how to water-ski. While they were sitting on the beach afterward, Jean heard Preminger screaming for her. Instinctively she turned and ran in the opposite direction. "Jean, stop right where you are," François ordered firmly. "Now walk calmly." Then he took her hand, quieted her down and led her back to Preminger.

Reluctantly Jean had already concluded that her long-distance romance with Paul Desmond was a decidedly one-way street. She accepted Moreuil's attentions with a mixture of relief and gratitude.

"You asked me about Paul," she wrote to Dawn Murray Quinn. "Well, it took me quite a while to realize it, but everything ended as soon as I left San Francisco. He didn't write, didn't call, didn't do anything. And I became a very bitter girl. But now I've met someone who has taken his place wonderfully—a tall, thin, very black-haired Parisian lawyer named François Moreuil. He is a count but his family doesn't use the title . . . He wants one day to be a film director. And he loves me. When I was sick here, he was my nurse. When I cry, he cries. He has such a lovely soul and, thank goodness, he speaks a perfect English."

Weiller expected Moreuil and his other houseguests, who often numbered thirty, to be in round-the-clock attendance. For his part Preminger expected Jean's boyfriend to keep his distance. Nonetheless, Jean and François succeeded in seeing each other on the sly. The secrecy added to the adventure. Jean later compared it to playing hooky.

Footloose and aggressively debonair, Moreuil was a part of the St. Tropez set, which borrowed its note of glamour and wickedness from Brigitte Bardot and Roger Vadim, its unofficial founders. He knew the haunts, the restaurants and the style. His volatility appealed to Jean's sense of drama and he had aplomb enough for two. He kept crazy hours, gestured wildly, flirted outrageously. He also gave her a turtle on a leash. Viewed from Preminger's sheltered world, he was freedom itself, and some of his confidence rubbed off on Jean.

Preminger continued to criticize back on the set. Impatient with one of her line readings, he ordered, "Say it the way *I* say it," and gave her the exact intonations he wanted for the next take. Jean obeyed, repeating the line with a thick Viennese accent. The crew guffawed. Preminger, taken aback, walked away, muttering that film was too expensive to waste.

Temperamentally, he was hardly the one to be filming Sagan's fragile tale. His heavy-handedness ran counter to the fleeting emotions of the characters, and the Technicolor treatment pulled the narrative beyond its natural limits. Preminger also brought a conventional morality to the story and insisted on punishing the characters for their dalliance, not exactly Sagan's attitude. With a retinue of friends, Sagan motored over from St. Tropez one day in August. The author watched the shooting impassively and left unimpressed.

Filming wound up that fall in the Shepperton studios outside of London. The final scene called for Jean's character to sit at her make-up table and apply a layer of cold cream to her face. Preminger wanted her totally expressionless, except for tears slowly welling up in her eyes. Simple as that was, it took all day and exhausted Jean.

The scene was not just an appropriate climax to a film that leaves its principal characters empty and adrift but also a symbol of Jean's relationship with Preminger. As an actress she, too, had retreated behind a mask and buried emotions which, only a year before, had seemed irrepressible. Her face, normally so animated, now froze before the camera. It would take her years to work her way out of the shell.

Already, part of the Seberg persona was inadvertently taking shape—that of the cool, detached beauty. Canny directors like Jean-Luc Godard would exploit that image of her in subsequent films. It always puzzled Jean, however, who pictured herself as racked with inner doubts and tumultuous emotions.

She was even more puzzled by the rumors that linked her romantically with Otto Preminger and had begun to surface in the newspapers. Preminger's rough treatment of her on the set failed to discourage the gossip. Instead, it added an unhealthy sadomasochistic tinge to the sniggering reports.

Preminger himself quashed them categorically many years later. "First of all," he said, "I must tell you that I never have any romantic involvement with any actress while I'm working with her. Maybe much later. Maybe before. But never during the film. It only creates trouble. This is one of my very real principles and I have very few real principles. Jean Seberg? It is out of the question."

In London, Jean stayed at the Dorchester Hotel again. François Moreuil had followed her there and, with him around, the city seemed less claustrophobic this time. They caught Sir Laurence Olivier's tour-de-force performance in *The Entertainer* and dined at the best restaurants. In her letters home, Jean marveled that François and his friends could actually discuss the merits of various restaurants for an hour before making a choice.

Filming completed, she and François took the boat train to Paris to meet his family. While it didn't quite correspond to the image of the French aristocracy she had formed in her mind— the Moreuils actually lived in slightly dowdy middle-class comfort—Jean immediately cottoned to François's mother, an alert, political-minded woman who would later get involved in Amnesty International. Jean often traced some of her political consciousness to the woman who would briefly be her mother-in-law. "If you don't busy yourself with politics," she told Jean, "politics will busy itself with you."

For the Iowa girl, life was taking on an exciting Continental dimension. Professionally, though, she was in limbo. The technical proficiency she had acquired—she could now hit her marks on the set and had learned how to "find the light"— didn't compensate for the emotional constriction she conveyed. Preminger held her contract and he wasn't disposed to talk about future projects. Since Hollywood was not beckoning either—indeed, Hollywood suspected that Jean Seberg was an overpublicized cipher—she concluded that her only alternative would be to settle in New York, take acting lessons and pray that the *Bonjour Tristesse* reviews might change her fortunes. It was a tenuous future, but she was bolstered by the fact that François insisted on accompanying her. And because, in her family's hierarchy of values, romance went hand in glove with marriage, Jean Seberg thought about marriage, too.

9

"He's just what you would expect a fine young Frenchman to look like. He's very nice. We enjoyed having him here very much."
—DOROTHY SEBERG

In a mid-October drizzle, her favorite kind of weather, Jean returned to Marshalltown bubbling with news of her film and her French boyfriend. The Sebergs had moved into their ranch house on a quiet circle near the Iowa Soldiers Home, but otherwise life in the town was unchanged.

She was expected to help with the kitchen chores, and Dorothy Seberg still lectured her daughter about keeping her room neat. Once again, the *Times-Republican* reported her first home-cooked meal (steak, salad, watermelon), thereby reinforcing the prevailing notion that home is a place where you rest and eat well. The Sebergs were struggling to follow their habitual patterns, but it was not always easy. The traffic before their house increased dramatically whenever Jean was home, and gawkers peered out of their car windows for a glimpse of the local celebrity.

A week later François flew to St. Paul, Minnesota, and Jean rented a car and drove up to meet him. With $800 in his pocket and no work permit, his prospects were dubious. Yet he had certain assets. He was a distant relative of film director William Wyler. His English was fluent (he had spent the summer of 1954 at Harvard University). He had a flair for meeting people and he was, in his own words, "madly in love with Jean

Seberg." Dressed in thin-soled Continental shoes and a navy-blue suit, as if for a Paris dinner, he stepped off the plane into the snow. After a few days together at a lodge in Minnesota, they went on to Marshalltown.

Jean's parents welcomed François warmly and he was on his best behavior, but it was a clear case of mutual astonishment. François's over-the-collar hair and his expansive gestures were, if not suspicious, at least highly exotic to the Sebergs. Jean tried to make a joke of it. "That's why I love him—because he has more hair than I do."

Nonetheless, Ed Seberg did his best to adapt and began serving wine at dinner. Jean showed the town to her boyfriend and introduced him to Carol Hollingsworth, who served Cokes. They attended the Junior College Players production of *My Sister Eileen* and visited Iowa State University. Early in November, Dorothy Seberg held open house to introduce François to over a hundred neighbors and relatives. Jean was seeing her hometown not only from her own greatly expanded perspective but from François's as well. She told friends that Marshalltown seemed smaller than ever.

On her last night at home Jean invited Dawn Murray Quinn over for a long chat. "Both she and François were tired and tense. They hadn't had much time together or any opportunity to talk," Quinn recalls. "Jean was afraid to go back to New York because of Otto. 'He just isn't human,' she told me. 'He buys me beautiful clothes, but never makes me happy on the inside. It's terrible, but sometimes I wish he would just die!'"

The following day Jean and François flew to New York, where she had sublet an apartment on the Upper East Side. Shortly after their arrival Preminger announced he was picking up the second-year option on Jean's contract, a month before its January 1 renewal date. It was hardly a vote of confidence, however. Preminger was not about to let the contract expire before Columbia had released *Bonjour Tristesse.*

Questioned about her acting future on *Mike Wallace Interviews,* then television's most visible hot seat, Jean replied, "It may be silly pride, but I won't quit."

The *Bonjour Tristesse* premiere was held at the Capitol Theater in New York on January 15, 1958. Perhaps in atonement for the *St. Joan* excesses, opening night was distinctly low-key. Ed Seberg came east with his son Kurt, then fifteen, and the two of them donned tuxedos to accompany Jean. The theater lobby was decorated with thousands of mimosa blossoms, but apart from Jean and Geoffrey Horne, a featured player in the film, the event drew few celebrities. Several days later, the Des Moines *Register* passed on the dispiriting news in an article headlined: OUR JEAN FAILS IN CRITIC POLL.

The advertising campaign took what was then a mildly sensational tack: "An eighteen-year-old girl looks back at that fabulous summer on the Riviera with five unconventional people competing for 'kicks,' pleasure and love." But it didn't help. While Jean was not attacked as savagely as before, most of the critics sided with the *Saturday Review,* which observed that "Preminger, apparently, has not succeeded in convincing Miss Seberg that she is an actress." *The New Yorker* called for "a good solid, and possibly therapeutic, paddling."

Again, Preminger resorted to publicity gimmicks. He flew Jean out to Hollywood and back one Saturday, just so she could meet with Louella Parsons, self-anointed guardian of Hollywood morals. The two had dinner at Chasen's, and Louella gushed afterward that "she won me over with her youth and her apparent wish to have me like her." Parsons had heard rumors and wanted to know if Jean intended to marry Preminger, then in the process of getting a divorce.

"Of course not. I'm old enough to be his mother," quipped Jean. Charmed, the columnist gave her a delayed Christmas present, her blessings and a vaguely ominous warning: "If you marry Otto after his divorce from Mary is final, you will have lost my confidence." Having Louella's confidence counted.

Jean was actually living with François at the time, an arrangement they were careful to keep secret from her family and the press. He never answered the telephone, and when journalists came calling, he disappeared. Anonymity was harder to maintain in Miami, where Jean was soon dispatched on a publicity junket. Each time a reporter knocked at the door of her suite at the Fontainebleau, François would hide out in the bathroom.

A child of American movies, François was dying to see Key Largo, site of the celebrated 1948 film starring Humphrey Bogart. Columbia had magnanimously provided Jean with a Lincoln convertible. On either side, however, big letters spelled out "Jean Seberg in Bonjour Tristesse." One morning the lovers slipped away to a drugstore, bought a roll of tape and covered up the offending logo. Dressed (or undressed) for St. Tropez, François put down the top, and they sped south to the Keys.

Before long a pair of policemen pulled the convertible over to the side of the road. "I could see the scandal," Moreuil remembers. "Jean Seberg arrested in a speeding car with a half-naked man. We tried to talk our way out of it, but the cops, real rednecks, wouldn't cooperate."

The discussion escalated into a shouting match. When the policemen threatened to cart François off to jail, he objected, "But I'm a French citizen!"

"Finally," Moreuil says, "Jean took over. 'You've yelled enough,' she said. Then she took a hundred-dollar bill from her purse, tossed it calmly in their direction and we were on our way again."

Moreuil chalks up the experience to an excess of youthful spirits. "We were wild kids just having a good time."

Jean's sentiments were more complex. Her whirlwind existence with Moreuil couldn't entirely distract her from the growing realization that she had failed in her second try for stardom. At nineteen, she was quite possibly washed-up. "She was feeling awfully insecure," says one of her New York friends from that period. "She really thought that Preminger was going to wave the magic wand. And it hadn't turned out that way. There was this terrible gap between what she wanted to accomplish and what she had actually done. She felt exploited and thought people were making fun of her, which, in a way, they were. It was heartrending."

Lessons were her only hope. She studied speech for several months with Alice Hermes, who appreciated her lovely manners and her eagerness to work but thought her "terribly shy and a little colorless." She took mime lessons from Etienne Decroux, Marcel Marceau's mentor and an acquaintance of François's. The Actors Studio, however, extended the greatest promise of renewal.

"I went to see Lee Strasberg," Jean told *Cosmopolitan*

many years later. "I was going through a psychologically painful period—very painful—and I really had difficulty walking into a room with three people in it. I said to Strasberg, 'I can't possibly stand up now and audition, but I've heard you let people audit. May I? I know I'll be so swept away by the excitement of what I'm seeing, and the experimentation, that I'll want to take part.'

"I found him an extremely aloof man. He said, 'That's true. We do have such instances.' And he told me to go home and write to the Actors Studio for formal permission to be an auditor. I did write—three times—and I never even got a reply. That was kind of the final blow."

The French reception of *Bonjour Tristesse* in March was somewhat warmer. *Cahiers du Cinéma,* the magazine for and by young film intellectuals, had put her on its February cover and called her "the new divine of the cinema." François Truffaut, then a critic with movie-making aspirations of his own, admired the fanatical control Preminger had exercised over his material, but his enthusiasm for Jean Seberg knew no bounds.

> When Jean Seberg is on the screen, which is all the time, you can't look at anything else. Her every movement is graceful, each glance is precise. The shape of her head, her silhouette, her walk, everything is perfect: this kind of sex appeal hasn't been seen on the screen. It is designed, controlled, directed to the nth degree by her director, who is, they say, her fiancé. I wouldn't be surprised, given the kind of love one needs to obtain such perfection . . . Jean Seberg, short blond hair on a pharaoh's skull, wide-open blue [*sic*] eyes with a glint of boyish malice, carries the entire weight of this film on her tiny shoulders. It is Otto Preminger's love poem to her.

Although Jean did not know it at that moment, the review marked a significant turning point in her career. The ground was being prepared for her emergence as a star on the other side of the ocean.

Intoxicated by the pace and unpredictability of New York, François kept up their "mad, erratic life." Days, he worked for an international law firm on Madison Avenue. Nights, he liked to see his French and Italian friends, go to parties and ferret out the newest restaurants. On an impulse, he would fill the apartment with bouquets from the florist. The next day he and Jean would be carting empty Coke bottles back to Gristede's for a refund. At the ASPCA they adopted a black-and-white cat for a dollar, christened it Bipp and had matchbooks made with "Bipp" on the cover. "Sometimes we had money. Sometimes we didn't. It didn't change anything," Moreuil now says.

When they attended the April in Paris Ball at the Waldorf, they sat at the same table as Senator John F. Kennedy and his wife, Jacqueline. With model Suzy Parker and her French husband, Pierre de la Salle, they vacationed for a week in the Virgin Islands.

Jean, however, would sometimes bolt from the parties, and friends would have to chase after her in the street and plead with her to return. One day in Central Park she found a dead pigeon and insisted that François, an amateur photographer, devote a series of photographs to it.

"She was very tense and nervous," Moreuil says of their life that year in New York. "She would wake up in the middle of the night, covered with sweat, crying, 'I'll never be an actress.' She wanted to be an artist in every sense of the word."

Through the actor Roscoe Lee Browne, François and Jean were invited to spend a June weekend at Steepletop, Edna St. Vincent Millay's 800-acre estate in upstate New York. The poet had died in 1950, and now Steepletop was maintained by her sister, Norma Millay, and Norma's husband, actor Charles Ellis.

"It was one of those faded, run-down mansions with rusted gates and grass growing on the tennis courts," says Moreuil. For Jean, it breathed with the spirit of Millay. She walked the grounds with Norma, sat in Millay's library and reverently fingered the pages of her notebooks.

"Norma and I often sat around and read poetry," says Browne. "Nothing planned—it just happened. While she was there, Jean picked up a Millay book and started to read aloud, too. It was a shy reading at first—she felt she was in the presence of experts—but it was lovely. After the poem, Norma just smiled. So Jean turned the page and read another. It was exquisite. There was one line, I remember, that meant so much

to her: 'This moment is the best the world can give/ the tranquil blossom on the tortured stem.'

"Millay, as a young girl, really did feel you could see the
grass grow. That was not unlike Jean's sensibility at all. Her
eyes were deliciously moist—with the clear crystal glaze of
tears one notices especially in women and children. She was a
very bright, delicate girl, not fragile at all. For me, 'fragile' is
what breaks in two. Jean's delicacy had a tough sinew, like a
flower coming through a rock."

Norma and Charles were unaware of Jean's travails as a
movie star, but they responded to her as a vibrant young girl,
and the weekend momentarily restored her battered sense of
worth. "Seated in that faded house with only a few people
around, I saw Jean truly happy," says Moreuil. "It was one of
the few times."

Back in New York, Preminger's specter was never far away.
Jean's friends feared that her relationship with him now bordered on the neurotic. She even trembled to take his phone
calls. "We simply had to get her out from under Otto's
thumb," says Moreuil. He and his employer, lawyer Claude
Lewy, approached Preminger about selling the remaining
years of his contract with Jean to Columbia Pictures. The
transaction was negotiated in August. Preminger reserved the
right (never exercised) to use her in one movie a year. Otherwise, he severed the bond with little regret.

"I liked her," the director said years later. "I was never
against her. We were never in conflict, but there was also nothing in common after those two pictures. I was in Paris a couple
of times after that, but I never called her."

Once she had worked her way through her "hate-Premin-
ger" period, Jean would acknowledge that he had instilled in
her a professionalism that stayed with her all her life.
She was never late for calls and avoided any show of temperament on the set. She recognized, too, that all the publicity,
adverse as it had been, had given her a name. But she couldn't
help adding, "He used me like a Kleenex and threw me
away."

Film critic Hollis Alpert, who knew her then, appraises the
Preminger legacy another way. "I felt that if Preminger hadn't

discovered her, she would have been on Broadway within a couple of years and eventually attracted the attention of a film company. Preminger interrupted her natural growth and development as an actress. He forced her talents and in the process destroyed her confidence."

In little more than a year, Jean Seberg had started at the top and worked her way to the bottom. That summer, however, a final wave of publicity was building for the unemployed actress. In September she would return to Marshalltown to marry the Frenchman one of his Riviera friends playfully called "the charming idiot."

Photoplay tape-recorded an interview with them beforehand and asked them their marriage goals:

JEAN: Money, fast cars, minks! No, seriously, a quiet, creatively alive life with friends.

FRANÇOIS: No.

JEAN: Okay, a quiet, creatively alive life without friends.

FRANÇOIS: A quiet noisy life with interesting dull friends, with fast slow cars and large small houses.

10

Leaning her head against his shoulder, Jean thought, "Dear God, thank you for making my dreams come true. I wanted to be an actress, and I've had my wish, and I've wanted to be a good wife, and now I'm Mrs. François Moreuil."

Raindrops tapped against the car window.

"I wish," Jean said in a whisper as she looked at her bride's bouquet of white rose buds, "I wish I could throw it to every girl who's ever put on a slicker and a rain hat and walked for blocks and blocks in the rain. . . . I wish all their daydreams could come true the way mine have."

—Photoplay

Jean wanted a simple wedding without fuss, so as not to upstage her sister, who had been married in Marshalltown only three weeks earlier. It was wishful thinking, however, to expect that either the press or the Marshalltown citizenry would stay away.

"She's made two movies, both bad, but she's still popular," explained Columbia publicist Martin Goldblatt. "It's just that any girl can look at Jean and feel she might do it, too. She gives hope to American teen-agers that someone might discover them."

Curiosity had been building in Marshalltown for weeks. It turned to serious gossip the day François went shopping at St. Clair-Krieger's Clothing on Main Street, tried on a pair of underpants and then stalked boldly out of the dressing room to ask Jean her opinion. Shoppers' jaws fell. Shortly after, Jean went for a fitting of her wedding dress—an oyster white silk moiré gown with an empire waist and a balloon skirt—designed as a wedding gift by Guy La Roche. François crouched on his hands and knees to check the hemline, and gossip redoubled.

With a flamboyance unusual for Marshalltown, he had taken charge of all the wedding arrangements. At a restaurant called Lloyd's, where the reception was to be held, he insisted on caviar in a silver bowl and a roasted turkey, deboned and put back together again. He gave Jean's aunt Eula Mae Seberg a detailed blueprint for the floral arrangements, yellow roses and ferns, that would bank the altar. In the private plane of Marshalltown millionaire Bill Fisher, he flew to Chicago to pick up cases of champagne specially sent from France.

"He was kind of a wild person, I'd say," muses one of Marshalltown's older residents. "At least he was pretty different from us people. That wedding created quite a stir, I can tell you."

The stir assumed the dimensions of a tornado as photographers and reporters from *Life, Vogue, Paris-Match* and the wire services as well as several newspapers and television stations blew into the sleepy town to immortalize what the *Times-Republican* unabashedly described as "perhaps the most celebrated social event in the city's history."

The Sebergs coped quietly, until one night François and Jean fell into a heated argument over the ushers' ties. A distressed Dorothy Seberg took her daughter aside and informed her that she didn't have to go through with the marriage. "But I do. There's been too much publicity not to," Jean answered.

Nerves had overtaken François, too, and he developed a cold sore on his lip. Telling him she'd get some medicine for it from her father, Jean darted off to the pharmacy and soon came back with a tranquilizer. François was unaware of what he was taking, but every four hours Jean reminded him, "Honey, it's time for your pill. It may not help the sore very much, but it will keep it from spreading."

Both the temperature and the humidity climbed near the

100 mark on the morning of the wedding, September 5, 1958. For once, Ed Seberg didn't go to the drugstore. But he slipped away early to help out at the pharmacy of the Iowa Soldiers Home, leaving his wife to carry on. By four o'clock, the appointed hour, close to a thousand spectators had congregated outside the Trinity Lutheran Church and were craning for a view of the bride. "Everyone came out to look," Hannah Heyle recalls, "but it was a little like looking at an automobile accident. The town had never seen anyone like François or his best man. A couple of days before the wedding, a bunch of the high school athletes threatened to go by the Sebergs' and drag François out of the house and give him a haircut."

Jean arrived at the church in a black Cadillac and disappeared into the basement with her wedding party. Photographers were allowed to take pictures before the ceremony while she was dressing. Walter Shotwell, a columnist for the Des Moines *Register,* later echoed the town's disapproval: "Oh, you couldn't see anything, really. It was just the idea. Iowa guys were not used to the kind of backstage intimacy Jean brought home with her . . . she still had a lot of the sweet Marshalltown girl in her, so it wasn't one of her better lines when she said, 'Okay boys, I think we should call it quits on the pictures now.' By then she was two years into her movie career and had learned a tough sort of lingo to go with her put-on blasé manner."

François pulled up shortly afterward and climbed the church steps twice for the benefit of photographers and TV cameras before realizing he had locked his keys in the car. A garage mechanic had to break the car window with a hammer to get them out.

Still, the Sebergs had managed to inject a few homely touches of their own into the wedding. Eight-year-old David carried the rings on a satin pillow embroidered by Frances Benson. In her shoe, Jean had sixpence from Mary Ann. The Marshalltown High School music teacher, Stephen Melvin, and Jean's girl friend Dawn Murray Quinn sang "O Lord Most Holy" while Mrs. Melvin, a bundle of nerves, played the organ.

In the heat, the twenty-minute ceremony dragged on interminably. The Reverend Rolland Christenson added to the discomfort by sternly warning the couple of the pitfalls ahead. "I suppose he was right. I can't say that anyone really thought the marriage would last," remembers one of the guests. "Everyone wondered why she wasn't marrying a good American boy instead. But the remarks did seem kind of ominous."

Dripping with perspiration, François kissed his resplendent bride on both cheeks, Continental style, and burst into audible sobs. "I was a young kid with big emotions," he recalled years afterward. "And I paid dearly for them."

The reception at Lloyd's was disrupted by a torrential thunderstorm, the worst of the season. The newlyweds sipped champagne out of a sixteenth-century goblet, another of François's touches. The guests toasted the couple, and several women collected the champagne bottles, remarking that they would make nice lamps.

Uncertain of their honeymoon plans—Columbia, her new employer, had put Jean on temporary hold for a trifle called *The Beach Boys*—the newlyweds were scheduled to fly only as far as New York that night. A police escort preceded them over the rain-soaked highways to Des Moines, while they drank champagne in the limousine. Jean's friends followed them to the airport for a final round of cheers and flashbulbs. Then, Hannah Heyle says, "We all dashed off to a nearby motel to catch ourselves on a television in the lobby."

Jean's role didn't materialize. So after forty-eight hours in New York, Columbia waved her on to France. She and François took a three-week honeymoon in St. Tropez at Paul Louis Weiller's estate, where they had met a year before. Already there were signs of strain. Moreuil remembers a dinner party given by Roger Vadim for a coterie of his friends. Vadim had achieved international notoriety by launching Brigitte Bardot in *And God Created Woman,* and his films, not to mention his private life, then passed for the ultimate in daring.

"It rained buckets that night," says Moreuil, "and we

had to stay over. Jean didn't like that at all. She had a strong puritan side and she was terrorized by these people. She hovered in a corner all the time and hardly said a word."

That fall, the twenty-year-old bride and her twenty-four-year-old husband moved into an apartment with a garden in the fashionable Paris suburb of Neuilly. François furnished it with heavy antiques from the Flea Market and heirlooms from the family cellar. Jean thought it looked like a museum and grew to loathe the musty decor.

The marriage was shaky from the start. "François was sort of an overgrown French version of a fraternity boy," she told critic Hollis Alpert. "He had a compulsion to go out every night to either a night club or some ratty Whiskey à Go-Go jukebox kind of place." For his part, François realized that his bride's insecurities ran even deeper than he had suspected. "She was either unhappy because she was making a movie or unhappy because she wasn't making one. It was always a drama with her."

In November, Columbia put her to work in a low-budget comedy, *The Mouse That Roared.* Filmed in England, the picture was a vehicle for a rising young comedian named Peter Sellers. A triple threat, he played a foot soldier, the prime minister and the grand duchess of a microscopic European country that declares war on the United States solely to qualify for lavish postwar American aid programs.

Jean's role—the daughter of an American scientist kidnapped inadvertently by Sellers' twenty-two-man army—was flat and colorless, although it did allow her to give Sellers his first on-screen kiss. "It's nice to be playing a human being for a change" was about all she could think of to say to reporters on the set. (Unexpectedly, the film proved a runaway success when it was released the following year. On a $400,000 budget, it went on to gross $2.5 million, and the New York *Times* acknowledged that "Jean Seberg looks better than she's yet looked.")

Columbia sent her off to Rome soon after, to attend the premiere of *Bell, Book and Candle.* As part of the publicity campaign, she was awarded an "Oscar" for Bipp, who was expected to forward it to Pywacket, the feline star of the film. "Isn't that silly?" Jean wrote Dawn Murray Quinn. "But the Italians loved it!"

In the months that followed the shooting, however, she rattled around in a professional and personal void, feeling increasingly alienated. François's determination to lead an active social life merely exacerbated her sentiments of irresponsibility and guilt. She was without friends.

"All those people who had surrounded me with fond attention suddenly disappeared—many forever. There were no more flowers at the hotel," she said a long time after. "The shock was greatest because I had divorced myself from life in Iowa. My girl friends had married and led lives that I no longer had any touch with. I was a stranger everywhere. It was as if I had been completely wiped away with a cloth, and I had to begin again to re-create myself."

The re-creation began humbly in Hollywood in the spring of 1959. For its contract players, Columbia then had acting classes run by an eccentric and gifted instructor, Paton Price, who had a reputation for "opening up" young performers and imbuing them with a sense of their potential. While they mulled over her prospects (one of them was *The Gene Krupa Story* opposite Sal Mineo), Columbia executives suggested that she study with Price. Leaving François behind in Paris, Jean took a small apartment on Olympic Boulevard in Los Angeles and, with trepidation, showed up in mid-April for her first classes.

Price held forth in what had been Irene Dunne's dressing room on the old Columbia lot on Gower Street. It was informally furnished like a living room, and the dozen or so students who came and went (among them Roger Smith, Don Murray and Robert Conrad) looked on it as a refuge from the studio bosses.

A former teacher at the American Academy in New York, Price had been a conscientious objector during World War II and had served time in prison for his beliefs. "He had strong liberal convictions," says actor Glenn Corbett, then under contract to Columbia. "Anyone who came in touch with him was affected by his thoughts. He tended to change your life."

Price was also one of the rare teachers to have formulated

techniques for film actors, who at the time usually learned their craft on the Broadway stage or operated on blind instinct. His theories were anchored in self-discovery. An actor couldn't play a character, Price felt, if he didn't first know and accept himself as a human being. Long before the sensitivity movements of the 1970s, he was encouraging his students to get in touch with their feelings and exorcise their anxieties. "I used to say that if you wanted to be a good artist," Price recalls, "you have to cut off your head and leave it at the door. You have to immobilize the intellect for the emotions to run freely." He believed the camera probed so relentlessly that "trying *not* to act was the objective."

Price was also an outspoken anti-puritan, partially in reaction to his own stifling upbringing in Texas. (He once said he would never accept a virgin in his class. "They are too hidden—to others and to themselves.") He often talked freely about sex and fostered a climate of acceptance and understanding.

On her first day Price invited Jean to do a simple rehearsal exercise with Don Murray. It required talking and listening not as a character, but as herself. "Jean was petrified," Price recalls. "She began hyperventilating almost at once. Although I hadn't heard the Preminger stories, it was obvious someone had traumatized her. I discovered that she had an enormous amount of information about acting, but no foundation. She was wasting all her energy in anxiety."

Little by little, Jean responded to his coaching. "At first," remembers Tony Brand, another actor in the class, "she dressed very proper, almost strait-laced. She wore high collars and had a kind of wide-eyed look about her. As classes progressed, you could see her loosening up. The clothes became more casual, and she started to laugh."

To get some mileage out of its starlet, Columbia sent Jean to Boston in May to replace an ailing Doris Day for the premiere of *It Happened to Jane*. Primed for Day, the crowds called out to Jean, "Hi, Doris," "Welcome to Boston, Doris." Jean waved obligingly and signed Doris' name in the autograph books thrust at her.

On her way back, she stopped in Marshalltown. At the

high school, she presented the Jean Seberg Award to Nick Nichols, now a graduating senior, and attended a production of *Daddy Long Legs.* If nowhere else, she was still a star in the eyes of the students. But she missed the stimulation and security of Price's class, and had to force herself not to cut short the two-week visit with her parents.

The acting lessons continued until June. By then Jean had come to view the former dressing room as a sanctuary and in her letters referred to her fellow actors as "the family." Price's urgings to "stand open to life" had checked her natural instinct to withdraw. "Preminger had punished her for being herself," says Tony Brand. "Paton rewarded her."

"Paton showered me with warmth at a time I really needed it," she said later. At critical points in her life, she would come to him for artistic advice and emotional comfort. Price himself never stopped believing in her goodness, even when her life turned sordid and desperate.

Early in June, Jean flew to Paris, via Copenhagen, her self-esteem on the mend. Gary Cooper was on the same flight, and Jean gleefully reported that he wasn't at all "closed up" (a Price term) and didn't say "yup" once.

"I happened to be passing through the Copenhagen airport that day," John Gielgud recalls, "and suddenly Jean came running over from the bar and said, 'I'm with Gary Cooper! You must come meet him.' She dragged me over and introduced me. Then we all went out to the plane with this flock of photographers and publicity people crowding around us. I must say I felt more important than I'd ever felt before. The charming thing about Jean was that she'd learned to be a star before she became an actress."

Back in Neuilly, her garden was in full flower. Bipp had borne a litter of kittens, and a duck, the gift of a mailman, had taken over the pond in the front yard.

At an anniversary party that summer for Françoise Arnoul, the French actress, Jean ran into "Herr Otto and his girl friend" and surprised herself by having a long, pleasant chat with him. "I think I'm beginning to overcome my DTs about him," she wrote Price proudly. She also kept her head among the occasional aristocrats she met through François. "One thing about these princes and counts and countesses," she told her mother, "they spill food down the front of them when they eat just like the rest of us." Hollywood, however, seemed far away. "Sometimes I feel like a split personality, and my dual lives are California and Paris," she confessed. "It's awfully confusing."

François, still employed in a law firm, was thinking more seriously than ever about a directing career. A revolution was sweeping over the French film industry. Young film makers—some barely in their twenties—had taken to the streets with hand-held cameras, shoestring budgets and a jagged, improvisational view of life. The papers talked of a "new wave." François, who had succeeded in meeting a number of *nouvelle vague* directors, wanted to be a part of it and was hard at work on a scenario.

The "big bad wolves on the second floor"—Jean's term for the Columbia executives—had pretty much written her off, and her only opportunity for work that summer seemed questionable at best. But one night François told her that Jean-Luc Godard was interested in talking with her. Like Truffaut, Godard had been impressed by her performance in *Bonjour Tristesse,* especially the potential for casual destruction that seemed to lurk behind her innocent features.

Godard had no script to offer her, but he did have ideas, often paradoxical and complicated. He had been inspired by a squalid, seemingly unexceptional account in the French press about a motorcyclist who had killed a policeman and then hidden out with his girl friend, who had squealed on him. Godard saw the story as the genesis of a work that would not only pay homage to the grade-B American gangster movie but also depict a new generation of rootless youth. Shortly before, he had worked with a twenty-six-year-old ex-boxer, Jean-Paul Belmondo, in a brief film, *Charlotte et son Jules.* He thought Belmondo, with his beaten-up boxer's face and catlike agility, would be perfect as the thug, Michel Poiccard. He wanted Jean for the girl friend, Patricia Franchini. The film would be called *A Bout de Souffle (Breathless).*

Jean found Godard "an incredibly introverted, messy-look-

ing young man with glasses, who didn't look me in the eyes when he talked." The seriousness with which he took the cinema—just a diversion in the United States—intrigued her, however. She said she'd think about the role. While she did, Moreuil plumped for her participation. So did Truffaut, who had written the original treatment. Belmondo later came by her apartment and they improvised a few trial scenes. Finally, Jean consented.

Godard sent a twelve-page telegram to the casting department of Columbia, seriously taxing his already minuscule ($90,000) budget. In it, he laid out his plans and offered the studio either $12,000 for Jean's services or half the world-wide profits of the film. At the same time, Moreuil tried another tactic: he flew to Los Angeles and informed Columbia executives that he would take his wife away from the cinema forever if permission were denied. "I'm a very rich man, you know," he told Columbia vice president Leo Jaffe. He wasn't rich at all, but he had read that Nicky Hilton had used a similar ploy to win Elizabeth Taylor's freedom. Columbia accepted the $12,000.

Jean still had her doubts. "Day by day," she wrote Paton Price at the beginning of August, "the scenario seems to be getting bigger and worse in every way. I had a talk the other day with the young man who'll direct it, and his theories on working with actors are unbelievable, really odd."

On the first day of shooting, August 17, 1959, she nearly walked out. She thought that the character of Patricia, a loose American student who peddles the New York *Herald Tribune* on the Champs Elysées, was unpleasant enough. When Godard explained that Patricia would not only betray her lover but steal his wallet at the end, Jean balked. Godard's apparent misogyny bothered her. "Godard *was* an unsettling type," remarks Georges de Beauregard, the producer. "And Jean did have a certain goody-goody side then." After a long discussion the script was modified—Patricia would not steal—and Jean was lured back.

Every day Godard would show up with a sheaf of greasy papers stuffed into his pockets and thrust a few pages

Jean's way. It was her script. Often when he ran out of paper, that day's shooting stopped. Since *Breathless* was filmed without sound—it was dubbed later—Godard would shout instructions to his actors, telling them, sometimes in the middle of a line, to move toward the window or go into the bathroom. At one point he hid his cameraman, Raoul Coutard, in a lidded mail cart and pushed him up the Champs Elysées, catching the pedestrians unaware.

After two weeks Jean wrote Paton Price: "I'm in the midst of this French film and it's a long, absolutely insane experience—no lights, no makeup, no sound! Only one good thing—it's so un-Hollywood I've become completely unselfconscious."

Sometimes there was no script at all, so the cast and crew would move into a café and discuss the different possibilities for the next scene. On one particularly sunny day, ideal for filming, the producer caught the company nursing apéritifs at Fouquet's on the Champs Elysées. By way of explanation, Godard complained of a toothache. The producer, irate, marched him off to a dentist. Filming resumed in earnest the next morning.

Jean later described her rapport with the quirky Godard as "distant but passionate." François, in fact, often operated as a go-between and even managed to wangle a bit part for himself as a photographer in a sequence filmed at Orly Airport. But Jean thrived on the antics of Belmondo, "one of the freest actors I've ever worked with." "It's pure genius," Belmondo would tell his friends. "I walk in the street. This guy films me with a camera hidden in a mail cart, and I say whatever passes through my head."

That freedom extended to the film's then audacious bedroom scene in a Left Bank hotel room. Restless as cats, Belmondo and Seberg circled the tiny quarters, walked on the bed, careened off each other emotionally, and ended up tussling under the sheets. It was the sort of scene that activated Jean's latent puritanism. What would her father think? And Marshalltown? Yet it was shot so offhandedly that her fears were mollified. (Also, she remained fully clothed under the sheets.) On *St. Joan,* hundreds had

watched her. Here in the tiny room there were only Godard, his cameraman, an electrician and a bewildered script girl, whose main concern was trying to keep track of the shifting dialogue. To Jean, it was like making home movies. Her hair had been shorn back to St. Joan length and required no attention. She wore hardly any make-up, and her wardrobe came from Prisunic, the French equivalent of Woolworth's.

By mid-September, Godard had finished filming. From the rushes, Jean concluded tentatively that the movie was "bizarre and interesting," but she wondered whether it would ever be shown commercially. It appeared to her to be a peculiar interlude in her career—nothing more.

Of course, *Breathless* would go on to be hailed as the most significant film of the New Wave and make cult heroes of its stars and director.

Apotheosis was still months away, however. Unaware of what lay ahead, Columbia summoned Jean to Hollywood for a grim little melodrama, *Let No Man Write My Epitaph.* Since her marriage was barely limping along, she went by herself.

11

*"I don't know if I'm unhappy because I'm
free, or free because I'm unhappy."*

—PATRICIA IN *Breathless*

Back in Hollywood, it became increasingly clear to Jean that
she had married for all the wrong reasons. She had been lonely
and beaten, and François had been someone to lean on. But
their temperaments were diametrically opposed.

"Jean didn't speak French and François didn't speak English," says Aki Lehman, the attractive Japanese divorcée who
was one of Jean's intimates during this time. "When they finally understood each other, they realized they didn't have
anything in common." Actually, Jean's French, although
heavily accented, had improved dramatically, while François
was perfectly proficient in English. Metaphorically, however,
Lehman was right: they didn't speak the same language.

The glib society in which François moved so adroitly only
intensified Jean's belief that she was getting nowhere with her
life. She was ill-equipped for the casual rituals of the party
circuit. She committed herself totally to her friends, grieving
over their problems and exulting in their joys. And she opened
her purse to them freely; in François's circle, that often meant
picking up the tab.

"In my bitter moments," she admitted to Hollis Alpert, "I
often think it was François's itchy desire to be part of the film
world, a director, if possible, that was his primary motive in

marrying me. Certainly, I wouldn't have existed in his eyes if I had been Miss Nobody from Iowa."

Friends also sensed a strong current of sexuality rising within her, straining against her Marshalltown ethics. Jean enjoyed sex but had trouble justifying her casual affairs. She would invest her whole self in the relationship and when it proved to be less than love eternal, she felt guilty and used. Her parents' abhorrence of divorce—there had never been one in the Seberg family—didn't help. It was like a lid on a boiling pot.

That fall she resumed lessons with Paton Price and grew especially close to Dennis Hopper, a fellow student who would later make his name with *Easy Rider*. Exaggerated reports of Price's unconventional teaching methods had upset Columbia executives, and his anti-studio bias ("He was always telling us not to sell out, to turn down the crap," says Tony Brand) was not calculated to win back their support. In November, Price was given his walking papers. Jean immediately volunteered her apartment, and the classes, life-giving for her, continued through the new year in her living room.

On November 13, her twenty-first birthday, Jean telephoned Marshalltown millionaire Bill Fisher, then passing through Beverly Hills. "You are my legal guardian," she told him, "and you are now going to buy me my first legal drink, which is what a guardian is supposed to do." Fisher and his wife took her to Romanoff's for lunch, persuaded anew that she was "one of the sweetest girls on the earth."

About this time, director Joshua Logan called her to the Beverly Hills Hotel to read for the lead in an upcoming Broadway play, *There Was a Little Girl*. Jean lost out, as she half expected to, to Jane Fonda, who was Logan's goddaughter.

Let No Man Write My Epitaph was the main order of business, though, and it started out badly. Thinking she already had the part of a Chicago society girl, she reported to Columbia only to discover that she was expected to undergo a screen test. She won over two young women who had never acted before, but the test was a sharp reminder of her lowly position on the lot. It also brought back painful memories of the Preminger ordeal.

This time, the part was hardly worth winning. Its only function was to provide a happy-ending-by-marriage to the saga of a sensitive youth (James Darren) growing up in a tough, drug-infested ghetto in Chicago. Because of illnesses among the cast and various production delays, filming dragged on through the new year. After the freewheeling adventure of *Breathless,* the studio system struck her as regimented and overbearing. "It seemed like there was someone popping me on the nose with a powder puff every five minutes," she commented.

Before the Christmas holidays François joined his wife in California and promptly set about rustling up a social life for them. "Her problem was that she didn't have any friends," he said, although he was not sure that there hadn't been a few lovers. "She was lost and alone, and she had an immoderate fear of solitude. I got her invited to places."

One of those places was the French consulate on Outpost Drive in Los Angeles, a Spanish-style villa cloaked with tropical vegetation and the pungent scent of jasmine. Being the dutiful Frenchman abroad, François dropped by to leave his calling card. He vaguely knew the consul general, an urbane forty-five-year-old diplomat named Romain Gary. François remembers one detail from that meeting because it was so incongruous. While they were having drinks, Gary spied his shoes and said, "What a nice pair of shoes! Do you mind if I try them on?" Several nights later Gary invited François to return with his wife for a dinner party. Jean didn't want to go. It meant getting dressed up and facing the curious, not to say patronizing stares of the other guests. François insisted.

Gary had a rich and colorful past. Proud of his Tartar blood, he claimed he was born on Russian soil, although sources variously note his birthplace as Lithuania, Poland and Georgia (Soviet Union). His Jewish mother was an actress whose greatest histrionic skills seemed to be reserved for life itself. His father, who may have been a Russian merchant, abandoned them early on. Relishing the mystery, Gary liked to imply that he was really the son of the Russian silent-film idol Ivan Mozhukhin.

What is certain is that by the early 1920s, mother and son had settled in Vilna, then a part of Poland. There she prospered briefly in the millinery business by sewing false labels into her hats and passing them off as the latest in Parisian finery. The deception was rooted—at least, partly—in her immoderate love of all things French, an appreciation she instilled in the young Gary as well. She also stressed to her young son that glorious things were expected of him. He would be an ambassador of France one day!

The millinery shop eventually failed, and when Gary was thirteen, mother and son emigrated to Nice, France. Often without money but never without projects, she survived by selling jewels that she said had belonged to her family, and by running a boardinghouse and telling fortunes. Her life was an extravagant exercise of wits, and her faith in her son's unique destiny was unflagging.

In *Promise at Dawn,* the autobiography of his youth, Gary admitted that his overriding desire was to vindicate the eccentric woman and boasted that his vaulting ambition had at least propelled him to first place in the Nice Ping-Pong championship of 1932.

During World War II, Gary escaped to England and flew a number of missions over Europe and Africa with the Free French Air Force. He came out of the experience with a broken nose and with the lower left side of his face partially paralyzed, which lent a certain ferocity to his features and gave him a crooked smile. He also emerged from the war with a limitless admiration for Charles de Gaulle, which would not hinder him in his diplomatic career. He was made a Compagnon de la Libération, an order that comprised a select band of war heroes who had fought at De Gaulle's side to free France from German occupation. Until the end of his life, Gary kept his leather aviator's jacket safely preserved in a garment bag. Sometimes, according to one friend, he would take it out and put it on in the privacy of his home to recall what he viewed as "the best moment of my life."

Throughout his diplomatic career—in Sofia, New York and then Los Angeles—Gary bracketed his official duties with writing, often snatching time early in the morning or late at night. In 1956 his sweeping novel of Africa in transition, *The Roots of Heaven,* won him a literary reputation equal to that of his wife, English novelist Lesley Blanch, whose acclaim rested on the romantic tale *The Wilder Shores of Love*. Some friends thought the Gary-Blanch marriage was in the nature of a mother-son relationship, or nurse-patient. Older than he by five years, she seemed to indulge his excesses, cater to his whims and even, it was said, close her eyes to his extramarital affairs. They were an improbable couple—she a vigorous, outspoken blond Englishwoman, he a moody, pensive Slav. But they were both considered intelligent and stylish company, and invitations to the consulate were sought after.

"Dinners there were sort of like Noah's Ark—two of everything," says playwright and lyricist Alan Jay Lerner. "They always had an interesting group of people and the conversation was a cut above anything else in Los Angeles. Romain was a great companion—a listener as well as a talker—and terribly interested in just about any subject."

When Jean and François showed up for dinner, Lesley Blanch made a dutiful fuss over the young starlet, who was there against her will, and then turned to her other guests. Jean, however, was immediately captivated by Gary with his Clark Gable mustache and thick black hair. "She went completely overboard," says Aki Lehman. "It was a question of love at first sight." François had the impression that Lesley Blanch, on the other hand, was "distant, lost in a dream—letting her child [Gary] play."

As the evening wore on, Gary was drawn to Jean's radiant naïveté, and her almost hopelessly unrealistic idealism touched him. In *Promise at Dawn,* he wrote: "In order to face life, I have always needed the comfort of a femininity at once vulnerable and devoted, tenderly submissive and grateful, which makes me feel that I am giving when I am taking, that I am supporting when, in fact, I am leaning." The words had been inspired by a childhood girl friend, but they could well have been applied to Jean Seberg.

Gary invited Jean and François back for several dinners after that. "I thought he was just being friendly," says François, but according to Aki Lehman, the diplomat began seeing the actress on the side almost immediately. If Lesley Blanch had any qualms, she kept them hidden. Her marriage to Gary had survived the perils of both the war and literary celebrity. Gary's novel *Lady L* was even rumored to be a portrait of her. And, too, Gary had a reputation—carefully nurtured, some felt—of being an inveterate skirt-chaser.

The tumult Jean felt upon meeting him merely confirmed her conviction that she had married the wrong man. She was attracted by the maturity of the diplomat, who was only eight years younger than her own father. Gary may have been a father figure, but he was much more, too.

"Romain exerts an extraordinary charm over women," observes a woman who knew him well then. "He has very blue eyes, large like a spaniel's, and they seem to say, 'Oh, the hopeless doom of me.' It's enormously appealing. Women invariably find themselves staring at him and thinking, Oh, if I could only wipe that poor, unhappy look from his face."

Jean continued to report to Columbia for work on her film. François played tennis during the day and lived it up at night. John Derek, then Ursula Andress' husband, taught him how to break bottles with a whip.

The Sebergs had no idea of the growing split in their daughter's marriage when they invited the couple home to Marshalltown for Christmas. Mary Ann was there with her husband, Ed, and the Sebergs anticipated an old-fashioned family holiday. If they sensed any tension, it was, like most things unpleasant in the Seberg household, not discussed.

In a year-end issue devoted to "The Good Life," *Life* published a hauntingly intimate portrait of Jean and François. One sees only their heads and bare shoulders. François is bent over Jean, whose eyes are closed in rapture. The Sebergs approved less of the photo than the caption: "The ties that bind a marriage together."

"You could tell the marriage was on its way out," says Lynda Haupert. To her old friends Jean seemed daring and worldly. Haupert now laughingly admits to being shocked that Jean didn't wear a bra under her dress at an indoor swimming party they all attended that Christmas.

A getaway trip to Las Vegas didn't help the ailing marriage. Jean wanted to see the Lido de Paris show, then a novel import from France. The idea bored François, and after Jean retired to their hotel room at the Sands, he gambled the night away. At one point he lost all of their money and their airplane tickets at the crap table, before recouping his losses and running his stake back up to $250 by 9 A.M., when they departed for Hollywood.

Reports of a split first surfaced in early January 1960 in Dorothy Kilgallen's syndicated column. Jean stoutly denied them. In fact, she and François had already come to a parting. They would live separately after returning to France. She did consent, however, to star in his first picture, which he hoped to direct that June.

Before François left the United States he stopped by the French consulate a last time. "I entrust my wife to your care," he said jokingly to Gary. "I didn't know," François added much later, "that he would steal her from me." In fact, in the days that followed, Jean and Gary attended the same parties and even slipped away to Mexico for a weekend together.

Jean also revisited the consulate one last time just before her departure toward the end of the month. "I told Romain I was going to miss him," she admitted afterward. "Somehow, I felt if I didn't tell him, I was going to by-pass something significant in my life."

Gary went on temporary leave from the diplomatic service that spring and also returned to Paris. Officially, it was to devote more time to writing. Unofficially, some friends thought, Jean Seberg was the reason. But their romance was especially ticklish. As a diplomat, Gary had to avoid even a suggestion of scandal. Discretion was all the more imperative because Tante Yvonne, as the French called Madame de Gaulle, was known for her prudery and the high moral tone she expected of her husband's representatives.

If Lesley Blanch tended to adopt a complacent attitude toward such matters, François did not. For all his antic spirits and what one observer perceived as "ambition oozing out of his pores," he was in love with his mystifying wife and hoped for a reconciliation. Jean's parents remained ignorant of the temporary separation, and that aggravated the actress' apprehensions.

When Hannah Heyle, Jean's high school friend, visited Europe in April, Jean took her to lunch and boldly introduced her to Gary. "Where's François?" Heyle asked, puzzled.

"Oh, busy with a movie," Jean replied.

"He's such a dear," said Heyle.

"Yes, isn't he," said Jean airily and avoided any further explanation.

Gary puffed on a thick cigar—a habit he had picked up from director John Huston—and looked benignly paternal.

Her domestic troubles and her liaison with Gary were progressively harder to hide after the March release of *Breathless.* Propelled by *Cahiers du Cinéma,* which two months before had put Jean on its cover for the second time, the film was a surprising success. It spawned controversies, fueled discussions and generally shook up the French cinema industry from top to bottom. Such intellectuals as Jean-Paul Sartre and Jean Cocteau felt obliged to enter the fray and tout the unconventional little film.

Overnight, Belmondo graduated to the forefront of French movie stars and Jean was vindicated at last as a serious actress. For the young French, she represented the ultimate in liberated womanhood.

Legions of girls began asking their hairdressers for "la coupe Seberg," the close-cropped hair style that was her trademark. (In later life, whenever she felt insecure or threatened, Jean would invariably cut her hair and go back to the *Breathless* look.) Her androgynous beauty—a forerunner of the unisex look of the 1970s—was the new ideal. Director Claude Chabrol, commenting later on the sexual ambiguity she projected, quipped, "It was almost as if you became a queer by looking at her."

Her career, which had flickered conspicuously and then died out, miraculously caught fire. "Suddenly every director in the business wanted her," says Philippe de Broca, who would use her in his next film. "The more expensive her price, the more desirable she became."

"I still don't know why I should have meant anything to the French," Jean noted later. "This strange awkward creature with rather bad teen-age skin and extremely short hair—what could she possibly have symbolized? . . . But it was a triumph in the funny old Hollywood style. Really, like a bad movie, only it was good. It was *fantastic* for all of us."

"For my generation, Jean Seberg was a reference point," muses Josie Yanne, an actress who subsequently became Jean's friend. "As much as Brigitte Bardot was the woman as object, Jean stood for the woman as free spirit. It really was the first stirring of feminism in France."

On the one hand, there was the Sagan mystique, born of *Bonjour Tristesse* and its depiction of a disillusioned teen-ager living for amoral pleasures. On the other, there was *Breathless* and its view of a couple of nonconformists ricocheting through society with little concern for its values. The two visions came together in the person of Jean, who seemed to embody an intoxicating liberty. "For us, she was the woman who went to bed with men and didn't torture herself about marrying them afterward," says Yanne. That image was inflated and compounded by a torrent of magazine articles. Jean's picture bloomed everywhere. It hurt not at all that she was an American. On the contrary. The informality of the United States, not so much disrespectful of tradition and history as simply unconcerned with them, added to her aura. She was modern. The enthusiasm of the French press was largely shared by the American critics, who hailed Godard's ability to capture life on the run and admitted to second thoughts about Jean Seberg. Pauline Kael rhapsodized: "As Jean Seberg plays her—and that's exquisitely—Patricia is the most terrifyingly *simple* muse-goddess-bitch of modern movies." Kael also pinpointed some of the contradictions that made Jean a French national heroine, as *St. Joan* had not:

"Patricia, a naïve, assured, bland and boyish creature, is like a new Daisy Miller—but not quite as envisioned by Henry James. She has the independence, but not the moral qualms or the Puritan conscience or the high aspirations that James saw as the special qualities of the American girl . . . she is so free that she has no sense of responsibility or guilt. She seems to be playing at existence, at a career, at 'love'; she's 'trying them on.' But that's all she's capable of in the way of experience. She doesn't want to be bothered; when her lover becomes an inconvenience, she turns him in to the police."

In reality, Jean was considerably less liberated than her screen image suggested. She had more regrets about the disintegration of her marriage than either Cécile or Patricia could ever have understood. Her startling success seemed to her as disproportionate as the drubbing she got for *St. Joan*. That success made privacy a near-impossibility. The French press wanted to know what Jean Seberg was wearing, thinking, doing. Whom she was seeing, as well.

"It was a difficult period for her," says Aki Lehman. "She didn't want to hurt François, but she was madly in love with Romain. She was strung out between the two of them."

The pressures mounted. "One night she became totally hysterical," François remembers. "She began breaking things up in the apartment. I put her in her Sunbeam and drove her to the American Hospital. On the way, she took off one of the high-heeled shoes she was wearing and smashed all the instruments on the dashboard. The doctors had to give her an injection to put her to sleep."

Soon after, she checked into a clinic for a rest under a psychiatrist's care. Gary and Moreuil agreed that she should go home to Marshalltown and sort out her thoughts away from the spotlight. They both also agreed to leave her alone during her hospitalization. But François claims that Gary, pretending to be a doctor, continued to visit her secretly while she convalesced outside Paris.

Jean flew to Montreal on a plane equipped with beds, then transferred to Chicago, arriving in Marshalltown on April 20. Reporters were told only that she was "recuperating from a kidney ailment brought on by overwork." When columnist Earl Wilson telephoned the house, she again denied rumors of a divorce.

Her parents—Ed Seberg especially—were dead set against the notion and made Jean feel that she was letting them down. But she painted a hopeless picture of her marriage and convinced them that François frightened her.

Her stay had its customary bucolic moments, which merely accentuated the distance she had gone in a few short years. She helped David make May baskets, and they flew a kite together. She went for walks and watched the birds. She even found time to apologize in advance for *Breathless.* "Yes, it has some naughty four-letter words," she told the *Times-Republican.* "But I don't say any of them."

François had scheduled the first day of shooting on his film for June 6. As the date approached, Jean grew uneasy about returning to Paris alone. She asked her mother to accompany her. But Kurt was graduating from high school that month, so Dorothy Seberg decided her duties lay at home. Frances Benson happily accepted the invitation, however. She empathized with her granddaughter, and furthermore, she had never seen France. Grandmother and granddaughter departed for Europe on June 3 and checked into a Paris hotel. The French press, keeping a close watch on Jean, noted that François was not at Orly to greet them.

A week later Harry Druker, Jean's hometown lawyer, filed divorce papers for her in the Marshalltown County District Court. François was not apprised of the action. In an article informing its readers of the proceedings, the Des Moines *Register* explained: "During her recent visit, Jean told friends that he [François] perferred urban living, was highly emotional and often insulting to her friends." Jean, the report continued, "preferred a quieter way of life."

12

"Jean Seberg has found her best role: herself."

—FROM A REVIEW OF *Playtime*

In the summer of 1960 Jean had three black-and-white films lined up back to back, all of them tailored to her accent and to her image as the representative American Abroad. She went immediately into *La Récréation (Playtime),* which Moreuil had based on a short story by Françoise Sagan—who, for once, gave her blessing. Then Jean would star in *Les Grandes Personnes (Time Out for Love)* for director Jean Valère. After that, Philippe de Broca wanted her for a frothy comedy about adultery, *L'Amant de Cinq Jours (The Five-Day Lover).* Before long, the schedules overlapped and Jean was working "like I've never worked before."

By Hollywood standards, they were all low-budget productions, unlikely to get a screening outside of art houses in the major American cities. Still, Columbia, pleased by her surge in popularity, revised her weekly salary upward and hiked her loan-out fee to $20,000 per film. To the young French directors who clamored for her, she usually represented their single biggest expenditure. Despite her rising income, Jean's finances were precarious. High living with François had eaten up most of her earnings. She had to budget carefully and restrain her natural inclination to send money and gifts home to her friends.

As she had feared, the filming of *Playtime* was stormy. She and François put on a polite façade for members of the press, who inquired whether the upcoming divorce didn't make for problems on the set. Once the reporters disappeared, however, tensions broke to the surface. They were compounded by the fact that Jean's leading man, Christian Marquand, was a close friend of François's and had never been particularly fond of Jean.

She was cast as the innocent daughter of an American NATO officer, enrolled in an expensive boarding school in Versailles and attracted by Marquand, the weak-willed sculptor who lives next door. The sculptor's mistress, an older woman, encourages him to seduce the gamine, knowing that infatuation will pass. It does. The American girl—disillusioned, but wiser to the ways of Europe—returns to school. Playtime is over.

With a few variations, this would become the standard Jean Seberg role for the next two years—a kind of virgin-temptress who tempts mainly by her overwhelming innocence. It was almost as if the Old World, tarnished and blasé, were taking revenge on the New World, which still permitted itself ideals and dreams. Yet something about Jean's presence righted the balance. She projected a capacity for wonderment that suggested she was alive in a way that the bored playboys and their disenchanted mistresses were not. She was awakening to life. They had already struck their compromises with it.

Because her participation had been instrumental in securing financing for the film, Jean later referred to *Playtime* as her "farewell present" to François. Privately, she described the two months' filming as "pure hell." Pictures taken on the set conjure up the mood: François is often smoking Gauloises furiously, and his brow is furrowed. Jean looks sullen and defensive. In one photograph she is giving him the finger. "We'd shout at each other all during the day and then I'd come home and cry all night," says François.

The completed film attested to his gifts as a director. Unfortunately, by the time it was released the following year, the market had been glutted with New Wave dramas. *Playtime,* with its emphasis on the familiar moral lassitude, was regarded as slender material.

During the filming, Jean and her grandmother moved in with her diminutive friend Aki Lehman, who ran a Left Bank antique shop on the Rue de Bellechasse. The adjoining apartment, equipped with a large modern kitchen, was an informal meeting place for young artists and struggling performers of all nationalities. Frances Benson was given her own room and zestfully took her place in this bohemian society—an Iowa embodiment of Grandma Moses. She acquired a taste for Alsatian wine, savored the Parisian cuisine, and to Jean's amusement, developed a coquettish side hampered not at all by a total ignorance of the French language. Having "spoiled her rotten," Jean saw her off to the United States at the beginning of August. Back in Marshalltown, Frances Benson immediately set down her impressions in a journal she presented to her grandchildren that Christmas. Its title: "24 Days of Ecstasy." She also moved out of the Seberg house, found herself an apartment, and a month from her seventy-ninth birthday, proudly asserted her independence.

Meanwhile, Jean had begun work on *Time Out for Love,* in which she was playing a nineteen-year-old girl from Lincoln, Nebraska, who wants to experience a great passion during her three-month stay in Paris. This time she falls in love with a jaded playboy who races cars for kicks. There are the usual triangular implications and the mandatory references to solitude, man's inability to love and the wasteland of success. At the end of the film she is seen on a train with her American boyfriend, heading for the boat that will take her to the States—sadder, as ever, but wiser, as French morality dictated.

In the role, Jean graduated from adolescence and braids to womanhood and a chic version of her *Breathless* look. Even in this gloomy-gray film, her appeal is clear. In one scene, set in a smoky Paris *boîte,* she dances a giddy Charleston. Momentarily drenched in bright white light, she stands out like a beacon in a sea of world-weariness, banishing lethargy and self-indulgence with her sheer youth.

"I've always thought of her as Alice in Wonderland," says Maurice Ronet, who co-starred in *Time Out for Love* and went on to make three other films with Jean. "She had the same delighted astonishment at everything she saw and everyone she met. Even when things got bad for her, she kept that openness. She was always a kind of Alice for me. Even at the end, when she was Alice in Horrorland."

Jean was on the set every day from 8 A.M. to 7 P.M. Then she would take a quick break for dinner before reporting back to Moreuil to complete the sound track of *Playtime,* which had run over schedule. That usually meant another four hours. At midnight she'd drag herself home exhausted. "God bless vitamins B_{12} and C," she wrote Paton Price, at the same time cursing the ineffectual French actors' union, which permitted such killing hours. Nonetheless, she preferred French film making to that of Hollywood. There were no producers breathing down her neck, and she relished the camaraderie between cast and crew, which Hollywood's rigid caste system made impossible. Between shots, she stole time for her French reading and was soon deep into Gary's autobiography, *Promise at Dawn.* "Gary's book is beautiful, lovely to read," she told a *Newsweek* reporter on the set. "As a birthday present, I sent him my own translation of two chapters, and he told me I had done a good job."

On September 20 the Marshalltown County Court granted her a divorce from Moreuil on the grounds of cruel and inhuman treatment. Jean heaved a sigh of relief that "that whole unsuccessful chapter of my life is closed."

François knew only that he and Jean were separated. He was editing his film in Paris when news of the divorce came over the radio. "It fell on me like a ton of bricks," he recalls. "I just sat there and cried." Later his hurt turned to anger at having been so cavalierly dumped, and he unburdened himself to the press: "She owes almost everything to France. She became a star in France. She became a Frenchwoman when she married me. But she took refuge in the States rather than apply to a French court when she felt it more convenient."

François had the divorce declared invalid in France, arguing that he had not been informed of the American proceedings. Then, charging adultery and naming Gary as the other man, he countersued for a French divorce. The courts eventually ruled in his favor and relieved him of any alimony payments.

The squabble enlivened Paris gossip that fall. There was certainly a touch of malice in the newspaper account that identified Gary as Jean's constant "chaperon," just as there was in the observation of one prominent film director who described the unlikely couple as "another Agnes and Arnolphe." The not-so-subtle comparison referred to the innocent virgin and the fatuous roué who tries to mold her to his specifications in Molière's *School for Wives.*

Jean was upset enough to write a friend in the States and swear: "Any rumors of my marrying anyone—and I know there are some—are complete lies. It's the last thing I want to do."

François thought otherwise. Returning to his apartment one day, he put all Jean's belongings on the landing and went out and bought himself a new bed. "I never saw her again," he says. "Maybe I was too young for her, or maybe she didn't love me as much as I loved her. But most of the time she was like someone from another planet. There was always a trauma. She was always running away. I think I changed careers and went into television as a direct result of her. I didn't ever want to have to deal with a movie actress again."

In later years Jean dismissed their marriage as "a youthful folly." Nonetheless, François had weaned her away from Preminger, taken her to France and persuaded her to make *Breathless.* He had also introduced her to the man who would become her second husband. For a bankrupt marriage, it had not been without remuneration.

Romain had temporarily taken an apartment in Paris on the Ile St. Louis, the fashionable island enclave in the Seine. Jean continued to give her address as Aki Lehman's antique shop on the Rue de Bellechasse. In letters to friends, however, she talked poetically about the pleasure of waking up with the Seine flowing beneath her windows. The antique shop was blocks from the water, but Jean was sure that no one back home knew Paris geography. And in Paris, Aki Lehman willingly acted as a cover, describing for reporters the quiet life she and Jean were enjoying.

The few who saw Jean and Gary together could not help but sense a deepening involvement. "You could get sunburned by the love between them," says Aki Lehman. Jean had brought new joy to Gary's life and given him a playfulness his friends had not seen in him for some time. Intellectually, Jean thrived in his company. She was intelligent and alert, but her formal education had stopped abruptly after high school. Through Gary, she was experiencing the wealth of European culture and thought. He gave her books to read, sent her to museums, and encouraged her to examine herself critically. "Jean liked to sit at his feet and address him as 'dear master,'" Hollis Alpert remembers.

In a French interview given then, she was asked to analyze this celebrated creature called Jean Seberg. Speaking of herself in the third person, she answered, "Jean Seberg has short hair. It's almost become a symbol for her. Now she's letting it grow out a little, and she's delighted because she hates going to the hairdresser. She is small. She has to be careful because she'll have a tendency in later years to put on weight. She has a beauty mark on her face and used to have a lot more of them. . . . I have the impression that on certain days she looks like a kid, on others like a very old woman.

"Morally, I know her less well. She is nervous, a little worried, rather unstable. Her character is more Slavic than American. Her timidity is often mistaken for coldness. In the social world, she feels out of place. From a professional point of view, she has to be careful to avoid facileness by always playing the same parts—charming little girls in charming little stories. She should really play the kinds of roles that attract her—clowns, easy women—roles that are the opposite of her personality. If she really wants to learn her craft, I'd advise her to do some theater."

It was a largely accurate appraisal, and Jean did explore several theatrical possibilities. Among others, she seriously considered appearing in a French adaptation of Arthur Miller's *A View from the Bridge,* as the orphaned niece of an Italian longshoreman. Inevitably, though, she would back off. While the stage attracted her, it also frightened her. She had perfected basic techniques for the camera—often through painful trial and error—but she never felt secure enough to give a sustained theatrical performance.

She tried to sort out her thoughts on the matter in an article she wrote for the *Oxford Opinion* which was published in England at the end of October 1960. The piece strongly reflects the teachings of Paton Price, but its writerly style is an attempt to emulate Gary's.

It is a very difficult craft, film acting. Understanding it intellectually means very little. Some of the most unbelievable actors are "intelligent" actors. A camera traps you, the true you—not a distorted reflection in a mirror, but a pure critical reproduction in a magnifying lens. It is difficult to lie to a camera. One's eyes are so enormous, one's breathing, mouth, smile are so evident. . . . On the screen, when an actor is false, the audience unconsciously recognizes it and refuses to *give* with him. We all know when an actress is really crying on the screen. On the stage, the vital question is if the actor makes *you* cry.

In the flush of success, she showed herself surprisingly aware of the pitfalls of her profession.

Perhaps, the day arrives when what he [the actor] has to offer is à la mode—the little-boy-lost quality of James Dean, Van Johnson's freckles, the soft-hearted gangster face of Bogart. What happens? The audience identifies him with this special personal quality, and the movie moguls capitalize and produce it on a mass market. He has, suddenly, no self to sell anymore; he has the carefully mimicked imitation of himself as he once was. And finally the public will feel this too.

Still, she admitted to a fascination with

a profession which few can leave even when they know their time has come. There is too much pleasure in being the caricature of life—the good guy, the bad guy, the *femme fatale*, the worried housewife. It's exciting and, oddly enough, real. For most of all there is a kind of masochistic challenge to see how far Humphrey W. Dumptey can climb before tumbling down to break his crown.

When the article appeared, she told friends it was one of her proudest accomplishments. Some of them suspected Gary's hand in the writing.

By October she had begun work on her third film of the year. *The Five-Day Lover* was a charming romp directed by Philippe de Broca, unique among the New Wave directors in that he made comedies. De Broca had a lightness of touch and a jaunty wit that would later turn *King of Hearts* and *The Man from Rio* into world-wide hits. Relaxed and ingratiating, he believed comedy such a perilous undertaking that he tried to make his actors as comfortable on the set as possible. ("You should never scold the dear children," he once theorized.)

Jean's role was a welcome modification of her usual image. De Broca put her in a brown shoulder-length wig and cast her as a young Englishwoman and mother of two, married to a stuffy but lovable historian. "Jean always liked to say that she was *une petite bourgeoise*," De Broca says, laughing, "so that's the role we gave her." With a difference. During the week, while her husband minds the archives, Jean's character, Claire, conducts a sprightly daytime affair with a frivolous playboy.

"Life's a bubble. When it touches earth, it's over," says Claire at one point. The line seemed to be the guiding principle for De Broca, who enriched his feather-light comedy with a strain of melancholy and a touch of satire. "Humor is always the hardest thing to understand in a foreign language," he says. "But Jean did. She was very gifted for comedy, and it's always surprised me that she never made more. She played the character of the free-spirited Englishwoman delightfully. Her leading man, Jean-Pierre Cassel, was more than a little bit in love with her. Frankly, I always felt there was a little wickedness to her delight. Jean was very flirtatious, and she could certainly tease men, string them along. She liked to leave a trail of broken hearts behind her, although it was never done with cruelty."

The filming was trouble-free, and De Broca came away with the impression of an ebullient girl who was taking her success in stride. "She was so completely the opposite of what she later became," he observes, "that I sometimes wonder if she didn't already have a double nature back then."

The Five-Day Lover enjoyed only a marginal success in France, but it was popular in art cinemas in the United States. Coming on the heels of *Breathless,* it revealed Jean in an entirely new light. She could be an admirably deft comedienne. *The New Yorker* was "astonished by the tact and delicacy with which Miss Seberg played her tricky role. She, it turns out, is an actress, and oh, how beautiful." Of her thirty-seven films, *The Five-Day Lover* remained one of the few that Jean spoke of affectionately later in life.

At the end of the year, she and Romain moved into a spacious apartment at 108 Rue du Bac, with an eye to buying into the building. For tax purposes, Jean had been advised to establish residency in France, and her romance gave her further reason to stay abroad. The Left Bank neighborhood they chose was elegant and prosperous, dotted with art galleries and antique shops. Luxurious gardens grew behind many of the thick stone walls. But the area was kept from being stuffy by the nearby Boulevard St. Germain, with its round-the-clock traffic of artists, students, writers, night owls, gigolos, tourists, hustlers and the occasional panhandler. Jean came to love the mix. Later she would drown herself in it.

Her liaison with Gary was attracting more and more attention. Publicly, Jean admitted her boundless admiration for his writing. She told one journalist that Gary was "the most noble person I know." But she hastened to add, "People generally forget that Romain Gary has a remarkable wife, who is my friend. You see, for the moment, I don't want any other role in life than that of a happy vagabond. After months of work, my only desire is for a vacation. I'm just waiting for January, when I can get far away."

True to her word, she left shortly thereafter, for a six-week tour of the Far East at the invitation of the Japanese film industry. What she didn't say was that Romain Gary was going with her and that Lesley Blanch, her "friend," was beginning to wonder if things weren't getting out of hand.

13

"Madame Gary Will Not Even Reply to Jean Seberg."

—TABLOID HEADLINE

Any residual doubts about Jean's emergence as a film star in France ended in February 1961. Within ten days, *Playtime, Time Out for Love* and *The Five-Day Lover* began their first-run engagements on the Champs Elysées. She received top billing in all of them, and one newspaper went so far as to declare an unofficial "Jean Seberg Festival."

If the films were not uniformly well received—the New Wave had crested rapidly—Jean herself could do little wrong. Reviewers were enchanted by her presence, so fresh and defenseless as to appear artless. "For the French, at least, I seem to express a basic melancholy, a sense of loss that says something about young women today," Jean theorized later, groping for an explanation of her appeal.

Her vulnerability on the screen was enhanced by the disarmingly gauche American accent she brought to the French language. "Jean Seberg, her cheeks polished like two pebbles on the beach, has such a seductive way of saying *'très bienne'* that one wants to applaud all her errors of diction," concluded a reviewer.

In Marshalltown, the *Times-Republican* ran a full page of stills from her French movies and regretted that Central Iowans would probably never have the opportunity to see the racy fare in their local theaters.

Early in March, Jean and Romain returned from their six-week trip to the Orient by way of Los Angeles and New York. The beauties of Bangkok and the picturesque bustle of Hong Kong had impressed her, but she informed friends that "India was tragic in its poverty and primitiveness." The trip had caused her to re-evaluate her thinking about the United States. "I find myself believing more and more in American culture," she told Hollis Alpert. "And I'm getting more and more fed up with those who pooh-pooh America. It's far and away the most humane country and the one with the least compromise. Whenever someone tells me, 'I don't really consider *you* American,' I'm ready to scream." She also said she was happy to rediscover peanut butter and pizza, her favorite foods.

In New York she checked into the Plaza Hotel and appeared on *The Tonight Show* (then hosted by Jack Paar), where she talked about her improbable comeback. The customary ups and downs of a long show business career had, in her case, been compressed into three roller-coaster years. But to the public, at least she seemed to retain her equanimity. "I've never been psychoanalyzed," she told a reporter, "but I believe that everything that happens to you up to twenty or twenty-one marks you so profoundly that you should cherish it—even the awful things, because they are what make you a human being." Ever mindful of her hometown, she went to the trouble of sending a congratulatory telegram to the Bobcats basketball team, which had won the state championship. The message was read aloud at the team banquet.

Dorothy Seberg had recently undergone surgery, so Jean flew home to Marshalltown for a quiet Easter week. She colored eggs with her brother David and visited relatives. Her mother found her "very happy and full of her recent trip to the Far East, during which she gained many new experiences." From her husband's example, Dorothy Seberg had learned to keep the deeper worries to herself. After Easter services at Trinity Lutheran Church, Jean's parents drove her to the Des Moines airport and saw her off to Paris.

Columbia had proposed a role for her in *Sail a Crooked Ship,* opposite Robert Wagner and Ernie Kovacs. But Jean, still leery of Hollywood and its pressures, backed out of it. "I'm a turtle crawling into his shell when I know I have to make good," she confessed to Earl Wilson. Her new popularity notwithstanding, she also had reservations about her French films. "I did my best and hope my work is simple and direct," she wrote Paton Price, her Hollywood mentor. "But my own sense tells me an actress is someone who acts and acts and acts. I need to study and I want to study." She offered to pay his way to Paris if he would coach her for a couple of months. Price accepted and flew over in mid-May.

The arrangement worked out badly. Price, who spoke no French, found Paris cold and the Parisians remote. Jean introduced him to Romain on his first night there; Price sensed a scorn that the writer took few pains to mask. Their dinners together were strained, and Price had the impression that Gary considered Jean's career negligible.

Jean had arranged for Price to see *Breathless, The Five-Day Lover* and *Time Out for Love*. Afterward, when they settled down to study, the teacher felt his pupil was too distracted and edgy to concentrate.

"It was a turbulent time for her," he recalls. "She desperately wanted Romain to marry her, although, frankly, I could never understand why. She alluded to it constantly. Her mind wasn't on her work. We weren't getting anywhere. After two weeks I'd had enough and decided to go home. Before I left, we all went out to dinner—Jean, Romain, a consular official and myself. Halfway through the meal, Otto Preminger and Tony Perkins walked into the restaurant. Jean just froze up, but she figured she'd have to say something to them eventually. On the way out, Gary and I walked ahead, and Jean stopped by their table. When she joined us on the sidewalk, Gary wanted to know what Otto had said. 'Oh, he asked me if you were my husband yet,' replied Jean. 'Then he said he'd see me at the next divorce.'"

Gary spun around and threatened to go back into the restaurant and punch Preminger in the nose. Jean restrained him.

"I don't know if she had been joking or not," says Price. "She could be very mischievous, and she was certainly doing all she could at the time to get Romain to marry her."

Aki Lehman has a different view of this period. "Jean was insanely happy. Her career was going well, and she was secure in her relationship with Romain. The early sixties were a fabulous time in Paris. We did a lot together. We'd go shopping and visit the museums and the art galleries. Jean loved jazz, so we'd go to all the concerts. She learned how to cook in my kitchen. It was a wonderful friendship. 'Aki,' she'd often say to me, 'you're my tranquilizer.'"

Through her friend, Jean had entrée to a society of young artists and musicians—among them entertainers Bobby Short and Hazel Scott, who appeared regularly in Paris; the poet Gregory Corso, who introduced them to Allen Ginsberg; and the sculptor César. Roman Polanski, then a struggling director, came by the antique shop, as did Jones Harris, Ruth Gordon's son.

Sometimes Jean dropped in on novelist James Jones and his wife, Gloria. Their Ile St. Louis apartment, according to one habitué, "attracted the brightest and most interesting Americans on the Continent." "She met all the big names in Paris," says Lehman, "and she was terribly observant. She'd tell wonderfully funny stories about them. What was refreshing about Jean was that she had never become spoiled, and she had meanwhile developed a fantastic thirst for knowledge. Gary did a lot for her in that respect, making her aware of paintings, books and music."

Together, Jean and Aki took art courses at the Louvre. As a reward for completing a course on Roman and Gothic art, Gary arranged to have her diploma personally signed by André Malraux, the Minister of Culture. A highly respected writer and statesman, Malraux was Gary's friend and idol. After Gary introduced Jean to him, she was beside herself. "One lunch with him," she bubbled, "and I don't care if I see anyone else." Malraux was equally taken with Jean, and they kept up a correspondence until his death in 1976. He told her she would be ideal for the role of Anna Karenina. If only he had the time, he said, he would write a screen adaptation of Tolstoy's novel for her.

Much of Jean's life with Gary was, by necessity, concealed. He was intent on side-stepping any compromising publicity;

but he also had long periods of self-absorption, when he was writing or moody and saw no one at all. He tended to keep to the company of a few fellow writers and diplomats, many of whom regarded Jean as a lovely ornament at best.

In addition, the formality of French social life occasionally frustrated Jean. Once she had conquered an initial timidity, she became the gregarious Midwesterner who poured out her soul to friends and acquaintances. "The French system seems to be based on saving the maximum of yourself for those nearest you," she complained to a reporter. "Perhaps that is better than the other extreme in Hollywood, where people give so much of themselves in public life that they have nothing left over for their families. Still, it's hard for an American to get used to. Often I will get excited over a luncheon table, only to have the hostess say discreetly that coffee will be served in the other room. I miss that casualness and friendliness of Americans, the kind that makes people smile."

Gary's marital status did not ease matters. Lesley Blanch was apparently willing, if not exactly content, to let her husband's affair with Jean run its course. "I'm sure they had a nice time for a while in the beginning," Blanch said much later in her life. "But nobody thought it would last. I certainly didn't. The young, pretty, determined girl—well, it's classic, very classic, isn't it? They were having an affair, but he certainly wasn't running off and begging for a divorce. I'm sure she was nice to sleep with. But she always saw where she could move on and do better."

On the contrary, Jean and Romain seemed to be settling in. That fall, a team of workers was in the midst of remodeling a large apartment they had bought on the second floor of 108 Rue du Bac. The couple hoped to be in by Christmas. "We are very happy," Jean confided to Paton Price. "But still no solution to his marriage problems and, I'm sorry, I was never known for my patience."

Eager to put its star to work that fall, Columbia was considering the possibility of casting Jean in *The Ugly American* opposite Marlon Brando, the hero of her adolescence. Although far from definite, the prospect struck her as too good to be true. While she awaited confirmation (fruitlessly, it turned out), she accepted a role in a Franco-Italian production *Congo Vivo.*

The curious film—part documentary, part love story—was to be filmed on location in the former Belgian Congo, which had recently gained its independence. Her trip to the Far East with Gary had fired Jean's zest for travel to exotic places. She was both giddy and apprehensive about visiting the new African state. On September 6 she departed for Leopoldville. After the long flight she was immediately taken by the lush tropical landscape and its people. "The Africans are so child-like and sweet," she wrote Dawn Murray Quinn. "And the babies: the women carry them on their backs—like little black beans. But as you read in the papers, they have a child-like brutality, too."

With her instinctive belief in fair play, she was offended by the wreckage Belgian colonialism had left behind, and she decried the horrendous poverty. "The Belgians bungled things badly," she told columnist Sheilah Graham later. "They wouldn't educate the natives. It was only last year that a colored doctor was able to practice. The Belgians built two universities that presumably were open to all. But to get in you had to know Greek, which automatically kept out the Congolese. The fact is the natives are basically very kind, and it is surprising after the treatment they received from the Belgians they are not more brutal."

To no one's particular surprise, filming of *Congo Vivo* was difficult. The heat was oppressive, the food and water suspect. Jean contracted a case of amoebic dysentery that would leave her irritable and lethargic months later. Fighting continued to rage over the fate of the mineral-rich Katanga province, which under President Moise Tshombe had seceded from the Congo. The United Nations was attempting to negotiate a settlement. But on September 18 the plane carrying UN Secretary General Dag Hammarskjöld to a meeting with Tshombe crashed in the jungle. The political situation looked more ominous than ever.

One day the crew and actors ventured outside Leopoldville to shoot a scene on a ferry. They ran up against a squad of Congolese soldiers, their guns trained on the apparent interlopers. The film-makers' explanations got nowhere; the soldiers refused to budge, so the crew turned back. As complications increased and the danger seemed to grow daily, the company retreated to Rome to complete the film.

The finished version of *Congo Vivo* would reflect the muddle. President Kasavubu and General Mobutu, the country's strongmen, had both consented to be "interviewed" in the film by an Italian actor, Gabriele Ferzetti, who played a foreign correspondent. Jean, whose role was developed in flashbacks, was the frigid, suicidal wife of a Belgian colonist. Awaiting her return to Brussels on the eve of independence, she drifts into an abortive affair with the Italian journalist, but she is unable to consummate it due to the lingering trauma of having been raped by a Congolese. Critics would point out that the love story in which Jean figured had nothing to do with the tribulations of a country's struggle for independence, and they would dismiss the work as misguided.

Romain flew to Rome in October to join his lover, who would soon celebrate her twenty-third birthday. The Italian press, more persistent than the French, dogged them during their stay. Eventually the couple capitulated and allowed themselves to be photographed together for the first time in their apartment in Rome. Immediately speculation ran rampant: Lesley Blanch had secretly agreed to a divorce . . . Jean Seberg would be leaving her movie career to become a diplomat's wife . . . Romain Gary would be throwing over his diplomatic career to follow the young actress . . . The marriage would take place in three weeks . . .

In fact, nothing was definite. The idyll of the dashing diplomat and the actress some reports described as "glacial" was now officially in the open. That was all. Although a single woman elsewhere in the world, Jean was not yet free to marry in France, where the French tribunal would not grant her divorce until January. And Lesley Blanch wasn't even considering divorce.

The three parties were back in Paris by November. Jean had completed her film and busied herself shopping for furniture for the apartment on the Rue du Bac. Lesley Blanch had come from America to attend to last-minute details on her book *The*

Sabres of Paradise, a study of a Caucasian war resister during the time of the czars that was being brought out in French. Temporarily, she had moved in with a friend only blocks from her husband and her rival.

Elle, the French women's magazine, attempted to sort out the affair in a question-and-answer interview with Jean. Some observers felt that her answers delivered a veiled challenge to Lesley Blanch.

QUESTION: It seems that in America the notion of divorce is not the same as it is in Europe. What do you think of that?

JEAN: I'm for divorce. I think, in general, Americans are less sophisticated than Parisians.

Q: What do you mean by sophisticated?

JEAN: Here in Paris, even if people get along very well, they prefer to cheat on one another as much as possible. Each one has his little life on the side, and I don't like that. Americans divorce. It's more honest.

Q: If you had to get married in the near future, would you marry Romain Gary?

JEAN: I have no idea. All that I can tell you is that he's a marvelous man, a great friend for whom I have admiration and esteem, on the human as well as the professional level.

Q: Do you know the wife of Romain Gary, the novelist Lesley Blanch?

JEAN: Yes, I met her in California. She's a very nice woman, I must admit. But she's been separated from Romain Gary for a very long time.

Q: Do you expect a man to be responsible for you?

JEAN: Yes, I do. It's a man's job.

Lesley Blanch showed herself more discreet with reporters. "Romain lives nearby. It's very convenient," she said with only a hint of irony in her voice. Claiming her old-fashioned prerogatives, she added, "I'd rather not wash my dirty linen in public. Romain and I have been married for seventeen years. We met during the bombardment of England, and we've lived through some difficult times together. That doesn't come undone in a day or even a year. I have total confidence in Romain."

French show-business journalist France Roche later observed, "Romain put more stock in Lesley Blanch than people suspected then. Of course, he was flattered and excited by Jean Seberg, but he wasn't that eager for a divorce. Jean had a stubborn streak, though, and she was determined to have him. She'd drop all sorts of hints that they were going to get married soon. It was the tactic of someone who likes to suffer. Either you sleep with a married man or you don't. But to make him divorce and marry you, well, it is not the mark of a serene person. And there was very little serenity about her at the time. She went out of her way to look for drama."

A former actress, however, thought it was Jean who was being exploited. "Who was Romain Gary then? A poor, minor consul. Lesley Blanch had brought him into literary circles. The brains were hers. She was like a mother figure to him, and he was considered like a mother's boy. Oh, he had a moody persona that some found attractive. But it was really only through his relationship with Jean Seberg that he started to assert himself as this strapping macho type. All right, he may have found his manhood through her. But what was in it for her?"

The gossip had soon penetrated upper French diplomatic circles, confirming Gary in his decision to abandon that part of his career, at least until the scandal died down. In *The Night Will be Calm,* a personal examination of conscience he published in 1974, he attributed the decision to his loyalty to Charles de Gaulle. "I couldn't work next to Charles de Gaulle because I wanted to keep my sexual liberty . . . It was a question of rectitude. De Gaulle had an ethic of respectability for his public servants that I didn't want to take on myself. I had to choose between a double life and lies or refusal. These were my last young years—well, relatively young—and I wasn't going to sacrifice my nature and my love of life to ambition and the desire to make it."

The issue was intensified by the fact that Jean Seberg yearned desperately for a child and said so repeatedly.

14

> *"I'd like to slow down. My life has been like a*
> *45 record. Now I'd prefer 33⅓."*
>
> —JEAN SEBERG

Whatever Jean's image elsewhere, in Marshalltown she remained the sweet, talented hometown girl who had kept her head through the travails of stardom. There was always gossip, of course, and the usual small-town sniping, but on her visits home Jean did all she could to combat it. She would go to church with her parents, drop by to see her former teachers —or at least telephone them—and put in an appearance at Marshalltown High School. Although she now wore clothes by Givenchy, she would go shopping on Main Street and show her enthusiasm for the little things—the latest twist records or a knit cap—that she just couldn't get in Paris.

The Sebergs recognized the unusual destiny of their daughter, but they refused to believe that it had altered her character. They were not prideful people. On the contrary, their greatest aspiration was quiet respectability. One's accomplishments would speak for themselves, if any talking needed to be done. They had strong family ideals but their sights rarely extended beyond the community.

How could Jean confide in them? Little by little, she had turned to others for more worldly advice: her grandmother, Carol Hollingsworth, her lawyer Harry Druker, Bill Fisher, and later, Sol Serber, the local rabbi.

The *Times-Republican*—faced with covering a celebrity and

respecting the privacy of an upstanding Marshalltown family—glossed over the less savory reports about her. Usually Warren Robeson, now the city editor, would stop by the Seberg house just before Jean was to leave for Europe, chat amiably with her for an hour or so, and once she had left, bring the town up to date with a friendly article filled with homey details.

Consequently, the news of Jean's unconventional romantic life broke not in Marshalltown but in the Des Moines *Register* in January 1962. JEAN SEBERG, IDOLIZED, IS SADDEST AMERICAN blazoned the headline on the front-page story. A compilation of several French articles, it pictured her as a disillusioned homewrecker, chasing after another woman's husband and advocating divorce as the "honest" solution to everyone's problems. "I am not attracted by handsome men who flex their muscles and talk nothing but sports," it quoted her as saying. "What every woman wants is a thinking genius who is able to understand the feminine nature, too."

It was an inflammatory article for the Bible Belt. The general reaction was reflected in a letter to the editor, published the following week, in which Lewis J. McNurlen, a professor of sociology from Drake University, took it upon himself to lecture the young actress.

> Without necessarily trying to promote my field of study it would be safe to say that Miss Seberg could benefit from a good course on courtship and marriage. Using her term "honest," I find it difficult to believe that it is "honest" to "fall in love" with a married man. Love is not an innate behavioral response: It is something we do through our own choosing . . . Miss Seberg is an attractive, vivacious young lady. She should have such an extensive array of single suitors that married men would not have to be included on her eligible list . . . I regret that one of "our own" appears to be the victim of the "fate" that seems to befall so many people in the entertainment field. Her behavior does not appear to be in harmony with her home training and our "Midwest conservatism."

The Sebergs were mortified by all the fuss. When Jean visited Marshalltown late in January 1962, she instantly read the embarrassment and bewilderment on their faces. More for their sake than her own, she undertook to reply to the sociology professor.

How can any of us possibly believe we can understand a situation concerning three people—two of them from foreign lands—only on the basis of hearsay and gossip. For Professor McNurlen's information, I *have* studied sociology and "marriage and family life" courses (in fact, the Marshalltown High School principal will tell you I didn't get such bad grades in them either!), but my teachers never pretended to offer pat formulas to cover any occasion. They simply tried to prepare us to cope with the adult life awaiting us. . . .

I am proud to know Mr. Gary—he has many qualities I've been raised to admire. I know Mrs. Gary as well. Their private life and any personal difficulties they may or may not have do not—and should not—concern me in any way.

I suppose that after five years, I should be used to living in a glass bowl, but I don't think I ever will be really—and certainly my parents won't.

It was not the explanation the Sebergs would have liked. But explanations by Marshalltown standards were not possible. Jean's only recourse was simply to keep ever larger portions of her life to herself.

Breathless had, by then, made its way to a Des Moines cinema, amplifying her image as an amoral nonconformist. One of the Des Moines columnists had telephoned the Sebergs to say he didn't like the film. Mrs. Seberg had turned the caller over to her husband, who asked, "But tell me this—didn't you think Jean did a good job of *acting*?" Some of the townsfolk weren't sure it was acting. On the steps of Trinity Lutheran Church one Sunday, the minister took Jean aside and suggested benevolently, "Jean, why don't you come back to us for a while?"

"Jean felt there was no way her parents could fathom what was going on in her life then," says one friend. "If she could have broken away from them, maybe things might have been different for her. But whenever she came home, she was always trying to live up to this vision of the dutiful daughter. She developed a real split personality later in life, and I think a lot of it goes right back to Marshalltown. She was ultrasensitive and really didn't like to hurt people, but she kept coming up against the rigid expectations of her parents. She wanted to protect them, but protecting them meant hiding from them.

Half the time, the Sebergs didn't have a clue what was going on."

In fact, while Jean's parents fretted over the unseemly newspaper accounts of her liaison with Gary, she was concealing far more disturbing news: she was already carrying Gary's child. Since her religious scruples ruled out the possibility of abortion, her only option seemed to be to have the child in secret.

That decision would cause her untold anguish and drive the final psychological wedge between her and her parents. Morally, she no longer belonged to Marshalltown. Until the end of her life, however, part of her would struggle to maintain the impossible fiction of the good Marshalltown girl. When she failed, as she often did, she was filled with guilt and self-loathing. "Jean should have been born twenty years later, when sex and morality were freer," says Lynda Haupert. "With her upbringing, it was an awful stigma to be pregnant and not married. Jean wasn't ever really a liberated woman, but she tried to live her life as if she were."

Back in Paris that spring, Jean and Romain dined one evening with Joseph Roddy, a senior editor of *Look* magazine. His account was entitled "The Restyling of Jean Seberg" and presented a playful picture of the couple. Roddy had no doubts that the restyling was largely Gary's work.

Between courses, Gary told him that he was using Jean as the basis for a character in a new novel, in order to depict the unrealistic idealism he found typical of Americans in general. (The naïve character would appear in *The Talent Scout.*)

"But Jean loses her naïveté rapidly under my influence in real life," Gary assured the *Look* writer. "In the book, and maybe in life, too, she takes people for what they are on the surface. And she does this with frequently disastrous results. She can be in the middle of the most criminal sort of setup, and she can't see it. That's the American side of her character."

In describing them, Roddy was not the first to evoke the myth of Pygmalion and Galatea. Gary's attitude reminded many of the sculptor who fell in love with the enchanting statue of his own making, clearly Seberg in this case. At one point, Roddy reported, Gary reeled off the books he had given her to read:

"Pushkin, Dostoievski—"

"Just *The Idiot*," the girl noted.

"Balzac, Stendhal, Flaubert—"

"*Madame Bovary!*" Jean sang out. "That could have been me if I had stayed in Marshalltown one day longer."

"She is an absolutely marvelous reader," Gary claimed. "She always finishes the book."

"Except a couple of yours, sweetie," she jabbed, and the jab might as well have been a kiss. "What Romain thinks is that I'm still a dumb farm girl."

"I'm being absolutely serious about this," Gary went on. "She has brains and, what's more, intellectual curiosity. And when you think where she came from—"

"You mean to sit there and say Marshalltown High School is not an intellectual atmosphere?"

Toward the end of the conversation Jean turned serious and said to the man from *Look*, "I know that the greatest of actresses has about twenty good years of acting in her and that she will go on living for thirty or fifty years as a human being. So the conclusion I have come to is that I can't make acting my whole life . . . I'm lost to Debbie Reynolds roles, and I'm not going to give Liz Taylor a run for her money." Then she smiled sweetly and added, "Now you know absolutely everything about me, including the fact that I was conceived, born and married in Marshalltown and that I will probably be buried there in the fourth most beautiful cemetery in the world."

The Talent Scout, which appeared first in an English translation in 1961 and then in French five years later, throws a revealing light on the Gary-Seberg relationship. It is the story of Jose Almayo, a bloodthirsty dictator in an unspecified Spanish-speaking country, and the unnamed American who becomes his mistress and sets out to reform him.

The parallels between Jean and the mistress are unmistakable—from the upturned nose, the flawlessly white skin and the short-cropped blond hair to the hopeless sentimentality of her idealism. Like Jean, the character comes from a respectable Midwestern family, joined the NAACP when she was fourteen, composed dreamy verses in high school and writes long, confessional letters to her grandmother in Iowa. In her consuming need to justify her existence, Gary describes her as "having a struggling quality, the feeling of a bird beating its wings against a windowpane."

But the portrait has an unflattering side, too. Delicate of nerves, the character goes on long crying jags to get her way, drinks heavily and has a propensity for breakdowns. She is stubborn, and her soft, angelic features occasionally combine "in an air of almost reckless determination." Of her strong sexual appetite, the English translation observes discreetly, "She had true goodness in her—but it had taken him [Jose] some time to discover this because she was so willing in bed, and he did not think the two could go together."

Gary permitted himself to be more graphic in the French version. It depicts a sexually insatiable woman, dispensing caresses with the "humility of a faithful dog" and whimpering on about the beauty of lovemaking.

Jean was not merely Gary's creation, as the popular press liked to point out. She was his material, too.

15

*"I'm not the simple untouched girl I was when
I left home. . . . You're going to say I should
come home like a good little girl and be a nice,
demure, hypocritical piece of merchandise on
the marriage market, pretending I don't know
which end of a man is up."*

—CHRISTINA JAMES TO HER FATHER
IN *In the French Style*

Jean's life in the late spring and summer of 1962 is shrouded in
deep secrecy, apparently occasioned by the birth of Alexandre
Diego Gary, her son by Romain. Only Jean's closest confidantes knew that he was born that year in the middle of July.

Others were told—in time—that he had been born on October 26, 1963, in the French village of Charquemont. Using contacts he had developed in the diplomatic service, Gary would
have the proper legal papers drawn up to support the fiction.

Clearly, it *was* a fiction. During the months just preceding
that date, Jean was hard at work on *Lilith*. As late as September 22, 1963, a month before the official birth date, she was in
London on a publicity junket, receiving reporters who inquired
when she was going to marry Romain Gary. Photographs taken
that month in her suite at the Dorchester Hotel show her to be
enviably slim. "I'm like a whale when I get pregnant," Jean
confided later to her friends. A whalelike Jean Seberg would
not have gone unnoticed at the time.

For the first years of his life, Alexandre Diego was kept from the public eye, and only a few of the Garys' intimates were even allowed to see him. Stifling the urge to share her good news, Jean rigorously concealed the circumstances of his birth.

In March 1964 she sent congratulations to Lynda Haupert on the birth of her child: "Mom wrote that you hardly gained anything. Is that possible? Tell me the secret when my turn comes." It wasn't until July 1965 that Jean let Dawn Murray Quinn in on her secret, while taking pains to falsify Diego's real age. "I have a big surprise for you," she wrote. "Now hold on to your seatbelt. Romain and I have a two-year-old son. Really! He is a beautiful boy and his name is Alexandre, but we call him Diego. He was born shortly after our marriage, and because of that we have kept it very quiet. I imagine around this fall, it will come 'out,' but we will have avoided by then the kind of press we feared and it will be alright. I had him by Caesarean section. It's a rather fantastic story, but I'll have to tell you when I see you."

Carol Hollingsworth didn't find out until December of 1966, when Jean enclosed the child's photograph in a Christmas card. Jean could hardly share the true details with Marshalltown, but she did confide them to Paton Price. "Jean told me that she had deliberately gotten pregnant so that Romain would marry her," he says. "But naturally they didn't want the press to learn about Diego until his age caught up with his size. So it was hush-hush for years."

Jean had good cause for prudence. In the spring of 1962 Hollywood was starting to look her way again, willing to forget the Preminger debacles and the belittling reviews of the past. Columbia was eager to star her in a picture called *In the French Style,* based on two short stories by Irwin Shaw. It would be her first American movie in nearly three years and could mark a significant breakthrough. A scandal could jeopardize her career. The example of Ingrid Bergman and Roberto Rossellini still stood as a warning. Movie stars who had children out of wedlock were not accepted in the early 1960s.

That spring Jean underwent a long cure for the recurring amoebic dysentery she had contracted in the Congo. The treatments left her tired and shaky, but they also provided her with a reason to escape to Spain for a three-month "vacation," far from the prying eyes of the press. Gary had a house in Barcelona, where she could rest. Eugenia Muñoz, her maid, would accompany her. Eugenia's family was from Barcelona, so the arrangement seemed ideal.

"I am recuperating from my cure, which about finished me off for good," Jean wrote to Dawn shortly after her arrival in Spain in May. "But if it did that to me, it must have done worse to my amoebas, which are smaller. At least that's what we hope. All seems to be well, but I have to take it easy for a few weeks and decided to get away from the hurlyburly of Paris and take a little sun. . . . The Spanish are such absolutely lovely people—so clean, honest, proud and generally nice. It has been a revelation."

Gary had been invited to be a judge at the Cannes Film Festival, so he joined her later in the month. "I'm very happy generally and with Romain in particular," Jean chirped to Paton Price. The cheerful letters were deceptive, however.

When director Robert Parrish came to Barcelona for consultations with her about *In the French Style,* Jean was confronted with a dilemma. She couldn't appear in public in the final stages of her pregnancy, and yet she didn't want to lose the role, an important one. After much hesitation, Jean and Romain found a solution. She would receive Parrish in her bedroom. Pretending to have a broken leg, she slipped into bed. Gary placed a protective arch over her leg and the sheet formed a tent, which concealed her ballooning shape.

Parrish was convinced that Jean was "on-the-nose casting" for the film. Ironically enough, it told the saga of a small-town American girl who loses her virginity in Paris and then drifts into an aimless, empty life with the jet set. Jean had already made that film several times, but she hadn't made it in English yet. Columbia believed there was a large women's market in the States ready to gobble it up. Parrish, unaware of any trickery, informed Jean that shooting would begin late in August in Paris. He invited her to visit him and Shaw earlier that month for rehearsals in the mountain village of Klosters, Switzerland, where Shaw maintains a handsome villa. Jean accepted. Not long after Parrish's departure, she gave birth.

Eventually she confided in Vony Becker, wife of the film director Jean Becker, that Diego had been born in Barcelona, despite his papers. She also told both Betty Desouches and Raymonde Waintraub, two of her closest French friends, that Diego was a year older than his birth certificate maintained. In one of the last tape-recorded interviews of her life, she acknowledged that her son's birth sign was Cancer (July) and that he had been born on the seventeenth, early in the morning. But when the interviewer asked her the year, Jean changed expression and said abruptly, "Your questions are tiring."

"Jean was very pleased that she'd been able to pull it all off," says Paton Price. "It took a certain amount of guts. But Jean could be spunky when she had to."

Lesley Blanch, who according to one acquaintance had been "holding on for dear life," bowed before the inevitable and agreed to begin divorce proceedings. "Of course, pregnancy was a lever that a woman of her type would use," Blanch reflected many years later. "It is really rather naïve to think that she was going to get an abortion, I must say. She wasn't going to give up that handle. It was the classic gambit for someone like her, who was pretty and ruthless. Yes, that's how I'd describe her. Pretty and ruthless. She had no style or discipline, and she wasted a great deal of my ex-husband's time and money. I certainly gave the divorce as soon as it was asked. But I can tell you Romain wasn't rushing things up to then."

Dennis Berry, Jean's third husband, believes the birth was traumatic for Jean. She was uncertain when Gary would be free to marry her. The pregnancy flew in the face of every moral principle she had been taught by her parents. What could have been a joyful occasion was, by circumstance, secretive, sinful and lonely. "She gave birth in a dark room in Spain. How can you ever dismiss that?" Berry wonders.

At the end of July, Jean returned to Paris, entrusting Diego to the care of Eugenia Muñoz, who would become his surrogate mother and develop over the years a fiercely proprietary attitude toward the child. "Diego was pretty much raised by Eugenia," Aki Lehman admits. "When Jean wasn't making a film, Eugenia and Diego would come to Paris, but they spent a lot of the early years in Spain. Diego became very attached to the governess and grew up speaking Spanish. Jean learned the language just so she could communicate better with them."

Jean reported for rehearsal in Klosters in early August. Parrish has good memories of the easy rapport he and Shaw were able to establish with her. "She liked us and trusted us," the director says. "We worked on the script and dined together. Klosters is a beautiful village. Because of all that, we had no problems later on in Paris. We were all in it together."

Jean's respect for writers *per se* automatically extended to Shaw, a burly man who looked not unlike William Bendix and who hoped to reverse the damage that Hollywood had wreaked on his previous stories by producing this film himself. "We didn't find out until after the picture was made that she had been pregnant and given birth," says Shaw. "She seemed flustered at first when she arrived at Klosters, and I thought she looked a little plump. But I assumed it was from the summer. I remember asking her, 'Jean, you're not pregnant, are you?' She just laughed and said she'd lose the weight by the time we started shooting."

Jean made a quick trip to Barcelona to see Diego before embarking on the actual filming of *In the French Style* at the end of August. A few of the scenes were shot on the Riviera, but for the most part Parrish relied on the usual picture post-card sights of Paris for the exteriors and the Studios de Billancourt for the interiors.

"It sounds like five films I've already made," Jean told a French television interviewer. "But it's the best scenario and the most developed character I've had so far, excepting Joan of Arc." As Christina James, a plucky American art student in Paris, Jean was given more opportunities to reveal her acting range than any of her French films had allowed. Spread over four years, the script shows her first as a ponytailed innocent, dabbling away at bad canvases, braving Parisian snobbery and indulging in puppy love with a French teen-ager (Philippe Forquet) who is even less experienced than she. The years flash forward, and Christina emerges as a sophisticated plaything of the jet set, caught up in a round of parties and a rocky affair with a globetrotting journalist (Stanley Baker). Finally, tired of the sham and feeling shopworn, she returns to San Francisco to marry a doctor.

In the French Style was a summing up of Jean's American-Abroad pictures. Probably because it was written and directed by Americans, it struck more biographical resonances than her French films. Jean responded to them, especially in a long scene with her concerned father (Addison Powell), who fears that Christina has become an emotional transient and urges her to "quit escaping" and come home.

"It was a fairly deep and heavy scene," Powell recalls. "The father sees that his daughter is like a chip on the waves and wants to probe the extent of her injuries. She argues that she's no longer a child and knows which end of a man is up. We filmed it at night on a steep incline in Montmartre. Jean and I talked a lot about it beforehand. She admitted she'd had similar discussions with her own father. I mentioned that to Ed Seberg when I was teaching one semester at the University of Iowa. Ed nodded sadly and said the scene had been very real to him, too. But he liked the way Jean called me 'Papa,' in the film. 'Papa—that's what she always calls me, too,' he said."

Parrish, who had cast Jean for the type she represented, was surprised at the technical proficiency of his star. "She really had absorbed an amazing amount of knowledge about the art of film making for one so young. On top of that, just for sheer beauty on the screen, she was a joy to photograph. She was great for a camera—she acted with her eyes and mouth, all the things that are suited to close-ups. It was an up time in her career. She really pitched in and worked harder than anyone else."

Gary frequented the set, observing closely. He had been displeased by the Hollywood version of his novel *The Roots of Heaven* and had begun to nurture directorial ambitions himself. Powell thought he was "awfully good for Jean. They seemed to fulfill each other's needs. She needed his sophistication and learning. And for him, the middle-aged man, well, he had the support and love of a very beautiful woman, which isn't nothing."

Jean appeared in almost every scene of *In the French Style,* and while she was nervous about carrying the whole weight of the picture herself, in retrospect she admitted enjoying it "in an almost narcissistic way." Parrish and Shaw were old skiing buddies, and their friendship spilled over to the set. It was an American film, but the working climate was properly Continental. The reviews would be restrained—Jean's performance was more widely applauded than the film itself—but *In the French Style* would recoup its modest production costs.

Jean felt she had now exhausted the acting possibilities as America's surrogate expatriate in France. Her usual post-film letdown set in that November. "After a picture is over," she told a reporter from *Seventeen*, "I don't want to do anything until I recuperate from the emotional exhaustion. . . . Then in a couple of weeks, I'll be nervous if I'm not working, I won't be able to sit still. You have to be a little nutty—although that's not the right word—some sort of demon has to be in you—to keep going in this business, never knowing whether you are really going to make it. So far, pride has kept me going and some other crazy thing. I don't know what.

"I don't mean to sound unhappy or sad, because I'm not. I've been enjoying myself. I've grown up here in the most exciting years of my life. . . . No matter what happens, it's far better to be alive and doing things than be safe and dead somewhere back in the States, never having tried anything at all." It could have been Christina James talking.

Once again, rumors had begun to circulate that Jean was about to marry Romain Gary at last. In December she made what was her ritual statement to the French press. "I don't understand," Jean said to the newspaper *France-Soir*. "It's absolutely untrue. We're in exactly the same situation we've been in for the last three years. Romain Gary is still married, which cripples our plans. If we were married, we wouldn't hide it. On the contrary."

16

"I have just read an American critique which reproaches me for always being the same from film to film. I accept the criticism with one condition—the person who is making it hasn't seen Lilith!*"*

—JEAN SEBERG

Jean went to work almost immediately in January 1963 for Jean-Luc Godard, whose films usually spelled instant controversy. Godard was one of five international directors who had been asked to contribute a "sketch" to a film that would carry the overall title *The Greatest Swindles of the World.* A commercial undertaking, it was hardly his cup of tea. Nonetheless, he decided to resurrect the character of Patricia Franchini, who in the four years since *Breathless,* he figured, would have become a roving reporter for a San Francisco television station. His scenario, "The Big Swindler" ("Le Grand Escroc"), was set in the souks of Morocco. There the inquisitive Patricia meets and interviews a counterfeiter whose bizarre notion of charity consists of distributing phony bills to the poor. The sketch was filmed rapidly in Marrakech, but the magical accord between director and performers instrumental in making *Breathless* a hit was missing this time. Deemed the weakest of the five sketches, "Le Grand Escroc" was dropped from the film and eventually wound up as a short on French television.

Jean's return to Europe was more eventful. At the end of January she boarded the ferry at Tangiers for the Spanish coast. As the boat approached Algeciras, a powerful storm arose. The boat was blown onto rocks, and for thirty-eight hours was whipped by high winds and lashed by waves that held rescuers at bay. Into the night, Jean comforted the frightened Moroccan children on board, and with her new, shaky command of Spanish, acted as interpreter for the English-speaking passengers.

"I don't know what we would have done without Miss Seberg," said one British tourist. "She was absolutely wonderful, and kept us all going." Then, conferring the ultimate British accolade, the grateful woman added, "So calm!"

Jean chalked it all up to the continuing disasters of her career and joked that it was better than being burned at the stake. "We ran out of food and water yesterday," she told a reporter. "There was only wine to drink. But the captain gave us all a large tot of brandy before we were taken off this morning."

Shortly after settling back into her Paris apartment, Jean learned that Robert Rossen was interested in her for the starring role in *Lilith,* which he was adapting from J. R. Salamanca's novel and filming for Columbia. The year before, she had read and liked the novel, which in contemporary terms retold the myth of Lilith, the demonic first wife of Adam, who wanted to brand the world with the mark of her sexual desire. Jean hadn't even considered it as a possible role for herself, but now that Rossen had put out feelers, she had second thoughts. This might be the long-awaited chance to shatter the constricting stereotype of the young innocent abroad—a part that was not only devoid of interest but one that her own circumstances had rendered ironic, not to say ridiculous.

The film represented a departure for Rossen, who was known mainly for such gritty, virile films as *All the King's Men, They Came to Cordura* and *The Hustler.* His script showed how Lilith, an enticing young schizophrenic in a mental hospital, lures a well-intentioned orderly named Vincent into her web of folly and destruction. After rejecting dozens of scripts, Warren Beatty, then Hollywood's prince-apparent, had consented to play Vincent. But the picture would belong to the actress who incarnated Lilith. Vulgar, sensitive, girlish, cruel, flirtatious, spiteful—it was a uniquely challenging role. Lilith's sexual attraction to all humankind—men, women and children—promised a certain controversy as well.

Rossen was considering several names: Yvette Mimieux, who wanted the part badly; Natalie Wood, who didn't, having already played a mentally troubled character opposite Beatty in *Splendor in the Grass;* British actresses Samantha Eggar and Sarah Miles; and Diane Cilento, who exuded a wildness on the screen that made her Salamanca's choice. However, Columbia, pleased with her work on *In the French Style,* was putting heavy pressure on Rossen to use Jean.

With Beatty, the director flew to Paris that spring to consult with her in person. Jean tried not to let her eagerness show and slipped only once. In keeping with her *Breathless* image, her hair had been cropped short for "Le Grand Escroc." Rossen's secretary remarked tartly that Lilith should at least have long hair. "Really! I've always thought I looked very good in long hair," Jean snapped back. Rossen was amused. He agreed to give Jean the role. Something about her fresh looks intrigued him, something unsettling that was akin to a geological fault under a golden landscape, he noted later.

"Lilith is not a villainess. She's too much good gone bad," he explained to the press. "It's usually innocence that makes the sharp transitions to these psychotic stages, and it's the innocence that attracts Vincent. I think Seberg is just right for it. She'll be great. She's got that flawed American-girl quality—sort of like a cheerleader who's cracked up."

According to Saul Cooper, one of Rossen's assistants, the director was actually less confident—about the film in general and Jean in particular. "Rossen brought a tremendous burden of guilt with him to that film," he says, "presumably dating back to the days when he had been a cooperative witness during the Hollywood witch hunts. He had lost a number of close friends, and a lot of people turned their backs on him afterward. He carried this with him all the time. In my analysis, it was as if he felt condemned to pay the price of his guilt. He viewed *Lilith* as some kind of retribution and felt he deserved the little failures of the project as it worked out. He was extraordinarily talented, but he was also very insecure. Each scene was torture for him, and the shooting was fraught with emotion and conflict."

Jean was signed for a reported salary in excess of $60,000 as part of a revised contract with Columbia, which now wanted to keep her in its stable of stars. Entrusting Diego to Eugenia again, she traveled to New York at the beginning of April 1963 for pre-production work. Uncomfortable in Hollywood, Rossen had resolved to shoot his film entirely on the East Coast. Jean stayed briefly at the Sherry-Netherland Hotel, and for a while it was almost like the early days of glory under Preminger. "Flowers just seemed to arrive in steadily increasing proportions," remembers Kathy Wyler, director William Wyler's daughter, who had worked briefly on *In the French Style* and paid Jean a catch-up visit in New York. "It seemed like men had only to talk to her on the telephone—they'd send flowers afterward. She was very sexy then, in an unpretentious way. She seemed to glow, and that glow was very attractive to the male sex."

The glow, it seemed, masked genuine fear. Jean spilled it out one day to Rossen. "I was afraid," she said later, "that I could never do anything as good as I thought I could when I was seventeen. I was worried about the time gone by that you can never match." "It's not true," Rossen reassured her kindly, "You can only gain." Privately he anticipated difficulties with her performance and decided to shoot "round the clock" (simultaneously from multiple angles) so as to be sure to capture her best moments.

Salamanca, a professor at the University of Maryland, had laid his novel in the Maryland countryside, not far from Washington, D.C. Early in May the company went south for location shots. Most of the cast and crew were booked into a sprawling motel on the outskirts of the capital. Jean and Romain, who traveled with her, opted for the posh comfort of the Georgetown Inn, where he worked sporadically on a novel when he wasn't with her on the set.

Rossen filmed several bucolic scenes along the towpath of the C & O Canal and at Great Falls on the Potomac River. In Rockville, Maryland, he stumbled upon a stolid frame house that looked just right for Vincent's family home, and rented it, furniture and all. Since its wizened owner looked perfect, too, he hired her to play Vincent's grandmother. Using the townsfolk as extras, he shot the annual jousting contest in tiny Barnestown, Maryland; the medieval curiosity had somehow survived over the years as the state sport of Maryland.

Salamanca had modeled his sanitarium, Poplar Lodge, after Chestnut Lodge in Rockville, at the time one of the most expensive facilities of its kind in the country. It resembled nothing so much as an exclusive country club, and its clientele was viewed as "the elite of madness." The treatment it dispensed was novel in that it foreswore drugs and chemicals and relied on extensive daily sessions of analysis. Rossen arranged for his cast to visit the sanitarium and participate in several psychodramas with the patients. (Peter Fonda, who was playing a fellow patient, begged off, saying, "I'm crazy enough as it is.")

As she waited for the young patient who would show her through the establishment, Jean trembled noticeably. "I shook so much," she later recalled, "that I had to sit down and smoke a cigarette to steady myself and prolong the time before going from one wing to the next. I wanted so badly to make an honest film. All those movies in which the insane scream and yell and make wild faces—they're so ignoble and false. That's not madness at all. Madness is like a camera that goes in and out of focus—now sharp, now fuzzy. That's what hurts so much and makes for its fascination. Here were all these lost, brilliant, sensitive, kind people and suddenly they'd just go out of focus. There was this irrational violence just below the surface, and it was frightening—the way a high-strung horse is frightening when you know he can't control himself."

In "Lilith and I," a perceptive interview she gave to *Cahiers du Cinéma,* Jean described her encounter with a schizophrenic woman who called herself Rita / Sylvia. "If one said, 'Good morning, Rita,' she replied, 'I am Sylvia,' and vice versa. Besides this doubling, she took herself for God as well, and she complained endlessly of the work that that caused her. She knew how to do nothing but knit, and as she was God, she knitted hearts, lungs, ovaries, human organs." Not even Gary, Jean felt, could have invented such a personage.

Rossen especially wanted her to meet and observe a young woman who had once been a beauty queen and who incorporated many of the caged-beast mannerisms he envisioned for Lilith. "She received me in her room, completely hidden under the sheets—you could see that she was nude—her face included," Jean remembered. "Visibly she was masturbating. She said good morning to me. I returned her good morning and added that I was going to leave. She asked me why. I replied that it was impossible for me to speak to someone whose eyes I could not see. She asked me to stay, then to come back and see her. As I was leaving, she informed me of her intention to get up and say good-bye to me, and she got up, rolled in her sheet, her head hidden like a child playing ghost. She turned her back and stretched out her hand to me behind her. Then she said, 'I am going back to bed.'" Jean used some of the woman's extraordinary behavior for the final scenes of the film.

A young male patient asked her, "Aren't you the star of *Breathless*?"

"Yes," Jean replied. "Why do you ask?"

"Because you are so beautiful that you made me crazy."

On one visit Jean was introduced to another patient, Philip L. Graham, the brilliant but unstable publisher of the Washington *Post*. She chatted with him at length and came away puzzled: Graham, she told friends, didn't seem mad at all. Three months later he committed suicide, and she was dumbstruck.

"I developed a great respect for mentally ill people," she said. "They reminded me of very fine crystal that cracks because it's almost too fragile to be touched." Some of her friends thought that more than respect, she developed a fixation with the mentally ill. "She was really very deeply marked by the experience," says Aki Lehman, who visited her during the making of *Lilith*. "All these young people her own age with these incredible problems—she couldn't forget it."

Salamanca often saw her on the set while the company was in Maryland. He specifically remembers having lunch with her and Gary one afternoon at the rustic Comus Inn near Barnestown. "Jean had a lot of extravagant mannerisms. She smoked little black cigars and wore floppy hats and eccentric clothes—not defiantly, mind you, but more as a disguise. Of course, everyone in the inn was craning all through lunch to get a look at her. She had a childlike quality about her at the same time she had that thumb-the-nose insolence of *Breathless*. But it seemed to me that her affectations were the result of her great insecurity. She was very provincial, basically, and Gary was clearly educating her then in liberal attitudes. He indulged her affectations and may even have found them amusing.

"At one point he and I got to talking about a Brazilian writer. And Jean asked if his novel was written in Spanish, not knowing that Brazilians speak Portuguese. When she found out, she blushed terribly. But Gary just reached over and patted her hand. She was stylish and very feminine, and he obviously was very proud of her. Despite her attitudinizing and her attempts to be theatrical, there was a great sweetness about her."

Although long discussions preceded each scene, Rossen gave very little specific direction to his actors. He preferred that they steep themselves intellectually and psychologically in the overall climate and then let their imaginations play. Irritable on occasion, he was a perfectionist who would resort to as many as thirty takes to get the precise effect he wanted. For one of the film's most dreamily beautiful sequences—a picnic scene—he carefully explained Lilith's fascination with water and reflections. When the camera rolled, Jean delicately hiked up her skirt, waded into the water, stared at her reflected image and then, with almost childish wonder, bent over and chastely kissed the shimmering surface. It was an exquisite depiction of Lilith's enchantments, not to mention a perfect symbol for her schizophrenia.

As filming progressed and a darker side of Lilith emerged, a certain uneasiness began to pervade the set. The material was depressing. Morale declined. The tensions were palpable by the time the company relocated up north, on Long Island, where Rossen had discovered an uninhabited estate near Oyster Bay that fit his notion of Poplar Lodge. Convinced that Rossen was lavishing an inordinate amount of attention on Jean and the Lilith role (which he was), Beatty took to bucking the director every step of the way. The press had hailed the actor as the successor to James Dean, and he brought that brooding persona onto the set. He groused that Fonda had the sympathetic male role. Imposing his whims on the company, he kept his fellow performers waiting for hours until inspiration struck, then mumbled his way through the scene, leaving Rossen no alternative but to reshoot it.

"Warren is a brilliant, charismatic person," says Cooper, "and he made sure he got his share of the spotlight. He has the charm of the stalking cat, and he preyed on Jean with all his powers as a seducer. But nothing was ever what it seemed to be on the surface. He was busy playing games, manipulating people and situations. For Jean, it was a terrible handful."

Most of her scenes, redolent with sexuality, were opposite him, but his vanity was difficult for her and she had trouble adapting to his introspective, group-theater approach to acting. Before long, they were barely on speaking terms. "I'm dead—my hours are from 5:30 A.M. to 7:30 P.M.," she wrote Dawn Murray Quinn. "And it's such a rough role. Plus the fact that Warren Beatty's behavior is just unbelievable. He's out to destroy everyone, including himself." To another friend, she confided that Beatty gave new meaning to the word "complicated." "It's long and fatiguing," she wrote. "We lose a staggering amount of time every day."

Unbeknownst to the actors, the harried Rossen was slowly dying from a rare skin disease that left dark splotches on his face and body. The director popped pills endlessly, and the cortisone he was taking had ugly side effects. He collapsed several times on the set. "Sometimes he would fall asleep—in the middle of night shooting, especially," Peter Fonda recalls. "It made things very difficult. You'd be in the middle of a scene, and all of a sudden you'd hear him snoring. But Jean knew this was a big film for her. She worked extraordinarily hard. I think she sensed that she was doing something that would have lasting value—if not necessarily to the public, at least for herself."

In a fight scene with Beatty, animosities boiled to the surface. Lilith was called upon to slap Vincent roundly on the face. "You could tell something was wrong that day," Fonda says. "Warren kept repelling the slap with his arm, badly bruising Jean. He kept it up through take after take. It was really hurting her. I told him that if he continued, I'd beat the shit out of him. Columbia promptly sent someone down to the set to tell me that if I touched Beatty, they'd sue my ass." Fonda showed up shortly thereafter with several friends, black belts in karate, who positioned themselves menacingly on the sidelines.

At the end of July, newspapers reported that Rossen was closing the set of *Lilith* to observers so that he could film a love scene between Beatty and Jean, who would be nude to the waist. The announcement turned out to be the work of an over-zealous press agent, and Jean quickly set the record straight. "I have never done a nude scene or a nude-to-the-waist scene, and the way I feel about it, I never will. It's a decision every actress has to make. I'm not objecting on moral grounds. It's just that I didn't do it." (In fact, she was always slightly self-conscious about her body, and whenever a part called for her to bare more than her emotions, she would insist on some kind of protection.) Her denial didn't get half the coverage reaped by the initial announcement. However, *Confidential* magazine seized the occasion in an article headlined "Why Jean Seberg Won't Strip" to remind its readers of her unconventional relationship with Romain Gary. In Marshalltown, a pained Ed Seberg refused to put the magazine out on his drugstore racks.

Jean had a brief respite from the rigors of filming that summer when she and Gary received a call from the social secretary of the White House, asking them—on twenty-four hours' notice—to dinner with President and Mrs. Kennedy. Jacqueline was an ardent Francophile, and the President entertained more than a passing curiosity about General de Gaulle. Delayed by traffic and a stack-up at the airport, an embarrassed Jean and Romain arrived a half-hour late to discover that there were only two other dinner guests, speechwriter Richard Goodwin and his wife.

Gary recounted "My Dinner with Kennedy" in detail for the French publication *Candide*. He described Kennedy as young, alert and blessed by the gods, but felt that he carried intellectual lucidity to the point of chilliness. Focusing his steely-blue gaze on his guests, the President bombarded them with questions about everything from Belmondo and film making to

America's reputation abroad, all the while cataloguing their answers. "In my seven years in the United States," Gary wrote, "I have never encountered a brain that functions so implacably."

Jean related to her friends afterward that Jacqueline had taken her aside and asked if she planned to marry Romain Gary. When Jean said she might, the President's wife replied, "Don't. They lose all interest in you once you do." (Jacqueline later requested a print of *In the French Style* for a private screening at the White House.)

For Gary, the dinner was a journalistic coup. It also helped contribute to the shifting public image of Jean Seberg, who increasingly was being perceived as an international sophisticate. No longer the small-town girl, she dined with presidents, conversed with cultural ministers and hobnobbed with Europe's best minds. It was an exaggerated view, but it made good copy. Many of her friends sensed that Jean was ill at ease in Gary's circles and thought she suffered under an unspoken injunction to live up to Lesley Blanch's widely acknowledged brilliance. "I was at a lot of dinner parties with her in the sixties where no one even bothered to ask her what she thought," one actress and friend recalls. "She would sit there, looking vaguely bored through it all. If she happened to say something clever, everyone looked surprised. Nobody really listened to her. She was there because of Gary, and she always knew it."

Filming on *Lilith* ran well into August, and it left Jean emotionally bankrupt. She had gone deeper into herself for the role than any she had played before or any that would come after. It was not acting so much as a journey in self-exploration, during which she discovered a startling and sometimes awesome potential within her.

"There are times in that film when what you see on the screen is Jean herself—pure and unadulterated," says Betty Desouches, Jean's close friend who observed her during the making of several French films. "In her other roles, you know immediately when she is acting. In *Lilith,* she is being. There's so little between her and the role that it's almost spooky."

"Two films in her career are the key to Jean," says Dennis Berry. "They are *St. Joan* and *Lilith.*" *St. Joan,* he believes, called upon all her intrinsic idealism, although she was too young at the time to express it adequately on the screen. "In the late sixties she tried to become St. Joan in real life," Berry says. "And her crusading led her into total despair."

Like the enigmatic Lilith, she would spend much of the final year of her life in a succession of mental institutions, gripped by madness and yet curiously aware of its strange theatricality. "I don't know whether Jean was a true schizophrenic at the end," Berry says, "but she certainly had no defenses against the world by then. Some of the psychiatrists she was working with thought that she was actually trying to go back to the role of Lilith. She knew it had been the crowning achievement of her career. It was almost as if she was trying to hide in the role."

In the late summer of 1963, uncertain of the fate of *Lilith,* Jean went back to Paris to dub the French version of *In the French Style.* Columbia then packed her off to London during the third week of September to promote the film. Jean received reporters in her suite at the Dorchester Hotel and astonished them by admitting that "I've found happiness and love in Paris, and very soon I hope I shall be married. He [Gary] is writing a book now, so I imagine we shall have to wait until it is finished. But what does it matter, since the decision has been made." The announcement and pictures of her looking thin and elegant hit the Paris newspapers the next day.

On October 10, Jean and Gary took out a marriage license in Paris. Six days later they slipped away unnoticed to the village of Sarrola-Carcopino on the Mediterranean island of Corsica. Accompanied only by their witnesses—a French air force general and his wife—they were married by the mayor in a brief civil ceremony, after which they disappeared into a waiting car and sped away from the sun-bleached town. Later that day, they flew to Nice. Jean was almost twenty-five, Gary forty-nine.

Deprived of more pungent details, one Paris newspaper headlined: THE NEW WAVE LOVES THE FIFTY-YEAR-OLD SET. Another, with a kind of lip-smacking glee, reported Gary as saying, "I owe children to posterity." Officially, Diego was born ten days later.

17

"Jean Seberg has become a lot more than just another dumb blonde. Perhaps there is still hope for Kim Novak and Tippi Hedren."

—*Life* MAGAZINE

For Americans, the Cinderella story had begun when Otto Preminger tapped Jean with his magic wand to play Joan of Arc, and the scathing reviews had pretty much symbolized the stroke of midnight. The French interpreted the fairy tale differently. For them, it began with Jean's marriage to Gary. He was the one, they felt, who had taken the radiant innocent of the New Wave and molded her into an elegant woman in the Continental mode. Perceived as an alliance of American beauty and European savoir-vivre, it was a replay, on a lesser scale, of the Grace Kelly–Prince Rainier romance.

Jean entered her *haute couture* period, shopping regularly at Givenchy and Dior. She engaged a maid and a part-time secretary, drove a Jaguar and dashed off genteel notes on pale-blue stationery bearing the monogram *JSG*.

The Garys' apartment—strictly off-limits to the press—was said to be handsomely decorated with Giacometti-like sculptures on slate floors and with abstract paintings on the stark white walls. In French women's magazines Jean dispensed beauty tips and decorating secrets. She even took a course in Japanese flower arranging.

"The French lapped it up," says Barbara Sohmers, then an American expatriate actress who had appeared in *In the*

French Style. "If you're not French, you're considered only half-finished. When Jean married Gary, the general thinking went, 'Well, good. Now she'll have someone to take the rough edges off her.'" During her rocky marriage to Moreuil, Jean was widely quoted as saying, "Frenchmen think you have to break in an American woman like a horse. You have to comb it, run it, train it and beat it . . . The ultimate compliment is that you don't act like an American at all." Her observation still held true, although Gary, wise in the ways of the world, was subtler in his methods.

Once his relationship with Jean had been sanctioned by law, Gary occasionally let himself think about resuming his former career. At times he complained that writing was an unre- lievedly solitary occupation and he envied those with more gregarious professions.

"Did I tell you Romain will probably go back to the diplo- matic service?" Jean wrote to Carol Hollingsworth early in February 1964. "I know he misses it and they'd like him back, probably as consul general somewhere for a year or so, and then ambassador. This means that a certain party I know from Iowa who can't even make her own bed properly is going to have to learn how to run gigantic houses and plan meals. Ugh! But it's an exciting life and a wonderful way to see the world. And the people at the Foreign Office say it's perfectly alright for me to carry on an acting career."

Gary's sights were fixed on the consulate in New York, a position that he hoped would be open in a year's time. On February 18 the couple was invited to lunch with General de Gaulle. According to a letter she wrote, Jean was excited about seeing "the secretive old man" in the flesh and thought the invitation augured well.

Meanwhile, she had been signed for a French chase film, *Echappement Libre (Backfire)*, which would pair her and Jean-Paul Belmondo once again. The announcement conjured up huge expectations in France. (Precisely because he feared the inevitable comparisons to *Breathless*, director Jean Becker had hesitated a long time before casting Jean.) Belmondo had quickly climbed to stardom, while Jean's marriage had further endeared her to the chauvinistic French.

He was cast as a scrappy smuggler, darting all over Europe

in an effort to unload three hundred kilos of gold concealed in his Triumph. She, posing as a photojournalist (Swedish mother—American father, to explain her accent), was the cool-mannered accomplice with whom he would eventually fall in love. The movie traded on Belmondo's image as a street fighter with charm. But it presented a new Jean: sexy, stylish, smoking thin cigarettes and downing whiskey, all the while looking mistily enigmatic and very much above the chicanery.

The film required nine weeks of shooting and took the company on a zigzag through Europe and the Near East. Romain accompanied Jean throughout the trip; beginning in Mégève and the snow, they went on to Barcelona and the sun. Becker lived it up with the crew at night but remembers Jean and Romain staying mostly to themselves (although she did develop a flirtatious relationship with one of the cameramen, an aspiring director named Costa-Gavras). Throughout the filming, Becker and his wife, Vony, often found Jean unaccountably "perturbed"; they later learned that she had a child she was hiding for mysterious reasons that seemed to go well beyond an actress' vanity.

At the end of March the company pushed on to Athens, Beirut and Damascus before returning to Paris. Romain introduced Jean to the Greek islands. Captivated, she impulsively bought a fisherman's shack on Mykonos for $3,000. Yet to become the St. Tropez of Greece, the wind-blown island was sleepy and picturesque. Jean's address there—c / o Joseph the Tailor—suggests the rustic mood that prevailed then. Because of the distance from Paris and the erratic political climate in Greece, she used the cottage less than she had anticipated. (After the junta seized power in 1967, Jean's political principles prevented her from staying there herself, but she would regularly lend the house to friends.) Nevertheless, for the French press, it was the Garys' unofficial hideaway.

Their marriage was being depicted in near-idyllic terms. *Jours de France,* a popular general-interest magazine, imagined the scene:

Rue du Bac, a man, pen in hand, works twelve hours a day on his new novel, *Les Mangeurs d'Etoiles* [the French version of *The Talent Scout*]. At dusk a young woman, tired but smiling, returns home from the set where she has been acting for eight solid hours before the cameras. She tiptoes up to him, encircles the man in her arms and in an irresistible tone of voice asks, "May I see the first draft of your chapter, Monsieur Author?"

This is the happiness of the Garys. This summer it will have Greece for a backdrop. In the Cyclades, they have bought a minuscule shack—white, isolated, burned by the sun. Like all couples who are sufficient to one another, the Garys—everywhere and forever—want only to be together.

There was at least one blot on this desperately romantic canvas, and Jean set out to remove it. To that end, she invited her parents to Europe. Flying petrified Dorothy Seberg, and Ed disliked leaving his drugstore for any extended period, but Jean overcame their reluctance and persuaded them to visit her and Romain in the summer of 1964 on the Spanish island of Majorca.

Romain met them at the airport and drove them to the villa in the hills. As the car pulled up, Jean came out the door with a child at her side. "Papa, Mama—meet your grandson!" she called out with a broad smile.

It was the first the Sebergs knew of Diego. They were thunderstruck, although Dorothy Seberg later said that she had understood the situation before Jean even opened her mouth—the resemblance between Diego and Jean's younger brother David was so striking to her.

Jean explained the delicate circumstances to her parents and swore them to secrecy, a needless precaution given their natural reticence. A close friend of the Sebergs who didn't learn the story until many years later says, "Dorothy took it very well, all things considered. But there's no pretending it wasn't a shock to them, especially Ed, who always thought of Jean as a virgin even after she'd been married three times. Of course, they were excited about having a grandson, but I don't think they ever reconciled themselves completely to the circumstances of his birth."

Long afterward Dorothy Seberg would compound the confusion surrounding Diego's birth date. Subtracting yet another year from his age, she would say he was born in October

1964—a properly respectable remove from Jean and Romain's marriage.

Backfire was released in September and attracted long lines in France. Reviewers dismissed it as a conventional film, however, and it had only a fitful commercial life elsewhere.

Becker, who later in the decade got to know Jean well, already appreciated the air of faintly amused superiority she projected on the screen and often in life. "Jean had a beguiling way of putting herself above the throng," he says. "There was nothing offensive about it. She had a kind of detachment, and her best movies took account of it. As long as she stayed out of the melee, she had a surprising simplicity and clarity about her. She could look over at Romain and come up with the most deliciously ironic statements about him, as if he were deaf. And it was never hurtful. I always thought she should have lived her life that way—slightly apart from things."

Jean was never a "hot" actress but she could be entrancingly cool. When a role allowed her to keep her distance from the heat of emotion, she was in her element. Godard, intuitively sensing that, had had her play the unconcerned, unconnected Patricia in *Breathless.* De Broca had put her into a comedy—essentially a cool form—and in *The Five-Day Lover* allowed her to remain blithely above conventional morality. In *Lilith* it is a similar detachment—which allows her to emote at the same time she is *observing* herself emoting—that accounts for the hypnotic fascination of the schizophrenic character she plays.

Before that film came out, however, there were indications that it might meet with less than universal approval. Paralyzed by premonitions of failure, Rossen had taken an excessively long time to edit. In August *Lilith* was submitted as the American entry at the Venice Film Festival, where Columbia hoped it would receive the kind of highbrow accolades that would compensate for its less-than-commercial subject matter. The chairman of the festival selection committee was displeased with the entry, made disparaging public remarks about it and indicated that the Americans might prefer to submit another film in its place. Claiming that his work had been judged prematurely and unfairly, an angry Rossen yanked it out of the competition.

Lilith received its first screening on September 19, 1964, at the New York Film Festival, where scattered boos pierced the polite applause. They were a portent. The film would be grossly underestimated by American critics, who were unsure of its point of view, generally overlooked the story's mythological underpinnings and, in some instances, compared it unfavorably with *David and Lisa,* an inferior work.

Time carped that *Lilith* was an attempt "to deliver the same old Hollywood sexology in a fancy wrapper," while *The New Yorker's* Brendan Gill, who had previously identified himself as a charter member of the Jean Seberg fan club, wrote "the less said about *Lilith* the better."

What praise there was went to Jean for a performance the New York *Times* described as "fresh, flighty and fearsome." Most reviewers, in fact, declared her incontestably photogenic and disturbingly mysterious—and conceded, seven years after *St. Joan,* that she was an accomplished actress.

But the film played to empty houses. *Cahiers du Cinéma* championed it in France and put it high on its list of the year's best films—to little avail. *Lilith* drew crowds only in Scandinavia. Its failure proved an immense disappointment to Jean. *St. Joan* had been a failure of inexperience. This time, however, she had felt in full possession of her talents. By rights, *Lilith* should have catapulted her to American stardom. Instead, once again she was the darling of art cinema aficionados and a few intellectual critics. More than ever, she rued the unpredictability of her profession.

Even her hometown was less than appreciative. "The average viewer," wrote the *Times-Republican* when the film opened in November, "may come away still wishing to see Marshalltown's pride in something light, bright and frothy with a touch of corn that we Midwesterners like in our entertainment."

Jean remained a stalwart defender of *Lilith* all her life, citing it as her finest work. "It marked her more than any of her other films," says Raymonde Waintraub, a dental hygienist who knew her well. "Jean was endlessly fascinated by insanity

and the insane. Whenever she made new friends, she'd somehow arrange for them to see *Lilith*. It was almost like a ritual.
That film said something about her, something that she wanted
all her intimates to know and share."

In late 1964 Jean had another role to fall back on—that of the
cultured wife of a respected writer and diplomat. Jean later
called it "acting like a lady," and for a while she took to wearing Grace Kelly chignons. Like most upper-class French-
women, she was not expected merely to entertain; she "presided" over social gatherings.

"Jean was the last great love of Romain's life," says a prominent actress who dined with them often. "But he was a strong,
egotistical man, very much concerned with his public image,
which he shaped carefully. I don't think he ever really gave
Jean credit for what she was. He brought her into a world that
treated her as an object. She'd have to give dinner parties, and
she didn't like that at all. She found herself with people far
older than she was, and their conversation bored her. Romain
was always a little patronizing with her, and she was quite
sensitive to that. Frankly, I thought it was a far more destructive period for her than most people like to think.

"Jean never had to fight for a career. The way she was chosen by Preminger, the overnight triumph of *Breathless*—it had
all taken her by surprise. She never felt worthy of her success,
and as a result she let herself be molded by others. She had a
son, but even there, Romain made her feel inadequate, as if an
actress wasn't capable of bringing up a child. So the governess
was given all the responsibilities. I don't think that sort of thing
would happen today. Young people don't have that kind of
malleability. But Jean wouldn't strike back or take a stand.
Romain was always telling her what was good for her. She
allowed herself to be overruled all the time."

Jean had not yet come to those conclusions herself and
gamely tried to be a *femme du monde*. To reporters, she denied
that Gary influenced her career. On the contrary, she said, he
insisted on erecting a barrier—"the Berlin Wall"—between
her career and their life together. She dismissed the disparity
in their ages by retorting gaily, "Oh, I'm too old for *him*." His

ceaseless curiosity about people and events, she explained, kept him youthful, while her basic seriousness of character made her old—or at least older—before her time.

"Romain just wants people to be what they are," she said. "He has taught me how to accept myself."

18

"Jean Seberg's saga is now one of Hollywood's happiest success stories."

—Los Angeles *Times*

Hollywood, which had never quite understood Jean Seberg, understood elegance, or thought it did. Early in 1965, the elegant new Jean Seberg was summoned back to Los Angeles for *Moment to Moment,* the first of two films she would make that year under the protective wings of the studios.

Envisioned as a romantic suspense drama, *Moment to Moment* might have fared better if Alfred Hitchcock had been at the helm. But he wasn't. It was the seventy-fifth film of Mervin Le Roy, who produced and directed it for Universal. Under Le Roy's guidance, it came out looking less like a film than a shop window. And Jean was the mannequin—impeccably dressed by Yves St. Laurent, flawlessly made up, her blond hair lacquered to withstand the fiercest gusts.

The plot was pure contrivance. Jean was Kay Stanton, an errant wife living on the Riviera who appears to have accidentally shot the Navy ensign with whom she has had a brief fling. Not long after she has dumped his apparently lifeless body in a ravine, the ensign turns up again, a victim of amnesia. In the course of their investigation the French police enlist the aid of Kay's husband, a psychiatrist on sabbatical from Columbia University, to help the sailor recover his memory. Therein the suspense: Will the ensign blurt out the truth? In keeping with Hollywood's official morality, Jean's character suffered the anguish of the unfaithful, although the emotional turmoil took little toll on her tailored appearance.

Moment to Moment was, in many ways, characteristic of the synthetic roles Hollywood offered Jean. The studio bosses liked her for her drawing power in the European market, but she wasn't one of the "types" they understood. Usually she was clamped in a wig, painted and polished until she shone like a new car, and plopped into a two-dimensional part that ignored the gnawing contradictions under her placid exterior. For Hollywood, she represented a kind of bush-league Grace Kelly. Only Rossen had tapped the inner tumult.

Filming of *Moment to Moment* began on the Riviera in January in such made-for-Technicolor locales as the Colombe d'Or restaurant at St. Paul de Vence, the village of Mougins, the flower market at Nice and the beach at Cannes. More accustomed to low-budget movie making, Jean was astounded by Hollywood profligacy. According to one estimate, Le Roy was spending $25,000 a day on the Riviera. Cameras had to be transported from Paris, a dozen wind machines from Rome, Jean's sleek sports car from Lyons, and the English-speaking extras from Paris and London. Universal's prop department even provided palm trees to remedy the lapses of Mother Nature, who had failed to grow them in the properly photogenic places.

When the weather proved unseasonably chilly, Le Roy simply pulled up stakes (and his trees) and returned to the Universal lot in Los Angeles, where he had his own stretch of Riviera built for $350,000—nearly four times the cost of *Breathless*, Jean noted.

If she was not yet a full-fledged American star, the publicity department at Universal acted as if she were. Overlooking her brief appearance in *Let No Man Write My Epitaph*, it touted *Moment to Moment* as her triumphant entry into the Hollywood fold. Swathed in a sealskin coat trimmed in mink, the lost urchin of *St. Joan* had come home in style. Universal arranged a round of lavish parties and receptions to get the word out.

Jean inherited Doris Day's dressing room—a sumptuous trailer equipped with a full kitchen—and Le Roy, properly respectful of her "arty" reputation abroad, treated her with the deference due visiting royalty. When real royalty, in the person of Princess Margaret, came by the Universal lot on her 1965 good-will tour of America, Jean was placed at the head table and Romain exiled to a lesser one. Through a seating mix-up, Jean failed to take her assigned place next to Margaret's husband, Lord Snowdon. A red-faced studio official blamed her for the faux pas: "We were told Miss Seberg wouldn't sit there unless her husband were allowed to." "How dare anyone accuse me of such bad manners?" Jean fumed. Indeed, her manners sometimes seemed to be all that Universal had hired her for.

Befitting her new status, Jean and Romain rented a large, rambling house high in the hills of Coldwater Canyon. It had a swimming pool, of course, a four-car garage, an elaborate cream-colored conversation pit and a spectacular view of smog-enshrouded Los Angeles. "It's the kind of house that you enter and immediately look for the poodles," Jean joked, but its size allowed Eugenia and Diego to stay conveniently out of sight whenever company called.

If Hollywood wanted to make amends for the past, Jean was not one—publicly, at least—to bear a grudge. "I have every reason, I suppose, to be hostile in my attitude toward the movie industry and what it did to me when I was younger," she philosophized to a reporter from the New York *Times*. "But the strange thing is that I am not especially angry about it. My husband scolds me about this. He says it's a character flaw." Present at the interview, Gary said nothing at all. He was absorbed in correcting proofs from his publisher. "Romain has an amazing talent," Jean felt obliged to explain. "He can be in the same room and ten thousand light-years away."

Jean's attitude toward Hollywood was more complicated than her apparent willingness to forgive and forget. "When she arrived here, Jean had had no successful Hollywood experience," says Chuck Belden, her American agent at the time. "She put up a brave front, but it was whistling in the graveyard. I met her the first day on the set, and she was scared to death.

"Everything was magnified in Jean. There was never any middle ground with her. Either she laughed off Hollywood or she was totally impressed by it. Money was a joke with her, and yet she was overwhelmed that there was so much of it here and loved the fact that all her expenses were taken care of. She was intensely curious about this place—its power struggles, the gossip. People like Mervin Le Roy or George Seaton fascinated her, because they were the pioneers of the industry.

"On the other hand, she complained constantly that she wasn't allowed to function creatively, that her pictures were dumb and her roles even dumber. Deep down, I think she really wanted to make it in Hollywood and erase the Preminger stigma once and for all. But she just couldn't seem to get this place in perspective."

In some ways Jean remained the small-town girl who had spun fantasies in the darkness of the Orpheum Theater on Main Street. One day Cary Grant stopped by her table at the Universal commissary. "So nice to see you," he cooed. "You see, Jean, I put on a clean shirt just for you." Jean was speechless before the dapper star, prompting a nearby reporter to quip that she looked like "Richmond after it had been taken by Grant." At her first Hollywood premiere she was equally wide-eyed when Joan Crawford chatted with her briefly.

Jean's feelings for Le Roy occasionally approached the reverential; this was the man who had directed *The Wizard of Oz* and *I Am a Fugitive from a Chain Gang.* But she had trouble reconciling that reputation with his conduct on the set of *Moment to Moment,* where he seemed little more than a technician going through the motions.

"Mervin had come out of the studio system," says Arthur Hill, then a reigning Broadway actor, who played Jean's understanding husband. "He was one of those who invented it. He tried to be courtly, but underneath he was still a newsboy from San Francisco. He knew a lot about the cosmetics of acting. He'd counsel you not to move your lips too much, and he was absolutely right. But when it came to understanding what went on inside an actor, he didn't pretend to have an idea. 'Okay, let's have a good scene now with lots of energy,' he'd say to us. After a while we realized that's what he said before *every* scene.

"Jean would just look at me each time and smile. Maybe one of her problems was that she was too bright to be an actress. She didn't have enough ego. She could always see the ridiculousness of the situation a little too clearly. Before long it dawned on us both that we were trapped inside this 1937 movie. Only it was 1965."

Jean appreciated Le Roy's gentleness, but sometimes he displayed a crassness that brought her up short. Paton Price was on the set the day Jean was to play an important scene with Hill: the psychiatrist has come home to his jittery wife, who is pretending that nothing is wrong. "Le Roy went up to her beforehand," recalls Price, "and said, 'Honey, I want you to play this scene like a nun that's just farted.' Well, Jean was no prude, but she was very much a lady. Her sensibility was offended."

Universal had been unable to find a suitable co-star to play the ensign and settled on Sean Garrison, a newcomer who was nervous and stiff in the role. He towered over six feet, and Jean had to stand on a box to embrace him. "About halfway through the shooting," Chuck Belden recalls, "Jean realized she'd been had; she was carrying a major motion picture all by herself. But she laughed and tried to make the best of it." As she had feared, however, *Moment to Moment* flopped at the box office. "Jean Seberg is too young to be getting bad Lana Turner parts," sniffed one reviewer.

For Gary, the stay in Los Angeles was an opportunity to renew acquaintance with a city he thought "dynamic and beautiful," catch up on old friendships, and explore the possibilities of film writing, an ambition he entertained simultaneously with his desire to resume diplomatic duties. A sometimes acute observer of America, he sensed healthy stirrings in the nation. The old certainties were withering away. What he perceived as a salutary questioning had spread among the younger generation. America seemed to be taking measure of itself. Opposition to racial injustice was on the rise. Pockets of resistance to the Vietnam war had formed. Gary believed the country was less sure of itself but also less smug.

He had put many of those impressions into a novel, *The Ski Bum,* which Joseph Levine wanted to film. Gary hoped to write the screenplay. "It's about a generation of kids whose parents know nothing but certitude," he explained, and he could well have been talking about Jean. The novel's French title, *Adieu Gary Cooper,* better symbolized his point: the end of the old America, tranquil and secure. "Cooper was the strong, quiet American who always wins in the end," he elaborated. "But the world has suddenly become an American responsibility. America used to get involved, then withdraw. This time, there is no withdrawal."

It was more than coincidence that Jean was frequently mentioned for the lead in *The Ski Bum.* She, too, had begun to question the established order of things and to welcome change. By the time the film was made, however, under other auspices and with other actors, it would bear little of the Garys' imprint.

Jean had become a fierce defender of Kennedy's presidency, which until his assassination had seemed to embody for her a new American awareness. Once while taking tea in her dressing room, Hill casually suggested that history might reevaluate Kennedy's sainted place in the national life. Jean tore into him. Hill never forgot her anger, which struck him as completely disproportionate to what he considered an offhand remark.

A discouraged Jean completed *Moment to Moment* late in March, fully aware that it would not be a breakthrough. She packed up house and family, which now included Sandy, a huge mongrel dog that tended to urinate on the furniture. Romain was suffering from a painful hernia of the esophagus that required prompt medical treatment, so she had time for only a brief visit to Marshalltown and a couple of plays in New York: *Luv,* which delighted her, and *The Odd Couple,* which didn't. (Romain went alone to *Fiddler on the Roof* and dismissed it as "schmaltzy and fake Yiddish.")

Hollywood had put on a welcoming face and paid her generously, but Jean was leery of the coddling, and the rampant commercialism bothered her. With a sense of relief, she went into a low-budget caper film, *Un Milliard dans un Billard (Diamonds Are Brittle),* upon her return to Paris. The first feature of a young Swiss director, Nicholas Gessner, it let her play a svelte member of a gang of international jewel thieves who are outwitted by a dreamy bank teller (Claude Rich). Gessner saw it, not inappropriately, as a European version of a Blake Edwards comedy. The pretty packaging was similar, although the moral—crime *does* pay—was not. The role required only four weeks of Jean's time in Lausanne, Geneva and Paris, and it earned her respectable enough reviews in France.

"It was thanks to Jean that I got my film career started," Gessner remembers gratefully. "She was a bankable name then and willing to take a risk. 'I was lucky with a new director once,' she told me. 'Why not try again?' She could look at herself—as an actress and as a human being—almost as if she were another person. She wanted to appear very much in control. Yet she'd hint at this great vulnerability underneath. She had a way of implying that there was something more than she was telling you, something beyond the words, something that you alone could understand. It gave her a special intimacy and was very flattering to a man."

The bespectacled director also believes that Jean had "her political antennae out" by then. Later that summer, riots broke out in the Watts section of Los Angeles, tearing a big hole in the fragile racial fabric of the United States. "Jean went on at great length about it," Gessner continues. "She said there was a new world coming and that artists had to make their contribution. I thought she was overdramatizing a bit. Despite this large, bourgeois apartment they had in Paris, both Romain and Jean made a point of fitting into that hip, leftist slot.

"I had the impression they were very happy together, at least superficially. I remember going by to see Jean one day after filming, and since I was early, I stopped into a café first. Romain was there, but he seemed in a complete haze. When he finally spotted me, he removed a pair of earplugs and said, 'It's terribly noisy here, but the coffee is so much better than Jean's. You won't tell her, will you?' He could be very paternal when he wanted to."

For the summer months Jean rented, sight unseen, a villa in the Mediterranean town of Roquebrune. When she and Romain got there they discovered that it sat between the railroad tracks and a national highway, at a considerable distance from the beach. Romain complained of the impossible working conditions, so they hastened back to Paris, where Jean read, wrote letters and mulled over her career.

Paris in August was far from unpleasant. It was empty of Parisians, who pursue their traditional summer holiday with a vengeance, and its streets were peaceful and inviting. While Romain remained closeted in his study, absorbed in his writing, Jean went for long strolls but experienced a growing restlessness.

"I'm going through a phase where I'm a little tired of acting," she wrote Dawn Murray Quinn. "It will pass, but I think it's mainly a disappointment over the quality of roles and scripts one sees. Sometimes I wish I had another, second 'craft' to have satisfaction from and not be dependent on just acting."

Early in August she received word that Hollywood wanted her back for *A Fine Madness,* a promisingly unconventional comedy about a rebellious Greenwich Village poet and his tussles with an uncomprehending society that tries to lobotomize him. Sean Connery, then, in full glory as James Bond, would play the rebellious poet; Joanne Woodward, his harried wife; and Colleen Dewhurst and Patrick O'Neal, the psychiatrists who set out to cure him.

Jean was a last-minute addition, and her role—she was cast as O'Neal's neglected wife—was secondary. Her salary was not. Warner Bros. was shelling out $125,000 for her. While not in a league with Connery's $500,000, it was still $25,000 more than Woodward was receiving to play a lead.

Jack Warner had okayed the expenditure to placate director Irvin Kershner. Just before *A Fine Madness* was to go into production, Warner had whisked away the chief cameraman, Haskell Wexler, for a more prestigious property, *Who's Afraid of Virginia Woolf?* Kershner was irate, and Jean was the unofficial sop to his anger.

Kershner, who prides himself on nothing else about *A Fine Madness,* believes it was beautifully cast. Of Jean he says, "She really fit the role, a sort of gilded-cage housewife who looks a little uptight but can be very refined, if necessary. Oh, I heard a lot of stories to the contrary, but that was the Jean I knew. Of course, she was a limited actress. She lacked the technique for Hollywood. Because of the casual, kind of improvisational way films are made in France, you can come off the street and do pretty well. In Hollywood, it's different. But her character, this slightly indignant woman who wants her husband to pay more attention to her, seemed to be an extension of her own Midwestern, middle-class background. I thought she had a quality that was just right."

"I don't know if I'm a good actress, but I'm becoming an expert at packing valises," Jean commented to a reporter from French television before leaving Paris in mid-October. In Beverly Hills she and Romain moved into another sumptuous house—this one on Loma Vista Drive—and with expectations revived, she reported to the Warner Bros. lot. The film turned into yet another disappointment for her—a blend of cockamamie comedy and antiestablishment satire that failed to jell. The script was perpetually rewritten under orders from Jack Warner, who didn't understand the offbeat project or its seriocomic tone, and apparently was under the impression that his studio was producing a James Bond action picture. Daily, Jean's role made less and less sense and the filming was, by several accounts, almost chaotic.

"It was a very unpleasant project for her," says Chuck Belden. "Jean was terribly unhappy and threatened to quit several times. But after the Preminger experience, she was afraid to open herself up to charges of unprofessionalism, so again she muddled her way through."

"She called me up frantically several times during that film," says Paton Price. "They'd cut all her good scenes. She didn't know what to do. 'You can't compromise yourself out of existence,' she complained. She was learning that Hollywood is a marketplace. What sells is what goes."

The Warner lot, today one of the world's busiest, was almost eerily silent in 1965, a victim of television. The palatial dressing rooms stood vacant and shuttered. *Virginia Woolf* was the only other film in production that fall. It, however, was rumored to be a blockbuster, what with Mike Nichols directing and Elizabeth Taylor and Richard Burton playing Edward Albee's disputatious couple.

Naturally, *Virginia Woolf* was strictly off-limits. CLOSED SET was posted over every entrance to the sound stage, and uniformed guards enforced the ruling. All this piqued Jean's curiosity. With O'Neal, she would frequently slip past the guards, tiptoe onto the set and from afar observe Nichols rehearsing his fabled stars.

"I suppose we could have wangled permission," says O'Neal, "but Jean preferred to sneak in. We were like two excited little kids who'd creep down the stairs at night to watch their parents' party. Sure, we were making this charming little comedy of our own, but it was as if these were the adults, the grownups, and they were doing the real thing. Jean would giggle like a child, afraid we were going to get caught. It was almost a game with her.

"Her reputation as a woman who made racy films in France didn't seem to have anything to do with her. She really was a little girl from Iowa. Her mother and father came to visit us on the set once. When you saw them—this pouter pigeon kind of lady and this Grant Wood stick figure—and then you looked at Jean, a beautiful girl married to a man twice her age . . . well, it was unlikely, that's all. She was the most unlikely person to be a film star."

Every Friday night the actors from *A Fine Madness* congregated informally in the screening room of the Beverly Hills Hotel to watch a movie that one of them had selected. "The rules were loose. The film could be an all-time favorite or one that you'd always wanted to see," says O'Neal. "Paul Newman would come with Joanne, and they'd always bring beer and popcorn. Romain showed up with Jean." Most of the selections acknowledged the wealth of Hollywood's past. When it was Jean's turn, she opted for *The Lady With a Dog,* a haunting, beautiful little black-and-white Russian film based on a Chekhov short story.

"Sometimes," Joanne Woodward recollects, "Jean would talk very strangely about this child she had, a child of hers and Romain's. I never quite understood it. They'd sent it away or put it out in the country. It seemed such a curious tale coming from this sweet, seemingly simple girl. Paul and I had known Romain when he was married to Lesley Blanch and thought he was a brilliant man. So we figured there must be something more to Jean than met the eye. Romain wouldn't have been interested in just another pretty girl."

By December *A Fine Madness* was into its final weeks and Jean's role had been reduced to moments of petulant foot stamping, peevish complaining and endless cigarette smoking. In her single unconventional scene, she and Connery frolicked like playful seals in the sanitarium ripple bath, a sequence *Playboy* magazine felt worthy of a double-page spread.

From the start, Jean had made it clear that she would not perform in the nude. So the wardrobe department concocted an elaborate skintight body stocking for her. Unfortunately, that's what it looked like. Eliminating the body stocking and using flesh-colored pasties seemed to be the only solution. Jean still hesitated.

Connery had trouble understanding her scruples. He, after all, usually walked around his dressing room stark naked. "Sean desperately wanted to make that picture live," Kershner recalls. "So what he did was order up several bottles of champagne. While the crew set up the shot and filled the tank with water, he got Jean soused. When we were ready to shoot, he just kicked off his shorts, jumped in and pulled Jean in with him. The champagne kept flowing all afternoon. By the end of the day Jean's pasties had flown off, and she was laughing and splashing around in the water and having a wonderful time."

For Jack Warner, however, the film was a complete puzzlement. Once shooting was completed, he threw Kershner off the lot, commissioned a new score and had the film cut to his own tastes. In this instance, Jack Warner's tastes were not those of the moviegoing public.

"The film's a mess," says Kershner. "I can't watch it even today."

Jean's disenchantment with Hollywood was nearly complete. She didn't like Los Angeles or the smog. ("It could be eliminated easily, but for political reasons, it hasn't been," she explained to a French television interviewer.) Repeatedly dismantling and setting up a household strained her nerves and upset Diego and Eugenia. She felt incapable of entering into the round-the-clock social rituals that help sustain, if not advance, a Hollywood career.

"There are none of the friendly, family feelings that I get

when I work in France," she mused. "In France, you know if you're making a movie, you're going to sit around waiting in a café, which is not disagreeable. Here, they give you some superb trailer with a Frigidaire and a stove. I keep expecting to find a warmth to the work in Hollywood which doesn't exist. The unions have imposed so many people for each job there is no longer a sense of personal responsibility. I'm a lot less nervous when I get up in the morning to go to work now. But some of the joy has gone out of acting for me."

On *A Fine Madness,* a team of make-up artists and hairdressers labored to keep her blemish-free and wrinkleproof. In France, her friend Phong Maitret often dabbed on the make-up in the rest room of a café. At twenty-seven, Jean thought she liked it better that way.

19

"If you don't fit one of the categories—the lady, the sex kitten, or the white-toothed ingénue—you have a lot of trouble finding work."

—JEAN SEBERG

Around Christmas, Jean's thoughts usually turned to Marshalltown and the excitement that had filled the stucco house on 6th Street: the carolers who dropped in for hot chocolate, the frantic last-minute search on Main Street for a gift that would please her father and yet not violate his native sense of thrift, the spicy aroma of Swedish cookies that wafted out from the kitchen. It was the one time she allowed herself to wax nostalgic about her hometown and her family, both of which had seemed so claustrophobic when she was growing up. "She loved celebrations," says Betty Desouches. "On holidays, birthdays or Christmas she was like a little girl again, and she made a big fuss over them." Indulgently, Romain let her carry on, although he didn't share her sentimentality and thought that the enthusiasm was misplaced. She chided him for being "a Scrooge," noting that "he never gives anyone a gift."

Christmas was also a time to shower Diego with attention, partly in expiation for her long absences during the year. Eugenia exerted a firm and steady grip on the child, who viewed his real mother—according to one friend—as "some magical fairy princess who passed through his life now and again." But on his birthday and especially at Christmas, Jean reclaimed her motherly role. Many of Jean's acquaintances thought it was

161

just that: a role. "Whenever she wrote me a letter, Jean would go on at great length about Diego and what he was doing and how much she loved him," says Vony Becker. "But in life, it was completely different. She hardly bothered about him at all." (Not until 1976 would Jean admit in one of her letters to the awakening of her "gut maternal instincts" and add: "They have been a long time coming.") Still, she would try to create the illusion of a closely knit family in the Rue du Bac apartment at Christmas. She sent out greeting cards, promising in each a longer letter to come, put up a big tree and decorated the apartment, convincing herself that "the excitement in Diego's eyes when he counts all the presents makes it worthwhile."

In a metaphor that works better in the French language, the press portrayed Jean's marriage to Romain as *une plage de bonheur*—"a beach of happiness"—in an otherwise storm-lashed life. But intimates of the couple believe that by the end of 1965 it was evolving into more of a father-daughter relationship. Publicly, Mrs. Romain Gary displayed all the poise and chic expected of that personage. Privately, she was insecure and restless, and looked to the writer mainly for the approval she had once sought from Ed Seberg. She greatly admired Gary's intelligence, and despite her denials to the press, relied on his guidance in her career. She was perpetually doubting her worth, while he, at fifty-one, was casting an ever longer shadow, not only as a novelist but also as a journalist who profited from Jean's far-flung movie locations by filing reports on the state of those corners of the world.

There were drawbacks to the union. If Jean had cajoled her way into the marriage, as some suggest, she couldn't always quell her suspicions that she was accepted in certain circles primarily because she was Gary's wife and not for any of her own accomplishments. (In France, movie stars are not the social catches they are in the United States.) Much as she admired Romain's talent, it excluded her. At times when Gary was absorbed in his writing for weeks on end, she would feel adrift and aimless. Sometimes she tried to make a joke about it and giggled that Romain had to wear shin guards to dinner to protect himself from the kicks she delivered under the table whenever that distracted, preoccupied look came into his eyes.

"Because of her family and Diego, it had been very important for Jean to get married," says Dennis Berry. "But Jean told me that once that had happened, they became sexually uninvolved very quickly. She would say that all she used to do was sit around the house, waiting for Gary to finish his writing. She was alone a lot, and it reminded her of the times Preminger had shut her up in a hotel room. Loneliness was one thing Jean couldn't tolerate.

"Gary was like a distant protector and father figure for her. It was very important for her to get recognition from him. She kept seeking it, long after we were married. If she got it, which wasn't often, it would put her in a state of joy.

"Jean had always wanted to be a writer herself, and I think she could have been a profound one. She had a wonderful natural gift. But Gary never took those aspirations seriously. Why should he? Still, I believe if she could have written one work she was really proud of, it would have kept her going in life. Gary would always tell her to concentrate on her acting instead."

Acting, unfortunately, was proving less than rewarding. Jean repeatedly chalked it up to the absence of good women's parts. Those that did come her way, she complained, didn't serve her personality. Yet her personality was ambiguous. She bridged two worlds and belonged fully to neither. After she had lost the dazzling freshness of her youth and the breath-catching vulnerability that went with it, her image became less definable. With maturity she had gained refinement and an apparent sophistication, but the Continental veneer could be confusing. On the one hand, it never entirely concealed her basic American wholesomeness, prompting Vincent Canby to observe in the New York *Times* at her death: "Even when she was wearing couture clothes, she possessed the idealized radiance I associate with the clean-scrubbed, Lutheran Middle West of her youth." On the other hand, the European veneer suggested that she was collected and very much in control of herself, a creature of restraint who had mastered the apparent contradictions of her life.

163

From a dramatic standpoint, she could be mistakenly viewed as slightly bland. Even her French agent, Olga Horstig-Primuz, believes "she was a very good actress, but she just wasn't all that different. She never really had a success to match *Breathless.* New people came along, as they always do; she made a number of bad films in a row; and before long her career just started slowing down."

When people remarked on the assurance she exuded, Jean usually looked dismayed and accepted the compliment with a faint air of incomprehension. As she told *Cosmopolitan* several years later: "People have a strange picture of me. I'm not at all the steady, calm person they seem to think I am. That's part of the masquerade that will never cease to amuse me. I'm not really serene; I'm a nervous wreck. I suppose the mystique about me, the aura of serenity, is due to my upbringing, to some kind of puritanical self-control—you know, smiling on the outside, cracking on the inside. I don't show it, but I really am an extremely keyed-up person. I often find myself quivering, and I really have to get a grip on myself. An article about me, recently, said that I was extremely mature, and that I knew exactly who I was and where it's at. But I don't! I'm so hopelessly confused. . . ."

Excepting *Lilith,* few of her movies at this time allowed her to delve beneath the cosmetic calm, and the conditions of her life with Gary demanded an unruffled dignity.

Perhaps it was that image which made her seem right for her next film, *La Ligne de Démarcation* (*The Line of Demarcation*). The story dramatized French resistance to the Germans in a village that straddled the line between unoccupied and Vichy France during World War II.

At the suggestion of producer Georges de Beauregard, who had fond memories of her from the *Breathless* days, director Claude Chabrol cast Jean as the stalwart, not to say noble, English wife of a French count (Maurice Ronet). With total aplomb, Jean's character helps two Allied spies make their way over the line to freedom, a deed for which she is eventually arrested by the Nazis.

Filmed in February and March 1966 in the Jura region of France, *The Line of Demarcation* dealt with a subject of some moment to the French. But Chabrol insisted on treating it tongue-in-cheek, tinkering with the traditional canvas of French heroism so that it reflected his own cynical ambiguity.

"Jean had the goodness to act in that nonsense," he says now, eyes gleaming devilishly in the chubby face that gives him the appearance of a cagey schoolboy. "It was a ridiculous film. No, it wasn't. It was clever in that it respected the given orders and disobeyed them at the same time. I consider it my only dishonest film. There weren't eighty resisters for every bastard. The proportions were not duly respected. But Jean brought a certain *vraisemblance* to the role, a remarkable clarity, if only by the shape of her face."

The final scene is characteristic of Chabrol's approach. The gallant townsfolk have gathered on the bridge that links the occupied village with free soil. Whipped, they rally their spirits by singing the "Marseillaise." Slowly the camera pulls back on this patriotic tableau to reveal the swastika flapping gently from a flagpole. At the premiere of the film in Paris, Chabrol recalls with wicked amusement, the audience was peppered with war heroes and patriots who jumped to their feet at the first measures of the "Marseillaise." Seconds later, to their chagrin and Chabrol's amusement, they realized that they were standing up for the Nazi flag.

Jean later confessed her bewilderment over the project in the British monthly *Films and Filming.* "Chabrol is such a strange man. I think with *La Ligne de Démarcation* he believed that he was going to make almost a parody of the Resistance, and of that whole period of French life. . . . I also suspect—knowing Claude, and liking him for this—that he probably had heard that we might be able to shoot this story in a place where there was a very comfortable hotel with an absolutely superb restaurant. When you make a film with him you can't help putting on weight. You spend the morning in the make-up department, . . . deciding what you're going to ask them in the kitchen to prepare for everybody to eat that night. Otherwise I don't really know why he made that film."

The Line of Demarcation created surprisingly little stir in Paris, but it was successful in the provinces, where audiences tended to overlook Chabrol's mockery and swallowed the film as a tribute to the French underground. As a result, Chabrol was prompted to cast Jean and Maurice Ronet the following year in *The Road to Corinth,* a spy film in which, with his habitual craftiness, he mocked all the conventions of the genre.

That March, Jean resumed her role as Mrs. Romain Gary and accompanied her husband on an extensive tour of Poland and Hungary, where she listened appreciatively to his lectures and attended numerous official banquets. Vilna was no longer a part of Poland, but the writer was still regarded as a native son. "The Poles have been wonderful, very hospitable and full of humor. They seem to love R.'s books," she scribbled in a note home before boarding a train from Warsaw to Budapest. On a shopping spree, Jean bought a stuffed animal for Diego. When she showed Romain the colorful postcards she intended to send to her friends, he dryly informed her that they were actually Polish Christmas cards. On the trip, Jean was recognized less often than she was elsewhere, but young people still mobbed her. Usually, they clamored for the latest rock-'n'-roll records, which she obligingly promised to send them from France.

In May she made her annual trip back to Marshalltown and brought Warren Robeson and the *Times-Republican* up to date on her career. "What I miss most," she said, "are the long, hot Iowa summers and the times I used to spend on Uncle Bill's farm." Her deeper thoughts about the United States were less bucolic, although she didn't share them with the editor. On her return to France, however, she told a reporter, "In the United States we have a tendency to replace culture with Freudianism; the way you appear intelligent is to talk about your neuroses. I was very struck by this during my last stay there. The guilt complex continues to dominate American psychology. I know very few creative people—creative in the true sense of the term—who don't end up on the psychiatrist's couch."

That reflection betrays the influence of Gary, who tended to reject the heavily Freudian interpretation of human behavior and the arts. It also unwittingly suggests the vague pangs of guilt Jean experienced whenever she visited her parents. She felt that she had failed them, let them down in some basic way. Mary Ann had a conventional life the Sebergs could understand and appreciate; it was a reflection of their own. Jean's wasn't. It appeared exotic and vaguely mysterious to them, and Jean read their incomprehension as veiled criticism. "Whenever she was going to see her parents," says Berry, "she'd be nervous for days beforehand."

Marshalltown had seemed much the same as ever, but Jean appreciated the change that was going on elsewhere in America. Young people were less fettered, more willing to buck the established ways. As she explained it to the French, "Things are beginning to happen there. Bob Dylan, an authentic poet, has become the symbol of a rising generation looking for new values. As for the Vietnamese war, you're finding young men who don't want to fight, some of them from the highly patriotic families of the Midwest where I come from. The beatniks are almost respectable. Ginsberg gives lectures in the American universities now. It's incontestable. America is waking up."

By contrast, her career was decidedly dormant that August. With no more promising prospect, she accepted a role in *Estouffade à la Caraïbe* (loosely translated as *Revolt in the Caribbean*), an adventure picture that would take her to South America for two months. Her co-star, Frederick Stafford, was a strapping Austrian who was beginning to make a name for himself in Europe as a James Bond knockoff.

Diego and Eugenia were packed off to Spain, and Sandy farmed out to friends. It was the height of the rainy season when Jean and Romain arrived in Cartagena, Colombia, and the heat was oppressive. They stayed in a luxury hotel, its grounds bordered with palm trees and other luxuriant vegetation. But Jean couldn't help noticing the squalor just beyond. "It is the end of the world," she wrote Paton Price, "full of misery, crime and poverty." The slums of Cartagena triggered both her compassion and her indignation. "If I had lived in South America," she reflected later, "I would have fought with Ché."

Shooting began early in the day to avoid the intense heat. Nevertheless, the actors' make-up ran off their faces in rivulets. Ice packs didn't help. Equipment shipped from France was delayed in transit or held up interminably at customs. A particularly photogenic cove turned out to be infested with sharks. When Jean slipped into the water for the camera, two frogmen had to swim alongside to keep them at bay.

Jacques Besnard, the stocky director, has no illusions about the film. "It wasn't important at all. Jean played the dutiful daughter of a mobster, daddy's little girl, who eventually bucks her father and joins Stafford in a rebellion against the country's dictator. Frail and helpless, she becomes strong fighting beside her man. I think that transformation appealed to her, simplistic as it was. Frankly, I could see no other reason why she accepted the role."

In Besnard's favorite scene, a native village comes under attack, panic erupts and everyone flees, leaving a lone black child in the middle of the square. While bombs go off all around, Jean's character dashes back and saves the child. "It was a bit of a cliché, I suppose, but Jean played it beautifully. Her hair was cut short and dyed even blonder than it was in *Breathless*. She looked so fresh," Besnard says admiringly. "Almost as if she had just been unwrapped."

The debilitating climate left Jean more exhausted than her appearance indicated. She had discovered several lumps in her breasts, and fearing cancer, she consulted her doctor when she returned to Paris. He removed twenty nonmalignant cysts and told Jean they could recur. But she dreaded the treatment— heavy doses of male hormones, which sometimes produce facial hair as a side effect.

"It scared her terribly at the time," says one friend. "Romain, especially, made a big thing of it and told her she needed someone to take care of her. Personally, I thought that was just his way of keeping her tied down for a few more years. He made Jean feel incapable."

20

"What I love about acting is that it is a lot like the circus."

—JEAN SEBERG

In the spring of 1967, Gary accepted a post as an adviser to the Ministry of Information. He was responsible for formulating new cultural programs for the French national television and for developing and maintaining smooth relations with the Ministry of Culture, headed by his long-time friend and model, André Malraux. Jean applauded the change. "I think it's good for him to be active in public service again," she said. "He gets so lonely sometimes shut up writing in his office." Gary accepted the job on two conditions: flexible office hours and liberty to travel. That left him free to accompany Jean to Athens, where she was to star in Claude Chabrol's new film, *La Route de Corinthe (The Road to Corinth)*. Deciding that Diego was "husky and jolly," Jean once again left him behind with Eugenia. "It's awfully hot there," she rationalized, "and there's nothing but hotel life, so I think he's better off in Paris."

The Road to Corinth was an elegant-looking but empty-headed pastiche of the countless spy films that had sprung up, like mushrooms, in the shadow of James Bond. It called for Jean to pursue her husband's killers, and with the help of Maurice Ronet as a special agent, to unravel a diabolical scheme to sabotage NATO radar installations in Greece. The flagrant inanities of the scenario notwithstanding, the two months she and Romain spent in the Greek capital and surrounding countryside represented, for her, a period of almost undiluted happiness.

"Jean was full of fun and gaiety," says Betty Desouches, who visited the set frequently. "But she had a pensive side to her as well, and often the two got mixed up. She was the sort of person who could be depressed in the midst of a gale of laughter. It was a seductive combination, and I liked her immediately. Romain seemed more relaxed then I ever saw him afterward. He had a beard then, and he looked like an amiable buccaneer hovering protectively by her side."

A friend of Maurice Ronet's, Desouches had a warm strength that appealed to Jean. During lulls in the shooting, they scampered off to visit the monuments or the marketplaces, where they bought silly hats from the expansive merchants. Jean organized fishing expeditions and an overnight boat tour of the Greek islands.

"She was the regular little busy bee," Ronet recalls with a laugh, "astounded and amazed by everything she saw. In spite of the huge differences between them, she and Romain seemed to have a real understanding of each other. I was having difficulties then envisaging life with another person. One day I opened myself up to Romain and asked him how he did it. 'My only goal in life, as far as Jean goes, is to earn enough money so that she'll be well off when I'm gone,' he said. 'That's why I drive myself so hard. It's only for her.' I believed him implicitly."

Chabrol regaled his actors by treating *The Road to Corinth* as a colossal put-on. Disguising himself as a Greek Orthodox priest named Alcibiades, he put himself in the film, then had himself brutally bumped off in a cemetery. Carrying black humor one step further, he instructed his assassins to wash their "bloodstained" hands in a font of holy water.

"This film has been hard, hard work. Up every day around 5 A.M. and the old eyes are getting weaker and weaker under those awful arc lights," Jean wrote to Carol Hollingsworth. "But I'll be miserable when it's over. It's the most fun I've ever had (which, alas, doesn't mean it will be the best film) and

I've done comedy with a freedom and relaxation I've never known before. Chabrol loves actors so much that you feel a positive force coming to you from him while you work."

She rediscovered her sense of make-believe, which Hollywood had pretty much paralyzed, and insisted on doing such minor stunts as driving her own motorcycle and leaping onto the back of a moving truck. At one point the sweaty villain of the film hooks Jean's character to a crane and dangles her high over the Corinth Canal. Jean's double, an earnest Greek woman who had cut her hair and dyed it blond, peered over the edge of the cliff bordering the canal, down to the blue-green waters three hundred feet below, and balked.

"Okay," Jean volunteered, "I'll do it. But only if you don't tell Romain beforehand."

Although Chabrol let himself be persuaded, he first insisted on testing the equipment himself. The rotund, near-sighted director taped his glasses to his head, slipped into a harness and swung out over the canal, to the raucous applause of his crew.

"Let yourself go limp and drop your head," he counseled Jean when her turn came.

Giggling nervously, Jean took her place in the harness. Abruptly, the overzealous crane operator jerked her off her feet, and she found herself rocking back and forth in the void. "Let me down, let me down," she screamed shrilly. Panic-stricken, the cameramen stopped shooting, and the crane operator hastily maneuvered her back to land. As Chabrol rushed forward, fearful and concerned, Jean beamed broadly and asked whether she had played the moment with sufficient gusto. The cameramen turned sheepish: the sequence would have to be reshot. This time, when Jean let out her piercing wails, the film kept rolling.

"Actually, I was scared to death," she confessed later. "But once I'd done it, I was very proud. For the same sort of reason, I suppose, that men do stupid things like shooting lions and feeling proud of it. Just showing off, I think. Exhibitionism."

A French television show, *Les Coulisses de l'Exploit,* normally dedicated to the adventures of mountain climbers and deep-sea divers, included her daring stunt in one of its telecasts. Jean boasted that she was becoming "just like Belmondo," who always refused to use a double.

The Mediterranean sun had rejuvenated her. With her short hair, she resembled a tow-headed boy on a Midwestern farm. "She is twenty-eight, but she looks seventeen," reported a disbelieving visitor.

During one scene, shot at the Athens Hilton, Jean ran into Harry Druker, her Marshalltown lawyer, and his wife, Rose, who were on their way home from a visit to Israel. That night they all had dinner together. "Jean and Romain were living in the most magnificent apartment. It had a picture-postcard view of the Parthenon, which was reflected in the pool outside," recalls Mrs. Druker. "She didn't have a touch of make-up on, and she was dressed in one of those long, flowing robes the Greek women wear. She was absolutely breath-taking in that setting. As a girl, Jean had spent a lot of time at our house, dreaming out loud about the day she'd be a famous actress. I reminded her of that and said, 'Your fairy tales really did come true, didn't they, Jean?' She smiled and put her arms around me. She was so beautiful and unassuming, I almost wept."

The sunny interlude was over by the end of June, when Jean and Romain went back to Paris. For all the fun it had been to make, *The Road to Corinth* was a fast flop at the box office. Even Chabrol would admit, years later, that "Its charm may be a bit too confidential."

Jean was distressed to find that Diego now relied entirely on Eugenia and would throw violent tantrums whenever his mother tried to take over. It was time, she decided, for one of the parties Diego adored. The child had begun painting in kindergarten, so Jean organized an exhibition of his work. She covered the walls and stairwell of the Rue du Bac apartment with his efforts and invited her friends in to view them. The guests oohed and aahed appreciatively and then snapped them up at five francs apiece. "He's a lousy painter," Jean observed afterward, "so he may well have a bright future in art."

To solidify their renewed relationship, she and Diego spent the month of July together in the Spanish town of Puerto Andraitx, on the island of Majorca. There, Romain was building a summer home, to be called Cimarron, but construction had lagged behind schedule. Jean rented a spacious villa in the rocky hills and invited Vony Becker and her children to share the house with Diego and her.

Becker warmly recalls that summer as a lazy, uneventful vacation—with a single exception. One day the brakes on Jean's rented car gave out. The vehicle hurtled down a narrow, winding road and across a busy highway before smashing into a stone wall. Miraculously, Jean and her passengers emerged shaken but unhurt.

Becker makes no apologies for being a devoted housewife who relishes order and the little rituals of family life. "Later on, Jean heaped scorn on me for all that," Becker says. "By then she was living in total chaos and couldn't be bothered to pick up a shoe. But curiously, I think that's what Jean really appreciated about me. There were times when she needed to play housewife and mother. Deep down, she was always looking for a simpler life, and she never outgrew her nostalgia for that ideal Marshalltown family she was supposed to have come from."

The vacation mended the rift with Diego, but Jean concluded that he was "terribly sensitive and easily hurt, with specially tuned antennae." She resolved not to leave him with Eugenia for such extended periods of time again.

That summer she was offered a role in a Bob Hope comedy, *The Private Navy of Sergeant O'Farrell.* The salary tempted her, and so did the location—Puerto Rico masquerading as an island in the South Pacific. But the role did not. She turned it down, disappointed anew at the dwindling opportunities for a serious actress.

Her professional frustrations weighed heavily on Romain at the same time they fueled his ambition to direct her in a film himself. During his years as consul in Los Angeles he had labored on the screenplay of *The Longest Day,* and his friendship with director John Ford extended onto the set, where Gary sometimes acted as Ford's unofficial assistant. Since his marriage to Jean, he had continued to soak up movie-making techniques and now and again even doctored her dialogue. Although they had vowed to keep their careers separate, the moment seemed opportune to join forces.

Gary went back to his short story, the sparse and symbolic "Birds in Peru," which had received wide attention when it was first published in *Playboy*. He thought it could be developed into a vehicle for Jean. Universal was willing to put up the money and give him a shot at directing. If Jean had been patently misserved by most of her films, this one, Gary announced, would finally reveal the full scope of her talents and personality. Who knew her better?

Birds in Peru would turn out to be the most perplexing and, some say, demeaning film of Jean's entire career. Her role: a frigid nymphomaniac, vainly seeking fulfillment on an isolated beach littered with the carcasses of exotic birds.

21

"She gives the best performance of her life. I didn't have much to do to get it out of her because she felt the part admirably."

—ROMAIN GARY

Despite its seemingly scabrous subject matter, Gary entertained lofty notions about *Birds in Peru*. If it was a film about frigidity and nymphomania, it was also something more. He saw his heroine, Adriana, as possessed by a particularly poignant, not to say poetic, form of madness. Her frigidity seemed to him "the very definition of the impossible, the tragic." The frustrations of her plight spoke to him in symbolic terms of the never ending, never satisfied quest for human fulfillment. "I have always been haunted by that particular failure of love which only redoubles and exasperates the search and pursuit of love," he admitted in his book *The Night Will Be Calm.*

Whatever its broader implications, *Birds in Peru* told a very explicit story of a haunted woman fleeing her sadomasochistic husband, a millionaire who has vowed to have her killed if she succumbs to her nymphomania again. The threat does not prevent the driven Adriana from giving herself successively to several fishermen, to the proprietress of a seaside bordello, to a loutish customer there, and to a seedy adventurer who, at one point, saves her from drowning herself in the sea.

In scene after scene, Jean would be obliged to portray a woman on the brink of orgasm—fighting sweatily for fulfillment and all the while loathing the very act she cannot complete. The moaning and groaning would be intense.

The French board of censors, which ruled on the propriety of all scripts, recognized the delicate nature of the material but gave its approval, expressing confidence in the taste and discretion Gary would bring to the film. "I am not entering this as a lark or as a vacation from the writing table," he announced shortly afterward. "I hope—if my film is well received—to divide my time between writing and directing. There will be no wild sex scenes. But as the emotional strain on Jean in certain tense sequences will be heavy, I am closing the set during the shooting of them."

"I have it in my contract," Jean assured columnist Radie Harris, "that I'll never play a scene in the nude, even if my husband demands it."

Filming began at the Studios de Billancourt outside Paris early in October with a blue-ribbon cast that included Danielle Darrieux as the madam, Pierre Brasseur as the possessive husband, and Maurice Ronet as the washed-up adventurer. Later in the month the company migrated to a deserted stretch of white-sand beach on the south coast of Spain, not far from the Portuguese border.

The location was primitive, emptied of even the last straggling vacationers. The nearest grocery store opened only twice a week, but a few itinerant vegetable and meat peddlers occasionally passed through, their cries triggering a stampede among the local housewives.

"We're living in a rather plain little summer house, and we can't get the hot water to function," Jean wrote Carol Hollingsworth. "Last night Celia [her maid] and I heated two canisters of water so Romain could take a sorely needed bath. The first days it rained here and was awfully depressing—our cars and the camera equipment kept sinking into the sand."

The weather remained obstinately uncooperative during most of the shooting, multiplying Gary's problems as a first-time director. A certain lassitude overtook some of the cast and crew, who felt cut off from the world. Jean described Brasseur as "the original *monstre sacré*—huge actor's baritone voice, looks a little like Orson Welles" and reported that he "drinks, drinks, drinks when he doesn't have anything more interesting to do. The other afternoon, we had to abandon any scenes with him in them."

Faulty equipment ruined five days of work. One of the sets, a seaside shack hammered together out of fresh wood, warped and swelled in the rain and collapsed in a heap. Gary spent one morning trying to coax a recalcitrant condor, trucked in from the Seville zoo, to look properly menacing. Observing his efforts and the profusion of dead birds strewn on the beach, presumably to underscore the film's symbolic import, one wag renamed the production "Gulls and Dolls."

"Jean was marvelous and tried to keep everyone's spirits up," Ronet recalls. "The wife of one of the machinists died while he was there, and Jean was wonderful with him—warm and generous." When Diego visited during a break in his schooling, she made a point of showing him a good time and worked hard to strengthen their new relationship.

But the film took an emotional toll on her that is immediately visible in her performance. Shoeless and dressed in a beaded green evening gown, she is exceptionally beautiful as she wanders along the beach. But she keeps her arms rigidly pressed to her sides and her face frozen into a mask. Her expressions are limited to a series of tics and grimaces. In only one other film is her self-consciousness quite so painfully obvious: *St. Joan.*

"It was a very trying experience for Jean," says Betty Desouches, who was present for most of the filming. "Romain really wanted to shock people with that film, and Jean had an intrinsic modesty. She also had a lot of hang-ups about her body, and it was terribly difficult for her to do some of those intimate love scenes—especially knowing they'd been written and were being directed by her husband. Romain and Jean would huddle together between shots, discussing Adriana's perverse motivations and the manner in which she subjugates all the men in her life. There was something distinctly unhealthy about the whole project."

Back in Paris, work on the film dragged into December and left Jean, once again, pondering her own conflicts—as an actress, a diplomat's wife and an American abroad. She hadn't been home in nearly two years, and as she told one columnist, she feared that "the American side of me is suffering."

In one of those sudden twists that characterized Jean's career, Hollywood came to her rescue. Inspired by the gargantuan grosses of *The Sound of Music,* the studios had suddenly put all their faith, plus princely sums of money, into musicals. Paramount had earmarked a then-staggering $15 million to bring *Paint Your Wagon,* a middling Alan Jay Lerner–Frederick Loewe collaboration to the screen. Lee Marvin and Clint Eastwood had been signed to play miners in No Name City, an all-male boom town during the Gold Rush. They would end up sharing the same wife, the only significant female role in the raucous extravaganza. Although Paramount was cool to the idea of Jean Seberg portraying the wife, both Lerner, who was producing, and Joshua Logan, who was directing, thought she would be ideal. In March 1968 they asked her to come to Hollywood for a screen test. Ordinarily Jean would have said no; since the Preminger days, she dreaded the ordeal of a screen test and preferred to forgo a role rather than open herself up to the trauma of potential rejection. But she read the script that Paddy Chayefsky had fashioned, cottoned to the role of Elizabeth, who struck her as "a nineteenth-century flower child," and this time leaped at the opportunity to prove herself worthy.

"I've got a colossal case of stage fright," she jotted on a card to Vony Becker. "But few illusions. Shirley MacLaine will end up getting it."

"Jean came into Joshua Logan's office wearing a real pistol— her husband's .45 automatic—to get into the mood," says Lee Marvin, who had negotiated a $1 million salary for his participation. "I thought, What kind of a cuckoo bird is this? Yeah, she wanted the part, all right. I said, 'What the hell, I'm here, I'll do the scene with her.'"

For the test, they played a part of Elizabeth's wedding-night scene. Marvin began by ripping off the front of her wedding dress; with firm, quiet dignity, Jean stood up to him. The test went well (and the scene proved to be Jean's strongest moment in the film itself). "I was impressed," Marvin allowed afterward.

"We wanted to make sure there would be nothing unduly salacious about the film. After all, here was a woman living with two miners," says Alan Jay Lerner. "Jean had a definite, womanly quality that was right. There was nothing cheap about her. It's my experience that every woman has about sixty percent little girl in her, and as they get older, they just become older girls. But with Jean, that girlishness was amalgamated with the very womanly qualities of compassion, understanding and empathy.

"The movie was going to be made in Oregon over a six-month period, and I knew that Romain was working on a number of projects in Paris at the time. So I said to him, 'Look, you're a friend of mine, and if I offer the part to Jean, I don't want to be instrumental in affecting your marriage in any way. If so, I just won't offer it to her. I don't believe that theater and motion pictures are the beginning and end of the world.' He replied, 'No, if that's what she wants to do, I want her to do it because her happiness is mine.'"

Jean did want to do it. She signed for a salary of $120,000, rented a stately home on Arden Drive in Beverly Hills, and started taking singing lessons in earnest, even though she would have only one number in the film—"A Million Miles Away Behind a Door."

Meanwhile, Gary was encountering difficulties with *Birds in Peru*. When he submitted the edited version to the French censors for final approval, the board reversed its earlier position and by a vote of 10 to 9 banned the work from French screens. (*Birds in Peru* later had the distinction of being the first picture to receive an X rating under the Motion Picture Association of America's newly formed production code.) Gary was incensed and appealed the decision directly to the Minister of Information, for whom he was still working. The minister overruled the board, but Gary relinquished his government post shortly thereafter.

Jean missed the premiere of the film, which was France's entry at the Cannes Film Festival that spring. But Paton Price vividly recalls her first reaction to it at a private screening she arranged at Universal in May while she prepared for *Paint Your Wagon*.

"She came over to our house that night and had dinner," says Price. "Afterward we all drove over to the studio. Jean had invited several close friends and some of her celebrity acquaintances to the screening. She had seen a rough cut of the film and believed she had reason to be proud of it. But it wasn't what she expected at all. The film opened with a head shot of her, her head being pushed against the sand in that telltale sexual rhythm. Immediately, Jean tensed up. It got worse. At the end of the film, she said, 'Get me out of here fast.' She didn't want to see anyone. She stumbled out of the screening room and ran to the car. We never discussed the film after that. It was so bad. And that Romain would do that to her! It was the most embarrassing moment I ever spent with her."

With few exceptions, the reviewers would share a similar sense of bewilderment and indignation. "Under the guise of bourgeois respectability, Romain Gary permits himself just about anything," said one. The French satirical review *Le Canard Enchaîné* suggested that maybe De Gaulle might want to organize a showing of "his friend's dirty picture" at the Elysée Palace. Because Gary had specifically conceived and developed the project for Jean, some observers couldn't avoid reading personal meanings into it. "There is a biographical side that is troubling," admits Claude Chabrol. Several of Jean's friends considered the work flatly insulting and felt that Gary had taken advantage of her. Echoing their feelings, one critic wrote: "If we remember that Jean Seberg is Romain Gary's wife, we shall fully measure the depths of the abyss into which he has fallen."

The tumult, far from producing a *succès de scandale,* seemed only to promise a *scandale.* Olga Horstig-Primuz believes the film seriously harmed Seberg's career in France. Whether it contributed to the erosion of her marriage is matter for speculation. In any case, the marriage was beginning to come undone in 1968. Increasingly, Jean was going her own way, and her way led back to the States.

"The superb thing about Romain," she said several years later, "was that he created this Frankenstein. He pushed me to develop my own tastes. This invariably created conflict." Gary himself was deeply preoccupied in the early months of 1968 with the mounting domestic attacks on the French government, attacks that would erupt into student protests and workers' strikes in May of that year. Ever the fervent Gaullist, he was torn between the problems of his adopted homeland and those of his wife. He was to shuttle back and forth across the Atlantic no less than six times before he and Jean would conclude that their lives had diverged and that their marriage was, as Gary put it, "losing inspiration and color." For both of them, other winds were blowing.

22

"The most sound advice Otto Preminger ever gave me was to never lose my roots."

—JEAN SEBERG

Although she had yet to step in front of the cameras, the announcement that Jean had been signed for *Paint Your Wagon* momentarily galvanized her career. A pack mentality has always governed Hollywood, and the pipers were saying that at twenty-nine she was a comer. Flooded with scripts, Jean accepted a small role in *Pendulum,* a low-budget police melodrama with a social conscience. It told the story of a Washington, D.C., police captain (George Peppard) who plays free and easy with civil liberties until he himself is falsely accused of murdering his unfaithful wife—played by Jean. While her character would disappear in the first third of the film, Columbia was willing to pay her $100,000 for a month's work. After rehearsals on the Columbia lot, director George Schaefer had scheduled two weeks of location shooting in the nation's capital, beginning at the end of April.

Just before she was to leave for Washington, Jean received a late-night call from Marshalltown. Her eighteen-year-old brother David had been killed in an automobile accident. He had taken a friend out for a Sunday night ride, and on a bend south of Marshalltown, the car had veered out of control, skidded eight hundred feet and crashed into a ditch. The two youths had been found dead in a patch of burning grass. Jean immediately flew home to join her grieving parents. The following day Romain jetted in from Paris for the funeral. Dorothy Seberg was in a state of near-collapse, and there was ugly talk that the parents of the other teen-ager might instigate a lawsuit. Jean insisted that her parents follow her to Washington to recuperate.

It was hardly the peaceful interlude she envisioned for them. On April 4 the airwaves crackled with reports that Dr. Martin Luther King Jr. had been assassinated. Washington erupted like a tinderbox. Crowds of vengeful blacks took to the streets, fires broke out in several of the commercial districts, and looters carted off the spoils. A thick layer of smoke, the volcanic ash of anger, hung over the city while the white population retreated behind locked doors like victims of a medieval siege.

"It is horrible," Jean wrote her friend Vony Becker in France. "The indifference of the white population is almost total. Instead of improving conditions in the ghetto, they are buying arms to defend themselves. You get the impression of being in a profoundly sick country which doesn't believe in its illness. Even Romain, who judges America less severely, senses a disturbing malaise."

The metropolitan police informed Schaefer that they could no longer protect his crew and counseled him to pack up his gear. Several of the extras, costumed as police officers, had already been roughed up by rebellious crowds. On his final morning in Washington, Schaefer made a last-ditch effort to get the footage he needed to establish the film's locale: Jean hailing a taxicab at Lafayette Square, opposite the White House, and then riding past various monuments to Capitol Hill. Even in the edited version of the film, Schaefer could not entirely erase the tumult that had overtaken the city. Through the window of the taxi, a cloud of black smoke, almost dagger-shaped, suddenly looms in the sky—an inadvertent intrusion on the carefully ordered universe of the cinema. Given Jean's subsequent involvement with the black movement, it seems an eerie premonition.

The Peppard-Seberg pairing struck relatively few sparks on screen and even fewer off. Jean told friends that the actor was always on the make and not easily discouraged. Peppard remembers it differently. "As an actress," he said, "she was defensive, hesitant, almost like a child thrown among grown-ups. But away from the set, there was this almost condescending feeling she gave me, as if she were more experienced and sophisticated than I was—and I'd seen a lot. She was having troubles with her marriage, which is not hard to tell when you are working that closely with someone, and she stayed very much to herself. At the same time, there was this curious kind of come-on, an aura that said she wanted to get involved. It wasn't schizophrenic, but there were clearly these two sides to her."

Back on the Columbia sound stage in Los Angeles, Jean had her one big scene with him, a bedroom spat that, to her bewilderment, Peppard wanted to invest with sadomasochistic overtones. The slaps he gave her were, she felt, unduly rough. "It was a pretty torrid scene for those days," Schaefer recalls. "Jean had on a flimsy robe, and she and George rolled around a good deal. We showed as much as we decently could. Jean felt very modest about it and didn't want to do the scene without some protection. So wardrobe put some flesh-colored pasties on her. Editing the scene was sheer murder. Just when you'd get to the moment you wanted, you'd see one of those pasties popping up over George's shoulders. Jean could be very proper. But she was absolutely gorgeous, and I always thought she must have had a million boyfriends along the way. I can't imagine anyone not making a play for her."

Pendulum received decent, if unspectacular, notices, mostly for the timeliness of the script, although it prompted one reviewer to wonder "if Jean Seberg is going to be cast until the end of time as a compulsive bedmate."

Years later Peppard tried to make sense of the Jean Seberg he had known: "A lot of movie performers lead their lives as if there is going to be a happening—success or fame—that will make things fall into place. Yet as they achieve those things, they see it changes none of the personal problems. Disillusionment sets in and with it a desire to put that fantasy to work where it *will* make a difference. Jean was like a number of actresses who suddenly get religion, turn bitter and drink, or throw themselves headlong into causes."

In one respect, though, she was significantly different. "Jean," Romain Gary once observed, "is the only being I've ever met in whom racism provokes total indignation, a kind of suffering."

Columnist Pete Hamill remembers her at a Beverly Hills party about this time. Jean detached herself from the disparate guests—Robert Kennedy supporters, black activists, rock-'n'-roll personalities, all momentarily united under the double banner of liberalism and celebrityhood—and engaged him in a discussion of Vietnam. As he described the encounter:

> We wandered out to the pool and sat on a rock ledge in the smoggy night air, and for two hours I tried to tell her about Vietnam. She had a scrubbed blonde beauty about her, her hair cut short in the style she wore in *Breathless.* She wore no makeup, and asked straight, intelligent questions. She didn't flirt. She shook her head a lot, appalled by the details, and her hands kept kneading each other. An aura of tension came off her like mist.
> "It's all connected, isn't it?" she said at one point. "Vietnam, the oppression of blacks in America, all of it."
> "What do you mean?"
> "I mean that it's all part of the same disgusting racism," she said. "If we were fighting the war against Swedes, we wouldn't be doing these things. But because it's Orientals, we can do anything. Like Hiroshima being bombed, instead of Berlin."
> "Maybe."
> "There isn't much maybe about it, is there?" she said. "It looks very clear to me!"

As Jean's liberal views became known, she was often solicited for her money and her signature, both of which she tended to give willingly. She helped canvass funds for former athlete Jim Brown's Negro Industrial Economic Union, which aimed at establishing black-owned businesses in the ghetto. She attended a gathering for Coretta King and Ralph Abernathy, who had replaced Martin Luther King as the head of the Southern Christian Leadership Conference. Her acting teacher, Paton Price, long a pacifist himself, contributed to the honing of her opposition to the Vietnam war and through him she would meet David Dellinger, the prominent peace activist. She also publicly voiced her support of Dr. Benjamin Spock, the baby doctor turned war resister.

"Back at seventeen, I believed in the Midwestern and the

Protestant way," she told one reporter. "If one felt deeply, that was enough to make everything come out all right. I still try to keep a little of that spirit, but it is now coupled with action. The strong belief in itself isn't enough. I've learned the hard way."

Romain was largely disenchanted with Hollywood liberalism and regarded it with the full skepticism of his fifty-three years. Movie actors, like Marlon Brando, who attached their star to a cause struck him as the worst kind of exhibitionists. But he was equally distrustful of those radical groups that pinned their cause to a star. In *White Dog,* a partly fictionalized account of Jean's activism, he expressed disapproval bordering on contempt. The idealistic battles of youth were far behind him. Jean was dragging him back into the arena, and he shrank from the inevitable pain and deception. "I have never met a more typical American idealist," he said of her. "That is to say, an easy mark."

Toward the end of April, Gary was invited to meet with Robert Kennedy, who was recuperating from an early setback in his presidential campaign at director John Frankenheimer's Malibu beach house. Jean went along and was impressed by Kennedy's warmth and charm. He was far more accessible and human, she informed people afterward, than his brother John had been.

Just back from a swim, Robert Kennedy sat cross-legged and barefoot on the floor and talked easily and intelligently about the racial climate in the United States. "I remember that Jean talked a lot that day too," says Alan Jay Lerner, who along with several other show-business personalities attended the luncheon. "She was on a soapbox for all the minorities, the underprivileged who were getting less than a fair share of life. At one point Kennedy finally had to tell her to be quiet. He did it in a very jocular way, though, almost fatherly, the way one tells a child to be quiet. Jean was involved with the causes of just about every underdog that was. She was a very compassionate girl."

That compassion was genuine, but its roots were complex. Since childhood, Jean had tended to identify with the alienated, those people who by temperament dwelled on the fringes of society or who had been relegated there by circumstance. Preminger had divorced her from her peers—the under-thirty generation that was giving vent to that alienation in the streets and on the campuses—and she had come of age abroad, under unique and artificial conditions.

The social and political unrest that seethed in America had a reality to it, however brutal, that mattered to her in a way her movie career did not. All at once she was catching up with the youth she'd missed in a country she'd lost contact with. For one who had long questioned her own worth, the challenges of those days were as inviting as they were treacherous.

Gary returned to France early in May to face his fifty-fourth birthday and a riot-stunned Paris. A month later Jean traveled to Baker, Oregon, the town nearest the secluded valley which was the location for *Paint Your Wagon*. Jean and her maid, Celia, settled into a green clapboard bungalow with chintz curtains, and Sandy and the four cats were put out in the fenced yard. A small sleepy town, Baker reminded her, not unpleasantly, of Marshalltown. She gushed that a nearby barn was every bit as inspiring as a Gothic cathedral and thrilled to the deer that came down from the woods to feed. "I am rediscovering a little of my childhood here," she wrote to Vony Becker. "This part of America is truly appealing. I guess I'm just a country girl at heart."

The filming of *Paint Your Wagon* was less agreeable. At colossal cost, Australian set designer John Truscott had built two versions of No Name City—a bleak encampment of tents mired in mud, which, once gold was discovered, would be transformed into a brawling boom town packed with saloons, dance halls and bordellos. To provide a fittingly cataclysmic conclusion to this tale of pioneer greed, several of the miners would burrow under the buildings for gold dust that had slipped between the floorboards, and No Name City would suddenly sink into the ground. Consequently, the sets rested on a complex system of hydraulic lifts and rockers which allowed the buildings to tremble persuasively, collapse spectacularly, and if additional footage were needed, spring back into place.

The crew alone numbered more than 250, and the ranks were further swelled by a contingent of Chinese extras, several

187

Indians, a musical group called the Nitty Gritty Dirt Band, teams of horses and oxen, and a trained bear. Since the overland trip from Baker required up to three sometimes hair-raising hours by automobile, Lerner had arranged for two helicopters to ferry his cast back and forth, considerably compounding the expense, estimated at one point to be $80,000 a day.

Lerner and Logan had worked congenially together the previous year on the movie version of *Camelot,* but they crossed swords almost as soon as they set foot in the pine-dotted valley. There were rumors that Logan was to be replaced, and while they proved untrue, the filming was plagued with intrigues. Demoralized by Lerner's incessant intervention, which he felt undermined his authority, Logan directed the opus with what he later termed "joyless industry."

Although Jean's role had been highly coveted, it was less than fully fleshed out. To make up for the inspiration lacking in the screenplay, Logan advised her to keep the image of a stalwart pioneer woman in mind. Remembering that her grandmother had scrubbed farmhouse floors at thirteen, she chose the strong-willed Frances Benson as her model.

If the hills were not necessarily alive with the sound of music, they were awash with hippies who had converged on the valley almost as soon as the first call for extras had gone out. Their scraggly tresses, Lincolnesque beards and handlebar mustaches made them ideal for the crowd scenes, and, at $20 a day, they came cheap. Every morning several hundred would show up on the set, where a casting director patiently screened out those who were too drugged to work. Those who remained were fitted into the costumes that the Paramount wardrobe department had thoughtfully shipped ahead in shapes and sizes to meet every possible contingency.

During the interminable waits between shots, Jean often played cards with the youths, engaged them in long conversations, or whenever a guitar was brought out, simply sat in their midst and sang along.

"Some of them were strung out on drugs and in pretty bad shape," Logan remembers. "Others had babies they were trying to raise in the woods. Jean naturally sympathized with them—partially because she was young, but also, I think, because she felt that 'there but for the grace of God . . .' She never quite believed all this magical movie stuff that had happened to her. One Sunday we all attended a hippie wedding by a waterfall. Jean helped organize it, brought a cake and was matron of honor."

Some of the hippies made their way into Baker and knocked at her door. Jean obligingly offered them steaks and showers and, to Celia's distress, collected their dirty clothes and put them through the laundry. "Never let it be said," she joked, "that Jean Seberg would refuse a hippie a bath." Hearing the tales, columnist Rex Reed promptly branded her "Mother Superior" of the flower children.

"You'd think I was a charter member of the hippies, the way people reacted to reports from Baker," Jean later commented. "Everybody talks about gaps—communication gaps, generation gaps, believability gaps. There is really only one gap, and that is a compassion gap. It exists between all of us."

The production's carnival-like atmosphere was enhanced by a steady flow of international journalists who sensed that the combination of a remote location and professional discord might make for lively copy. In most of their accounts Lee Marvin was depicted as soused; Clint Eastwood, remote; and Jean, the placid eye at the center of the storm. As usual, it was a misreading of her personality.

Despite her apparent equanimity—co-star Ray Walston thought she was one of the most "unobtrusive" stars he had ever worked with—Jean had moments of pure despondency, when what she called the "black Swede" in her took over and she behaved like "an Ingmar Bergman character."

"There are days when I see no reason whatsoever for me to have been put on this earth," she told reporter Joan Barthel. "And this is such a big picture. Even Lee was scared at first. Because in a sense our careers are all at stake, and it's a very big load, particularly for Lee and Clint. There's less pressure on me because I'm that new-old girl they brought back, although I must say, if I really am bad a second time around, they may not be very forgiving."

Jean had continued to take singing lessons on location for

her number, "A Million Miles Away Behind a Door," which composer André Previn had written to supplement the original Frederick Loewe score. When it came time to film the song, Eliot Daniel, her voice teacher, saw all his patient coaching efforts vanish. Under a mounting attack of nerves, Jean's voice became shaky and tremulous. Reluctantly, the decision was made to have her voice dubbed for the song. Jean was disappointed, especially because she had written her long-time friend Dawn Murray Quinn to say that it looked as if the many hours of high school choir practice might finally pay off.

Instead, Jean mouthed the words to the song, a celebration of log-cabin domesticity, as she went about her nineteenth-century housewifely chores with stately grace. As soon as Previn saw the rushes, he called Logan from Los Angeles to tell him that the pace was entirely too languid. He would send up a new recording of the song in the proper tempo. Logan dutifully reshot the scene to Previn's specifications, but admitted afterward, "I couldn't tell the difference, and I don't think anyone else could. But it was typical of that film. No one tried to hold it to a budget. It was the most flagrant throwing away of money I've ever seen."

Jean relied on her friendships with Marvin and Eastwood to get her through the chaos. Despite Marvin's heavy intake of alcohol, she described him as "adorable, one of the most inventive actors I've ever worked with." Occasionally, though, when she would accompany him to the bars in Baker, she would secretly instruct the bartender to water down his drinks after the third one. "Clint Eastwood," she wrote a friend, "is extraordinarily handsome and very calm in the Gary Cooper style. He's a good pal."

Eastwood was, in fact, more than a pal. Says Logan: "There was a very warm feeling between Clint and Jean after their first meeting up there. He was certainly an attractive guy and she was beautiful, and they—how shall I put it?—enjoyed each other. They were always very proper in front of other people. But one day Jean told me that she was crazy about him. Clint had a very publicized marriage at the time, and she said it probably would never work out. But still . . . I suppose it was one of those things that could only happen on location."

Eastwood's career, like Jean's, had been salvaged in Europe, where a series of spaghetti Westerns had made him an international star. His chiseled good looks and laconic manner were quintessentially American, however. In Baker he opted to stay on a ranch and sometimes helped slop the pigs. When rumors of their relationship began to suface, Jean quipped, "People talk if we pet the same pigs together. We better stop petting the pigs."

"Jean used to tell me that if she had ever wanted to go back to Marshalltown with someone her parents would have approved of outright," says Dennis Berry, "that person would have been Clint Eastwood. She'd say, 'He's the sort of man who does his own dishes.'"

Far from mending the rift in their marriage, Jean's enforced separation from Romain merely deepened it. "He's going through a terrible human transition right now," she admitted to Rex Reed. "He's fifty-four years old, and despite his service to France and his own war record, he feels he was never properly assimilated." To Vony Becker she confided, "Between us, I don't know what kind of a man I am going to find when I see him again."

She saw him in mid-August. Back in the States to promote his latest novel, *The Dance of Genghis Cohn,* he flew to Baker to join his wife and Diego, who had arrived shortly before for a summer visit. Gary's stay was brief and stormy. Early one morning in the Lerners' kitchen, he confronted Eastwood and challenged him to a duel. Nothing came of it, however. Several days after Gary departed, Jean called her publicity agent, Jerry Pam, in Los Angeles.

"She told me it was urgent for me to come up there and see her," Pam recalls. "When I arrived, she confessed that she was madly in love with Clint Eastwood and that she had decided to get a divorce from Romain. She really believed Clint was going to leave his wife for her. But she said that Romain was a lovely man and that she wanted to protect him under the circumstances. So I should get together with him and work out as friendly an announcement as possible."

That announcement hit the papers on September 17, 1968; it attributed the breakup to the demands of Jean's career, which would presumably keep her in the United States for a minimum of two years. "In spite of my love for Jean and America, I do not wish to become an exile," Gary's statement read. The marriage had been a joyous one, he added, and they were divorcing "if only to preserve the happy memories of the past."

Ironically, Jean's romance with Eastwood barely lasted out the shooting of *Paint Your Wagon*. In October, dropping temperatures and the threat of early snow sent the company back to the Paramount lot, where No Name City was partly reconstructed at additional expense. By then the affair was clearly over. Feeling abandoned, Jean rattled around the house she'd rented in Coldwater Canyon.

"Once they got back to Paramount, it was as if Clint didn't know who she was," says Pam. "Jean couldn't believe that he could be that indifferent to her, after everything that had gone on in Baker. She was a very vulnerable woman, and it was a terrible trauma for her."

Jean shared her disappointment with only a few friends, but a year later she publicly alluded to Eastwood and the role he had in terminating her marriage. "I broke up our marriage," she admitted to columnist Roderick Mann in Rome. "I got a crush on someone else, and because I'm a bad liar I had to tell Romain about it. There was no sneakiness about it, and that's one of the reasons we've managed to remain friends. The sad thing, of course, is that my confidence in this other person was misplaced. It didn't work out. He was the absolute opposite of Romain, an outdoor type, a kickback to my days in Iowa, perhaps. It was marvelous while it lasted. It's always a bit of a shock to discover that people aren't sincere. Perhaps I have to grow up a little."

Dubbing her the Martha Mitchell of show business for being so outspoken, gossip columnist Joyce Haber relayed the information to readers of the Los Angeles *Times* and added: "Who's the man? I'll give you a hint. It isn't Lee Marvin."

On the surface, the divorce arrangements were supremely civilized. "Even I am a bit appalled by it," Jean confessed. She would be given custody of Diego, but both she and Romain agreed the child should have a European education. So that he would not suffer unduly from the split, they decided to divide their Rue du Bac apartment in two. Jean would live in one half, Romain in the other. Diego could shuttle freely between them.

That fall she wrote her friend Vony Becker again. "There is no one else in my life, at least no one you'd call someone. Romain and I have left one another on the best possible terms. I'm leaving empty-handed. I want nothing. Why should I when I can earn my own living? I want only the happiness of Diego, and my one fear is that Romain will take him away from me completely. I love them both, but I was no longer able to live with lies. That's all. Nothing else has changed."

The Hollywood press tried to link Jean with Jean-Claude Killy, the French Olympic skier, when he passed through Los Angeles promoting a new line of sporting equipment. But aside from five days of whirlwind dates, their friendship amounted to little more than fodder for the gossip columns. In mid-October her mother and aunt paid a visit, and Jean busied herself by taking them to Disneyland, Chasen's, the Farmer's Market and a taping of *The Joey Bishop Show*.

Jean was recognized in the studio audience by Sammy Davis Jr., one of Bishop's guests on the show, and was asked to take a bow. Afterward Davis invited Jean and her relatives out to dinner. Dorothy Seberg was still grief-stricken over her son's death, and the entertainment Jean arranged provided only passing distraction. The depth and persistence of her sorrow worried Jean.

These worries contributed to Jean's customary post-film depression as *Paint Your Wagon* ground to a lumbering halt. Her correspondence at the time refers to the monotonous life in California, which was turning her into a recluse, and the depersonalization of the movie industry, which took all the joy out of her work. According to several friends, Jean was drinking more than usual and was taking Valium to calm her nerves.

"Without a man, I'm like a ship without a rudder," she confessed dispiritedly. Logan has another image of her then. "She reminded me of those roly-poly dolls that children play with," the director says. "The kind you knock over and they wobble and bob on the ground before slowly righting themselves— only to be knocked over again."

23

"*I get tired of seeing black school children being educated by and entrusted to the people who once enslaved us. I get tired of black preachers lying about God and the things He is going to do one day. I get tired of black movie stars—and white ones—being projected as our leaders. I get tired of presidents who continue to promise black people civil rights. I get tired of being told American ex-slaves are better off than other black people in other countries. I get tired of hearing about black churches being bombed and little black girls killed. I am tired of being tired, and of saying it.*"

—HAKIM JAMAL

On February 29, 1968, about the time Jean arrived in the States for the *Paint Your Wagon* screen test, a column appeared in the Los Angeles *Sentinel,* which served the black population clustered in East Los Angeles, Watts and Compton. It was written by a Hakim Abdullah Jamal and in clarion terms called for the establishment of the Malcolm X Foundation.

Compton is only a thirty-minute drive from Beverly Hills, but its shabby dwellings are light-years from the opulence of the film community. It is unlikely that Jean was aware of the article, but before the end of the year, its author would irrevocably alter her life.

He was born Allen Eugene Donaldson on March 28, 1931, in

the slums of Roxbury, Massachusetts, seemingly destined to become yet another victim of the ghetto. Hooked on heroin at a young age, dishonorably discharged from the Army for drug use, dunned for child support by a wife he had abandoned, his early life presents itself as an unbroken string of personal failures and skirmishes with the law. Things momentarily looked up when he married Dorothy Durham, an attractive, strong-willed woman from Georgia. She was a distant cousin of Malcolm X, and eventually Donaldson converted to the Muslim faith, kicked the drug habit and adopted a new name. "Jamal," he informed people, means "beautiful."

By the early 1960s he had moved his new family to Los Angeles. There, he worked sporadically as a linotype operator for the *Herald-Examiner* and, occasionally, for a publisher of pornographic books. Following Malcolm X's lead, he formally renounced the Muslim faith to make his own way in the surging and often contradictory tides of the awakening Black Power movement. After Malcolm X's assassination in 1965, he found his niche as a self-appointed guardian of the memory and teachings of the slain leader. Dorothy Jamal had barely known her controversial relative, but Jamal took a more proprietary view and unabashedly presented himself as "the cousin of Brother Malcolm X who served him loyally in life and in death."

Tall, thin, sporting a single gold earring and a lamb's-wool cap, Jamal cut an arresting figure when he shouted his Black Power views on the cheerless street corners of Compton. He cultivated a beard and a mustache, which seemed only to emphasize the hollowness of his cheeks. Sometimes he wore glasses, as Malcolm did, only Jamal's had nonprescription lenses. By 1968 the Los Angeles *Sentinel* was publishing a column under his by-line twice a month. The articles mixed watered-down teachings of Malcolm X with a fair amount of rabble-rousing and an even greater amount of self-promotion.

The February 29 column laid out his plans for the Malcolm X Foundation, which, at first, seemed nothing more than a study and cultural center where "articles such as Malcolm's desk, articles of clothing and notes of speeches that Brother Malcolm planned to deliver at future times" would be on display as a source of inspiration. Over the months, however, Jamal's vision expanded to include a "photography lab" for jobless teen-agers who had overcome their drug habit, and a Montessori school for children aged two to six.

That his vision far outstripped the realities of the foundation's resources—it never had enough money and functioned out of a succession of ill-equipped storefronts on Compton Boulevard—merely fired his rhetoric to greater heights.

Jamal knew how to talk. He could bait whitey, flail the Uncle Toms and castigate the system with a belligerence that pleased his audience every bit as much as it disturbed Compton's predominately white police force. Even those acquaintances who dismissed him as a con artist begrudgingly admired his charisma. One day he casually strolled into a Compton bank with a broken-down shotgun in his hand, calmly conducted his transaction and sauntered out—to the consternation of the tellers. At meetings he would whip out a pistol and place it conspicuously on a table before speaking. Once he refused to speak at all until an American flag hanging in the room had been removed from his sight.

For all his street savvy, Jamal also liked to mingle with the famous and boasted openly of his friendship with Marlon Brando. His interest in the Hollywood celebrities he assiduously badgered and courted for financial support was not solely monetary, however. He had a kinship with them that transcended race. Jamal was a showman too.

By the fall of 1968, the Malcolm X Foundation and the Montessori school had made inroads into the Compton community —partly because Hakim Jamal was a tireless promoter but also because his wife possessed a level-headed strength and had assumed the daily responsibilities of running the school. Housed in a bungalow on a weedy lot with an empty, cracked swimming pool in back, the school had an enrollment of approximately two dozen black children. From a poster on the wall, a determined Malcolm X gazed down at the classroom while Medhu Trivedi, a mild-mannered Indian woman from Bombay, glided among the desks, encouraging her students in their lessons.

Parents were expected to help out—escorting the children on field trips, monitoring the classroom, buying and delivering the milk for snack break. By Jamal's order, parents also had to foreswear narcotics if they expected their children to remain in the institution. "I know if they're off or on," he warned. "I was an addict for ten years until Malcolm took the needle out of my arm."

The serenity of the classroom contrasted violently with the militancy that Jamal brought to the storefront headquarters of the Malcolm X Foundation several blocks away. There, he harangued and he goaded. Sometimes he would conduct trials of members he suspected of using drugs. Those found guilty had their heads shaved. Lest an "enemy" try to smuggle guns onto the premises, he decreed that each meeting be preceded by a shakedown—of brothers and sisters alike—at the door.

Urgency was an intrinsic component of Jamal's psychological make-up. He believed in brinksmanship. To depict the foundation on the verge of collapse, not to mention outside subversion, was one way to keep it alive. At the same time, Jamal was plainly enhancing his own stature when he painted himself as a target of vengeful drug dealers; of irate Black Muslims who resented his independence, just as they had resented Malcolm's; and of the Compton police force, which actually did view Jamal's activities with alarm.

Jamal seemed to thrive on the paranoia that by 1968 was eating away at the Black Power movement. Operating on the principle of "divide and conquer," the FBI had infiltrated most of the major black groups and from within fomented rivalries and factionalism. The tactics were part of Cointelpro —the bureau's term for its secret counterintelligence program. Jamal was not a big fish in those troubled waters, but the FBI judged him "armed and dangerous" nonetheless and kept him under surveillance. His dossier in the Washington bureau was more than an inch thick, and growing.

Still, a large measure of the persecution Jamal felt was self-induced. "He was always positive that he was going to be put away the very next morning by *them*—that wonderful word," says Shirley Sutherland (then the wife of actor Donald Sutherland), who lent her support to several of the black groups in

Los Angeles. "I'd get some pretty strange telephone calls from him that usually began, 'If you don't hear from me tomorrow by noon . . .'"

"Hakim would go around saying that people were after him because of his connection with Malcolm X," says his wife, Dorothy. "After a while I think he really came to believe it. He would talk all the time about getting shot at in the streets. But if he had been, I would have heard about it from other people, too."

"Jamal would rap with everybody," adds one of his Compton friends. "His main point was that the white man gives you only what's bad for you—drugs—never meat and potatoes, which are good for you. But sometimes he'd say the weirdest things to get up against your head. He could look you straight in the eye and ask, 'How many meals have you missed? Do *you* know what it is like to have hunger pangs?' And he didn't know from poor. He'd never missed a meal growing up. But that was his style. I remember one of the girls used to say, 'I know he's lying, but I just love the *way* he lies.' He had a lot of sway over people, and meetings were always packed. There were still white merchants on Compton Boulevard in those days, and here was the Malcolm X Foundation right in the middle of them. It got a lot of attention."

To some, Jamal's fears were given momentary credence when, early on the morning of October 22, 1968, fire broke out in the foundation's headquarters. By the time the Compton fire department arrived the building had been seriously damaged, and Billy Pye, a foundation member who was sleeping there, had been badly burned. The fire inspector attributed the blaze to a short in the electrical system. Jamal rejected that explanation. It was, he claimed, a bombing, and just more evidence of a larger conspiracy against the black community as a whole.

In the dramatic style that invariably linked his destiny with that of Malcolm X, he told reporters, "We at the foundation have taken two hundred black children off dope, and those who push drugs want to destroy us. It's also a case that black people in Compton have begun to listen to us and apparently there are those who don't like it. We received threats by mail. So did Malcolm. His house was bombed. So was our office.

Malcolm was killed approximately a week after his house was bombed. This is what has me worried, because it's the same tactics that killed Malcolm."

Not everyone accepted the parallels. Jean Seberg did.

Shortly before the fire, she had met Jamal on an airplane coming from San Francisco, where he had been lecturing at a college. He had sidled into an empty seat beside her and struck up a conversation. "Jean was extraordinarily open. She had great curiosity, and she was always trying to make connections between things," says Paton Price. Before the plane had landed in Los Angeles, Jean had volunteered her help in Jamal's crusade.

Dorothy Jamal remembers her husband announcing upon his return, "I think we've got another supporter for the school." Without naming Seberg, he told his wife that he'd probably have to spend some time in Beverly Hills. That didn't surprise her. "Hakim loved being around movie stars more than anything else," Dorothy says. "He was always dropping in on them. He'd just show up, without an invitation and sometimes without even calling first. I think it bothered some of them after a while."

On the weekend of November 9, Dorothy learned who the new supporter was. Jamal telephoned from Lake Tahoe. "He told me he'd gone there to see Sammy Davis Jr. about getting some money for the foundation," she says. "Then he said, 'By the way, guess who's also here. Jean Seberg.' After that, Jean got on the line and said to me, 'I just want you to know that after that awful incident, Hakim is safe.' He'd gone and told her that the foundation had been bombed and that someone had shot at him, and she'd fallen for it."

However, there was no talk of shooting in the call that Jamal placed to his Los Angeles friend Barbara Nash that same weekend. Barbara and her husband, musician Don Nash, both considered Hakim, for all his theatrics, "a basically good person." Their Tarzana ranch house was one of the few places at the time where politically active whites and blacks could meet and talk in an atmosphere of relative trust; Jamal was a frequent visitor.

"Do you know Jean Seberg?" he asked.

"Yes," Barbara answered.

"What do you think of her?"

"She's a movie star . . . she's very beautiful . . . Why?"

"Because," Jamal said, bursting into laughter, "she's sitting here right beside me."

According to an interview Jean gave the following month, she was convinced that Jamal's life was in grave danger and had taken it upon herself to find him a haven. Learning of the "bombing," she had immediately telephoned Sammy Davis Jr., who was then appearing at Harrah's in Lake Tahoe. In addition to his show-business career, Davis had an interest in a charter-plane service. At her request, Jean said, Davis put a jet at her disposal to get Jamal out of Los Angeles.

Jean and Hakim stayed several days at the Nevada resort. His paranoia was catching. Jean began to think they were being followed by suspicious-looking cars, and she noted darkly that their telephone calls were sometimes abruptly disconnected.

From the start, Jamal had had no difficulty interesting her in the fate of the Montessori school (in *White Dog,* Gary described Jean as having an acute case of "sympathy at first sight"). She would go on to be one of its most zealous supporters. But her concern extended further, to Jamal's wife and six children—all of whom, he told her, lived in constant fear for their lives. "Jean would catapult herself from one thing to the next," says Diane Bonnet, a close friend during this period. "She was always pushing herself. In Paris, with Romain, she had pushed herself intellectually. Now she threw herself into saving the Jamals."

At the heart of the matter, however, was her relationship with Jamal himself, a relationship that would soon become so entangled, psychologically and sexually, that it is simplistic to picture Jean as the helpless victim and Jamal as the ruthless manipulator. Sometimes Jean's idealism went so far beyond the bounds of reason and judgment as to become a virtual invitation to a form of spiritual rape. She carried within her the guilt of her Lutheran upbringing (and what Gary called "its inbred poison of original sin"), and the more conspicuous guilt of a movie star who felt she had an embarrassment of riches.

Giving helped appease her long-standing inadequacies. In the process, she was also purchasing experience.

Paton Price, who insists that Jean's generosity was above reproach, says, "Now and again, I sensed in her an appetite for crisis living. Under the Sunday school honesty she projected, some form of make-believe persisted. Jean had a mischievousness about her—it was one of her charms—but it did cause trouble. Often she would do and say things for effect, as if she were performing. I sometimes wondered if she was making a drama out of her life when there was none. More and more, I think, she felt she had to live at the apex of things, not the slow, steady life. But it wasn't the basic person at all. Her need for excitement contradicted the sweet reasonableness that most people loved in her—myself included."

Jamal did more than offer her a focus for the compassion she had earlier lavished on the hippies in Baker and the teen-aged misfits of Marshalltown. He gave her the chance to play the role of high emotion that had eluded her on the screen, and to participate in a drama next to which her films paled. It was *St. Joan* in modern dress and with an integrated cast. The very extremism of the relationship with Jamal was its attraction; the danger—real or imagined—its seasoning.

"Jamal was the one passionate love of Jean's life," Dennis Berry admits candidly. "I think she loved him more than she loved me. Certainly more passionately. That has to be recognized and said. I don't know why most people involved with Jean want to dismiss it. It's true. He had a number of strong qualities. At the same time, he had a serious identity crisis, and he ended up in a very scary way. He did some strange things with Jean toward the end. They were both psychotic together. But that often happens with passion of that intensity. Two people devour each other. They lose track."

When Jean returned to Beverly Hills from Lake Tahoe, she made a point of reaching out to Dorothy Jamal and her children. "Jean tried to be my friend," Dorothy acknowledges. "I guess she figured it was necessary if she was going to keep Hakim. She brought me a watch on a necklace that I've still got. It's broken now. I thought she was very sweet at first. She chatted with me about her life and kid and the nanny. She told me about her affair with Clint Eastwood, although now I think it was just to reassure me that there was nothing between her and Hakim. She was very pretty, but not strong, except, I found out, when she drank. Then you'd have thought she could change the world. It just amazed me that she had come as far as she had in the movie industry."

One day not long after returning from Tahoe, Jean rented a limousine and took Dorothy Jamal and her children to Disneyland. Diane Bonnet tagged along with her two children. "Jean was not very good with money or organization, so she said, 'Here, Diane, you take the money.' My daughter remembers it well because it was the first time she'd ever seen a hundred-dollar bill. Jean loved the Small World ride, with its animated dolls, and she insisted we all go on it first. Then we all got right back on a second time. We bought the children Mickey Mouse hats, and on the way home the limousine was filled with helium balloons. Jean was great fun to be with. When she was there, she was there."

Fun did not divert her from her purpose. In earnest, she began to drum up support for the Montessori school and seized every opportunity to promote Jamal among those well-heeled friends who might conceivably help out. Jamal couldn't ask for more. Vanessa Redgrave, an early convert, paid a visit to the school and pronounced it a success. Later, she would introduce Jamal to people she knew in sympathetic London circles.

Jean was not just the "easy mark" in Jamal's life that some observers took her for; she was a star player in his continuing drama of self-aggrandizement. It was not so much her money he wanted, although he never turned money down, as the opportunity to share in her fame. Jamal bragged that he occasionally went hiking with Wally Cox, was on a first-name basis with singer Nancy Wilson, and had once engaged James Baldwin in a dialogue about blackness—even if *they* perceived the "friendship" in far less intimate terms. When Marlon Brando said he'd like to meet with the Black Panthers, Jamal jumped at the chance to act as the go-between. Now he let the Panthers know that he could introduce them to Jean Seberg.

Founded in 1966 by Bobby Seale and Huey Newton, the Black Panther Party had taken shape in the relative obscurity of Oakland, California. As a political party, its doctrine rested on a ten-point program to break "the oppressive grip of the white power structure on the black community." It was the seventh point—a call for an immediate end to police brutality and the murder of black people—that had made the Panthers controversial and, in some quarters, openly feared.

Arming themselves with lawbooks and guns, they had begun by trailing the Oakland police on their rounds and intervening, whenever an arrest was imminent, to make sure that the suspect was not being harassed and that his constitutional rights were respected. For many members of the police force, such action by a black group constituted outright provocation.

When Seale and several Panthers marched with their (unloaded) guns into the California State legislature on May 2, 1967, to protest a pending gun-control bill that they felt was aimed at emasculating the black community, the party leaped to national prominence. Much of white America recoiled at this new image of young black men—berets cocked on their heads, guns at their sides, their fists raised in a gesture of defiance—and viewed them as the harbingers of revolution.

By the fall of 1968 the battle lines had been clearly drawn. On one side: the Panthers, whose numbers had swelled to 3,000, according to some estimates. On the other: the police, or "pigs," as the party dubbed them, and the hidden might of the FBI. Confrontations and shoot-outs multiplied so rapidly that some liberals began talking of the government's systematic persecution of the Panthers. After Huey Newton was sentenced in September 1968 for manslaughter in the shooting of an Oakland policeman, a large segment of American youth, both black and white, united in "Free Huey" rallies and demonstrations across the country.

Whatever position one took, the Panthers were by then inextricably woven into the national consciousness—that crazy quilt that included mini-skirts and pot, rock music, napalm, and a belief that for better or worse, the pillars of society were coming down.

Temperamentally, Jamal was ill equipped for the Panthers' strict party discipline. He belonged to an older generation and was reluctant to abandon his personal ambitions. The trappings of the good life tempted him too much. While few doubted that the Panthers were deadly serious, Jamal's militancy had a touch of P. T. Barnum. Still, he maintained friendly relations with the Panthers, even if their code name for him, "the Lone Ranger," reflected a certain scorn for his independent ways. He sometimes attended their meetings and spoke at their rallies. And he reminded people, whenever possible, that he had been present that spring day in 1967 when Betty Shabazz, Malcolm X's widow, visited the office of *Ramparts* magazine in San Francisco under Panther guard. That visit had resulted in the first armed stand-off between the Panthers and the police. Celebrated in print by Eldridge Cleaver, the event had since acquired the dimensions of a historical milestone in black consciousness. Jamal relished his place in history.

He was present, too, the night of November 17, 1968, when the Friends of the Panthers, a group of white liberals headed by Shirley Sutherland and author Don Freed, sponsored a benefit at Los Angeles Trade Technical College to marshal support for Huey Newton's defense fund. Folk singer Phil Ochs performed first, and then Seale and Raymond "Masai" Hewitt, the Panthers' Minister of Education, addressed the crowd of 2,000. Afterward Jamal made his way backstage and informed Seale that he could arrange an introduction to Jean Seberg.

The two Panther leaders, along with a dozen or so of their men, drove to Jean's house in Coldwater Canyon that night. Jamal later reported that Seale boasted on the way, "We took Marlon Brando for ten thousand dollars. We can take Jean Seberg for twenty thousand."

Seale was not exactly sure who Jean Seberg was. Nor did he recognize Vanessa Redgrave, Jean's houseguest at the time. With a few drinks under his belt, he began mimicking the British actress' accent, and inquired bluntly why she didn't talk like everybody else.

"Vanessa just flipped out. She couldn't believe that there were some cats who had never heard of her before," says one of the Panthers present that evening. "Man, we'd go to these Beverly Hills parties; half the time, we didn't know who the hell we were meeting. So we'd walk in, take a quick look around, and say, 'Whatcha got to drink?' Flipped 'em out every time."

Seale remembers that the two actresses bombarded him with questions. "Jean was a very alive, alert person," he says. "She understood that we were a direct political party, founded to organize the people against their oppressors. She wasn't asking if we were violent or not. She knew where we were coming from."

Jean was especially enthusiastic about the Panthers' attempts to set up a free breakfast program for ghetto children. As with Jamal's Montessori school, children won her instant sympathy. Unhesitatingly, she pledged her support.

The "rapping" went on until the wee hours, and Jean offered to put up Seale for the night. He declined. Party business kept him flying from city to city, often on a few hours' notice. "I had a plane to catch that morning," he says, "so the brothers drove me to a pad across town near the airport." It was the only time the Panther leader ever saw Jean Seberg.

Jean entered another world entirely when she returned to Marshalltown for the Thanksgiving holiday, the first family gathering since David's death. Before leaving California, she turned over her house to Jamal and his family. With its swimming pool and other creature comforts, it would provide them with a pleasant change from the grim surroundings of Compton. It was also "safer," she reasoned.

Marshalltown, sleepy as always, seemed to dwell in a neverland of ignorance so removed from the frenzy of Los Angeles as to appear unreal. The pervasive contrasts in her life loomed sharper, more irreconcilable, than ever. Jean rarely discussed her political activities with her parents, but over the holidays she welcomed the opportunity to talk with a *France-Soir* correspondent who had flown to Marshalltown to interview her. She told him of Hakim Jamal, the "bombing," the threats on his life and her efforts to harbor him in Lake Tahoe. It was all part of what she called "Operation Love," her singlehanded attempt to prove to Jamal that all white Americans were not "blue-eyed devils" and that trust could be established between the races.

"Hakim considers that he doesn't have a chance for survival," she said. "I hope with all my heart that he is wrong.

But I can tell you this. If he is killed, or his wife or one of his children, I will understand the anger of the blacks and will participate in violence myself."

The correspondent noted the palpable anxieties of the Sebergs, worried for a daughter who was "mixed up in things they don't understand." Impressed by Jean's stand, he filed a near-heroic account of her mission. The article appeared in the Paris daily several days later under a banner headline: ACTRESS JEAN SEBERG MENACED: IN THE UNITED STATES SHE HARBORED A BLACK AND HIS FAMILY, THE COUSIN OF THE ASSASSINATED EXTREMIST LEADER MALCOLM X.

Joyce Haber's gossip column in the December 3 issue of the Los Angeles *Times* featured a less dramatic item. It stated simply: "Jean Seberg is really some girl. She just had, as houseguests, Jamal X [*sic*] and his six children. Jamal X is the brother [*sic*] of the late Malcolm X."

In Jean's mind, 1968 was no time for idle gossip. She was convinced that Jamal was the target of dangerous conspiracies. By association, she too felt marked. She informed friends that her telephone was tapped, and would frequently leave the house to make calls from a public phone. Chuck Belden once called her up and pretended to be a policeman. Jean took the joke poorly. "Don't you ever do that again," she scolded him.

"There was always a tone of danger when Jean talked about the Jamals, a feeling that 'they are out to get us,'" says Diane Bonnet. "It was never exactly clear who 'they' were. The FBI? The Mafia? The same people who had killed Malcolm X? The danger was less apparent to me than to Jean. She had a sense of drama and blew things up. But I never once doubted that that was how she felt."

In mid-December, fired with new purpose at the onset of her thirty-first year, Jean returned to Paris to spend Christmas with Romain and Diego. After her departure a rental agent stopped by to check up on the house in Coldwater Canyon. She was dismayed by what she found: "The draperies were ripped, the furniture scarred. There was even an iron in the backyard. It was like three families had been living there."

The agent wondered what had gone on. "Jean seemed like such a sweet, insecure girl," she said.

24

*"You know the old story of the chameleon.
Put him on green, he turns green. Put him on
black, he turns black. But if you put him on
plaid, he explodes."*

—JEAN SEBERG

Hakim Jamal was not one to leave a contact unexploited. Jean
Seberg represented access to a larger and, from what she told
him of France, more sympathetic world. While many of the
celebrities he chased after eventually tired of him and closed
their doors, Jean burned with the flame of true commitment.
She believed it imperative that his name be known abroad—
not simply because his work was meritorious, but because
wider recognition could shield him from the plots and counterplots that were no less real to her for being vague and unidenti-
fiable.

Telling his wife that he had a series of speaking engagements
in New York City, Jamal boarded a plane at the Los Angeles
airport on January 24, 1969. His real destination, however,
was Paris. And his address there: 108 Rue du Bac.

Prior to his arrival Jean tried to stir up interest, informing
friends of his accomplishments and alerting journalists that he
would be giving a lecture at the Cité Universitaire, the student
complex on the outskirts of Paris. Jamal was impressed by the
French capital, especially its tolerant racial climate. He was
amazed that a black man and a white woman walking hand in
hand was a matter of complete indifference to most French

people, but he failed to adapt his rhetoric to the freer circumstances.

"Jamal came on very strong," recalls Vony Becker, who attended his lecture with her husband. "He told extraordinary stories and raged on about the need to kill all the whites. Jean just sat on the edge of her seat and listened to him in a trance. She was enthralled. Things were never gray to her, and she loved to be part of movements. She could have such good judgment about some things. But in other areas, she had no will power at all and let herself be swept away."

The audience, composed largely of African students, was less than receptive. Jamal's "hate whitey" rabble-rousing seemed overly dramatic and slightly irrelevant to them. Several of the journalists who'd come as a favor to Jean wrote him off as a cipher, and Julia Wright, the daughter of black author Richard Wright, stood up and challenged his credentials. By what authority, she asked pointedly, could he speak for the Panthers? Stung, Jamal had his friend Barbara Nash in Los Angeles send copies of the newspaper article that confirmed his presence at the office of *Ramparts* magazine two years before. Wasn't it there that the Panthers had first shown their claws? Wasn't he part of the crowd?

Jamal's connection with Jean Seberg had not gone unnoticed by the FBI. Capitalizing on Jamal's trip abroad, one zealous bureau official proposed a scheme to discredit them both. Although much of the information amassed in Jamal's voluminous file is blacked out today for "security" reasons, one document from February 1969 notes: "In memorandum of 2/13/69 . . . it was recommended that the Crime Records Division attempt to place information with a reliable press contact relative to actress Jean Seberg's relationship with Abdullah Jamal." Appended was the following "information," presumably destined for the gossip columns:

It was a cold day in January when American actress Jean Seberg met her tall, dark friend at Orly airport outside Paris. The warmth of the greeting suggested something more than a business relationship. He is Hakim Jamal, a black activist from Los Angeles. A few days later, they turned up in London, where Jamal appeared on television. Now she is back in the USA, but he lingers on in London. What is going on?

Few things aroused J. Edgar Hoover's wrath as much as sexual misconduct, of which he considered interracial intercourse a prime illustration. But the FBI plan was apparently not implemented. Penciled in at the bottom of the memorandum is the question: "Did Mr. Hoover approve doing this?" And Hoover's squiggly disclaimer: "I did not. Such matters should always be approved by [Clyde] Tolson or me."

By mid-February, Jamal had moved on to Vanessa Redgrave's house in London. Known for her strong leftist leanings, the British actress had long considered Malcolm X "an inspiration." A picture of him hung on the wall of her living room. As his "cousin," Hakim Jamal qualified for her respect and hospitality. Redgrave introduced Jamal to her brother, Corin, and his wife, who in turn brought him to the attention of their own friends. Years later Jamal would boast about hobnobbing with London society and recount that he had escorted the willowy Vanessa to the premiere of the film *The Magic Christian*. There, he said, he chatted with David Frost and Lord Snowdon, and pressing a brochure for the Montessori school into Snowdon's palm, brazenly asked, "Hey, by the way, would you give this to your sister-in-law?" (Snowdon's sister-in-law was, of course, the Queen of England.)

Meanwhile, Jean had returned to the United States to start work on *Airport* for Universal. It was the last picture she would make in the United States, far and away the highest grossing, and by general critical consent, one of the worst. Adapted from Arthur Hailey's bloated best-selling novel and directed by Hollywood veteran George Seaton, *Airport* had a glossy, all-star line-up: Dean Martin, George Kennedy, Helen Hayes, Maureen Stapleton, Jacqueline Bisset, Van Heflin, Burt Lancaster and Dana Wynter. But the real performers were two 707s—one crippled in mid-flight by a bomb and unable to land at fictional Lincoln Airport because of the second, which was stuck on the runway in mounds of snow.

From the standpoint of her contract, *Airport* was Jean's high-water mark. Her salary was $150,000, plus $1,000 a week in expenses for four months. She was guaranteed no less than fourth billing (and got third), and the studio put a car at her disposal. Artistically, it was the nadir in Jean's career as a Hollywood wind-up doll. She was cast as the airport's efficient public relations person, in love with sodden (and married) Burt Lancaster. When she was not chasing after a mischievous Helen Hayes, a cute little stowaway, she stood around in various posh airport offices and lounges looking detectably bored. Her performance prompted critic Gene Shalit to quip that she appeared to be competing "for an Oscar for 'Facial Immobility in a Movie Based on a Novel.'"

Jean had few illusions about the project. She detested the gray mini-skirted uniform that was her costume and carped that it made her look like a clown. She considered her role insipid. "They aren't interested in me," she told Paton Price one day. "They want a puppet." When Price urged her to get what she could out of the part, she shrugged, "Why should I? They treat me like garbage."

"The most stimulating thing about any of the American movies I've done," she reflected later, "has been the money. On the whole, I have fairly miserable memories of what I let be done to me when I go to Hollywood. I let them turn me into something I'm not. I've been Miss Submissive. I seem to have no will, no way of coping."

Location footage was filmed at the Minneapolis–St. Paul International Airport in the subzero cold of late February and early March. Then the company returned to the Universal lot, where a full-sized mock-up of a 707 occupied most of the sound stage.

Jean stayed largely to herself during the shooting. Helen Hayes, who won an Academy Award for her cameo, thought her "a bit of a recluse," while Lancaster, with whom Jean had most of her scenes, claims to have little recollection of her. Before the cameras, she went through the motions. Afterward she shut herself up in her dressing room.

"She wasn't happy with the material," Harvey Laidman recalls. He was an assistant trainee director on the film, and his duties included keeping tabs on Jean at all times and escorting her back and forth between her dressing room and the set. "Jean—and it was always Jean, never Miss Seberg—didn't seem to be comfortable in the company of the bigwigs, unlike Lancaster, who wasn't happy unless he was in a crowd of a hundred, telling a long, complicated story while everyone else was waiting for him. She never hung around with the other stars. She seemed to have the most fun when it was just one-on-one. Most of the time when I went to get her in her dressing room she'd be lying on the couch joking like crazy with her make-up man or the hair stylist. She had a lot of fun with them. I thought she was a regular girl—really a terrific, sad, giving person. Later I read about all the radical things that were supposed to be going on in her life then. It amazed me. I never thought that Jean in all her gentility could get that worked up. She didn't seem to have the energy level."

Peter Fonda saw her socially now and again during this time, and connects her disenchantment with acting to her political activism. "She seemed a little helpless. No, that's not the right word. There wasn't enough for her to do," says the star of *Easy Rider.* "I could tell her work wasn't satisfying her. The essence of acting is being able to share with everyone else on the set that particular moment. I think Jean's causes gave her that daily sense of necessity, of being needed and being able to share."

Away from the set, her life had a different tone entirely. Her relationship with Jamal had quickly intensified. She paid his delinquent dues in the linotypists union and frequently lent him her car. They had nicknames for each other. He was "Streetman." She was "Pudding Face." Maureen Stapleton was at Jean's house one night when Hamal telephoned. Sensing an opportunity to promote the cause, Jean handed over the receiver and said, "Talk to my friend."

"He was a surly son of a bitch," Stapleton recalls, "and I said all the wrong things. But he made me mad and I told him off. Jean turned white and tried to shush me up. The next day she showed up at work and said, 'He wants to speak to you again.' 'Tell him to get a nine-to-five job first,' I said. 'Then I'll talk to him.'"

Sometimes Jean and Jamal met for their trysts in a small out-of-the-way apartment on South Crenshaw Boulevard. The

Los Angeles police arrested a violent mental patient in the shabby neighborhood one day. From behind a clump of bushes, Jamal took pictures of the struggle, using a telephoto lens. Spotting him, the police came over to investigate. They were surprised to discover that he had a companion. Hidden with him in the foliage was Jean Seberg.

Dorothy Jamal was still unaware of their liaison, although she sensed something was awry one evening early in March when Jean threw a birthday party for the Jamals' twin daughters: "Jean was drinking a lot that night, and when Jean drank, she could be terribly aggressive. At one point she turned to Jamal and said, 'I don't like that hat.' She was referring to his lamb's-wool hat that he never took off for anyone, only to go to bed. She yanked it off his head. In its place she put a Mickey Mouse cap that the kids had brought from Disneyland. 'There, that's better,' she laughed. Hakim never said a word. He let her do it. I couldn't believe it. I hit the roof. He was at the stage where he suffered anything she wanted."

Jean and Dorothy continued to share an enthusiasm for the Montessori school, however. Those who saw them together that spring considered them friends, and when Jean went out at night, she sometimes arranged for the Jamals to come along. The first week in April, they all attended a fund raiser for the Panthers at the Ash Grove, then a popular coffeehouse on Melrose Avenue. A film about the life of Malcolm X was shown, and later a collection was taken up. Jean pulled a $100 bill from her purse, then turned to author Don Freed, seated next to her, and whispered timidly, "Do you think that's enough?"

Freed, who had interested a number of Hollywood stars in the fate of the Panthers, remembers Jean as being "more vulnerable than most." Sometimes he wondered if she wasn't looking for emotional sustenance in an arena unlikely to provide it. "Most of the Hollywood people drifted away when things became hot," he says. "Only the politically committed and the fools, as in fools for Jesus, stuck it out. Jean stuck it out."

Her generosity was unrestrained. She bought a yellow bus for the Montessori school and deposited $5,000 in a personal checking account for Jamal. When Billy Pye, Jamal's sidekick,

Butterfly Toe Dance. Jean is fourth from right.

High school production of Sabrina Fair *starring Jean Seberg.*

ABOVE: *With Otto Preminger on set
of* St. Joan.

LEFT: *At the moment of hair cutting
before first screen test.*

RIGHT: *Fitting for armor for* St. Joan.

Soldiers lighting funeral pyre for burning at the stake.

At Maxim's in Paris.

Marshalltown Homecoming Parade 1956.

Jean with Carol Hollingsworth and former classmates.

Family at Marshalltown reception. From left (seated): *Grandma Benson, Dorothy, Jean and David. Ed, Mary Ann and Kurt stand in rear.*

With Françoise Sagan and Preminger during filming of Bonjour Tristesse.

Marriage to François Moreuil.

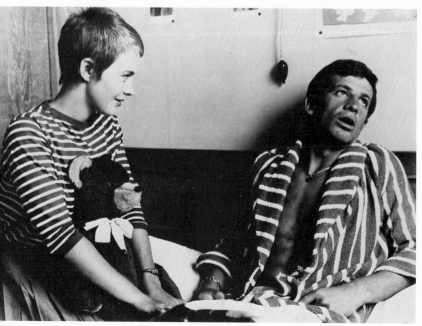

With Jean-Paul Belmondo on the set of Breathless.

On a visit to Marshalltown with Romain Gary.

Paint Your Wagon *with Clint Eastwood.*

With Dorothy and Diego in Marshalltown.

At Riverside Cemetery at burial of baby daughter, September 1970.

Gale Benson and Hakim Jamal, 1972.

With Dennis Berry in Marshalltown.

With Ahmed Hasni.

1979.

got married, she paid for his weekend honeymoon at Marina del Rey. According to the FBI, by 1970 her contributions to the Panthers amounted to $10,500 in checks alone. Her cash donations were harder to account for. "She was a pushover for any hard-luck story," says one friend, "and she was constantly extending her purse."

Throughout her life, Jean sent $200 a month to Frances Benson, slipped checks into letters to her friends and arranged "scholarships" for their relations. She helped set up her Vietnamese make-up lady, Phong Maitret, in a flower shop in Paris, and on one occasion lent Paton Price $25,000 so he could purchase several hundred acres of land in Northern California. Sometimes the generosity had a reckless impulsiveness to it. When a chauffeur once complained about the dismal circumstances of his life and his wife's threadbare wardrobe—nothing of course, like the elegant clothes that movie stars got to wear—Jean took off her fur coat, tossed it on the seat beside him and said, "Take it."

Not everyone was willing to follow her example. Early in April she arranged for Jamal to speak to a group of Price's friends and students in hopes of replenishing the coffers of the Montessori school. Held in the cluttered poolhouse that Price used as a studio, the meeting went poorly. Informing his listeners that he had a pair of guns in the briefcase at his side, Jamal launched into a heated attack. "You hate me, your father hated me, your grandfather hated me," he railed while several dozen guests shifted uneasily under the onslaught. Jamal had brought two of his children with him, and when he obliged them to take up his anti-honky diatribe, Price found his pacifism sorely tested. He stomped out of the studio, and several guests followed him.

Jean put greater hopes in the fund raiser she was scheduled to give in her own home on April 16. She spent weeks beforehand on the telephone to guarantee a good turnout. Jane Fonda showed up, as did Paul Newman, Joanne Woodward, Lee Marvin, James Baldwin, a very pregnant Vanessa Redgrave and her lover Franco Nero.

"Just about every well-known liberal in town was there," the wife of a prominent attorney recalls. "But frankly, I'd just as soon forget those days. We were all such patsies. We thought brotherhood was just around the corner."

Jean had counseled Jamal to keep the rhetoric low, and Diane Bonnet judged the evening "cool and efficient, compared to the debacle at Paton's." At one point, Redgrave interrupted the cocktail-party chatter and made a short speech about the Montessori school, assuring everyone that it was producing miraculous results. Dorothy Jamal says the affair netted very little cold cash, however. "The two rooms were packed with wealthy people," she remembers. "But I think we raised only fifteen hundred to two thousand dollars, which wasn't considered successful at all. Other organizations got a lot more from those very same people." (Jean later talked her Marshalltown friend Bill Fisher into anteing up $5,000.)

Although Jean was emotionally entangled with Jamal, the volatility of his views disturbed her and she realized that her political sympathies were shifting more and more to the Panthers. "Jean would say of Jamal that he was a romantic black Muslim who believed in the macho myth of guns but had very little political sense," says Dennis Berry. "She found the Panthers' positions much more understandable, and she especially believed in their right to self-defense. She had extraordinary esteem for Huey Newton until the end—yet, at the same time, she was in love with Jamal. There was always a romantic excitement about Jean when she talked of those days. She was trying to lead life in extremes then because that's what she thought living was all about."

By the spring of 1969, the ranks of the Panther leadership had been decimated, and control of the Los Angeles chapter had passed to Raymond "Masai" Hewitt, a deep-voiced intellectual of Marxist persuasion, sometimes identified as the political theorist of the party; and Elaine Brown, his girl friend and a part-time singer and composer whose steely strength and no-nonsense attitude would earn her the nickname "The Queen of the Panthers." Hewitt was tall, muscular and alert (the Panthers called him "Bright Eyes"), and the leanness of his body seemed to carry over into his thinking. Jean appreciated his reflective nature and his sharp, ironic appraisals of the times; Jamal, she felt, made up the rules as he went along.

Brown, who would take over the leadership of the entire party in 1974, is abrupt on the telephone. "I loved Jean. She was going through a lot of pain then, and no one helped her," she says in a clipped, edgy voice. "Now *I'm* going through a lot of pain, and I'm putting all that behind me."

For his part, Hewitt appreciated Jean, too. "She was 'good people.' She understood what the struggle was about, and she wanted to help."

One measure of Jean's involvement is revealed in a letter she sent eighteen months later to Charles Garry, the Panthers' attorney and a long-time defender of radical causes:

> Since the early part of 1969 (Elaine Brown, "G," B. Seale and others could remember date exactly) I have done what I felt I could to help the Black Panther Party for Self Defense. My efforts in militant areas or civil rights date from the age of 14 or 15 when I adhered to the Des Moines, Iowa, Chapter of the NAACP, and have inevitably progressed since then towards a deeper involvement in view of the tragedies occurring daily in our nation. I mention, and as normal, my paying for transport for the Free Breakfast Program, the paying of bail monies (to E. Brown or G. Glendoe) and hospital bills for the delivery of babies, as R. Masai Hewitt can confirm, and when I could, the offering of bed, food, and psychological peace to a besieged people. I have tried, in brief, in the past to be a friend and a good one.

Dorothy Jamal adds that "Jean was always renting cars for the Panthers, who generally tore them up." Jean also prevailed upon her friendship with director Costa-Gavras to procure a copy of *Z*, his acclaimed film about revolution in Greece, so that the Panthers could screen it at a benefit in San Francisco before it went into general release.

Her house in Coldwater Canyon became a regular stop for the Panthers, who made the rounds of Beverly Hills two or three times a week, often late at night. The Panthers generally traveled in groups, and while they were usually looking for nothing more consequential than food or drink, a donation to pay an overdue phone bill, or a signature on a document—what Don Freed calls "all the middle-class things they couldn't do easily"—their fierce demeanor and battle dress threw

Celia, Jean's maid, into a state of panic. She would start at the sound of the doorbell, and with mounting trepidation usher in the unexpected visitors.

From what Jean confided in him, Dennis Berry believes her allegiance to the Panthers went even deeper. "Jean was a woman for revolution. Not in any Marxist way, it wasn't that clear or definite," he says. "But she was for extreme stands that could change things. She was much more politically courageous than a lot of people were. The Panthers may want to reduce her involvement because, one, she's white, and two, she committed suicide, and say that she was just a Hollywood star who gave money. That's not true. She told me she helped organize meetings and made speeches at them. She was very close to several of the Panther women and wrote poetry with them. Some of them told her she should have been black. But she went further. I know that she bought and handled guns for them. She kept saying how important it was for them to have a means of self-defense. And she hid them when the police were after them. She took illegal positions, risking jail because of her beliefs. In a way, she has the same past that a terrorist does."

Jean concealed the turbulence in her life from most of her white friends. From the outside, it appeared that her movie career was in high gear. She had already lined up her next part, the lead in *Dead of Summer*, the second feature of a talented young Italian director, Nelo Risi. And although the cast of *Airport* was, in the opinion of one member of the crew, "phoning their parts in," shrewder observers were predicting that the film would be a blockbuster. One night, resplendent in a Mexican dress she had purchased in the Spanish quarter of Los Angeles, Jean turned up at a party that costume designer Edith Head threw for the *Airport* cast and eclipsed the other guests with her poise and distant beauty.

Actually, her life was seriously splintered, and the pieces didn't seem to fit. Jean was relying on liquor and tranquilizers to maintain her apparent composure and to quell the tensions.

"For a white person who wanted to help, there was a terrific gap to bridge," says Shirley Sutherland, who, like Jean, would be hounded by the FBI for her support of the Panthers. The police had purposely stepped up the number of arrests, while Hoover had thrown the FBI's Cointelpro into high gear. Just about any tactics were acceptable as long as they produced results. What the FBI wanted, and got, was a climate of discord and mistrust.

"Initially, all the money we raised went into the breakfast program," says Sutherland. "But the next thing you knew, someone had been arrested and the Panthers needed a little bail money. Just a small sum at first. Then in a couple of months, the whole thing escalated. The bail money got bigger with each arrest, and priorities were turned around one hundred and eighty degrees. It became a question of defense funds and lawyers and endless discussions about who shot whom. Somehow, the conversation never came back to the ten-point program.

"You found yourself tossed in and out of two worlds, and neither side seemed to know that much about the other. When you lent your car to someone, you weren't certain what you were opening yourself up to. Before long, you realized there were just one or two individuals you could trust. I never understood how paranoid I was until I left the country later on.

"But I think what got to you most then was the rage and the impotence. It's such a tiny distance from Beverly Hills to Watts—I drove back and forth I don't know how many times—but the two worlds didn't have anything at all to do with one another. You'd go to get someone out of prison, or you'd find yourself caught in a riot, or someone had just been shot on the street. And as you went back to Beverly Hills, you'd stop in a restaurant to regroup or just sort out your thoughts. And the restaurant resembled one of those movie sets where Susan Hayward comes through the door in a clean linen suit. Ten minutes away, it was like a war, and here people were asking one another if they wanted salt with their margaritas. The frustration! You just wanted someone to try to understand what was going on in that town—forget about Vietnam or any other place—and you felt like standing up and screaming.

"I'm sure there were times when Jean thought the only friends she had were Hakim and the Panthers. And I can understand that she probably thought she had more in common with them, and was closer to them, than anyone else. But the tragedy is, she wasn't. Because in the end, it was their organization and you were just supporting them. For fear of being Uncle Toms, the Panthers were not always terrifically understanding about whites making decisions. They rejected some real cooperation. You were there for the money. But it had to be that way. It was something you just had to accept."

Jean was not able to maintain that distance. She was swept up in the cause, and not only desired the security of belonging but expected certain emotional comforts from her commitment. "I was a sucker," she said many years later. "I would run to people with my arms open and my purse in my hand. They always took the purse. Never the arms."

Further complicating the situation, her relationship with Jamal was coming to light by May 1969. Just how is not clear. Hillard Hamm, the burly, large-toothed publisher of the *Metropolitan Gazette* in Compton, may have been one of the first to signal, in print at least, that Hakim was not sticking to the straight and narrow path he preached.

"Hakim was like a chameleon," Hamm says. "When you were alone with him, he could be the nicest guy in the world. But outside, with the other guys, he was a changed man. I thought he was raising a lot of hell on the Compton streets."

In the "Notes of Interest" column Hamm ran on the front page of his paper, he posed a loaded question: Which Black Power leader in Compton was talking black but sleeping white? Hamm claims that he got his information—that Jamal was living it up at night in Beverly Hills—from someone "high up in the L.A. Police Department," and that it created "quite a stir at the time."

A faulty sprinkler system in Hamm's storeroom destroyed most of the back issues of his paper, including the one in question. Unfortunately the *Metropolitan Gazette,* then a throw sheet distributed free from door to door, was not preserved in any library, either. But Hamm maintains that "my article sort of broke Jamal's back in Compton. He knew what I was talking about. He was living quite well, I'm told." Several of Jamal's acquaintances also cite the article as being instrumental in the dissolution of Jamal's marriage and of the Malcolm X Foundation.

Dorothy Jamal's suspicions were growing daily. "Hakim was spending less and less time at home. The kids were used to seeing their father at night, and they started asking questions. People would call me up and say they saw Hakim and some white woman in a floppy hat riding over on Crenshaw Boulevard."

She hired a private detective to trail her spouse and bluntly told Jean to leave Hakim alone. "Jean accused me of being a sick woman," she says. "She told me it wasn't that at all. That I was making it all up. I think that infuriated me more than anything else. After that, she wouldn't answer my calls, or she'd take the phone off the hook for hours."

Consequently, Dorothy telephoned the Chasin-Park-Citron Agency and presented her case to Wilt Melnick, who had replaced Chuck Belden as Jean's agent. Melnick told her there was nothing he could do. In mid-May, frustrated and angrier than ever, she called Ed Seberg. "I knew he had a drugstore in Marshalltown," she explains. "So I got his number from Information. I told him, 'I've got six kids and your daughter is breaking up my marriage. You have to have some influence over her. Make her stop.' It was a mistake on my part. He was her father. There was no way he was going to believe me."

An irate Dorothy Jamal called up many people that month. Some did believe her. "The troubles began when Sister Dorothy found out about Jean Seberg," Billy Pye admits. "Sister Dorothy was a real 'law' type, and the Malcolm X Foundation was supposed to be a family-type organization. We had a basic rule we were trying to follow. You know . . . the man-woman thing . . . not sleeping with whites. Jamal said he was sleeping with Jean Seberg to get money for the school. I understood him when he explained that you couldn't always tell people how you came by the money you got. Everybody had his own ideas, though."

When Dorothy called a meeting of the foundation and revealed her husband's activities, the news split the membership down the middle—some siding with the wronged wife, others sticking with Jamal. With his typical exaggeration, Jamal later said, "I had to pull a gun on my own men—Oscar, David, all of them! The organization broke up after that. It affected everybody terribly."

The Malcolm X Foundation barely lasted out the summer, although Dorothy Jamal would keep the Montessori school running until early 1970, when it, too, died for lack of funds. "I don't think Jean Seberg set out to destroy the organization," she says now in a flat tone of voice that has long since supplanted the old fury. "But she did. It was the only good thing that Compton ever had."

In late May of 1969, however, Dorothy Jamal continued to hound both Hakim and Jean in an attempt to put a stop to their affair. "One night Hakim told me he was going to quit the organization and just devote his time to fund raising. I knew what that meant. That meant he was going over to Jean Seberg's. Since she wouldn't take my phone calls, I drove over there myself and found his car, hidden in a dead end near her house. I knocked at the door, and Masai Hewitt answered. He was in his shorts and had a gun in his hand. Jean was standing behind him in a negligee. 'Oh, it's the mad lady, she's come to get me,' she screamed. I said, 'The mad lady only wants to talk to her husband.' Meanwhile, Hakim had disappeared out the back, jumped into his car and raced home before me. Masai kidded me about it later. 'Jean Seberg is so afraid of you,' he said. 'Every time she takes a drink, she sees you all over the place.' Masai was very much in the picture by June."

In the last year of her life Jean admitted to a reporter from the *International Herald Tribune* that she was having affairs with "two black nationalists" at that time, although she did not name them. Jamal was one. Hewitt, who, ironically, had been an early member of the Malcolm X Foundation before joining the Panthers, was the other. The FBI, which tapped telephone conversations between Jean and Masai, would quickly reach the same conclusion. But the FBI would put the information to work.

"What a way to go down in history," says Hewitt, who now works on a construction crew. "The black man who went to bed with a white woman!" He shakes his head and chuckles inwardly. Then he adds, "Who was sleeping with whom is not the real issue. The issue is, What was the FBI doing there in the first place?"

As much as the FBI was aroused by the Panthers' political

stance (Hoover would brand them the greatest threat to the internal security of the United States), it was equally outraged by the morality of party members, who openly and freely slept with one another. A kind of sexual indignation informed the bureau's views and lent the hot white heat of righteousness to its campaign.

Panther morality—more felt than formulated—rested on the fact that the Panthers truly considered themselves to be in a state of war against the police and the FBI. "When you attended fifty-two funerals in three years, it gave you a whole different outlook on things," says one member. "The Panther women understood this too. Because they felt the danger. They had seen children and wives gunned down by the police indiscriminately. So you lived every night as if it was going to be your last. Every woman you slept with was the last woman you were ever going to sleep with. Every affair was the last affair. No one thought about who belonged to who. The idea of jealousy was absurd. That was something the FBI never understood, never could understand. Because there really was a lot of love in that party. And it was never going to be destroyed from within."

Contact with the Panthers not only gave Jean a heightened sense of the moment, it added a certain piquancy to the sexual act. Despite her opulent life style, she consistently entertained romantic notions of herself as an outcast. Sex was one way of reinforcing her kinship with other outsiders; at the same time it repudiated the strict Sunday schooling of her past.

The FBI took another view: she was not merely a collaborator with the enemy; she was a wanton collaborator. The average white male agent in 1969 found that thought intolerable.

Early in June 1969 G. C. Moore, the FBI official in charge of extremist groups, recommended that "an active discreet investigation be instituted on American actress Jean Seberg who is providing funds and assistance to black extremists, including leaders in the Black Panther Party." The Immigration and Naturalization Service was instructed to search her luggage at customs, and her photograph and personal data were circulated to FBI field offices.

Jean's fears were becoming uncontrollable. She was caught

in an explosive racial climate, pursued by a jealous wife and targeted by the FBI as a Panther sympathizer. In her agitated state, it was all but impossible for her to separate fact from fiction. Jamal's propensity for high drama and the late-night Panther visits merely exacerbated her paranoia. Jean later described this period in a letter to Paton Price as "a long nightmare where you don't really know, and probably never will, where the truth is" and confessed that it was "hard to believe all that madness was happening to me."

The ominous signs multiplied. She received several phone calls threatening blackmail. She discovered a pistol planted conspicuously on a table in her house. One afternoon she returned home to discover that her cats had been poisoned. In *White Dog,* Gary alludes to some of these events and attributes them to the jealousy of "sisters" who resented the presence of a white movie star in a black movement. (But *White Dog,* while purporting to be a first-hand account of Jean's radical activities, is self-serving and factually unreliable.) There are other possible explanations. A former FBI agent whose disenchantment with Cointelpro caused him to quit the bureau says, "There's no doubt that the FBI bugged the hell out of her." Another observer points out that Jamal's own theatrics frequently veered out of control and recalls a meeting at which Jamal staged a shoot-out with blank cartridges and actually fell to the floor in mock agony.

For Shirley Sutherland, it was "Kafka time" in general, and it seems clear that Jean was trapped in that awful warp. Emotionally unstable, she clung desperately to her idealism, the very idealism that laid her open to exploitation. By her own admission, she was "in crack-up shape."

Just after nightfall on June 6 Jean bolted from her house, threw a few of her possessions into the back seat of her car and raced over the Hollywood hills to Paton Price's house in Studio City. Price opened the door to a Jean he had never seen before—breathless, disheveled, eyes wide with terror.

"They shot at me," she babbled. "Let me spend the night."

She thrust a package hastily wrapped in brown paper at Price's wife, Tilly, and said, "Please, Tilly, throw this away right now."

Tilly obeyed while Paton, at Jean's insistence, hid her car in a neighbor's garage. The Prices could make little sense of Jean's ramblings, but eventually they quieted her down. Tilly got a nightgown for her and put her to bed.

"I never pried into the lives of my students," Price says. "Both Tilly and I respected Jean a great deal. We figured she'd tell us what she wanted us to know. One thing was apparent that night. Jean fit badly into the world of intrigue and back-alley rendezvous. She was in a terrible mess."

The following morning Jean had regained some of her composure and assured the Prices, who had scheduled a trip to Northern California, that she would be all right on her own. They hesitated, but Jean insisted they stick to their plans.

On a table when they returned two days later was a note from Jean, thanking them for the refuge and saying that she had left for Rome to begin work on her new picture.

Later in the day, while Tilly Price was cleaning up the house, she went out to the trash. There was the package Jean had brought with her. Curious, Tilly unwrapped it. Inside was a man's shirt.

"It was pink," she says, "and it had great bloodstains on the collar and the cuffs." The Prices never learned who the shirt belonged to, nor how the stains had gotten there.

Not long after, FBI headquarters in Washington alerted Rome and Paris that "subject departed Los Angeles one P.M. June Nine last via TWA flight eight four zero for Rome, Italy. Seberg exchanged Los Angeles to Paris ticket for oneway ticket to Rome and is traveling under name Mrs. J. Gary. Subject reportedly will stay at the Excelsior Hotel in Rome."

25

Having fled from a situation in which she was no longer able to distinguish fact from fantasy, Jean was called upon in *Dead of Summer* (alternately titled *Heatwave*) to portray a woman prey to the wild imaginings of her unsettled mind. It was an all too appropriate assignment. The months in Los Angeles had shaken her profoundly, and her own thoughts were confused and perplexing.

In the third week of June 1969, she departed for Agadir, Morocco. The seaside city, leveled by an earthquake eight years earlier, was being rebuilt as a vacation resort, and the combination of desert scenery and the massive concrete constructions struck director Nelo Risi as an evocative setting for his strange film.

Dead of Summer chronicles twenty-four hours in the life of a schizophrenic woman (Jean) haunted by nightmares in which she has killed her husband, a boorish German architect. Escaping from their claustrophobic apartment one day, she wanders over the inhospitable terrain, tormented by the heat and the sand. A band of Arab urchins swarms over her sports car, and a sinister figure offers her a poisonous snake wrapped in a newspaper. She takes refuge in a clinic, where her unsettling visions recur. Returning exhausted to her apartment the following morning, she discovers the police examining her husband's corpse. True to her nightmares, she has been a real killer all along.

The cast and crew stayed at a luxurious Club Méditerranée facing the sea. But the heat, unbearable at times, sapped Jean's strength. On several occasions during the filming, she nearly fainted in the blistering sun. The local customs, for which she usually displayed such enthusiasm, could not distract her from the chaos of her personal life.

The Panthers were at least trying to stay in touch. One FBI memorandum notes the efforts of a Panther woman to place a call to Jean Seberg in Azazik, Morocco. When the international operator informed her that there was no such place, the puzzled Panther allowed as how maybe she had the wrong spelling and agreed to check it on a map.

Jean's health was deteriorating, and to her chagrin she discovered more cysts in her breasts. The hormonal treatments had proved ineffective. Three weeks into filming, she flew to Paris for a second operation. Her doctors still hesitated to link the growths to cancer, but they counseled her to keep a watchful eye on the problem.

Celia tended to her during the brief recuperation. Since Jean was in virtually every scene of *Dead of Summer,* her illness was a serious setback for the director, who was obliged to take his crew back to Rome.

Not yet fully recovered, Jean rejoined the film at the end of July and rented the elegant villa on the outskirts of Rome where, movie tradition had it, Richard Burton had first succumbed to Elizabeth Taylor's charms. There, Jean attempted to put together a semblance of family life. Diego arrived for a ten-day visit, and Ed and Dorothy Seberg came over for a vacation.

"Always at the back of my mind," Jean told columnist Roderick Mann, "is the romantic belief in the perfect relationship, in the ideal family life—mother at the piano, children round the fire—you know the sort of thing."

It was little more than a romantic fiction. The film prevented her from spending much time with her parents. The Sebergs were dismayed to find that Diego spoke practically no English.

They were not avid sightseers—their idea of fun was to stay at home, play dominoes, talk—and the splendors of Rome were a poor substitute for the family holiday they had envisioned. They fretted about their daughter's peace of mind.

Using a properly Italian comparison, Jean admitted that her emotions were all mixed up—"like minestrone." Divorce from Romain was difficult to accept, and occasionally she entertained notions of a reconciliation. "Right now," she told Mann, "I'm forcing myself to live in a kind of deep freeze. I run away if I see someone. It's worse than when I was eighteen. Perhaps I've just become overly cautious from having hurt and been hurt, and finally realizing that love is not some sort of a game . . . And yet I've got to start living again, I've got to make new friends."

With relief, she completed *Dead of Summer* on August 18. Of all the films she made in the latter half of her career, it was the one she preferred. Her physical beauty was at its apogee, not yet showing the ravages of pills and liquor. *Dead of Summer* would go on to win honors as the best film at the San Sebastian International Film Festival. (Curiously, though, while the film depended largely on her performance, the best actress award would be given to someone else.) It was not *Lilith,* of course, but the role allowed Jean to explore a schizophrenic mind and the madness that mesmerized her. In that sense, the film was prophetic.

Variety applauded *Dead of Summer* as "an art house murder mystery," but most American reviewers considered it arcane and obscure. "I don't know how she keeps finding her way into these imported fiascoes," scolded Rex Reed. "Must be rough these days for Americans in Paris." Which was an understatement.

Tired and depressed, Jean repaired to Majorca to recuperate alongside Romain and Diego from the accumulated months of anguish. Suddenly the marriage didn't seem so salvageable. "Romain has shown himself to be a true and good friend," she reflected. "So there's no animosity, only a little sadness as we have both come to realize that time and separation didn't arrange things between us in any way. I guess deep inside I still sort of hoped things would work out, but they haven't and won't, so it's best to clear the path and get the legalities out of the way and protect the affection that is left."

Paramount had scheduled its gala premiere of *Paint Your Wagon* for October 15 in New York City and expected Jean to attend. She was not excited about the prospect. Other obligations were harder to side-step, however, especially those she felt toward Bill Fisher, who had entered her name in the Preminger talent hunt thirteen years before. The Fisher family, determined cultural boosters, had given Marshalltown a new community center and theater, the Martha Ellen Tye Playhouse, named for Fisher's sister. The complex was to be dedicated the second week in September. As Marshalltown's most celebrated citizen, Jean felt duty-bound to appear. "I owe everything to Bill Fisher and Carol Hollingsworth," she conceded graciously at the black-tie opening. Nervously, Jean gave a short, halting reading from the stage, and the community players performed one of the sketches from Robert Anderson's comedy *You Know I Can't Hear You When the Water's Running.*

Fisher is charitable about her contribution. "Movie actresses are not at their best behind a podium," he remembers.

Obligations fulfilled, she retreated again to Majorca. She was in no mood to show up for the *Paint Your Wagon* festivities and pleaded ill health as an excuse. From what she had seen of the rushes, the hoopla surrounding the film far outstripped its merits, and she thought that too many opportunities for comedy had been passed over. Joshua Logan agrees. "It was an important film until everyone saw it," he remarks jovially.

Paint Your Wagon's hang-the-cost mentality grated on most critics. The love story that might have humanized the musical was lost in so much static, empty spectacle. The reviews granted Jean her extraordinary beauty, but little else. Pauline Kael put it better than most in *The New Yorker*: "Jean Seberg has become a pale, lovely, dimpled movie queen—a synthesis of Bibi Andersson and Stella Stevens, and with that worn, somewhat used look, like Ava Gardner's, which makes her more humanly beautiful than in her French films. But she's barely alive in a musical: she can't sing or dance; she can hardly move. Her eyes are as coolly blank toward Eastwood as toward everyone else. Why should we care if these two get together? They are so devoid of romance or passion they're like the unpeople at the end of *1984*."

Residents of Marshalltown didn't express it in those terms, but they wondered, whenever Jean's films came to town, what had become of the vivacity she had once brought to *Sabrina Fair*. "People here always knew she was so much more animated in life. They'd ask themselves what had happened," says one of Jean's hometown acquaintances. "It never seemed like Jean Seberg up on that screen!"

Jean would later blame the FBI for the slowdown of her career and the unaccountable delays her European films underwent in reaching the American market. *Paint Your Wagon* was just as good an explanation. Unlike her little flops, which passed unnoticed, *Paint Your Wagon* flopped big and dragged Jean down with it. Although *Airport* had yet to be released, it would in no way salvage her reputation. For all practical purposes Jean, at thirty-one, had reached the end of her career in the United States.

Her relationship with Jamal was also tapering off. In June of 1969, Dorothy Jamal had threatened her husband with a divorce suit. She says that "Hakim came running back, assuring me that Jean Seberg could never come between him and his family." Dorothy was not entirely convinced, especially when Jamal left the country in the fall on one of his vague missions, announcing his plans to write a book about his life.

"I continued to stay on Jean's back," Dorothy Jamal admits. "I wasn't going to let her off the hook that easily." Soon Romain entered the fray and fired off a sharp telegram ordering Dorothy to quit the harassment.

Eventually, Dorothy believes, "Jean just got fed up with all of Hakim's lies." The strong sexual attraction did not compensate for the irreconcilable political differences. Jamal seemed reckless to Jean.

"He [Hakim] is in many ways a fine person," Jean admitted in a conversation with Panther headquarters that was monitored by the FBI. "But he is hopeless. I mean he doesn't really relate to what the party is about." Jean also revealed in a subsequent conversation that Jamal had called her in the fall and dramatically announced his intention to marry her. "I just, you know, turned him off and tuned him out completely," she said. As a result she came to believe that her brusque refusal had "turned him back into his whole racist bag."

Although Jamal surfaced later in Jean's life, he was not about to carry a torch. Early in 1970 in London he met Gale Ann Benson, a twenty-five-year-old divorcée and the daughter of a former Member of Parliament. Aimless and depressed, she became Jamal's constant companion and busied herself, as Jean had once done, winning him converts and press coverage.

In the United States, the war between the Panthers and the police continued to escalate. From afar, Jean followed events with dread and disgust, attended meetings and tried to raise the ever needed bail money. She thought of herself as "the Panthers' honky representative in Europe." Even if the title was self-styled, the Panthers appreciated the money and gave her a code name—Arisa—to use whenever she called.

Jean's own financial future was less than secure. While she had been well paid in Hollywood, she had thrown her money about carelessly. Shifting trends in the movie industry did not augur well. The phenomenal success of *Easy Rider,* that low-budget saga of hippies on the road, had once again turned studio thinking inside out. The push was on for inexpensive, independently produced motion pictures. Barely on the screen, *Paint Your Wagon* looked like a relic from another world. For the next five years, actors would dominate films, and male-oriented plots would offer few opportunities for actresses. Jean read the signs and resigned herself to a dwindling income. She was still able to command $100,000 for appearing in *Macho Callahan* (largely because her contract had been negotiated before the release of *Paint Your Wagon*), which Bernard Kowalski would direct in Mexico. It was the last of her grand Hollywood salaries.

In that scruffy Western, she played the vengeful widow of a Confederate colonel who tracks down her husband's killer, Macho Callahan (David Janssen, then on a crest of popularity from the television series *The Fugitive*). They have a brutal showdown. Macho beats her up, rapes her and takes her prisoner—none of which prevents the poor woman from falling in love with him and sticking by him when the bounty hunters close in.

Jean tried to convince herself it was "a good woman's role." It wasn't. And for once her beauty would not save her. She looked bruised and worn in the part, her eyes often bloodshot. The fight with Macho Callahan left an unattractive gash on her cheek.

Arriving with Celia in Mexico City on December 2, 1969, Jean immediately went to work. Kowalski appreciated her willingness to spend long hours in the saddle and to shrug off difficulties with a quip. "We had a good relationship. She spoke fluent Spanish and made a point of getting along with the Mexican crew and her Mexican driver, who was pretty inept. At one point she contracted a strange disease that turned her gums and tongue totally black. She made a joke of it. She'd go around the set, asking 'Anybody want to kiss the lady with the black tongue?'" (The symptoms appear to have been linked to a deficiency of adrenal hormones; this may have accounted for the spells of listlessness Jean experienced later in life.)

Diane Ladd, who played a dance-hall hostess, was struck by Jean's many contradictions. "She was terribly sensitive, almost like a little girl. We shot in a village outside Mexico City one day, and they set up tables for the cast and crew to eat. These skinny dogs wandered over, and Jean started to feed them off her plate. Someone snapped that you didn't do that—not when there were people going hungry. Jean looked awfully hurt and didn't eat for two days after that. But she also had a worldly side and adored shocking people. She would tell me all the movie gossip—what producer had given the clap to what actress—and my mouth would fall open. She was certainly miles ahead of poor little me."

Shooting halted for Christmas. On an impulse, Jean and Celia caught a jet in Mexico City for Chicago, where they chartered a second plane, which was forced down by fog in Waterloo, Iowa. A taxi transported them the remaining sixty miles to Marshalltown. Pulling up at three o'clock on Christmas morning, Jean rapped at the door and sang out, "Is there any room at the inn?"

It was an exhausting trip, and the three-day stay scarcely gave them time to catch their breath. But for Jean, Marshalltown was one of the few reference points in a life that seemed to have lost its center.

Keeping watch, the Omaha office of the FBI noted that Jean established contact with Panther headquarters in Oakland over the holidays. (The following month she would respond to the Panthers' pleas of insolvency with a $2,500 contribution.) The Omaha agent's report included a clipping of the usual *Times-Republican* article, in which Jean innocuously talked about her career and expressed her desire to come home in the spring "for a longer visit and a bit of a rest." As a chilling footnote, the agent referred to her as "a sex pervert."

In mid-January 1970, *Macho Callahan* moved north from Mexico City to the province of Durango, which had the sort of rugged, mountainous scenery that corresponded to Hollywood's image of the Old West. Apart from several sprawling ranches, the economy depended on the Cerro del Mercado, a mile-long mountain of almost pure iron ore. The divisions between the wealthy few and the multitudinous poor were blatant, and the province seethed with unrest. Groups of striking workers camped at the mine entrance to block any shipments of ore. University students swelled the ranks. Businesses and shops closed down, and the city of Durango was rife with demonstrations and protests. On January 20, government troops had to be parachuted in to restore order.

Bernie Kowalski and producer Martin Schute recognized the need to maintain a diplomatic posture. Violence could scuttle filming, while the governor of the province could, if angered, entangle the project in endless red tape. The best tactic was to go about business calmly, irritating neither side.

Jean's sympathies lay, as usual, with the downtrodden. Drawing on her impressions, she later composed a heartfelt poem in French about Durango: the arrogant mansions of the rich, protected by high walls encrusted with shards of glass; the hovels where the poor huddled under the covers, drank mescal, and made babies. The poem concludes: "Almonds have eyes like these children,/And the children, the eyes of misery."

From all appearances, filming was progressing smoothly. One morning, however, co-star David Janssen approached Kowalski and said, "Look, Jean is making me just a little nervous. What she does with her life is her own affair. But I went by her house the other night, and it was filled with revolutionaries. She is putting them up, and she wanted me to take some of them at my place."

Shortly afterward Kowalski and Schute received a phone call from the Mexican Ministry of the Interior. "We were informed," says Kowalski, "that it had recently come to their attention that Miss Seberg was involved in rallies and meetings supporting the student revolutionaries, and that she had even donated some of her money—eleven thousand dollars was the figure I seem to recall—to their cause. If she continued, they said, they would be forced to deport her, shut down the picture and ask us all to leave." (Kowalski now believes that Jean's chauffeur was an informant for the Mexican government.)

Schute took Jean aside and explained the situation. "One knew that she was a left-winger and that you had to tread carefully with her," he says. "She surprised me by being very apologetic, embarrassed even. She was enough of a professional to know that a couple of million dollars were at stake. She agreed to stop right away."

"Jean was a very spirited lady—an adventuress in a way," says Kowalski. "I think the film brought that out in her. A funny thing happens when you do a Western or a period piece. Because the actors are wearing cowboy boots and riding horses, they begin to think they're really living the period they're filming. They go around drinking more than they should and being just a little rowdier. It was sort of like that with Jean. Her revolutionary activities seemed, well, a kind of child's play."

Actually, revolution was bound up in her mind with notions of romance. During her stay in Durango, Jean had an affair with one of the student revolutionaries. She delighted in introducing him surreptitiously one night to Kowalski as "El Gato," the man behind the student strikes, and Schute remembers her sneaking him into a cocktail party upon completion of the film.

He was tall and slender, with a dark mustache, and he spoke a Jamal-like rhetoric, directed in this instance against the capitalists who were plundering Durango's resources. Jean allowed herself to think, for a few weeks at least, that she was madly in love with him.

The student would probably have been nothing more than a passing fancy in her life—an on-location escapade quickly forgotten—if Jean had not realized, shortly after her return to Paris in early March, that she was pregnant.

26

This is to furnish information that subject, a beautiful, internationally known white American actress with black extremist relationships and sympathies, is reportedly a sex pervert.

—FBI IN-HOUSE MEMORANDUM

In a life already heavy with drama, the most agonizing and destructive remained to be played out. It revolved around the paternity of Jean's second child. Although she was in the throes of divorce proceedings in the spring of 1970, Jean was still officially Mrs. Romain Gary and shared the Rue du Bac apartment with the writer. Legally, if not biologically, the unborn infant was Romain's. Later he acknowledged Jean's pregnancy as the fruit of their reconciliation after she had returned in early March from filming in Durango.

In the final year of her life, however, Jean explained the situation to Jane Friedman, a reporter from the *International Herald Tribune*. The two met at the home of one of Jean's friends outside Paris. As Friedman wrote afterward: "She said she fell in love with Carlos Navarra, a Mexican 'revolutionary,' while shooting 'a bad movie named *Macho Callahan* in Durango.' Miss Seberg said Mr. Navarra was the father of the child she was expecting when she returned to Europe in mid-1970. 'I didn't want to abort,' she said. 'Romain said he would assume fatherhood.'"

Gary attributed the confession to her agitated mental state and claimed that by then Jean was saying anything outlandish that crossed her fevered imagination. Nonetheless, her admission seems to be supported by several telephone conversations Jean had with the Black Panthers in California in the course of 1970. (Transcripts of the conversations, wiretapped by the FBI, and in one instance, a tape itself, were made available by the bureau under the Freedom of Information Act.)

On April 21, 1970, the Panthers' Elaine Brown placed a long-distance collect call to Paris, waking Jean up at three-thirty in the morning.

"I'm sitting next to a friend of yours," Brown announced.

"Who's that? Johnny Appleseed?" asked a sleepy Jean.

"Yeah," Brown replied with a laugh. "Would you like to say hello?"

Masai Hewitt then came on the line, and he and Jean discussed Panther business. Before long, the conversation worked its way around to personal matters. Hewitt was startled to learn that Jean intended to have her baby.

"After not knowing and not knowing what to do about it, I'm going to go ahead, too," she told him.

"When?" he asked.

"In the fall. I'm like in the fourth month so I have a nice long wait ahead. I guess it's that year, you see."

"I guess it's all right," Hewitt replied.

"I guess, yes. I think it's all right . . . I'm happy about this, really . . ." Jean agreed. "I ran into a thing that scared me legally about my other son. I was afraid I was going to lose custody, you know, if my former husband got wind of it and got upset about it. And I talked to him about it and he was really very civilized and very nice about it. So it's really good, you know. So everybody you know sooner or later I guess is going to have a big tummy."

"I'm going to try not to have anything to do with it," Hewitt rejoined.

"Listen." Jean laughed coquettishly. "I'm afraid of you. You're a liar."

"I really didn't know."

"No, but I'm really happy. That's kind of the best surprise you could have. That's terrific. She told you what I call you, didn't she?"

"Yes, but I can't remember."

"Johnny Appleseed."

"No, she didn't tell me that."

"Yes, planting your little seeds around."

Hewitt's reputation was fairly well known among the Panthers. He had fathered a child by one of the Panther women and subsequently married another, Shirley Neely, who at that moment was carrying his child. It made for an admittedly awkward situation. All too neatly, the FBI could conclude that Jean, who had also been close to Hewitt during her last months in Los Angeles, was pregnant by him.

But the telephone banter was not what it seemed on the surface. Hewitt, in fact, had long thought himself sterile and told Jean so. The birth of one child and the prospect of a second had surprised him as much as anyone else. Jean's way of congratulating him was to call him Johnny Appleseed and to tease him for being "a liar." It was not a declaration that he had fathered her child.

Elaine Brown came back on the telephone, and Jean elaborated on what she had told Hewitt. "I'm going to go ahead with it."

"You aren't!" Brown exclaimed.

"I am."

"What made you make that decision?"

"Because I was really depressed about a million other things, so I talked to him one night, with Romain, you know, with my ex-husband, and I told him the truth, and he was really very civilized and very nice. He said it's ridiculous. If you want it, go ahead."

"So that's beautiful."

"Yes, it really was. I was surprised and really relieved," Jean said. "So, slowly but surely, I'm turning into a balloon."

"I know the feeling. Have you talked to the other one?"

"No, I have had no word. I've had mail, you know, but it's almost impossible, phone communications with him and everything. The last time he wrote he thought he was going to be put in prison, you know, in jail. But he wasn't sure. And that's the last thing that I've heard. So we have to be as, you know, very kind of cool about it, kind of relaxed."

What the FBI didn't pick up on—or chose pointedly to ignore—was the obvious time sequence. Jean was "in the fourth month" by April 21, which meant that the child's conception had occurred during her stay in Mexico. The "other one" she referred to in the conversation was a far more likely candidate for fatherhood. Two facts were reasonably easy to ascertain for anyone knowing Hewitt's whereabouts early in 1970, as the FBI did. Mexico was not part of his itinerary that year, and Jean was reporting daily to a movie set in Durango.

Nevertheless, the FBI perceived an opportunity to sow further dissension. Leaking the information—whether true or false—seemed guaranteed to cause the maximum damage to Jean, her career, Hewitt and the Panther cause. It would also scare away other celebrities disposed to supporting the party.

According to one former FBI agent who worked in Los Angeles at the time, the mood in the field office there was fanatical. Cointelpro was not the creation of an anonymous bureaucracy run amok but the calculated extension of what many agents considered a personal vendetta. "In the view of the bureau, Jean was giving aid. and comfort to the enemy, the BPP," he says. "The giving of her white body to a black man was an unbearable thought for many of the white agents. An agent whose name I will not mention, for obvious reasons, was overheard to say a few days after I arrived in Los Angeles from New York, 'I wonder how she'd like to gobble my dick while I shove my .38 up that black bastard's ass?' I later learned that the comment was in regard to Seberg. I was shocked at the licentious talk in the squad room area about the Panthers, Seberg and Jane Fonda. I was used to foul language after nearly twenty years in the FBI, but the conversation of these agents was grossly offensive."

Six days after the April 21 telephone conversation, Richard Wallace Held, son of the FBI associate director and the case agent in charge of Cointelpro activities against the Panthers, cabled FBI headquarters from Los Angeles with a proposal:

Bureau permission is requested to publicize the pregnancy of Jean Seberg, well-known white movie actress, by ____ [the name is deleted from documents supplied by the FBI, but independent sources confirm it is Raymond Masai Hewitt] by advising Holly-wood "Gossip-Columnists" in the Los Angeles area of the situa-tion. It is felt the possible publication of "Seberg's plight" could cause her embarrassment and serve to cheapen her image with the general public.

It is proposed that the following letter from a fictitious person be sent to local columnists:

> I was just thinking about you and remembered I still owe you a favor. So—I was in Paris last week and ran into Jean Seberg, who was heavy with baby. I thought she and Romaine [*sic*] had gotten together again, but she confided that the child belonged to ____ [position deleted] of the Black Panthers, one ____ [name deleted]. The dear girl is getting around!
>
> Anyway, I thought you might get a scoop on the others. Be good and I'll see you soon.
>
> Love,
Sol

> Usual precautions would be taken by the Los Angeles Division to preclude identification of the source of the letter if approval is granted.

Headquarters cabled back its agreement on May 6:

> Jean Seberg has been a financial supporter of the BPP and should be neutralized. Her current pregnancy by ____, while still married affords an opportunity for such effort. The plan sug-gested by Los Angeles appears to have merit except for the tim-ing since the sensitive source might be compromised if imple-mented prematurely.

The sensitive source was nothing more than its continuing wiretap of Panther headquarters. But to protect that source and

> to insure the success of your plan, Bureau feels it would be better to wait approximately two additional months until Seberg's preg-nancy would be obvious to everyone.

In the Los Angeles office at the time were special liaison agents responsible for clandestinely planting information with radio and television stations, newspapers and the movie studios. The FBI, which in 1979 conducted its own investigation of the smear campaign, maintains that the special agent in charge "has stated that he is as certain as possible" that the rumor was not passed along.

However, less than two weeks after Held's memorandum, a typewritten "tip" was passed to Joyce Haber, whose gossip column ran five times a week in the Los Angeles *Times* and was syndicated in almost a hundred newspapers. It read: "Informant sez Jean Seberg is four months pregnant by Ray Hewitt, know as 'Masai,' and identified as present Black Panther Minister of Education. Informant sez she has sed she plans to have the baby." A copy of the tip reveals that there was a note across the top: "Joyce, I don't know if you care, but this comes from a pretty good source." The note was signed "Bill Thomas," who was then the city editor of the *Times* and is now its editor.

Haber recognized the tip for what it was: a potential bombshell. But since it was sent to her by a highly placed colleague and seemed to carry his guarantee of legitimacy, she made only a few routine efforts to check its veracity. Still, she felt it wisest to protect herself by turning it into a blind item—one that omits names, all the while providing enough clues to make identification of the subject a foregone conclusion. It was the lead item in her column for Tuesday, May 19, which carried this headline: MISS A RATES AS EXPECTANT MOTHER.

> Let us call her Miss A, because she's the current "A" topic of chatter among the "ins" of international show-business circles. She is beautiful and she is blonde. Miss A came to Hollywood some years ago with the tantalizing flavor of a basket of fresh-picked berries. The critics picked at her acting debut, and in time, a handsome European picked her for his wife. After they married, Miss A lived in semi-retirement from the U.S. movie scene. But recently she burst forth as the star of a multimillion dollar musical.
>
> Meanwhile, the outgoing Miss A was pursuing a number of free-spirited causes, among them the black revolution. She lived what she believed which raised a few Establishment eyebrows: Not because her escorts were often blacks, but because they were black nationalists.

And now, according to all those really "in" international sources, Topic A is the baby Miss A is expecting, and its father. Papa's said to be a rather prominent Black Panther.

When the FBI scheme came to light years later, Haber (who was fired from the *Times* by Thomas in 1975) admitted her shock and horror but maintained, "The FBI did not plant me directly because I don't know anyone in the FBI. . . . That plant was given me by someone who is very reliable—a journalist. Good God, I never would have run it even blind! I think it is horrible. I liked Jean very much. She was a real human being, as so many people out here are not."

Haber's subsequent comment to *Time* magazine had an ominous ring, though. "I am beginning to wonder," she said, "who my best friends are." Since then she has steadfastly refused to name Thomas as her source, although her bitterness toward the *Times* remains acute. "I'll take my knocks from anyone I wrote about during those years or from any government agency," she says, puffing intensely on a Marlboro. "But what the *Times* did to me was the worst by far." What the *Times* did, she seems to suggest, was to let her take the rap single-handedly.

Thomas does not deny that he sent Haber the memo. "That's my handwriting," he says, relaxing in his spacious office. He's not sure who passed the rumor to him, however. "It probably came from someone on the police beat. I used to get fifteen or so tips like this a week—that's a rough guess. It sounded kind of cockamamie to me. I was not interested in it as a story at all. But it's the sort of stuff that, when it comes over your desk, you pass it along."

In 1976, *Times* reporter Narda Zacchino did an investigative series on Cointelpro dirty tricks. One of the rumors she attempted to track down—unsuccessfully—was the Seberg smear campaign. "When I heard that it started with an item in Joyce Haber's column, I was surprised," says Thomas. "Frankly, I could never decipher Joyce's column at all. My concern at the time was, 'Jesus Christ, did *we* run that item?' We tried to trace the memos then, but we never found anything." In response to the FBI's protests of innocence, however, Thomas suggests that with or without official sanction, it is entirely conceivable that the damaging information leaked out "in a casual conversation."

What is certain in the Byzantine affair, however, is that by 1970 the FBI considered Jean Seberg an important voice to be stilled. The same day Haber's column appeared, Hoover circulated reports on Jean's activities to John Ehrlichman, President Richard Nixon's White House assistant for domestic affairs; Attorney General John Mitchell; and Deputy Attorney General Richard Kleindienst. On June 8 the *Hollywood Reporter,* the trade newspaper of the motion picture and television industries, followed up on Haber's insinuations: "Friends wondering how long Jean Seberg will be able to keep that secret—or if she'll want to," it noted in its chatty "Coast to Coast" gossip column.

The dichotomies in Jean's personality had become more pronounced than ever. Depending on the circumstances in which they knew her, her friends seem to have been talking about different persons entirely. In the early stages of pregnancy at least, Jean appears to have luxuriated in her condition. When she was carrying Diego, she had been obliged to go into hiding. This time she was a mother-to-be for the world to see. She engaged in the usual speculations about the sex of the child (she hoped for a girl) and its personality (its size, she thought, indicated a certain independence). She tried out different names on her friends. "She'd come by the house a lot then," says Vony Becker. "We'd go shopping together and pick out baby clothes. She really was having a wonderful time. It was like she was playing the role of the pregnant woman. She loved the idea of being needed."

Jean and Romain's divorce came through on July 1, but she let it be known that they would probably remarry after the child's birth. Haber's article had greatly troubled her, and her doctors had warned that the pregnancy would be a difficult one. Jean was resolved to bring the child safely into the world.

There were other sides to her life as well. By letter and telephone, she remained in contact with the Panthers and tried to promote their cause and welfare in Paris. The party was undergoing a serious ideological split that summer. A militant faction had rallied around Eldridge Cleaver, the Panthers' Minister of Information until he had jumped bail in 1968 and fled with his wife to Algeria. From Algiers, Cleaver was advocating an increasingly revolutionary doctrine that eschewed cooperation with whites altogether and branded integration as pie-in-the-sky idealism. The objective, Cleaver felt, was to foment outright revolution in America.

The West Coast Panthers, under Seale and Newton, saw themselves working within the community, combining their resources with other groups that also were fighting for change. "Eldridge thought there was no way we'd win all the lawsuits. He wanted guerrilla units blowing away the motherfucking cops," scoffs Seale. The ideological rift often translated into violence, and there was mutual fear among the Panthers that one faction would try to eliminate the other. Europe was one of the battlegrounds.

Jean was only a tangential figure in the conflict, but she absorbed the fears as a blotter does water, and considered herself embroiled in the intrigue. Haber's article was proof to her that both her person and reputation were in jeopardy, although just where the next attack was coming from she was unsure.

That summer Jean hired a young Frenchman to be her bodyguard. He remembers going to meetings with her in Paris, at which Jane Fonda, Elisabeth Vailland (wife of the French author Roger Vailland) and a constantly changing cast of radicals were also present. The lives of Jean and of Jane Fonda, then married to Roger Vadim, presented some striking similarities: both spoke fluent French, acted in their husbands' movies and enjoyed a wide popular following abroad. Both had begun to support the Panthers actively at about the same time in Hollywood; both would also be targets of Cointelpro.

But although their paths often crossed, theirs was never a particularly close friendship. Privately, Jean found Fonda "too disorganized" in her political activism, and their approaches differed diametrically. Fonda took to the platform, made public declarations and generally worked in the spotlight. Jean remained in the background and shunned public actions and press conferences. Nor was it in her nature to strike back like Fonda. She was, more and more, influenced by Gary's belief that there was something false, not to say ludicrous, about a star proclaiming her solidarity with the masses. Sometimes Jean made a joke of it all. "I'm the Jane Fonda of the poor," she once told a friend.

There was another aspect of Jean's personality which flowered whenever she returned home: the unaffected small-town girl who rhapsodized over the joys of corn on the cob fresh from the fields, or a cold slice of watermelon consumed greedily on the back porch. It was not provincial blindness that prevented Marshalltown residents from perceiving in Jean her true depths and contradictions; it was simply that whenever Jean visited, she experienced a sentimental reawakening to the traditional values of the placid town.

She wanted Diego to know that kind of life, and on July 3 they boarded a jumbo jet from London for a Midwestern holiday. The stay began with the traditional Fourth of July celebration at the fairgrounds and concluded a week later with Dorothy Seberg's sixtieth birthday party.

Jean took her son swimming every day. He went for pony rides and tried his hand at miniature golf. Mary Ann came west from New Jersey with her two daughters, and the noise of their youthful games enlivened the tidy neighborhood. Jean informed her parents that she and Romain were reconciling. The prospect of an additional grandchild warmed them almost as much as the sight of Diego on a swing in the backyard. Ed Seberg delighted in sharing his favorite pastime with the sensitive boy: fishing from the banks of the Iowa River.

Even Jean's career was a matter of pride for the Sebergs. *Airport,* although critically lambasted, was the most popular box-office attraction in the nation the summer of 1970. As Jean informed the *Times-Republican,* Romain was busy writing a second script for her—an adventure film about the drug trade—which would be shot sometime after Christmas. That, too, seemed to confirm the reconciliation.

Dorothy Seberg redoubled her efforts in the kitchen, and Jean, already pleasantly round, joked that she would be a whale by the time she left. "It seems all we've done is eat," she laughed gaily.

Lynda Haupert dropped in for a visit and recalls Jean's mischievous good spirits. "I had on a pair of clogs and a mini-skirt—mini-skirts were in then. I was trim, my hair was up, and I looked the best I'd ever looked. Jean asked to try on my clogs. Then she said, 'Oh, heavens, Lynda, they really are much too big for me,' with this sly smile of hers. It was kind of a putdown, but not really. More this attitude Jean took to let you know that she was amused by you, but that she'd been there already. It was a look she gave me all her life—kind of ironic and mocking, loving and superior all at once."

From the outward signs, the Sebergs were enjoying a typical family reunion, as carefree and expansive as the summer skies that stretched out to little wisps of white clouds on the horizon. However, even Marshalltown would feel the impact of the drama that was brewing.

Jean and Diego returned to Europe on July 11. Four days after her departure the *Hollywood Reporter* carried another item in its "Rambling Reporter" column: "Hear a Black Panther's the pappy of a certain film queen's expected baby, but her estranged hubby's taking her back anyway." The sniping was getting closer.

Jean's fears, momentarily quelled in Marshalltown, surfaced again in France. She sometimes doubted that the Panthers' European friends were all that friendly. There was troubling talk of schemes to encourage black GIs to go AWOL and then smuggle them out of Germany. On several occasions Jean was asked to supply a van for that purpose. She continued to stick by the West Coast faction, sent them another contribution, and when told that Hoover intended to publish a list of well-heeled Panther contributors, blithely shrugged off the threat. Still, she felt on slippery ground and wondered if the machinations weren't getting out of hand.

Hewitt passed through Paris that summer on his way to Algeria for discussions with Eldridge Cleaver. During his brief layover at Orly Airport, Jean expressed some of her fears to him. Laughingly he replied, "Well, we're not in a popularity contest."

Her unsettled mental state was making a difficult pregnancy even more difficult. Diego had been delivered by Caesarean, and her doctors repeatedly told her that she would need all her strength for a similar operation. If she could make it successfully through the seventh month—mid-August—the child would stand a decent chance of surviving, but tranquillity was mandatory.

She tried to relax in Majorca but slowly sank into despondency instead. The reconciliation with Romain, she realized, was a reconciliation in name only, a legal nicety to protect her unborn child and Gary's reputation as a member of the French establishment. "Jean had a genuine desire to re-create things between them," says Dennis Berry, "but she sensed that this man was only interested in the public aspects of the relationship. She felt completely alone and estranged. They were sleeping in separate bedrooms. She couldn't understand why she was having him be the legal father of her child. It all got to be too much for her."

Late in the evening of August 7 Jean swallowed an overdose of sleeping pills, slipped out of the villa and headed in a daze for the beach. At the water's edge she slumped to the sand, unconscious. She was discovered by Celia, who, unable to sleep that night, had gone for a midnight stroll.

Jean was rushed in an ambulance to the Juaneda Clinic in Palma, and doctors hastily pumped out her stomach, barely saving her. Gary fended off the inquiries of the press. "Jean awoke yesterday complaining of stomach cramps," he said. "She took some tablets to ease the pain, but her condition became worse. She nearly died in the ambulance on the way to the hospital, but she is feeling much better now."

Jean was able to talk to the press several days later. Propping herself up in bed, she seemed to radiate contentment. "It is wonderful," she told a stringer for a British paper. "We (Romain and I) are completely reconciled—ironically, just when our divorce papers are coming through. During the last eleven months, things have changed, and we are back together and very happy."

Although doctors tried to reassure her that they had saved the unborn child, Jean was unable to banish either doubt or guilt from her mind. Romain persuaded her to go to Geneva, where the hospital care was more reliable and Hubert de

Watteville, one of Europe's finest obstetricians, would be near at hand if further complications arose. Mid-week, Jean was discharged from the Palma clinic. Shortly thereafter she flew to Geneva via Paris.

After consultations at the hospital, she went on to the Blauherd Garmi Hotel in Zermatt, the fashionable ski resort on the Italian border. She was under strict instructions to rest. Peaceful and remote, the village could be reached only by cable car. The air was bracing, and the nearby Matterhorn provided an impressive view.

Jean was joined there by her French bodyguard, and together they periodically translated Panther documents into French. Sometimes she would take out a large notebook and desultorily scribble away at a novel about Hollywood that she had tentatively named *Twinkly,* Panther jargon for a star who lent support to the cause. Her depressions would not abate. "The one thing I can never forgive Romain," says a friend, "is that he didn't go with her to Switzerland."

Meanwhile, news of Jean's hospitalization and her reconciliation with Romain had reached *Newsweek* in New York, which contacted Edward Behr, the magazine's Paris correspondent, for an update on the actress. It would go on the "Newsmakers" page, a chatty, generally light-hearted section about celebrity doings. Behr was unable to reach either Jean or Romain, but says that "A lot of Seberg rumors were floating around then. So I made a couple of phone calls." One, he claims, was to Pierre Lazareff, the publisher of *France-Soir* and *Elle.* The other was to a source he identifies only as "a close friend of Jean and François Moreuil."

Sitting down at the typewriter on August 13, Behr dashed off a brief piece and cabled it to New York. His entire report:

> Jean Seberg has recovered sufficiently from her pregnancy complications to leave the Majorca Clinic where she was undergoing treatment. She was unavailable for comment and Gary is in Africa working on aye [a] reporting series for *France-Soir.* Close friends feel that she and Romain Gary will remarry in the near future and all concur that they have seldom been closer than in the last few months, sharing their Ile de la Cité [*sic*] apartment and attending parties with friends as man and wife. Gary expects to direct Jean Seberg in aye movie called *Total Danger,* which he has been work-

ing on, as soon as she is able to work again. (It's about drug trafficking.)

Strictly FYI, the child Jean Seberg is expecting is not by Gary but by aye black California activist who figured prominently in her life at one stage, and whose name eye [I] haven't been able to discover. Also FYI, one of the reasons they might remarry is that Gary, with considerable chivalry, wants to do everything he can to protect Jean's child from possible discrimination and psychological trauma arousing out of this situation.

Regards,
Behr

Behr says that "no malice was intended. It was meant to be an upbeat item. And the rumors were definitely not for publication. It's one of those things you put into a report to show that you know more than you've written. I learned my lesson, in that respect."

Usually Kermit Lansner, the editor of *Newsweek,* personally checked over the entire contents of his magazine before sending it to the press. At four o'clock on August 14, according to one account, the editor stepped out of his office briefly to test a new motor scooter he had recently purchased. It was, he hoped, an answer to the agonies of New York traffic and the hours he wasted in the chauffeur-driven limousine that *Newsweek* routinely put at his disposal. On a test ride down Madison Avenue, the scooter skidded out from under him and he twisted his knee. Lansner telephoned his secretary that he would not be back in the office that day. The final editing of the "Newsmakers" items fell to less conscientious hands, and through a series of apparent slip-ups, the rumors that Behr had filed off the record found their way into print.

Consequently, *Newsweek*'s August 24 issue, on the newsstands August 17, asked its six million readers:

Can a small-town girl from Iowa find happiness in Paris? It seems so, despite the ups and downs of her marriage. "It's wonderful," smiled movie actress Jean Seberg, 31, when reporters looked in on her in a hospital in Majorca, where she was recuperating from complications in her pregnancy. "We are completely reconciled—ironically just when our divorce papers are finally coming through." She and French author Romain Gary, 56, are reportedly about to remarry even though the baby Jean expects in October is by another man—a black activist she met in California.

Jean was stunned when she read the article two days later in Zermatt. All the earlier reports had coyly beaten around the bush. *Newsweek* had actually named her and at the same time offered specific details about the father of her child. Indignant, Romain called her that same day to inform her that they would bring a massive lawsuit against *Newsweek*. Jean immediately alerted her parents by cablegram: "Please don't be upset by Newsweek item issue Aug. 24, page 31. We are preparing huge slander lawsuit and will win. My New York lawyer will call you to reassure you."

The Sebergs, who had been out of town when the story broke, were flabbergasted by the situation. In addition, the Des Moines *Register* had reprinted *Newsweek*'s allegation, and the gossip in Marshalltown was building to a crescendo. The Sebergs had always been leery of publicity, and this report was as unfathomable to them as it was humiliating. Ed Seberg groped for an explanation. "Jean tried to help a black activist group in California last summer," he told the *Times-Republican.* "But when she found out they were trying to use her, she dropped them, and now they're trying to get back at her and hurt her." In his mind, apparently, it was all linked up with Hakim Jamal, his wife, Dorothy, and the Montessori school.

Later the same day, August 19, using her code name Arisa, Jean talked twice with the Panthers in California. She wanted Hewitt and the others to know about the *Newsweek* article and the lawsuit she and Romain intended to initiate. Both conversations were monitored by the FBI. The first was with a Panther woman, and the transcript reads in part:

ARISA: Now first of all, my baby is due in late October and I can prove through a movie studio and through the press that nine months earlier in February I was reporting every day to a set to do a picture in Mexico.
—Right on.
ARISA: Secondly, they do not even say there are rumors that she is expecting a baby by another man, a black activist. They say it as a fact.
—Right on.

ARISA: I have given instructions to a very prominent Establishment liberal lawyer in New York to begin an extremely heavy and extensive and costly lawsuit for this defamation and intrusion in personal affairs, all the shit you can imagine.

—Uh huh.

ARISA: There is a very good chance of making a lot of money if I am lucky enough to get this baby into this world, because I've been having trouble, you know?

—I understand.

ARISA: Yeah, so the initial thing is, of course, right now, is my health and to get through all this shit.

—Right on.

ARISA: Now, the second thing I want him to know about and I want him to also know that you know and he knows [is] that if there is a lot of money coming out of these [this], you know where a great part of it will go.

Jamal also figured in the conversation. Jean had heard that he was writing a book, purportedly titled *A Sugar Coated Bullet.* In it, she was given to understand, he was planning to malign certain white actresses who had participated in the Black Power movement. If the rumor was true, the book couldn't come at a worse time—just when she was undertaking a lawsuit against *Newsweek.*

Jamal had never entirely forgiven Jean for switching her allegiance to the Panthers. Nor could he forgive the Panthers for eclipsing him. After all, the Malcolm X Foundation was dead, while the Panthers were seemingly in the vanguard of the black revolution.

Although he never actually wrote *A Sugar Coated Bullet*— some suspect it may have been an idle threat on his part—he did bring out the following year a benign biography, *From the Dead Level,* in which he recounted his life and spiritual adventures with Malcolm X. Dorothy Jamal dismisses that book as "exaggerated." Nonetheless, that August, Jean legitimately believed that Jamal was bent on personal revenge.

As the FBI transcript shows, she was demoralized, her energy was ebbing and she feared for the child.

ARISA: Well, it's a very bad situation because a week ago I was in a clinic and, you know, with a lot of glucose and transfusions.

—Right.

ARISA: And if I get through the end of this month then the child will be over seven months and he can possibly live.

—Right on.

ARISA: But I've been in a bad situation.

—OK.

ARISA: And it's been a very lonely one because I've been through it, you know, really like completely alone.

—I understand.

ARISA: . . . I'm really just a mess, and I'm on my back most of the time.

Still, she volunteered her help if any Panthers were planning to come to Europe and offered to send some "little baby things" to Shirley Hewitt, who was expecting to give birth any day. With *Newsweek* attacking her from one side and "the situation of the cultural nationalist writing this book, which came like a knife in the stomach," her mind was reeling. Arisa/Jean Seberg concluded, "It's a very cold world."

Hewitt called her back shortly afterward. Jean reiterated her fears about Jamal's book and assured him, "I'll go to war on it. I mean it. I mean I'll go to war on it on any level, legal or otherwise." Although she made no further mention of *Newsweek,* she told him that Gary had just come out with a book (*White Dog*) that was "quite frank about my involvement, you know, on a certain level." She was also worried about a letter, critical of the party, which she had recently mailed to Hewitt. "It's a criticism I felt had to be made, you know, even [though] I'm not in the party or anything." In the wrong hands, it could be used against her.

What runs through the conversation—above and beyond the particular worries of the moment—is the ache of a woman trying to keep from drowning in feelings of abandonment.

ARISA: I need moral support right now. This is like getting hit over the head with a hammer.

HEWITT: Shine it on. It ain't nothin'.

Seconds later she repeated the plea: "I'm in a very low moral situation." Comfort was not forthcoming. Instead Jean ended up promising her continuing support, pitiful as it was in her disturbed state. More than ever, it seems, she just wanted to belong.

Precisely what happened over the next thirty-six hours is difficult to ascertain. Even Jean's closest friends don't know for sure. In her feverish and depressed state, it appears she became convinced that her bodyguard was a traitor, part of the nebulous conspiracy aimed at eliminating Huey Newton if he ever set foot on European soil. Jean would tell people how the bodyguard amused himself by running a switchblade lightly over her stomach until she had to beg him to stop. Then, minutes later, he would start the torture all over again. Gripped by a fear of betrayal, she began to think that there was a plan afoot to link her with Angela Davis, who, only weeks before, had been placed on the FBI's Most Wanted list for allegedly smuggling guns into a California courtroom.

In later years the stories grew in magnitude, and Jean would describe her stay in Switzerland in even more surrealistic terms. She would tell how she had been detained by force and put to sleep, only to awaken with minute transistors implanted in her ears. "That way," she explained desperately, "they could capture anything anyone said to me, even if you whispered. It really happened! I didn't know how to get away. I had only one defense—to make people believe I wasn't Jean Seberg but her double for the next film."

Jean provided only a slightly more clearheaded appraisal of events in a letter she wrote several months later to the Panthers' lawyer, Charles Garry, in which she informed him she would be withdrawing her support from the party.

> I do not trust the friends of the Panthers or in fact, the sincerity of very, very few Panthers themselves . . . My reasons for this conviction are multiple, but one is that four times—twice by phone to my residence at Pt. Andraitx, Majorca, and once from California, I believe, plus once in a Geneva hotel—a certain either neurotic or malevolent Frenchman, his Panther girlfriend, and a member of the Panther hierarchy tried to link me with Miss Angela Davis. During the conversation in the Geneva hotel, the gentleman had a tape machine running which I noticed (a small cassette machine on which he had supposedly a friendly message from the Panther "sister"). I am not necessarily implicating people, but I

251

am stating certain facts. I have never met, known, seen, or spoken with Angela Davis, although I do know she received in July my Paris phone number via Masai Hewitt and may have tried to reach me while I was in Majorca. The point is, all of these conversations occurred approximately at the time of, or just after, the FBI announced their search and put her on the wanted list. I find it, to say the least, a wee bit strange. I will not, ever, even as a friend, deal with unreliable or neurotic people or those I suspect are snakes or cowards. And there may possibly be a word far graver than any of these and with more tragic consequences. I feel enough people have died—good people—and I will have no part of such games. There are many other reasons, but no need to go into more detail. I believed, I tried, I helped humanly when I could. I beg our mutual friends to take care of themselves, their brothers, sisters and children, as the divisions in this country become each day wider.

The actual plots and counterplots that gave rise to Jean's paranoia have been obscured by time and faulty memory. In the curious dual attitude she later adopted, Jean would refer to them as both "childlike and child-killing." On August 20, 1970, however, she was in a highly agitated state. She had slept little. She felt rejected, with no one to turn to.

Then the contractions began.

That evening a helicopter flew her to the Cantonal Hospital in Geneva. Immediately, doctors injected powerful sedatives into her veins in an attempt to render the uterus dormant and prevent the child from being born. The stories she babbled in her drugged state made little sense to the hospital staff. On August 23 she wrote a letter to Paton Price, telling him that

I am fighting like a lioness to save the child I am expecting who, as you probably already know from bullshit lies in newspapers and specifically the last *Newsweek,* is a cause célèbre for racist America before even being born. I am in the hands of the best obstetrician in Europe and if anyone can save this situation and this innocent creature who already seems to be a revolutionary and is a little too anxious to get out into this insane world and try to help change it, then it is this doctor. Paton, I have to make this short, for the second goddam day I am being taken up to the delivery room for special intravenous liquid they try to give to stop the contractions . . . Screw the money you owe me, Paton. Use it for whatever you need it for, keep building strong and loving young men and women. Please help them know that every single person can change things a lot. You'll hear from me later.

She did not have time to mail the letter. That day Jean Seberg gave birth by Caesarean to a girl weighing less than four pounds. Doctors immediately put her in an incubator and gave her less than a 20 percent chance of survival. For two days, the infant clung to life. She died early in the morning of August 25. Witnesses reported that the child was light-skinned and appeared to have Caucasian features.

The horrors did not stop there, however. Shortly after Jean had been wheeled from the delivery room, several of her Panther friends appeared at her bedside, and from what she later said, tried to take her credit cards, her money, her typewriter and the keys to her car. One of them had a gun. "He showed it to me and said, 'Here, Jean, look. This is the best gun in Europe,'" she recounted. "I took it and turned it over in my hands. Stupidly. Without thinking. My fingerprints were on it. He could kill anyone with that gun and furnish proof against me."

Sedated as she was, Jean was in no position to sort out the truth. According to one friend, "the hospital officials thought she was crazy. It was an absolute nightmare for her." Jean was persuaded that infiltrators were everywhere. From her hospital room she frantically telephoned a Panther sympathizer in New Haven to warn her that "your friends in Europe are not your friends" and to urge Newton to take every precaution in traveling abroad.

Across the top of the unmailed letter to Paton Price, she scribbled hastily: "2 days later. My baby is dead. Tell David Dellinger to warn Huey Newton that the pigs control entirely the European Panther contacts. I am of no utility to the party at present." She mailed the letter this time—not to Price himself but to Eliot Daniel, her vocal coach on *Paint Your Wagon,* with instructions to deliver it to Price personally. It was just one of six letters she wrote in her desperation and sent by circuitous routes to the United States, hoping to get a message through.

Director Jean Becker also received an urgent phone call from Jean, who told him the Panthers were mistreating her. She needed his protection and begged him to come quickly. Anticipating a fight, Becker took a friend with him when he flew to Jean's side. But Gary, who had got there earlier, had cleared Jean's hospital room of all dubious visitors, had had the phone disconnected and had stationed guards outside her door. By the time Becker arrived, there was nothing to see (if there ever had been) other than a pack of journalists waiting for a follow-up story on Jean Seberg's deceased child. Becker wondered what had happened. He knew from experience that Jean had a tendency to magnify the events in her life, and he asked himself "if Jean and Romain weren't already imagining some wild drama of their own."

Dennis Berry heard the stories often during his marriage to Jean. Although he, too, is not sure of exactly what happened, he has no doubts "that there were black Panthers at her bedside, and a blond bodyguard who made her touch this gun repeatedly. I knew when Jean was telling the truth and when she was delirious. In this instance, I believed her. Something traumatic happened to her in that hospital room."

Although her baby had lived barely two days, Jean gave her a name that was, in essence, an identity—Nina Hart Gary. Nina, after Gary's resilient and courageous mother. Hart, after John Hart, her distant ancestor who was one of the signers of the Declaration of Independence. In her mind, the child was the victim of scurrilous rumors and a sick, racist society.

Gary shared her outrage and wanted the world as a witness to the child's death. In Geneva, he took up his pen and wrote a fierce indictment of *Newsweek,* which he titled "The Big Knife." It was a passionate *J'accuse,* published in the August 28 edition of *France-Soir.* "There was a time when the mother and child were sacred," it began. "Men owed them aid and protection. . . . No more. This is the time of the cutthroats." He related the gossip that had appeared in the press and speculated on its base motives:

Since the age of 14, this daughter of the Middle West has supported the right to dignity of blacks of her country. Therefore, it was necessary at all costs to explain her horror of racism by sexual penchants. It was necessary at all costs to prove that a white woman who still believes in the American dream of justice and fraternity, the dream of Jefferson and Lincoln, was actually interested in blacks because they are, in the minds of the crazed racists, the tempting symbols of the forbidden fruit.

In no uncertain terms, he laid the blame for Jean's miscarriage at *Newsweek*'s doorstep:

> Several hours after reading this infamy, Jean had to be transported by helicopter to the Cantonal Hospital in Geneva, where she has just given birth, 63 days prematurely, to a little girl who, at the moment I am writing this, is struggling against death with all of her 1,700 grams of white flesh. This little spark of life is mine by all the laws of France. But *Newsweek* cares little for the laws of our country. This publication operates according to more convenient laws—those which, for 50 years, have assured the prosperity of the Mafia. . . .
>
> It is three o'clock in the morning. We will have to wait, wait, wait, before knowing whether this attempt at slaughter in the Manson style . . . will be rewarded with success. But already a Dante-esque carnival of legal doctors, witnesses, and lawyers swirl about this little being, trembling in its incubator . . .

There was a dramatic postscript: "August 25, six o'clock in the morning. The doctor has just come in. The child is dead."

While most of Jean's friends shared Gary's indignation, some questioned the wisdom of his article. Jean needed quiet solace. The drama in her life had exploded out of control, and they saw Gary's prose as kerosene on the flames. In a way, his literary reputation as a pugnacious idealist demanded that he go to battle yet again. "There is a lot of the self-appointed savior in Romain," comments one acquaintance. "He has an important public life. He likes scandalous actions, but only when they are well orchestrated and well presented. Jean's scandals were messy and uncontrollable. He wanted to tidy them up."

It was also important for Gary to state in print that the child had been born sixty-three days prematurely, which would have placed conception in early March—after Jean's return from Mexico—not in mid-January, as she herself claimed. Gary was attending to details that could prove embarrassing.

At the beginning of September, the writer returned to Paris to occupy himelf with the legal aftermath of Nina's death. Grief-stricken, Jean remained in the hospital several more days. Although she and Gary had a public scapegoat in *Newsweek,* Jean would wonder until the end of her life just what role the sleeping pills had played in her child's death. The thought would cause her ineffable guilt.

Among the many friends she had summoned to her side was Guy-Pierre Geneuil, a bushy-mustached gypsy from Montmartre whom she had known casually since *Breathless* days. Guy-Pierre had a hearty, ribald sense of humor that refused to give in to her depressions. A veteran of the French-Indochina War, he was also stockily built and quick with his fists. Jean hired him to be her new bodyguard. For the next few months he would not leave her side, and slept either in the same room or in an adjoining room with the door open.

Upon Jean's release from the hospital, Geneuil accompanied her to a Geneva mortuary where Nina was embalmed; a photographer took pictures of the child, and some of them turned out to be of Jean holding the infant in her arms. Then Jean went by a limousine equipped with dark curtains to Lausanne, where she would recuperate from the ordeal. To ensure her anonymity, Guy-Pierre had bought her a long blond wig and dark glasses. Jean checked into the Beau Rivage Hotel under the name of Madame Médard. The staff was under strict instructions to keep her real identity secret.

Diego and Eugenia came for a short visit, but Jean stayed mainly in her room. Because of her Caesarean, walking was painful, but Guy-Pierre says she was also fearful of the outside world and saw assailants lurking everywhere. After a few days she had recovered sufficiently to take her meals on the flowery terrace overlooking Lake Geneva. As her strength came back, a singular, burning need possessed her. She would bury Nina Hart Gary in Marshalltown.

27

"I suffered from gossip in the press—a nasty rumor circulated about me. It was a terrible shock for me during a precarious pregnancy. The wound is still there. It's a difficult thing to forgive."

—JEAN SEBERG

Gary's indictment of *Newsweek* stirred up a flurry of articles, as expected. Publicly at least, *Newsweek* stuck by its scoop. Most of the French press rallied to Jean's defense, although in its gallantry it seemed incapable of avoiding either bathos or sensationalism.

JEAN SEBERG WEEPS FOR HER BABY, KILLED BY HATRED, screamed a typical headline. "IT WAS MY DAUGHTER," SAYS ROMAIN GARY, shouted another. *Minute,* a notorious right-wing weekly, took another tack. It its issue of September 3, 1970, it announced: THE SHADY ACCIDENT OF JEAN SEBERG; IS A BLACK PANTHER THE FATHER OF HER CHILD?

The *Minute* article was a sorry regurgitation of misinformation and errors that tried to go *Newsweek* one better. The real father of the child, the publication insinuated, was Hakim Jamal. After presenting its muddled evidence, it then concluded: "The most confusing thing of all is why the young actress of *Breathless,* having embraced the cause of the black militants, would be floored by the deductions that have been drawn from her actions."

That question was on other minds as well. From the start of

her career, Jean had had to endure the drubbings of the press. Why should the latest round, scurrilous as it was, have so completely annihilated her? "At the time," says Edward Behr, "it seemed like such an overwhelming reaction, considering that it came from one who had professed a highly developed sense of racial consciousness and whose private life was fairly well known. I was rather appalled by the enormity of the aftermath."

"I wondered about it for a long time," says Raymonde Waintraub. "Jean talked so much about those stories. What did it matter if they'd accused her of having a black baby? I finally figured it out. It was simply because it wasn't true. It was an outright lie. And the truth was very important to her. If it had been a black baby, Jean would have admitted it. I have no doubts about that. She was traumatized by the falsehood."

"Jean really was one of those rare people," explains another friend, "who were raised to be good, and who thought that if you were, the world would be good in return. It seems inconceivable in the light of her experience. And yet that's the way she was until the end of her life."

More than any other place, Marshalltown symbolized that ethic to her, even though the town was often spiteful and cruel and probably no better or worse than any other place where human beings gather to live and suffer. In Jean's mind, however, taking Nina home had become more than a duty. It was a necessary reaffirmation, however macabre.

The second week in September, her nerves shattered, the frightened actress boarded a Swiss Air 707 in Zurich for the harrowing pilgrimage. Guy-Pierre Geneuil, her omnipresent bodyguard, tried to reassure her that she was safe and that all her assailants had fled. Jean would not be placated. Several days before, extremist members of the Popular Front for the Liberation of Palestine had hijacked three European planes bound for the United States, diverted one of them to Cairo and the other two to a "revolution airstrip" in Jordan. Now the hijackers were threatening to blow them up—passengers and all. For Jean, it was just another sign that menace lurked everywhere.

To steady herself before the flight, she downed several

Valiums with whiskey. Once she and Guy-Pierre had settled into their first-class seats, she took several more and encouraged him to do the same. As the plane soared over Europe on its way west, she drifted in and out of a fretful sleep. Mid-flight, she roused herself and told her bodyguard that she was going to wash her hands.

"Minutes later," Guy-Pierre recalls, "Jean burst out of the lavatory, completely nude, trailing the bandages from her operation. She was screaming that the plane was being hijacked. 'They're after me! They're trying to kill me! You must turn the plane back!'"

Fear rippled through the first-class cabin. Then the passengers realized what was happening. Embarrassed, they averted their gaze from the raving actress and tried to pretend that nothing was amiss. Guy-Pierre struggled to get Jean dressed and back into her seat. Eventually she calmed down, but for the rest of the flight she continued to toss back the tranquilizers. By the time the plane landed in Chicago she was in a stupor, barely able to stand up. O'Hare Airport, the world's busiest, was noisy with travelers jostling one another as they rushed along the seemingly endless passageways. Guy-Pierre had to put Jean in a baggage cart and push her through the throng so they could make their connecting flight. "There were cops throughout the terminal," he remembers. "Jean came to all of a sudden and spotted one who was black. 'Traitor!' she yelled at him. 'You're black. How can you be a cop?' Then she started flailing out at him, as if she wanted to get his gun. It was a terrible scene. Pretty soon some other cops came over and threatened to arrest her. I had to push her into the Lufthansa lounge to quiet her down."

At the Des Moines airport Dorothy and Ed Seberg were confronted with their bedraggled daughter and a bodyguard who spoke hardly a word of English. The anxious parents drove them quickly back to Marshalltown and put Jean to bed in their own room. Guy-Pierre was given the spare bedroom. Ed Seberg set up a cot in the basement for himself. "They were very hospitable people," says Guy-Pierre, "and they treated Jean like a princess. But I don't think they ever knew what was really going on."

Jean regained some of her composure in the following days, although the fear that she would be killed was seared in her mind and would, in fact, stay with her until the end of her life. One of her first acts at home was to withdraw officially from the Panthers, which she did in a rambling letter dated September 11 and addressed to Charles Garry. After enumerating her reasons—her mistrust of all but a few of the Panthers; the presence of infiltrators in the ranks; the prospect of a controversial trial ahead—she could not help herself from concluding the letter with a desperate plea. "It may come too late," she wrote. "I do not know precisely the friendship any Panther members may or may not have with Arab leaders. I presume, without knowing, that they surely know some of them. I beg them if they can to intervene for the safety of the perfectly non-involved people aboard the captured planes now held by a Palestinian revolutionary movement. Please consider this. Perhaps through a simple personal contact on a human level, one of you can save these people."

She then wrote to the Reverend Jesse Jackson, the charismatic black minister who was attracting widespread attention for his work with the Southern Christian Leadership Conference. She informed him of her upcoming action against *Newsweek* and pledged half of any libel settlement to the SCLC "to be used as you and Rev. [Andrew] Young see fit."

Part of this money, she hoped, would "go to Cesar Chavez, to certain Puerto Rican areas, to the group of American Indians which you feel are most concerned about the welfare of their people, and to Huey P. Newton or his lawyer Charles Garry to care for the orphaned and oppressed, including families of black militants."

In the event that the settlement was significant, she requested Jackson "to please ask your friend Harry Belafonte, a friend of long ago of JS, to apply them in the areas he chooses and this includes the Caribbean and the Appalachian poor."

It was a tall order. "Jean was always trying to do it all by herself—save the world," says Harry Druker, shaking his head.

Jean passed hours on the telephone, consulting with lawyers and pouring out her sorrow to friends. Late one night, after she had been drinking, she placed a long-distance call to Joyce Haber, whom she held personally accountable for Nina's death. "This is Jean Seberg. How are your children?" Jean asked when Haber picked up the phone. She then proceeded to berate the columnist for printing a vicious lie. "How does it feel to be a murderer? I don't know who your sources are, but they are wrong. Better watch out, lady! You goofed!"

The one-way conversation rambled on for several minutes before Jean concluded ominously, "You're going to get something in the mail soon—a fetus!"

Haber, whose position on the powerful Los Angeles *Times* had earned her a fair share of enemies, was inclined to dismiss the call as that of a crank. "I used to get all sorts of weird calls, but that was one of the weirdest," she says. Among friends, however, Jean proudly owned up to the act. It was, she explained, the least she could do for Nina Hart Gary.

The child's body arrived in Marshalltown on Wednesday, September 16, in an oak casket lined with lead, and was taken to the red-brick Avey Funeral home, two blocks from the courthouse square. "Jean was sure there was a bomb in the casket, and the mortician was afraid to open it. So I did," says Guy-Pierre, who later told the French press he believed that the child was of Mexican-Indian parentage.

The open casket, with its tiny body, was put on display on Thursday and Friday, until the afternoon burial service. Friends and neighbors were invited to call at the funeral home. Jean hired a photographer from the *Times-Republican* to take pictures.

Not everyone understood why she had brought Nina halfway around the globe to be buried. The Sebergs themselves had privately disapproved of the idea and considered it a prolongation of an unfortunate situation better forgotten. Bill Fisher defends her actions: "It's perfectly understandable. Home was always a magnet to her. Marshalltown is a small town, and the people are real people who can be suspicious and talkative. If Jean hadn't come home with the baby . . . well, I don't know that I can finish that sentence."

Many of the Sebergs' closest friends stayed away, out of a sense of discretion and compassion. Marshalltown had its

261

share of curiosity seekers, however, and they filed through the funeral home to check out the color of the child's skin. "The gossip was fierce," says one resident. "The open coffin didn't do much good. The mouths were still yapping. People were positive, even with the open coffin and the baby staring them in the face, that the child was black."

"That town was quick to believe the worst," concurs Rabbi Sol Serber, an energetic and robust man whose commitment to activism is clearly indicated by the sign on his desk: "Behold the turtle, who makes progress only when he sticks his neck out." Serber has since moved to Waterloo, but in 1970 he was one of the few liberals working for social change in Marshalltown. During her stay, Jean went to him often for comfort and advice.

"She was a very unhappy and disturbed person then," he admits. "She felt she was a disappointment to her parents—she knew she hadn't made it artistically—and she wanted them to be proud of her. She heard all the gossip going around, and she was afraid it would hurt them. In my talks with her, she was always this little girl who went away from Marshalltown but never really left. Being put down by her community, WASPy and conservative as it was, was one of the things she just couldn't seem to overcome, even though I think she knew in her heart that she could never be a part of it again. It was sad."

The day before the funeral, Jean and Guy-Pierre drove to the nearby Tama Indian reservation. Several hundred Mesquakee Indians lived on the compound, the squalor of which contrasted dramatically with the fertile and prosperous farms nearby. Jean would tell people that she could read a look of extinction in the Indians' eyes, a look that invariably moved her to tears. That afternoon she invited them to come to Nina's funeral.

Paton Price and Tom Malinchak, one of Jean's Hollywood friends, flew to Marshalltown for the simple service, which began at three-thirty Friday afternoon. "I could tell Jean was under enormous tension," Price says. "But she was in complete control of herself. She projected great dignity and poise. About ten minutes after the service began, several dozen Indians filed in quietly, walked down to the front and took their place among the surprised mourners." They had brought talismans with them, and Guy-Pierre claims that at their request he slipped several of the charms into Nina's coffin before it was closed forever. The Reverend Marvin Johnson made a short plea for brotherhood, and Mark Adams, a promising Marshalltown music student, sang "Jesus Was a Carpenter," accompanying himself on the guitar. (Jean found his song comforting and would later arrange a two-year music scholarship for him. "That keeps him two years away from Vietnam," she reasoned.)

There was one conspicuous absence that day: Romain Gary. To those who asked, Jean explained that he had taken ill just as he was boarding a plane in Paris. "She was embarrassed by that," Price says. "Somehow, it seemed to lend credence to the notion that the child was not his." Gary would later brand the whole idea of flying home with the child as "sick."

After the service, the body was taken to Riverside Cemetery. The leaves of the tall elms had begun to turn and the late afternoon sun glinted off the pond just beyond the entrance gates. With its gentle hills and unpretentious memorials, the cemetery seemed to justify the pride the townsfolk took in it. Four pallbearers lowered Nina's casket into the earth, only feet from David Seberg's final resting place. The unadorned headstone reads: NINA HART GARY AUG. 23–25, 1970.

The *Times-Republican* carried a front-page account of the service and burial, with a picture of Jean and her mother walking arm in arm to the gravesite. The Des Moines papers had briefer accounts. Otherwise, the funeral went unreported. Jean was baffled and hurt. The press had been eager to spread the rumors about her pregnancy. With an assist from Gary, it had widely publicized Nina's death. Now that she had come home to face down the ugly gossip and to bury her child before the world, no one seemed to care. She sent Paton Price a copy of the *Times-Republican* article and added a handwritten note in the margin: "UP and AP didn't want the story. Are they that scared of *Newsweek* or something?"

Price had tried to convince a few Hollywood celebrities to come with him to the funeral and "troop the colors," as he put it. His efforts were in vain. Jean Seberg was no longer important to them. "It's not as if she had an international stature," Gary later remarked ruefully. "She was absolutely in despair that nobody believed her crusading for blacks was done in good heart."

In Hollywood, all that Jean's misfortune seemed to provoke was a macabre joke, which momentarily enlivened the cocktail party circuit:

"Did you hear where Jean Seberg's baby is buried?"

"No, where?"

"In Paris, next to Alexandre Dumas and Guy de Maupassant." (The celebrated French writers were both mulattoes.)

The following day Jean, Guy-Pierre, Price and Malinchak returned to the Tama reservation so that she could thank the Indians for their attendance. "On the way she saw a scroungy dog by the roadside and urged us to stop the car so she could take it home," says Price. "Stray animals, stray humans, she would have adopted them all."

That day Jean also wanted her visitors to see a 314-acre farm, eighteen miles south of Marshalltown, that she intended to purchase. She envisioned Black Angus cattle grazing in the pastures, and fields of corn and hay ripening in the sun. She justified her enthusiasm as a sound business investment, but the notion of owning a farm seems to have fulfilled a more basic need at the time. It was a link to the past and the carefree summers she had spent on her uncle Bill Benson's spread. It was also a bridge to the future. She would retire there. The whole family—especially Frances Benson—could come and enjoy it. Jean would be part of a community, after all. That October she put down $40,000 on the $227,550 purchase price and signed a ten-year contract calling for annual payments of $20,000. Jokingly, she called herself "La Baronessa."

During her stay in Marshalltown, Jean made one other significant purchase: a two-story, five-bedroom frame house on West Church Street, only blocks from her childhood home. Jean announced that it would be used to provide lodging, rent-free, for black athletes attending Marshalltown Community College because she knew they frequently encountered difficulties finding rooms in the town. The announcement set off a furor in the community and even alienated some of Jean's relatives who had trouble enough comprehending her support of faraway black causes and viewed her plans for the quiet, white neighborhood as an act of high treason.

To mitigate the criticism, Jean had the football coach call on the owners of the adjoining houses to explain her intentions. It did little good. Shortly after, complaints were lodged with the realty company that had arranged the transaction, with the police and with the Sebergs themselves. It wasn't just the noise, and the cars and the loud parties—no. White girls had been seen coming and going in the night. Just why, the irate neighbors demanded to know, was Jean Seberg running a common boardinghouse?

Jean listened to the objections politely but stood firm. "The purpose of the house," she wrote one neighbor who telephoned in high dudgeon, "is that they [the black athletes] should have a home in our town in the truest sense of the word. I checked the zoning laws of your neighborhood. A boardinghouse is a place where monies are exchanged for living there, which is absolutely not the case in this instance. The United States has very specific laws as to open housing, as well. I went into this rather carefully. As to your concern of noise . . . I do hope you will not be too disturbed and find the quiet and peace of mind which every human being should have the right to. I hope all goes well and I hope you will behave toward your neighbors as you want them to behave toward you."

The house was poorly maintained, however, and before long it became, in the judgment of one resident, "a complete shambles. It needed constant supervision, and Jean just didn't follow through on it after she left town. A year or so later she bought some siding for it because it was looking pretty rundown by then. But the community college never pitched in, really, and it never worked out the way she had hoped."

Some Marshalltonians began referring to it as "the Seberg house."

Rabbi Serber encouraged Jean and tried to keep an eye on the house. "She had this need in her, almost to the point of an obsession, to make the world a better place. All you had to say to her was 'people are being hurt,' and she was like putty. She could be used by anyone if she thought that person was sincere, and there were those who took advantage. I'd talk to her about kids on drugs or the problems of the elderly, and her eyes would just start to well up. A terrible civil war was going on inside her—she had this desperate need to get the world to care, and this overwhelming frustration that she couldn't do it alone.

"With all her personal troubles that fall, she met with the black leaders of the town, which led to the purchase of the house. She set up meetings with the Indians to see if there was something she could do for them. She conferred with community action people about the problems of low-income families. She couldn't reject anyone. She was a very giving person. The tragedy was, she expected to get back as much empathy as she gave."

Later on in life, Jean was possessed by a similarly feverish desire to help humanity. The frantic mood, her close friends came to realize, usually preceded a nervous breakdown. In fact, Jean was slowly losing contact with reality throughout the fall of 1970. The hyperkinetic activity on the heels of a personal tragedy seems to have been, in part, an attempt to stave off a paralyzing depression.

Instead of flying directly back to Paris at the end of October, Jean decided to go to Chicago first. Having transferred her allegiance from the Panthers to the Southern Christian Leadership Conference, she wanted to demonstrate publicly her support of the Reverend Jesse Jackson's "Operation Breadbasket." She chartered two small planes so that several of Marshalltown's black leaders and students could go with her to attend the service that Jackson broadcast from the stage of a former theater on Chicago's South Side. At sunrise on October 24 they gathered at an airstrip outside Marshalltown, Jean bid Ed Seberg good-bye and the planes took off.

Roger Maxwell was one of those who went along. "Jean was very tired that day," he recalls, "but everything seemed to be going just fine. In Chicago, Jean sat on the stage to one side of the pulpit. There was a huge youth choir in white shirts and jeans that sang. Then Jackson came on and preached."

Jackson's message took the form of a spirited exchange that

grew in volume and enthusiasm as two thousand members of the audience echoed his words:

Jackson: "I am—"
Audience: "I am—"
Jackson: "—somebody."
Audience: "—somebody."
Jackson: "I may be poor . . ."
Audience: "I may be poor . . ."
Jackson: ". . . but I am—"
Audience: ". . . but I am—"
Jackson: "—*somebody*!"
Audience: "—*somebody*!"

"After the service," says Roger Maxwell, "we went to a black restaurant for lunch. I think Jean was going to confer with Jackson later. Anyway, she and the Marshalltown group were all sitting at a table in the back when this white lady in a paisley dress came over and joined us. She said to Jean that she brought greetings from friends in Hollywood, but Jean didn't know her. The lady put her purse on the table and then she started asking questions—who we were, where we came from, how long we were staying. It was casual at first, but pretty soon she was coming on real strong. Jean had a worried look on her face and asked my wife, Bunny, to accompany her to the rest room. 'I think I'll come with you, too,' this woman said. Jean turned to Guy-Pierre and muttered something in French—something to the effect of 'the purse . . . move the purse.' I think Jean thought there was a tape recorder in it. Anyway, it was getting kind of tense, so I went over and told one of Jackson's staff, a gorgeous black woman, that she'd better check out the rest room.

"When they all came back, two of Jackson's security guards came over and asked the white lady, 'Are you ready to leave?' 'But I haven't finished my lunch,' she answered. 'You're ready to leave,' they said and escorted her out. Jean was pretty shaken up by it all. I was kind of naïve at the time, but looking back on it all now, I believe this lady was some kind of infiltrator."

Guy-Pierre was not so convinced. "Jean saw spies everywhere. But it was all in her head."

The Marshalltown contingent returned home that night. Jean

267

and Guy-Pierre remained in Chicago. "We were staying in a motel," he says. "One night Jean was cutting out pictures of her baby with a pair of scissors. Suddenly she turned on me and started yelling that *I* was a spy and stabbing away at me with the scissors. I wrestled them away from her and managed to quiet her down. Before long she was crying uncontrollably and saying how sorry she was. It was becoming a constant drama with her."

Eventually Guy-Pierre washed his hands of the assignment and returned alone to Paris. "I'd had it with her. She was living a novel of her own making. I called up Romain when I got back, but he was in Majorca. Eugenia answered. I said to her, 'Tell Romain I left Jean in a motel in Chicago. She's completely nuts.'"

On her own, Jean paid a brief visit to her sister in Cherry Hill, New Jersey, and then consulted with a lawyer in New York about her libel suit against *Newsweek*. He gravely informed her that it was not the open-and-shut matter she thought it would be. The trial would be long and messy and difficult. It would mean opening up her private life for public scrutiny. In all likelihood, she and Romain would have to take the stand.

"He said it would cost a million dollars and take ten years," Jean stated later, "He asked me if the bitterness was worth it. That's when I cracked up."

28

"Hakim was full of jive, but I really think he loved Jean in his way."

—BARBARA NASH

"I went crazy," Jean would say matter-of-factly when she looked back to November 1970. She spent most of that month in and out of a clinic in Paris, and her doctors regarded her mental state as grave indeed.

Exhausted and emotionally drained, she would go on long crying jags. She began to hear messages coming from the refrigerator, or to see them in crumpled pieces of aluminum foil. Ordinary passers-by transformed themselves before her eyes into CIA agents. Then, as she described it, her mind broke and she tumbled into a profound depression, unresponsive to outside stimulae. "At one point, he [the doctor] feared I would never snap out of this ghastly world I was hiding in," she admitted to Rabbi Serber. "My parents don't know about this. It was the result of many things—mainly the body insisting on its own time to recuperate rather than let me push it too fast and too far, plus the inevitable shock reaction, which hit even worse because it came so late."

She was treated with heavy doses of medication, and the drugs seemed to cast a glaze over her eyes and cloud her thinking. Recovery was slow and painful. "Faith helps," she told Serber, "when you haven't lost it, which, alas, I pretty much have."

Her friends were appalled by the physical ravages. She looked a ruin. Although overweight and puffy, she had the haggard, drawn appearance of a famine victim. "It was as if she were bloated and gaunt at the same time," says one of her regular visitors. "And she had a curious ailment I'd never seen before; the entire inside of her mouth and her gums were black as tar. I almost didn't recognize her."

When she could pull herself out of the depths, she would babble endlessly about Nina and the perversity of the press, which she blamed for killing the child. "Jean was absolutely stunned by that article. It had bludgeoned her. She would come back to it time and time again," reports one of her confidantes.

Maurice Ronet paid a call to the clinic that November and observed that "Jean was astounded, almost intoxicated, by the whole notion of injustice. She would speak of the hunger of little children and how it hurt her. At the same time she took such an exalted tone that you almost suspected her of playing a role. Already she was weaving this vast conspiracy between herself and the world."

The pervasive paranoia was hardly appeased by a visitor who unexpectedly emerged from the past. It was Hakim Jamal. He had been traveling in Morocco with Gale Ann Benson, who had converted to the Muslim faith, viewed herself as Jamal's disciple, but explained crisply, when asked, that she was his "secretary."

While in Morocco, Jamal had telephoned his wife in California. The Montessori school had long since closed down, and Dorothy Jamal was having troubles making ends meet. A proud woman, she resisted going on welfare, and eventually asked Shirley Sutherland to take her in. Dorothy demanded that Hakim send funds to help her and their six children.

To his friends, Jamal admitted, "There was only one place I could get my hands on some immediate money—and that's Jean Seberg." He had heard of the *Newsweek* article with its reference to a black nationalist and thought he might pick up a little publicity on the side—even if it meant swearing that Jean's child was not his. Selling his typewriter and his '54 Ford for air fare, he and Gale Ann flew to Paris. Jean was not at the

Rue du Bac apartment as he had expected, and Gary provided no clues to her whereabouts. By asking around, Jamal learned where she was. "So I drove to the clinic and there's Jean," he said. "She did a hasty make-up job, but she looked terrible."

Back in America, Jamal later described his visit as a mission of mercy. Predictably, it was a highly selective account; there was no mention of money or madness. "I called the hospital and was told that Jean was in bad shape and should not be bothered," Jamal told the press. "I didn't dig that answer, so I packed my bags and went to see her to find out if I could be of any help to her in her time of suffering and to find out if the black activist referred to in the article was me.

"When I walked into the hospital in Paris, there was Jean—crying and listening to the tape recording of her baby's funeral. Finally she told me the story of a little newspaper there [*Minute*] in France that linked her and I. It implied that I was indeed the father of the child.

"I looked at her—hurt and alone—crying for a child the world was ready to condemn. It wasn't enough that they just wanted to ruin her—they wanted to hang her, not on a cross, but 1970 style, in print. The next surprise came when she told me she was crying for me, as she knew the story would hurt me with all my friends in America . . . I stayed with her for hours, consoling her and reminiscing about old times.

"Watching her cry over her dead baby made me realize a lot of things. One: this woman with blond hair and blue eyes is completely different from me. But I wished I could have been the father of her child. She is a woman I am proud to say to the world I do love with the same kind of love that Jesus Christ spoke of, that Moses spoke of, that God himself speaks of. Perhaps the world feels Jean owes them an explanation. Well, maybe she does. But not with me. I prefer to leave them with what they deserve: dirty oceans, smoggy air, polluted rivers, wars, skinheads, segregation, hatred, discrimination. That is all they deserve. They made it, now die in it."

As usual, Jamal believed he was addressing the world. In reality, his remarks were published in the tiny Compton *Bulletin* under the guise of an interview that, some say, Jamal wrote himself.

The effect of his visit was far less calming then he maintained, even though Jamal boasted to Barbara Nash that "As soon as I arrived, [Jean] just cooled right down. She wasn't insane anymore," and claimed that the doctors were amazed at his miraculous powers.

Jean had recovered sufficiently to leave the clinic temporarily during his stay. One night shortly after her thirty-second birthday she, Gale Ann Benson, Jamal and Guy-Pierre, who had been summoned back into service, went to a Paris *boîte* where Memphis Slim held forth at the piano. In the cab on the way, Jean was singing songs, laughing gaily, and according to Jamal, "having a helluva time." She even did a tap dance on the cobblestone street when they reached their destination. Inside the night club, the mood turned sour. As the liquor flowed, the talk grew delirious, and long-smoldering jealousies broke to the surface.

Jamal's rhetoric never failed to mesmerize Jean, and she was all too easily drawn back into his world of intrigue. By this time Jamal had come to see betrayal everywhere. The Panthers had set him up. His men in the Malcolm X Foundation had set him up. He even felt that Jean, in her rush "to get to the top of the Panthers," had set him up. Yet paradoxically, that very climate of treachery drew Jean and Jamal together and fed the sexual attraction between them. More than ever, their desire seemed rooted in a mutual appetite for self-destruction.

Jean was smoking heavily that night. When the conversation got nasty and personal, she held her cigarette over Jamal's hand and suddenly crushed it out in his flesh. Sitting back, she watched, amused, while he cursed, as much in surprise as in pain. Then she lit up another cigarette and calmly proceeded to apply it to the knuckles of three of her own fingers. Long afterward she would show the scars to her friends and explain that it was her way of proving to Jamal that, unlike him, she could withstand the pain of love.

Jamal was incensed. Soon after, he avenged his injured pride by boasting that he had spent that night with Jean. When her whimperings about Nina droned on too long, he claimed, he had knocked her brutally about the bedroom and forced her to tear up her photographs of the child. "I told her I didn't want to hear it. I said, 'You killed that motherfucking baby. You killed that little fucking piece of rubber with them goddamn pills. How many pills do you think it takes to kill an embryo?' And I slapped the dogshit out of her."

He recounted a similar tale to Bob Logan, a lanky American actor who had recently become one of Jean's good friends. Furious, Logan told Jamal to lay off. "Man, you don't understand women," Jamal replied. "You have to rough them up now and again." Later Logan asked Jean if Jamal's tales were true. "He got angry. We had a fight, and he took a couple of swipes at me," she admitted sheepishly.

At any rate, Jamal and Gale Ann soon departed for London on a laissez-passer, Jamal said, arranged by Gary. Jean returned to the clinic. Before he left, however, Jamal volunteered his diagnosis of Jean. "It's not just the baby," he said. "Jean has a good girl and a bad girl inside of her. Sometimes the bad girl takes over completely. Tell the psychiatrists. Maybe they can work with her."

Nonetheless, Jean arranged for a $700 check to be delivered anonymously to Dorothy Jamal that month.

Early in December, out of the clinic again, Jean received another troubling visitor—her lover from Mexico, the man she called Carlos. Arriving in Paris with a swagger, he proudly asserted before several of Jean's friends that he was the father of Nina.

"I think he'd read about the baby in the papers and wanted to take up with Jean again," says Raymonde Waintraub, "but she was pretty embarrassed about him by this time. She wouldn't have any part of it."

"He rattled on about how he and Jean should have another baby," Bob Logan recalls. "Jean wouldn't go near him. She put him up in the guest room for a few days because he didn't have any money. Then she offered to pay for a hotel room. At long last he got the idea and left. It was incredible, the way she was constantly opening her pocketbook and her door to these strange people. Here she'd just gotten rid of Jamal, and then this one turned up! I could see the old malaise creeping over her. But I sensed Jean really wanted to be free of it once and for all."

Logan had an unusual address in Paris. He was living on Sterling Hayden's houseboat on the Seine. Three or four times a week he would drop by Jean's apartment to take a shower, then have tea and chat with her. Sometimes they played Scrabble. One day she showed him her medicine chest. A confirmed health-food freak, Logan was appalled by what he saw. "She had this vast array of pills she was taking every day to maintain her stability. I don't place much faith in pills, personally, and I asked her how they were working. 'The Valium makes my skin break out,' she said. 'This one gives me an appetite. This one makes me throw up.' It was a real nightmare. I said to her, 'Jean, do you want to try something?' She said, 'I'll try anything.' So I told her to flush them all down the toilet. 'We're going to get you a bicycle, a running outfit and some shoes.' And we did. All the pills went down the toilet. There was one she wanted to keep—the Valium, I think. It was the last to go.

"Her doctor went absolutely berserk when he found out. Romain sided with the psychiatrist and screamed that I was trying to kill her like the Black Panthers had. He threatened to have me arrested, which was ridiculous. Anyway, Jean was on my side.

"I had kind of a regimen going, and she started eating good food, too. Every day I'd bicycle out to the Bois de Boulogne, where I'd take out a rowboat. Pretty soon, Jean was coming along. She could hardly ride a bicycle. It surprised me, for a small-town girl. But she was willing! I think I'll always have this marvelous image of her, speeding down the Champs Elysées, totally out of control, wobbling in and out of the traffic, frightened out of her wits, her eyes filling with tears. But at the same time, there was this wonderful, crazy adolescent grin on her face.

"This went on for about five or six weeks, and Jean's body just went *pfffft*! I mean, the fat melted right off her. I was going by her place one morning and ran into Romain. 'You've worked a miracle,' he told me. 'Jean looks better now than she did when she was twenty-one.' I said, 'Don't give me the credit. Jean can be tough as nails when she wants to. It's all her.' And it was, too."

Since Nina's death, Jean and Romain had abandoned any further talk of reconciliation and remarriage. According to several of his friends, Gary found the tumult in Jean's life profoundly distasteful. In addition, Gary himself was under mounting pressure to complete the script for *Total Danger*, which had been retitled *Kill* and was scheduled to go before the cameras in early 1971. Myriad pre-production details had to be attended to.

Jean stayed briefly in an apartment on the Rue de Varenne while workmen installed a second kitchen in the Rue du Bac apartment. Thereafter the old arrangement prevailed: she and Romain would continue to live under the same roof—together, but apart, so that Diego could share his time between them. Publicly they struck the pose of the grief-stricken couple united against the mendacity of the world. But the relationship was far less secure than it appeared on the surface. Gary's *White Dog* had come out in English, and while the writer had taken pains to disguise the identity of certain characters, the disgust he felt toward some of Jean's Los Angeles friends was unmistakable. Paton Price had merited an especially savage attack.

Jean spilled out some of her deeper feelings toward Gary and the book in a letter to Price that December: "Ah writers," she said, "with their smugness and their terrible swift swords . . . their pens. How easy and fun it must be! Sometimes, I imagine them as little Stalins, legs spread wide, flashing whips gleefully at bent backs around the earth. Did you notice the knifing I get at the end, when he [Gary] comments on the young girl supposedly living in the eaves of the house in Paris. 'It's so nice to be able *at last* to respect someone.' That one hurt, too, Paton, ten years and one child later."

She called Gary "my home-grown Joyce Haber" and deplored the anti-American sentiments she perceived in the book. Then she added: "It is sadder than that. It is the hatred of someone who is incapable of loving anything or anyone except fictitiously, and that I know to be a fact . . . He has lost any hold he could have had over a naïve girl."

That hold would not be so neatly severed. Once her anger had subsided, Jean continued to look to the writer for approval, as she had in the past. More than anyone else, Gary had formed her intellectually, and he would remain a crucial influence in her life.

Logan readily sensed the discord between them. "Romain was an intelligent man, a brilliant novelist, if not scenarist, and a very strong man psychologically. I think Jean frustrated him no end because she was so flexible. Oh, she could be strong at times. But in many ways, she was this thin reed. Her eyes were being opened all the time. She was constantly learning things. Romain was learned. That was the big difference, and I always thought it was the main problem in the relationship."

In a candid radio interview he gave in 1975, Gary reached a similar conclusion. "By the time you're fifty, you've taken on the world. Several times over. You've lived," he explained. "All of a sudden you find yourself in the company of a young woman who's just starting out, who wants to forge her own relationships with the world. That's hard to bear. You see her making the same mistakes you made. She won't listen to your advice. And the more advice you give, the more you begin to resemble a sagacious papa. All of which means, after a certain period of time, that a husband and wife have turned into a father and daughter. That's the profound drama."

Jean tried to look ahead to Gary's film. She was determined to get back her strength and her figure, although she admitted that "I have lost a good deal of my pleasure at 'making believe.'" Inexorably, her thoughts returned to the events of the fall, and she talked about them so compulsively that Ronet affectionately nicknamed her "St. Joan of Arc of the Guerrillas."

Still, by mid-December Jean was able to write Dawn Murray Quinn and say that she was finally feeling "like someone who is coming out of a long tunnel on the way to health." Christmas, her favorite holiday, was approaching. "I am trying to be enthusiastic," she confessed, "but it is really not easy as so much has happened." To her, the world seemed etched with violence, and violence had taken a devastating toll in her own life, robbed her momentarily of her sanity and undermined her ideals. "It seems that people have to scream because no one listens when they whisper," said the broken actress, struggling to understand.

On December 29, 1970, the FBI placed Jean Seberg on its Security Index—Priority 3. Priority 3 was reserved for any individual who "because of background is potentially dangerous; or has been identified as a member or participant in communist movement, or has been under active investigation as member of other group or organization inimical to the U.S." In the event of a presidentially declared national emergency, she was marked as one of those the FBI would round up to safeguard the republic.

29

> *"I'm putting all the pieces together. I try to understand and apply what I can from the past."*
>
> —JEAN SEBERG

By February 1971 Jean had regained her svelte figure, but what she called her "appetite for living" was slower to return. She tried to be optimistic about *Kill,* her upcoming film, and looked to it to pull her out of the lingering depression. That had always been Ed Seberg's way. In times of difficulty or emotional stress, he would simply redouble his efforts at the drugstore. Convinced that you could only take a day at a time, he found a certain strength in the fact of work and the long-established routines of his life.

"Work heals and time helps," said Jean, wanting to believe. "But some things will never be the same."

Kill was hardly a peaceful project. Gary envisioned it as a crusade against the international drug trade, and in particular, those narcotics investigators who were actually in cahoots with the mobsters.

"I love life too much not to hate everything that destroys or corrupts it: pollution, safaris, intolerance. For me, drugs are the most terrifying means of abasement today," he announced. "Drug traffickers are the worst sort of assassins. Since I can't kill them myself, I'll kill them in the movies."

With *Kill,* he said, he would elevate the "cop" film to the realm of art. The tale would unfold at a vertiginous pace, his scenario calling for a dizzying number of chases, fights, stabbings, seductions, betrayals, tortures and bared bosoms, plus a final *danse macabre,* in which five barons of the drug trade would be machine-gunned to death in slow motion. "There will be twenty-seven cadavers in my film," Gary promised.

Jean would play the bored wife of an Interpol agent (James Mason) who is about to leave their quiet home in Switzerland for a high-level tactical meeting in Afghanistan with his international counterparts. Unbeknownst to her husband, Jean precedes him by twenty-four hours and links up with a sweaty American (Stephen Boyd) who has his own grudge against the dealers. What follows resembles the Perils of Pauline as the Marquis de Sade might have imagined them.

At the end of February, Jean and Romain left for Spain, where *Kill* was to be filmed—first in Madrid, then near Alicante on the Costa Brava—over a ten-week period. Jean had misgivings. The project seemed poorly organized, and the notion of Stephen Boyd as her leading man left her cold. (In one letter she summed up her reactions to him with a single word: "Ick!")

Mason had previously turned down the Pierre Brasseur role in *Birds in Peru,* finding it "terribly pretentious." Only out of a long-standing friendship with Gary had he consented to appear in *Kill.*

"It was not a film the making of which I cherish," Mason recalls. "The scenes were not terribly real, and Alicante is hardly the most agreeable spot on earth. After a while one found oneself wondering, 'How *long* is this going on?' From my observations, Jean was very quiet—placid, almost—and what I can only describe as on her good behavior. But the film didn't really need to have a woman in it. It was a man's film. I think Romain wrote the role for her only because he wanted to keep her career going. But much as he yearned to be an *auteur* in the cinema, he lacked the magic touch. None of the problems got solved."

In fact, Romain was frequently at odds with his producers, the brothers Ilya and Alexander Salkind, who were plumping for a gory commercial hit. According to one account, as the rushes were processed in Paris the brothers sent back their urgent recommendation: "More blood and tits." Gary exploded.

One day Ilya Salkind visited the set in Madrid, visibly concerned over the film's progress. "Do you think this film will be a hit in America?" he asked Bob Logan, who had been hired as an assistant.

"Ilya," Logan replied prophetically, "I'm not sure this picture will even be seen in America."

Gary didn't get along well with the lanky American, whom he accused of misunderstanding the film's black humor and generally sabotaging morale. After a vituperative exchange of letters with Gary, Logan quit. Jean was sorry to see her bicycling companion go.

She consoled herself by accepting the attentions of aspiring film director Ricardo Franco, a Spaniard nearly ten years her junior. Short, bearded and resembling "a cross between Ché Guevara and Toulouse-Lautrec," Franco had been a promising medical student before abandoning his studies for the cinema. Jean was amused by his appearance when she spotted him one night at the Santa Bárbara, a Madrid café popular with artists and film makers.

"Shalom," she called out mischievously as he passed by her table. A conversation ensued. Ditching her date for the evening, Jean left the café with Franco. For the next year, he would be her near-constant companion.

Although unprepossessing, he was kindly and bright. If some of Jean's friends referred to the pair as "Beauty and the Beast," others thought it was the kind of unthreatening relationship she needed at the time. "Jean was incapable of living without a man," says one, "and Ricardo followed her around almost as if he were her little pet dog." Romain approved, and he treated Franco like a son.

The pressures of *Kill* were not the only ones in Jean's life at the time. After consulting with lawyers, she and Romain had decided not to bring suit against *Newsweek* in the United States. The publication had already begun to assemble evidence justifying its assertions and was showing every sign of settling down for a long fight. Dorothy Jamal says that two representatives from the magazine paid her $1,000 for an "interview" and certain letters that Jean had sent to Jamal. Clearly, an American trial would be far more revelatory than either Jean or Romain desired.

Instead, they chose to bring suit in France, where truth is not an acceptable defense against the charge of defamation. There it would simply be a matter of proving to the tribunal that *Newsweek* had invaded their personal lives and cast a prejudicial light on Jean's character. Each of them was asking 500,000 francs (approximately $100,000) in damages.

Newsweek promptly countersued. Although the magazine asked for only one franc in damages for the accusations that Gary had leveled against it in *France-Soir,* the maneuver meant more legal headaches for the writer.

The trial got under way at the beginning of April and dragged on for six months. "You cannot conceive the baseness of *Newsweek*'s efforts to scare and coerce me into dropping charges," a dispirited Jean informed Paton Price. "They have even bought letters of mine, written to J, from his wife. And she, after selling them, was still sending me desperate wires to lend her money. It is all insane and ghastly and distasteful. I'm naïve. I still had some illusions about the ethical tactics of a magazine like *Newsweek.* I was wrong. Anyway, they printed a lie. Thus the struggle goes on."

Jean's hurt and deception stemmed from two factors: although she had had affairs with both Jamal and Hewitt, she knew, because of the timing, that Nina was neither's child. Factually, the magazine was wrong. But by impugning the paternity of the child, she felt, *Newsweek* had reduced her long-standing interest in civil rights to a sexual itch.

On her lawyer's advice Jean pressed her friends—even Jamal himself—for letters attesting to her interest in causes of all kinds, irrespective of race. Her lawyer planned to introduce them as evidence that Jean was, as she herself put it, "a good kid."

At the end of May the *Kill* company relocated to Tunisia for four days of supplementary shooting in an attempt to beef up the exotic look of the film, which, after all, was presumably unfolding in the Mideast. "I have very strong reservations about Romain's film, including my own work," Jean admitted afterward. "It was as if we were acting all alone and the disorganized setup wasn't conducive to standing open [Paton Price's injunction]."

The critics were contemptuous at the world premiere held the following year in Marseilles, a city that Gary chose for its importance in the international drug trade. "When it isn't wandering off into the worst melodrama, a nauseating pastiche of the most mediocre comic strips," one snorted, "*Kill* is stuffed with sadomasochistic sequences of aberrant eroticism." Another dismissed it as "probably the most puerile film the subject of drugs has ever inspired."

For Jean's friends, it was more than just another failed film. As they had during *Birds in Peru,* they shifted uneasily in their seats and asked themselves just what Romain was up to. "He seems to be taking digs at Jean and her revolutionary activities all the way through the film," says one. "It made me sick when I saw it. Jean was just coming out of a serious breakdown, and Romain in his great wisdom turned around and put her into a role where for ten weeks she was playing a woman who is hysterical, neurotic, paranoid, pathetic, and by the end of the film, almost catatonic. A woman who spreads her legs for the first man who comes along and finishes up as a gun-toting killer. What kind of therapy is that?"

Jean was circumspect in her criticism. "What Romain didn't realize when he wrote it was that the girl is almost perpetually in a state of fear and terror, so she tends to stay rather on the same pitch all the way through."

In the opening shot Jean is all but unrecognizable, wearing a bushy black Afro wig, listening to jungle sounds on a record player, patently bored with the tranquillity of her marriage. When Mason accuses her of being "into blackness again," she seizes a shotgun and fires a round of buckshot into the wall. It may be the most startling image of Jean ever put on film. Certainly it is the meanest.

Kill turned out to be Gary's last effort at directing. "I think it was always his biggest frustration that he couldn't seem to master the cinematic form," says an acquaintance. Although Gary consistently lauded Jean's talent as "the greatest," he was less capable of bringing it out on the screen than any of her other directors.

Jean repaired to Majorca in July for a lazy month on the sunny island. Romain immediately plunged into a new novel, and Diego set about learning to sail. He was now nine, and while he had his father's dark coloring, the soft, sensitive eyes were Jean's. The usual collection of dogs and cats roamed the property. Jean made a point of avoiding the newspapers, which only reminded her of the political tumult that had nearly destroyed her.

Not all the news was bad, however. The farm in Iowa appeared to be prospering. Thirty-eight calves had been born that spring, and the crops promised to be bountiful. She spoke of the farm in idyllic terms, but admitted that "I won't feel free and at peace until there's a good chunk of money to cover the payments."

For the first time in her life, finances loomed as a problem. Forced by necessity to be less choosy about her scripts, Jean nevertheless had good reason to accept a role in *Questa Specie d'Amore (This Kind of Love)*, which Alberto Bevilacqua would direct in Italy that fall. A prizewinning author, he had fashioned an intelligent and probing scenario from his novel of the same title. It told the story of a successful Italian businessman coming to terms with his empty present among the aristocracy, with his peasant past and with the nagging memories of his father, who had once led the fight in Parma against Mussolini's fascism. Ugo Tognazzi, one of Italy's finest actors, would play a triple role: the businessman, his father and (in flashbacks) the father as he had been forty years earlier. Jean would be his sleek wife, drifting through the sterile world of Rome society.

Ricardo Franco kept her company during the shooting in Parma and later in Rome. Jean also invited some of Franco's friends—among them a Cuban film maker named Fausto Canel—to share her villa in Rome. She had a mounting horror of solitude. The traumas of the past were all linked to empty rooms—the suite at the Dorchester Hotel in London, where Preminger had kept her a virtual prisoner; the Barcelona villa where she had waited out the final months of Diego's pregnancy, not knowing if Romain would marry her; the Zermatt inn where her worst nightmares had come true.

Having the young film makers around filled the emptiness and helped her face the future. She had hatched an idea for a movie scenario of her own, and in her spare time she and Canel worked on a first draft of a romance she would call *Frontier Palace*.

She still enjoyed a residual stature in Italy. One day Giacomo Ciarlantini, her Italian agent, arranged for her to meet a rising young Italian actor, Fabio Testi, in the hopes of squeezing some publicity out of the encounter. A strapping ex-seminarian and stunt man, Testi had set off a minor flurry as a rugged heartthrob. He quickly became enamored of Jean and persuaded her to take a small part in one of his upcoming films, *La Camorra,* which was scheduled to go before the cameras the following year.

Jean encouraged his attentions with the cool flirtatiousness that invariably enhanced her femininity, and soon was juggling Testi's favors with those of Franco. If Franco was properly obedient, Testi's jealousy was easily aroused. At parties his volatile spirits occasionally flared out of control. Convinced that Jean was betraying him, he stormed up to her villa one night, pounded loudly on the shutters and bellowed his suspicions to the world at large. "Jean did seem to exert a rather extraordinary charm on the male sex," Ciarlantini admits discreetly.

Despite her surface gaiety, the past was never out of Jean's mind for long. At times *This Kind of Love* came perilously close to her own experience. Early in the film her anxiety-ridden character learns she is pregnant and fears that she will be unable to carry the child, whose birth might effect an emotional reconciliation with her husband. Taken to a hospital, she miscarries. "I can only live a mutilated life," she drones tonelessly from the hospital bed.

It was the kind of scene that was unbearably painful for Jean to act, says Dennis Berry. Repressed memories of Nina, with all their attendant guilt, surged into her consciousness and threatened to jeopardize her hard-won mental equilibrium all over again. Indeed, her performance in the film at that particular moment is agonizingly real. Jean was not pretending to lose a baby. She was living it all over again.

For all its merits, *This Kind of Love* proved too specifically Italian in its concerns, and perhaps too literary, to get a wide audience. Even with Jean's name on it, the film did not receive a screening in France until 1980. Much as she tried to be cheerful about the future, Jean was turning into a figure of the past.

By October the trial with *Newsweek* was drawing to a close. On the fourth of that month Gary made an appearance in the Paris courtroom to make his final plea. He was hardly the diplomat of yore. One account at the time described him as looking like Anthony Quinn made up for the role of Paul Gauguin. He was dressed in a green suit and boots, and his sunglasses were perched on his graying hair, which now fell nearly to his shoulders. The 1960s had left their imprint on him. According to journalist France Roche, "Romain, in his fashion, had sort of fallen in step with the hippie movement, which shows both a certain flexibility and the lack of a sense of the ridiculous. The way he would talk about Woodstock being the music of our times, you almost suspected him of having been there in the mud with his sleeping bag."

But it was an outraged Gary, drawing on all his oratorical skills, who inveighed against *Newsweek*. "No one is more respectful than I of the rights and freedom of the press," he said. "But there is a problem, namely, knowing when this liberty becomes the fascism of the press. One is crushed when one has for an opponent a publication with a circulation of more than seven million. How does one fight that kind of pressure? The power of that kind of money? To give you a single example, I have been made to understand that as long as this trial continues, my books will not be published in the United States."

He painted his own attempts to right the balance in *France-Soir* as pitiful compared to *Newsweek*'s might. Then, tears in his eyes, his voice rising to the occasion, he boomed, "I ask you, sirs, what article could possibly avenge the death of a tiny infant?"

Gary was up against formidable competition in the person of Robert Badinter, France's most celebrated trial lawyer, who adroitly depicted the whole affair as utterly preposterous. The long, tiring trip Jean had taken from Majorca to Zermatt seemed to him a far better explanation for the loss of Nina than any "shock" produced by the *Newsweek* piece. "One would have to have the character, the anguish and the neuroses of

Romain Gary and Jean Seberg to claim that two lines of print caused the death of this child, and then qualify it as murder and defamation," he scoffed.

A decision was handed down on October 25. The court rejected Gary's accusation that the magazine had "killed" Nina, but acknowledged that both his and Jean's privacy had been violated. Gary's article in *France-Soir* was deemed forgivable, under the circumstances. *Newsweek* was ordered to pay damages totaling approximately $11,000, plus fines. "It doesn't seem like very much," said Ed Seberg when he learned of the decision. "I feel like I should have this much or more damages for what the story did to my wife. She has been upset ever since."

Although pleased with the moral victory, Jean was disappointed with the paltry settlement, which she had liberally earmarked a year earlier for her diverse causes. Nor did the trial exorcise the demons that haunted her. Over and over, friends say, she would steer the conversation around to *Newsweek*'s perfidy. Astonished and disbelieving, she was like a child who has learned for the first time that parents are fallible.

30

"I regret enormously that I had to divorce. I'm of a generation that believes in marriage. I'm just the marrying kind. Perhaps it would be better to live together and have a child, as the young do today. But I'd be incapable of it. That's my old-fashioned side."

—JEAN SEBERG

Sipping a glass of Sancerre wine, Jean leaned across the restaurant table and said to the interviewer, "I used to be attracted only to handsome men. But with age, I've discovered ugly men. And do you know something? They're nice. Men who haven't got everything going for them make much greater efforts than the others. They want to be better lovers, kinder husbands and more thoughtful escorts."

Then she let out a peal of laughter. "There's only one thing. You've got to overcome the barrier of being seen with them."

The mischievousness played well before an audience, but it didn't completely conceal the reality of her situation. Loneliness petrified her, and she required, at thirty-three, constant assurance that she was a sexually desirable woman. The pills and liquor she was consuming again had made her gain weight. On bad days, her eyes were puffy and lined. But she retained the iridescent complexion of her youth, her hair was now becomingly long, and she still passed for a handsome woman.

Jokingly, she admitted that she was an unrepentant romantic and said it ran in the family. In her ninth decade, wasn't

Frances Benson wearing high heels, writing dreamy poetry and waiting for Mr. Right to come along?

"Jean really had all the trumps," says her friend Raymonde Waintraub. "She was intelligent, beautiful and cultivated. She had a long-standing friendship with André Malraux, and he didn't talk to just anybody. Jean could have had any man she wanted. I always thought she should have continued to live with Romain, take lovers on the side and not tell him, although I think he might have tolerated it. But once Jean was through with a man, she was through. She'd divorce him and look for another. She needed the security of being married. She was a woman who was always in love—had to be in love—only it was never with the same person. All the time I knew her, her state never changed. Just the partner. It got to be very troubling."

For the time being, the diminutive Ricardo Franco filled the bill. And Fabio Testi.

Early in 1972 Jean was suddenly confronted with an awful reminder of a past that would not leave her. Since she had last seen them, Hakim Jamal and Gale Ann Benson had wound their way through Europe and the United States, although the zeal was going out of his mission and some of his friends believe he had reverted to drugs. Toward the end of 1971, the two had turned up in Trinidad at the commune of Michael X, a Black Power zealot who had failed to make much of a dent in London, had run afoul of the law and eventually fled to the Caribbean island. There, largely ignored by the populace, he concocted grandiose schemes of the black empire over which he would preside someday. In the hot, grubby compound, dementia and voodoo reigned in equal measure.

Gale Ann Benson was, by then, slavish in her worship of Jamal and looked upon him as God. Her new name, Hale Kimga, was an anagram of Hakim and Gale. One morning early in January when Hakim was away from the commune she was called into the garden, where she saw Michael X's men digging a large pit. As she stood at the edge and watched them toil away in the blazing sun, Michael X seized her from behind and stabbed her repeatedly in the chest and throat.

Spurting blood and gasping for breath, she was thrown into

the sandy pit and buried—no longer quite alive, but not completely dead either. Mystified by her disappearance, Jamal returned to Boston and professed total ignorance of the crime when the rotted body was unearthed late in February. Charges were brought against the demonic Michael X, who was captured in Guyana the following month as he fled through the bush toward the Brazilian border. He was tried and hanged for the savage murder.

Grisly accounts of the crime and the trial were splashed across the British tabloids for weeks. As Gale Ann's lover and Michael X's friend, Jamal landed back in the news, where he had always liked to be. Jean was sickened by the reports. She, too, had been Jamal's lover, participated in his crusade and experienced the paranoia that seemed to hang over him like a shroud. She, too, had been tantalized by the aura of danger he projected. Gale Ann Benson, however, had paid a ghastly, unthinkable price.

In later years Jean would romanticize Jamal and her relationship with him. At the end of her life he would take up permanent residence in her fantasies. But in the spring of 1972, he was a figure from a chilling past that she was struggling to put behind her once and for all.

Working on a new movie helped. Yves Boisset, an energetic young French director, had hired her for the only female role of importance in *L'Attentat (The French Conspiracy)*. In the tradition of *Z*, the film was loosely based on the Ben Barka affair. Ben Barka had been the leader of the leftist opposition in Morocco in the fifties and sixties and a fervent spokesman for Third World rights. In plain daylight on October 29, 1965, he was kidnapped in Paris by two policemen as he entered the Brasserie Lipp on the busy Boulevard St. Germain. He was never seen again, and many believe that he died under torture, the victim of a right-wing plot. The ensuing investigation implicated high-level Moroccan officials, a handful of French gangsters, and the Service de Documentation Extérieure et de Contre Espionnage, the French equivalent of the CIA. All told, it was a messy, shadowy affair that wrecked political reputations and shattered confidence in the French government.

For once, Jean was in stellar company: Jean-Louis Trintignant, Michel Piccoli, Roy Scheider, François Périer, Gian Maria Volonte and Michel Bouquet. Her role: a wealthy social worker with left-wing sensibilities and—intentionally—a Jane Fonda haircut. Even before it came out, *The French Conspiracy* generated heated discussions in France, and the controversy spilled over onto Jean's fading career, momentarily lending it luster. For three weeks of filming she would receive her last significant salary in France, approximately $40,000.

More than the money, the subject interested her passionately. Boisset wanted to show the unlikely meshing of disparate interests that cut across ideological lines and made temporary bedfellows out of politicians, journalists, spies and crooks. Behind the conspiracy and the cover-up, his film suggested, lay the long, meddlesome arm of the CIA. Jean agreed. "She had an excessive hatred of both the FBI and the CIA then," Boisset says. "But her thinking on the subject was ordered, rational, not what it became later on." In preparation for her role she made a concerted effort to lose weight, restrain her drinking and control her intake of tranquilizers. She slipped up once; she arrived drunk on the set and cost Boisset a day's filming. She was profusely apologetic afterward.

For the opening images of his film, Boisset took advantage of an actual anti–Vietnam war demonstration that occurred in January in the working-class suburb of St. Denis. Using a hand-held camera, he caught Seberg and Trintignant marching with the crowd. As the angry students and workers swept toward a phalanx of riot police determined to stand their ground, tempers exploded and the protest turned into a brawl that nearly engulfed the two stars. "No one knew we were filming that day," says Boisset. "If any of the protesters recognized Jean, they assumed she was there because of her political principles. She was very courageous about it. She plunged right into the fray."

During a lull in the filming she darted into a nearby shop. Minutes later she came back with a generous assortment of bonbons and goodies, which she distributed to the urchins who tagged along beside her.

Because of the film's controversial subject matter, Boisset met with little cooperation from the Paris police department, which systematically turned down his requests to film in the Paris streets. "No matter what we asked for, no matter what time of day, we were told that traffic conditions made it impossible to grant our request," he recalls. As a result, most of the exteriors were shot in the Paris suburbs or in Geneva.

One Paris locale was indispensable, however—the sidewalk in front of the Brasserie Lipp where the real Ben Barka had been abducted. When police flatly denied permission again, Boisset resolved to disobey their orders. He signaled his intentions to members of the international press, who showed up on the given day, notebooks in hand. Jean showed up, too. Although she was not in that particular scene, she wanted to be part of a common front with Trintignant, Volonte and Piccoli. Faced with the prospect of arresting the four stars and garnering unsavory headlines, the police backed off. Boisset got the needed shots.

The French Conspiracy, Jean's twenty-ninth film, was her last successful endeavor. While critical response was divided, the political thriller became one of the top box-office attractions in France that year. Its success did not reignite her career, though. "It was the subject matter people came to see," says Boisset. Still, he acknowledges wistfully, "Jean brought a great deal of honesty to her role. And it was the last film in which she was truly pretty."

By 1972 the commercial French cinema had long since discovered new idols, and Jean had reached a clumsy in-between age for an actress: she was neither an ingénue nor a character woman. Up to then, her career had more or less happened. Now it more or less stopped.

She took heart from certain lessons of the past. Where Preminger had failed with the resources of a major studio and his own considerable gifts for promotion, Godard, with no resources other than his own iconoclastic talent, had succeeded. *Lilith,* the least conventional of her Hollywood films, had been by far the most satisfying. She believed that renewal, if renewal there was to be, could only come from the risk takers and the innovators. In that respect she was an optimist, willing to stake whatever prerogatives and good will she had amassed in sixteen years on a perfectly unknown director and seemingly marginal projects. She didn't expect or want another *Paint Your Wagon*. But she did dream of another *Breathless*.

Dennis Berry represented that renewal to her. He was twenty-seven and broke, and his bushy hair and unkempt clothes gave him, at first glance, the appearance of a wild man. But closer inspection revealed the warmth of his eyes and a disarmingly boyish smile. Barely three weeks after Jean met him, he became her third husband.

Berry was an American, the son of film director John Berry, who had been blacklisted by Hollywood during the McCarthy era and, to salvage his career and peace of mind, had taken his wife and family to France in 1950. Six years old at the time, Dennis had been raised and educated in France and spoke English with an accent that sounded, to some, inexplicably Brooklynese. Alert and rebellious, he had helped man the soup kitchens at the Sorbonne during the May 1968 riots, which prompted author James Jones to use him as a model for Hill Gallagher, the idealistic young revolutionary and film maker in the novel *In the Merry Month of May*.

By sheer energy alone, Berry stood out in the checkered crowd of would-be directors, musicians and actors who haunted the cafés and bistros of St. Germain des Prés and Montparnasse. For all his brashness, he had a native gregariousness and a way with an anecdote that usually reduced his friends to helpless laughter. Much of his nonstop talk revolved around the cinema.

"Dennis could bend your ear for hours on end with the plot of the latest film he was going to make and how important it was going to be. They always seemed like rather bizarre, complicated films to me, the sort I'd never go see," says one of his former girl friends. "I thought he was too bright by half. But he was spirited and really great fun when he was around people."

In 1972 Berry was still trying to crash the movie portals. He had appeared as a gangster in the highly popular *Borsalino,* and his salary had allowed him to finance his first short, "Jojo ne Veut Pas Montrer Ses Pieds" ("Jojo Doesn't Want to Show His Feet"). A surrealistic effort—Jojo's girl friend perishes the day she sees his mysterious feet—the short had won several prizes, and Berry was eager to move on to a full-length feature.

He first spotted Jean at Castel's, the trendy Parisian bar and discotheque, dancing with Ricardo Franco. The disparity in their sizes amused him. With characteristic aplomb, he resolved to meet the star. Organizing a party seemed the best way, so he rallied his friends, invited a contingent of dancers from the Maurice Béjart Ballet company to lend a properly artistic tone, and then, by placing a few judicious phone calls, made sure that Jean would be escorted to the gathering.

"I was expecting her to arrive with some midget," he says with a laugh. "Instead, she showed up with this macho Italian movie star Fabio Testi. A real giant. I was horrified. For the first time in my life I didn't have anything to say. I just gaped at her."

Jean gaped back. "Then," she later recounted, "I surprised myself by doing something I'd never done before in my life. I turned to him and said, 'Will you come over here and kiss me?' And he did."

Before long, the pair was lost in conversation. Testi's ire built rapidly. Finally the Italian actor stormed from the party, slipped on the stairs on his way out and put his foot through a pane of glass, which merely redoubled his anger. "Once he'd gone," Berry remembers, "I told Jean, 'That man is really very dangerous, you know. He's beside himself and he's threatening to beat you up. You'd better go home with me.' I took her to this elegant town house where I was staying. And that's where we spent our first night. For all she knew, I was this nut who had a big mansion and peddled cocaine for a living. It wasn't until she discovered a screenplay at the foot of my bed that she realized I was a struggling film maker who just happened to be staying in a friend's nice house."

The screenplay was entitled *Howl.* "It struck a certain note of despair about our generation that gave me credibility in Jean's eyes," Berry says. "She told me she was so moved she had to take a Valium after reading it." Not long after, Jean was describing Berry to her intimates as "this lovely, zany, beautiful man who is a combination of Harpo and Karl Marx."

Romain was less captivated when Jean brought Dennis by one evening for dinner. Taking one look, the aging writer concluded that Berry was just another of Jean's follies. "Right there at the table, he told her that she was destroying herself, that she'd end up broke and alcoholic by the time she was forty, and probably commit suicide," Berry recalls. "I found out that he actually hired a private detective to follow me after he learned that I was having a love affair with Jean."

"I was convinced that he was another person using Jean," Gary later admitted. "I asked around and everybody said he was penniless and a scrounger. I could have killed him. Jean and I had our worst row."

Deeply smitten, Jean and Dennis escaped from Paris several weeks later for a weekend at St. Malo, the medieval walled city on the rugged Brittany coastline. At first the weekend did seem to draw its inspiration from a Marx Brothers movie. Jean drove recklessly, which made the hyperactive Berry even more nervous. An urban creature, he reacted to the customary sights of the countryside with astonishment.

"Look, there's a cow," he said as the car squealed around a bend. Then: "Oh, Jean, a tree! Did you see that tree?"

Calmly, Jean lectured him. "You're the most manic, nervous Jerry Lewis character I've ever been with. This is supposed to be a romantic journey, remember?"

By the time they pulled over for lunch in a small restaurant, they were both laughing. "For no special reason," says Berry. "We'd just look at each other and laugh. Like we were drunk or something. It was magical. When we got to St. Malo, Jean said to me, 'You know what I was thinking when we were laughing like that? I was thinking you'll never have the guts to marry me.' I said, 'I will if it's done immediately. Like tomorrow. Ever since I was twelve years old, I've had this mad desire to marry a movie star in Las Vegas.'"

"Anything but Las Vegas. It's so tawdry," Jean objected.

On March 12, 1972, they flew to Nevada. Since they had no American money with them, Jean put the entire trip, ring included, on her credit cards. Around midnight they were married in the Chapel of the Bells, one of Las Vegas' ubiquitous twenty-four-hour marriage mills.

While the minister performed the brief service, groans and shrieks echoed from the next room. The minister's children were watching a rerun of *Frankenstein* on television. It was every bit as tawdry and grotesque as Jean had anticipated. It was also utterly rejuvenating. "They were both on this huge high, this Great Gatsby spree," says Dennis' sister, Jan, who saw them in New York on their way back to Europe.

After the formality of the years with Romain Gary, it was as if the windows had been flung open on her life and a bracing gust of air had swept away the cobwebs. Dennis treated life as a lark, and Jean liked the change. With one impulsive move, she had wiped away a past heavy with consequence and tragedy. She was starting over.

For their first evening in Paris as man and wife, Dennis insisted on taking Jean to La Coupole, a Montparnasse restaurant that counted Jean-Paul Sartre and Eugène Ionesco among its regular clientele of bohemians and intellectuals. "Whenever Dennis was broke, he used to go there to eat," says one of his friends. "He knew everybody and usually could get himself invited for a free meal. If not, well, he'd convince the management to extend his credit. He managed to run up a pretty impressive bill. That's where he wanted to have his wedding dinner. Only this time when he walked in, it was different. He had Jean Seberg on his arm. With great flair he paid off his bill, ordered a magnum of champagne and offered it to the waiter and the maître d'hôtel, who had put up with him all those years."

"I suppose like everybody else, you're asking yourself what I see in Dennis," Jean said to one of her acquaintances not long after. "It's simple. He makes me laugh."

To another friend she blithely explained why they had eloped to Las Vegas: "We both had a hankering for tuna-fish sandwiches that night."

31

"Dennis was her crutch. He tried to take care of her."

—A FRIEND

Jean's marriage to Dennis Berry raised eyebrows in Paris. After having divorced Gary, a man twenty-five years older than herself, she had turned around and wed a youth six years younger. "She's just traded intelligence for sex," quipped one wag.

That wasn't all the gossips found suspicious. Who, they asked, was Dennis Berry? One more unemployed artist in a city overrun with the species.

Gary made a point of having a bottle of champagne and a bouquet of flowers waiting for the couple on their return from Las Vegas, but he maintained severe doubts about the union.

Jean felt disapproval emanating from many of her oldest friends as well—those who thought of her as a diplomat's wife and who felt her new marriage was a comedown. The solicitous tone didn't hide the cruelty of their remarks: "You're crazy, Jean!" "You're just being taken again." "He's altogether too immature for you."

"I suppose it was understandable," Jean reflected. "Dennis had been a flaming young man before I married him. And he certainly has an eccentric side. But I believe in loyalty. The way some of my friends reacted hurt me."

Many of them dropped by the wayside, unable to comprehend her thinking or to accept the distinct lowering of her social status. Jean was even dressing differently. High fashion and chic coiffures no longer mattered to her. She had switched to loose-fitting granny dresses and sandals; whimsy had replaced elegance in her wardrobe. "When I think that I tried for ten years to exemplify Parisian good taste only to find myself now in the blue jeans, white socks and sneakers I used to wear when I was sixteen—it makes me laugh," she said breezily.

A few good friends stuck by her. "Dennis really brought a grain of fantasy into her life," says one of them. "Romain was stuffy and pompous and constantly preoccupied with his image as a man of letters. By comparison, Dennis' youth was positively exhilarating. And he really worshiped Jean. He would do anything for her."

Berry, in fact, appeared to be a synthesis of the two male types that attracted her: the family man and the revolutionary. At one end of the spectrum was Ed Seberg. At the other, Hakim Jamal. All her life Jean aspired to the idyllic home life that Marshalltown represented in theory, if not in reality. At the same time, part of her yearned to participate in the excitement of change, artistic and political. She wanted stability and fled from it. If she rejected middle-class values as all too confining, too "bourgeois," she still hungered for the security they provided. Her desires were irreconcilable, but she could and did entertain them simultaneously.

At least temporarily, Berry satisfied the disparate requirements. For Jean, he was someone who would be acceptable both in Marshalltown and Compton, on the street corner and in the living room. "I don't have the guts, the nerves or the violence in me to lead the life of a terrorist. But I'm enough of a street person to be hip with them, to understand what makes them tick and get along with them," Berry now admits. "By the same token, I was willing to make my whole life with Jean Seberg. I'm a great believer in marriage. I anticipated the thirty or forty years we'd have together. I actually found myself wondering what it would be like for us then."

The euphoria induced by their mad elopement to Las Vegas lasted for several months and carried Jean through the filming of *La Camorra* that spring. Even though her romantic interest in Fabio Testi had obviously evaporated, she kept her promise to appear in his gangster film, which told of the corruption of a Neapolitan youth by an organization not unlike the Mafia. Her role as the chief gangster's mistress was inconsequential, and the film only slightly less grim than the slums outside Naples in which it was shot. Not always as diplomatically as possible, Testi avoided Jean during the two weeks she spent on the set. It didn't matter. She was filled with love and laughter. Once she'd honored her commitment, she and Dennis disappeared for a delayed honeymoon on the island of Capri.

Just as Gary had done, Berry introduced Jean to a new world. It was not the world of accomplished authors and well-mannered diplomats—each wearing his reputation like a pin in the lapel of a tailored suit. It was a society of artistic have-nots, those who lived outside the system and bucked it. Some of them had succumbed to the easy lure of drugs, which swept over Paris in the early 1970s. Others were nonconformists just for the sake of being nonconformists. What counted with them, however, was what they would do, not what others had already done. In their company, Jean blossomed with projects. She would write more scenarios herself. Possibly direct one of them. She would spend time on her poetry. Compose a short story.

"I always wanted to write, and I tried now and again," she said, "but with Romain, I had a hundred complexes." Not so with Berry; he urged her on.

During the summer of 1972, working on weekends with Fausto Canel, she quickly finished the scenario of *Frontier Palace*. It was a fanciful, light-hearted comedy about a film crew that descends upon a provincial French hotel, and the brief romance that blooms between the young hotel porter and the supporting actress, a pop singer named Lila Lowry.

Much of it was autobiographical. Jean modeled the porter after Ricardo Franco. There was a blustering movie producer, Richard Leidering—unmistakably Otto Preminger—who browbeats his performers. Jean put herself in the person of Lila Lowry, who is nervous about making her second movie because "I know I'm no good, but I can't help it. I just crawl into a shell when he shouts at me, and then I can't do anything." (Leidering/Preminger's defense: "I've yelled for twenty years. If I say so myself, I've made some outstanding films.") Canel says the script is almost pure Jean, and never so much as when Lila confesses tearfully to her young boyfriend, "Look, I'm a nice middle-class girl from Iowa . . . Oh la la . . . Sooner or later it catches up with you . . . You can take the girl out of the country, but you can't take the country out of the girl. It just hit me how true that is."

Jean subsequently received a grant from the French government to defray one third of the production costs. Unfortunately, she and Canel were unable to raise the other two-thirds, and the film was never made. With no more success, Berry was struggling to rustle up financing for his film, *Howl*. The going was rocky, and he abandoned the project to write an acerbic comedy for Jean, ultimately called *Le Grand Délire* (*The Great Frenzy*).

"There was something very strong between Dennis and Jean," says French actor Yves Benneyton, one of Dennis' pals. "She invested a lot of herself in him careerwise. I think she looked on him as a new Godard. Dennis was a hope for many of us. He had a great deal of raw talent and was always pushing for something new. He liked to take risks. After his marriage, he really changed for the better. He became more adult and responsible. He'd always had a very strong, dominating personality, but he sincerely tried to work things out. They were very happy together at first."

Romain's fear that Jean was being exploited yet another time proved groundless. Dennis had no interest in social standing or fancy trappings. Eventually Gary conceded, "Jean may have to pay the bills, but I reckon Dennis saves her a small fortune because he doesn't let her be taken for a ride."

Although Jean had earned more than $2 million in her career, Berry was understandably surprised to discover that she had relatively little to show for it: a vacation cottage in Greece; a farm in Iowa that was costing her more money than it was bringing in; and half of the Paris apartment, which she had helped buy but to which she apparently had no legal title. "I don't even have a place to call home," Jean often lamented to Berry. Gary's habit of popping in unannounced on the newly-weds, sometimes twice a day, didn't improve matters.

In an effort to replenish the coffers, Jean accepted a role in a grisly Spanish suspense movie, *The Corruption of Chris Miller*. Neither she nor Berry thought much of the script, which centered on a distasteful *ménage à trois*: a successful London fashion designer (Jean), her neurotic stepdaughter (Marisol) and the randy hippie (Barry Stokes) they murder one particularly gloomy night. This lurid effort called upon the actresses to wear diaphanous costumes and show as much cleavage as the Spanish censors then permitted. In its favor: Juan Bardem, the director, had a modest reputation for his craft, the film was budgeted at a respectable $1 million, and more significant, Jean's bank balance was low.

In August she, Dennis and Celia drove to Spain for the three-month filming. The experience was more unpleasant than they had anticipated. Not only was the material intrinsically worthless, but Bardem wanted to age Jean in order to make her relationship with her teen-age stepdaughter appear more credible. Seeing the rushes, Jean was upset by what she felt was a preponderance of unflattering shots. Dennis championed her cause. Before long the set reverberated with arguments and recriminations. "They really treated Jean like shit," Dennis says.

Worse, Bardem accentuated the sleazy sexuality of a voyeuristic script that suggested a lesbian attachment between Jean's character and the stepdaughter. Jean had not just landed in another flop; this time she actually appeared to be slumming.

When *The Corruption of Chris Miller* finally received a two-day screening in a New York art house in November 1979, Vincent Canby observed that Miss Seberg "gives an extremely sincere performance that is never particularly convincing. Once again, though, she gives dimension to a film of no great interest just because her presence is so unexpected. What, one keeps wondering, is this quintessentially American beauty, a woman who speaks in the flat accents of her native Iowa, doing in the middle of so much quintessential European decadence?"

That question would apply to the rest of her career.

Her salary from the film did allow her to purchase her own apartment once she and Dennis returned to Paris in October.

"I could have lived in one room," says Berry. "But Jean was a star, after all. Or she'd been one. And I really thought she deserved a place to sleep befitting her status."

They did not move far. In fact, they didn't even change their address. Jean merely bought another apartment in the Rue du Bac complex, in a building at the back, overlooking the court-yard. It put Gary at arm's length but still allowed Diego, once again in good health after a serious case of rheumatic fever, to shuttle back and forth. Jean appreciated the attention Dennis showered on the child.

At Christmas the Berrys traveled to Marshalltown for the holiday so the Sebergs could meet their new son-in-law. It was not exactly love at first sight. Berry's own family was loose and eccentric, accustomed to the erratic temperament of show-business types. Until McCarthy had done his dirty work, John Berry had been one of the bright young hopes of Holly-wood. His wife, Gladys, a friendly, slightly whimsical woman, was an actress herself, and she delighted in appearing in her son's strange films.

By contrast, Dennis found the Sebergs inexplicably re-pressed. The "lovey-dovey" façade they presented to the world, he thought, concealed long-festering resentments, and he felt smothered in the puritanical household. Ed Seberg now knew to serve wine at dinner, but it was tacitly understood that everyone would limit himself to one glass. On their side, the Sebergs were unprepared for Dennis' volatile spirits and con-cluded, between themselves, that he had "a terrible temper."

Bill Fisher seemed to express the consensus in Marshall-town, however, when he said, "Dennis was lively and fun, but he was too young to be called a gentleman."

To her parents' displeasure, Jean insisted on driving Dennis out to the Tama Indian reservation during their visit. He was surprised at the "mystical sensibility" she seemed to share with the Indians, who accepted her as one of their own. "Jean was truly moved by anyone who was in trouble," he says. "All people counted equally with her. Everybody had the same chance."

Later Jean gave the expected interview to the *Times-Repub-lican* and indicated that she wanted to return to Marshalltown in the near future and appear in a play at the Martha

Ellen Tye Playhouse. Berry would direct the production, she said, and local talent could fill the supporting roles. It would be her way of thanking the town for all it had done to get her started as an actress.

The idea was ludicrous and Jean knew it. Her parents and her new husband did not get along. The house she had purchased for the black students still stood as a reminder of the town's latent animosities. Dennis had been curious to see Marshalltown, but to him it was the end of the earth. If she had hoped to sell him on the solid virtues of the Midwest, the visit was a failure.

Before leaving, she bought a Marshalltown High School letterman's jacket for him. When he put it on, it transformed him, but not as she had expected. He looked nothing like the small-town star athlete Ed Seberg would have wanted for a son-in-law. With his unruly hair and the manic glint in his eye, Dennis bore a startling resemblance to an unrepentant hooligan from the wrong side of the tracks.

Nonetheless, it was a reinvigorated Jean who greeted the New Year. She had overcome the loss of a child and a crippling breakdown. She was free of her entanglements with the Panthers and the *Newsweek* suit. And she had a husband who strode boldly through life, pulling her along with him.

There was only one drawback. Her income was small and likely to become smaller over the years. She admitted that she and Dennis had married so quickly that they had never really discussed finances. While she was confident that their fortunes would change as soon as he made his first full-length film, she had to bear their living costs and provide him with pocket money.

Back in Paris, her apprehensions grew. Early in 1973 she got up in the middle of the night, slipped in the unlit hallway and broke her ankle. Confined in a cast for weeks, she wondered if and how she would ever work again. Overriding her principles, she wrote several friends reminding them of money she'd lent them in the past and hinting delicately that she herself anticipated financial difficulties in the months ahead.

Dennis refused to let her indulge in her pessimism. Whenever she fretted unduly about the future or her ankle, he would simply pick her up bodily and carry her off to the movies.

32

"I tend to involve myself totally in what I do, and I have changed a lot as an actress because I have changed a lot as a person. I wish I could say I have grown, but it depends on the director and the cast."

—JEAN SEBERG

At eleven o'clock on Tuesday evening, May 1, 1973, five men entered a shabby apartment building on Townsend Street in Roxbury, Massachusetts, and silently climbed the stairs to the third floor. On the second-floor landing, their way was blocked by a German shepherd, growling and baring its teeth. When one of the men tried to shove the dog aside, it lunged for the attack. The man pulled out a gun and shot the dog.

The intruders then bounded up the remaining flight of stairs and broke down the door to the third-floor apartment. As its startled occupant sprang from an armchair, they sprayed him with bullets. The impact of the shots ripping into his thin body sent him reeling. He crashed to the floor, and his lamb's-wool cap flew off his head. While a woman in the apartment shrieked in horror and disbelief, the killers bolted down the stairs, jumped into a waiting Toyota and sped away.

At forty-two, Hakim Jamal lay dead in a pool of blood.

The following morning one of Jamal's sidekicks from the days of the Malcolm X Foundation, a man by the name of Kidogo, blamed the slaying on the De Mau Mau, a radical black organization founded by discontented veterans of the Vietnam war. Since returning to the Boston area, Jamal had worked on and off with the group, but antagonisms had developed, and he had come to dismiss its members as "not fit to eat at my table." They, in turn, charged that Jamal was betraying "the purity of the black revolution."

Although motives for the killing were unclear, Kidogo explained that "the fact that Jamal was married to a white woman might be one of the reasons for the falling out." The explanation begged a technicality: Jamal was still married to Dorothy, and his white "wife" of the moment was but one in a string of mistresses.

For the police, it was just another instance of the factionalism and violence that periodically rocked the troubled suburb of Roxbury. Three of the De Mau Mau brothers were eventually arrested, and after a stormy trial, found guilty of first-degree murder and sentenced to life imprisonment.

Coming little more than a year after Gale Ann Benson's savage murder, the news of Jamal's death hit Jean doubly hard. "She was extraordinarily depressed by it," says Dennis Berry. "This black man she had loved had been killed by his own race for going with a white woman. Jean realized that it was something that could have happened to him while she was part of his life. That scared her terribly; at the same time, she felt awfully guilty about it."

As Jean's own perceptions of the late sixties grew progressively distorted, Jamal acquired even more heroic proportions in her mind. All that was opportunistic and manipulative about him would be forgotten. He was a victim of the racism they had combated together—the same racism that had killed Nina, doomed the Mesquakee Indians to extinction and flooded the ghetto with drugs in order to keep blacks in a state of stupor and dependence. For Jean, it was all related.

One indication of the metamorphosis that Jamal underwent in her head is found in a curious diatribe against drug addiction that she wrote for the newspaper *Libération* in February 1978. Embedded in the stream-of-consciousness prose is a thumbnail sketch of Hakim Jamal as Jean had come to see him: "Hakim Jamal, ex-addict, jailbird, Black Muslim, the most beautiful man who ever walked the earth in our time; he is dead, my Jamal. Eight bullets in the stomach while he was seated in a rocking chair, his family around him. Three junkies back from Vietnam did it. OK. Extenuating circumstances. But you killed him, my Jamal."

By then she had turned Jamal into a holy outcast, the saintly victim, a solitary fighter in the sinister world of deadly conspiracies. The Lone Ranger, after all. Seeing herself in similar terms, she recounted how Jamal had trained her to use a machine gun and how the two of them, side by side, had shot police helicopters out of the sky.

In 1973, however, Berry's exuberance was still enough to hold Jean's despair in check. The hopes and energies she had once devoted to the black revolution she now invested in the new cinema they would bring into being. The studios were dead, the established French producers mired in patently commercial undertakings. The cinema she envisioned would spring from the generation that had fomented the May 1968 revolution in Paris and contested the country's stuffy bourgeois values, just as the hippies had done years earlier in the United States. The Berry's apartment was a meeting place. Motorcycles varoomed into the stately courtyard, and a disheveled and motley crew came and went at all hours. Celia disapproved and sought employment elsewhere, while the well-heeled neighbors clucked behind their velvet drapes and wondered what had happened to that sweet Mme. Gary. Jean relished their indignant looks and savored her role as queen bee of the ragtag group.

"Jean was very modest about herself and her accomplishments," says Betty Desouches. "She was truly touched if someone liked her. I think it even surprised her. As a result, she forgave people for a lot of things. Even the bums she took up with at the end of her life. She liked them because they liked her."

"She was remarkably open to people," Yves Benneyton agrees. "Jean had none of the trappings of the traditional star. She tried hard to fight her own myth. After ten minutes, you could be her good friend."

If there were signs of her underlying instability, they were subtle and not immediately perceptible to outsiders. However, when Jean and Dennis took a three-week Easter vacation at

St. Tropez with friends, one of them, a doctor, observed that Jean drank continuously throughout the day. While never inebriated, she was also never without a glass of wine. To others, she seemed less and less fastidious about her appearance and unconcerned about her weight, even though it could only further imperil her career.

Frédéric Mitterand, a nephew of the French socialist politician François Mitterand, had a vivid impression of Jean as "someone who was already injured and forcing things," when, in May, he approached her to be the godmother of his Left Bank repertory cinema, the Olympic. Like many of his countrymen, he cherished memories of *Breathless* and thought it would be appropriate to have Jean preside over the opening of his redecorated cinema. "She was no longer in vogue," he admits. "But we decided to organize a celebration as if she were still a star."

Across the narrow street he strung a banner reading WEL-COME JEAN SEBERG, and a small girl presented Jean with a bouquet of flowers as she emerged from a rented limousine. In the hall, clips from Jean's movies flickered on the screen, while a band played American marches in an adjoining garden and guests besieged the buffet.

Fortified with a couple of whiskeys, Jean mingled hesitantly with the crowd. "She had difficulty walking," Mitterand remembers, "because of her ankle, which she'd recently broken, and that seemed to enhance the air of fragility about her. She stayed for approximately an hour but then got terribly tired and had to go home. Still, I think the tribute pleased her." In subsequent years, Mitterand would make sure that *Lilith* was part of the changing bill at his theater.

Regular therapy sessions with a psychiatrist during this period seemed to help Jean deal with her insecurities. "She really understood that her life had to change, that her career wouldn't go on forever and she'd have to reinvent herself if she was going to survive," says one friend. "She had never been able to accept her childhood and what she considered its awful puritanism. She was distressed by the huge gulf between her and her parents. She had an immense capacity for self-punishment."

The Sebergs' visit to Paris that August stirred up all the latent anxieties. "Jean felt trapped by them," says Dennis Berry. "They'd stay around the apartment and refuse to go out unless we all went out together as a family. Jean could never bring herself to say, 'Look, tonight I've got plans. Why don't you both go out by yourselves?' She just seemed to lose all her individuality and energy around them."

Before the Sebergs returned to the United States, they announced to Dennis and Jean that they had a present for them: in Jean's name, they had pledged $1,000 to Trinity Lutheran Church in Marshalltown. For Jean, such a gift was just another indication that her parents didn't understand her and probably never would. Berry judged it a hollow gesture by which the Sebergs wanted only to prove to their community that Jean was still part of it. He was relieved when the visit was over. If Jean was, she couldn't bring herself to say so. Not yet.

To her friends she presented a less troubled face, and most of them believe it was a relatively happy time in her life. She could be flirtatious and witty. She had wide-ranging interests, from politics to jazz, and four languages at her command— French, English, Spanish and Italian. She and Dennis liked to wake up at four in the morning, fix themselves a snack, and then chat for a couple of hours or dream up films before drifting off to sleep again. Whenever old acquaintances or friends of acquaintances passed through Paris, Jean jumped at the chance to take them out to dinner, even when it meant picking up the check.

One of her fears was coming true, however. Berry's career had not gotten off the ground, and she had gone for more than a year without making a film herself. The scripts that *were* offered to her were dramatically worthless, or worse, pornographic. In November, strapped for money, she sold the farm in Iowa at a small profit; the notion of having a retirement property her whole family could enjoy no longer appeared all that important to her.

That same month she finally received a respectable film offer—to star opposite Kirk Douglas in *Mousey,* which would be shot in England by Daniel Petrie. Actually, the film was destined for ABC television as part of a weekly series of thrillers, but under the title *Cat and Mouse* it later played movie houses elsewhere in the world.

The script's principal novelty was that it permitted Douglas, who normally incarnated more stalwart types, to be seen as a retiring biology professor who turns into a psychotic killer after his wife (Jean) divorces him and remarries, taking their son with her. The final sequences had him pursuing her through a darkened country house.

Douglas was full of suggestions when exterior filming began in Canada. He and Petrie had established a lively working relationship by the time Jean joined the production at Pinewood Studios in England. Petrie, who remembered Jean as the vital, assured woman he had met in 1961 at the Cannes Film Festival, was not prepared for the change that had come over her. "In spite of the fact that she had just married a handsome young man and seemed very happy about it, there was this enormous professional insecurity. She was almost spineless. Kirk is an old pro—you ring that bell and the horse rushes off to the fire—but Jean was just going through the motions."

One day, between shots, Jean startled Douglas by saying to him, "Sometimes I look back to the days I was making *St. Joan* and I think how much better it would have been if I really had been burned at the stake."

"Her remark astounded me because it came right out of the blue," says Douglas. "It wasn't a morbid death wish or anything, although I've since wondered. No, it was all quite matter-of-fact. She even let out a slight laugh afterward. Then she changed the subject. Jean had a very shadowy, enigmatic quality. You sensed that there was a lot going on behind the veiled curtains, a lot she didn't let you see."

Expecting Jean to contribute creatively to the film, Petrie was dismayed by her passivity on the set. While the electricians hung the lights one morning, he searched out a quiet corner to work on the script. Finding what appeared to be an empty room, he settled in and was deep in thought when Jean opened the door. Inadvertently, Petrie had taken her dressing room. He offered to move, but Jean insisted that he stay and curled up quietly in an armchair to read a magazine.

"After a while I began to sneak looks at her," Petrie recalls.

"There was such an aura of world-weariness about her, an awful sadness. I finally turned to her and asked, 'Jean, why don't you have any faith in yourself?'

"She looked at me as if I'd hit her with a hammer. Her face just collapsed, and she started sobbing uncontrollably—huge, copious tears. For about five minutes, she was unable to speak. I went over to her, put my arm around her and offered her a handkerchief.

"Then slowly she opened up. She talked about the awful diatribes Preminger had submitted her to and how those early experiences had shaken all the confidence out of her. I can't say that she was angry about it. She was trying very hard to be analytical. She told me about her marriage to Romain Gary and how she'd felt that intellectually she was out of her depth, and about the Black Panther affair and how it had been blown all out of proportion. She looked so utterly woebegone. I realized she had an abiding belief in her lack of worth.

"We talked for a long time that day. I wanted to convince her that it was all in herself. She was smart, she had talent. All that was required was an act of faith.

"A week or so later my wife and I went out to dinner with Dennis and Jean. Her walls were back up. There was no indication at all from her that we'd had this talk, not even a look in the eyes that implies a passing closeness. She was very conscious of her façade. And I began to think back to that very together, assured woman I had met in Cannes twelve years before, and I realized that that had probably just been a façade too. We wrote to each other a few times after that—polite notes. But because of our talk in the dressing room, I always felt as if I had a certain responsibility toward her. I felt terrible about it for a long time. She was a very moving lady."

There was no change on the set, however. *Mousey* was primarily a character study that depended on the electricity between its stars. "It was like the mating of two boiled eggs," says Petrie with a shrug of discouragement.

Jean later referred to *Mousey* as "my bread-and-butter picture of 1973." She had lent herself to it perfunctorily, almost as if she knew in advance that it would be shunted into a late-night slot on television and go largely unwatched. It was the kind of commercial undertaking she no longer believed in. But her salary was useful and would allow her and Berry to make the sort of films that did count: personal, committed, unorthodox.

On New Year's Eve she raised her glass to her husband and said with dramatic abandon, "I'm going to live this coming year as if it were my last."

33

"Actresses are a little like race horses. It's difficult for us when the race is canceled."

—JEAN SEBERG

Among the unconventional young artists and film makers who hung out in the Berrys' apartment, almost as if it were another café on the Rue du Bac, was Philippe Garrel. The son of Swiss marionettists, he was slight, tousled and unshaven, and his dark eyes seemed perpetually haunted. His shabby clothes usually bore the ashes from the stub of the burned-out Gauloise that dangled from his thin lips. A series of enigmatic, experimental films had earned him, by his twenty-sixth year, an unofficial reputation as "the pope of the French underground cinema." Not that he cared. Contemptuous of popular success, interested only in exploring the private recesses of his art, Garrel was more than content if his films recouped the cost of the negatives.

Often broke, he lived in a squalid flat furnished with a few pieces of rickety furniture, an editing table and literally thousands of cigarette butts, which covered the floor as thoroughly as any carpet. To some, his brooding manner suggested a kinship with the "cursed" French poets of the late nineteenth century—Rimbaud, Verlaine and Baudelaire.

Garrel liked coming by the Berrys' apartment, which had much the same electric atmosphere as the Actors Studio, or the Actors Studio as he imagined it. Although he sometimes appeared to be talking from another place and point in time entirely, Jean read genius into his self-absorbed manner.

"Jean had a very maternal attitude toward struggling artists," says one friend. "But with Garrel, it was something more. A sexual attraction? I'm not sure. But it was obvious she was drawn to the creative madness she sensed in him."

Early in 1974 Garrel said he wanted to use her in a film he had been mulling over for a while. Called *Les Hautes Solitudes (The Outer Reaches of Solitude)*, it became one of the most prophetic films Jean ever made. It was also infuriatingly impenetrable. Nonetheless, in the succession of black-and-white images, some of which have the inadvertent elegance of high-fashion photography, Garrel managed to capture much of the beauty and torment that was Jean Seberg.

At the start, Garrel knew only that he wanted to make a film on the theme of solitude with actors he judged authentically lonely. He had briefly explored the desolate terrain with a girl friend named Nico and with actor Laurent Terzieff. But his fevered imagination was fired by the notion of using Jean—the foreigner, living the solitude of exile; the political activist, trapped in the solitude of despair; the aging actress, facing the solitude of decay. The film quickly turned into a one-woman show.

Some of *Les Hautes Solitudes* was improvised on the streets of Paris. Much of it was shot in Jean's own apartment. Although she volunteered to put up the cost of the film—it amounted, Garrel says, to "about the price of a Volkswagen"—the director refused. He would shoot during the daylight hours until his film ran out, then spend his evenings trying to scrounge up enough money to buy stock for the next day. There were no lights, no sound, no story. Only images of Jean—fighting back the tears; sitting on the edge of her bed having her hair combed; huddled like a caged beast in the corner of a room; blowing out a candle; peeking out from under a voluminous hood and flashing a full, radiant smile; wiping the tears away; walking timidly into a café and then walking jauntily right back out again; or gazing melancholically from a window. Sad, tantalizing images because they show Jean lost in a private world, as shadowy and dense as the ocean depths, at the same time that she seems to be sending out a mute plea for understanding and acceptance.

One day, having secured enough film for a relatively protracted scene, Garrel asked Jean what aspect of her solitude she was interested in enacting. "I want to do a suicide scene," she answered him. "I think I'll do it in my bedroom. I'll do it with pills. And I want Tina [Aumont, who had a bit part] to come in and save me at the last moment."

Garrel set his camera rolling while Jean thrashed about in her bed, reached out for the bottle of pills and then began to wash them down compulsively with a glass of water.

"All of a sudden I had a terrible premonition," Garrel remembers. "I thought, She's taken the real thing. I was frightened, and a chill ran down my spine. I stopped the camera and shouted, 'Jean, what in the hell have you done?' She looked up at me, puzzled, and shouted back, '*Merde,* you've gone and loused up my big scene!' She had only swallowed aspirin, but her acting was so persuasive that I was completely taken in. I repositioned the camera, and we shot the scene a second time until the film ran out. Afterward I said to myself, She's done this before. She's played this scene with other people. And I told Dennis, 'I wouldn't ever leave Jean alone if I were you.'"

Garrel also took his own precautions. Several days later he filmed a short scene in which Jean, wearing a peignoir, embraced the cross she occasionally wore around her neck. "It was a way of protecting her," he says.

Les Hautes Solitudes, like most of Garrel's films, played only briefly in Paris to a handful of cultists, but it contains some of the most ravagingly honest footage of Jean. The full weight of her experience is reflected in her worn and lined face, all the more beautiful because of that. On occasion the resemblance to Marilyn Monroe is uncanny. Without explanation or commentary, *Les Hautes Solitudes* also reveals Jean flirting dangerously with insanity.

Berry sensed a deep complicity between the director and his wife. If he was not always sure what form it took, he was happy that Jean seemed to find the film rewarding. He liked Garrel and appreciated his apostolic fervor. Frequently the two of them would engage in long, convoluted discussions about art and the future of the cinema. Garrel remembers Jean's impatience one night while he and Berry debated the merits of Bernardo Bertolucci and Jack Kerouac. Feeling excluded, she drank throughout the evening, and the alcohol loosened her aggressions. As Garrel prepared to leave, Jean insisted that he stay for one more drink. Garrel said no. "Then stay while I have one more," she said. Again he declined. "Don't you think Philippe is being mean to me?" Jean snapped to her husband.

"On my way out the door," Garrel recalls, "I shouted *'Vive l'anarchie!'* Then I heard a crash. I looked back. Jean had taken a glass and smashed it on a table. With the jagged edge, she was slashing one of her wrists. Blood was flowing everywhere. Dennis took off his belt and made a tourniquet of it and yelled at me to hold it tight while he called a doctor. All the time Jean was crying, 'Let me go, let me go. I want to die.' I gripped the belt so hard that my hand was frozen stiff by the time the doctor finally arrived. He bandaged her wrist and gave her a strong sedative. It was a monumental scene. With all her intelligence, Jean just couldn't control her suicidal tendencies."

Shortly after, Jean checked into a private clinic for a week. Some of her friends were beginning to suspect that she looked upon the hospital as a sanctuary. The rigid, unvarying routines imposed temporary order on her life, and she secretly relished being the center of attention. More important, Berry believes, checking into a clinic of her own free will allowed Jean to view her instability as a physical problem, not a mental one.

When she returned to the apartment he encouraged her, almost as a kind of therapy, to seriously consider directing a film herself. Although Jean had spent nearly half of her life before the cameras, he knew that she felt victimized by her career. Preminger had nearly destroyed her talents; Hollywood consistently misused them. Gary's films had been exploitative and unsatisfying. Directing a film, Berry reasoned, might reassure her that she was actually in control of her destiny for once.

Jean had been toying with the idea for several years. Although *Frontier Palace* languished for want of financing, she did have thoughts for a short called "Ballad for the Kid." The idea had been suggested to her by an aspiring young actor,

Jean-François Ferriol, who carried his passion for the American West so far as to think, sometimes, that he was a reincarnation of Billy the Kid. Ever since he had visited an Indian reservation in Taos, New Mexico, he sported cowboy dress in the streets of Paris and considered the affectation the vanguard of a new vogue. Ferriol also yearned to be in a Western while he was still twenty-two, which, he reminded people, was Billy the Kid's age when he was gunned down.

What he and Jean imagined in their twenty-five-minute scenario was an encounter between Billy and a fading platinum sex goddess in the Jean Harlow mold who is called only Star and would be played, naturally, by Jean. The Kid, knowing he is fated to die but wanting a hand in his own death, delivers himself up to his love, Star, who obligingly shoots him in the back.

It was to be the meeting of two myths—the outlaw and the movie queen—and if Ferriol claimed to understand Billy the Kid, Jean thought she knew a thing or two about the fantasies of stardom. She put up half of the film's $10,000 budget, Ferriol the other half, which allowed them to pay a crew of twelve for a week's work. Jean contributed her services as actress and director for nothing.

Filming took place during the first week of July in an abandoned sandpit near Orly Airport that, rather miraculously, approximated the Painted Desert of New Mexico. Female directors were not exactly a rarity in 1974, but the notion that Jean Seberg, once Preminger's sacrificial victim, had been reborn on the other side of the camera captured the fancy of the press.

"It was a ten-thousand-dollar film that got a million dollars in publicity," boasts Ferriol. Not quite, but the New York Times seized the occasion to do a major profile of Jean. Newsweek and Time both carried items about the film. Articles appeared in the French and British press and sundry film journals, often accompanied by photographs of Jean in a sexy low-cut evening gown, peering through a viewfinder.

"People are making too much of this," she said as the publicity built. "It's just the realization of an idea I liked. It's not a big picture. I have no illusions about it. I'm not going to be onstage Oscar night. When it is shown to the audience, I would just like to say, 'Let me invite you into a little dream.'"

The little dream was laced with autobiographical references. Playing a vulgar, childlike sex goddess past her prime, Jean was alluding to the hype and heartache of her own career. She even alluded to Nina:

"How's our baby, Kid?" Star asks at one point.

"Ma'am, we never had a baby."

"Really? That's weird," she replies, a bewildered look on her face.

Star is not easily convinced, however. Putting her ear to the sand, she says, "I can hear him! I can hear him so well . . . our baby!"

"I told you once," the Kid snarls. "We never had a baby." And he slaps her face.

"Ballad for the Kid" was shown at several film festivals toward the end of 1974, and as part of a bill with two other shorts directed by women, had a brief engagement at the Olympic Cinema. But if the public had evinced a passing interest in the fact that Jean Seberg was directing her own film, it had little curiosity about the finished product.

"It's a failure," Jean said years later. "It was a mistake trying to direct and act at the same time. It made me completely schizophrenic. I just wanted to make a little Freudian film, but it turned into a round-the-clock struggle. I'd go home after the day's shooting and cry all night. People complicate the cinema so . . . Maybe I didn't work hard enough on it."

Far from replenishing her strength and confidence, "Ballad for the Kid" left Jean less assured than ever and several thousand dollars poorer.

Dennis meanwhile had secured a government grant to cover part of the costs of *Le Grand Délire,* and several producers were willing to provide the rest of the financing. It looked as if he might be able to go into production by December. One of the principal roles would be for Jean, who seemed eager to play it. While she waited for the pieces to come together, she accepted a part opposite Frederick Stafford in an Italian drama, *Bianchi Cavalli d'Agosto* (*White Horses of Summer*), which took her to Rome again. Berry, who stayed behind in

Paris, soon began receiving reports that Jean was behaving strangely on the set.

White Horses of Summer was a hollow account of an American couple whose marital difficulties come to a head during their vacation in southern Italy. Much of the script deals with the impact of their bickering on their impressionable son, who runs away to the nearby cliffs, accidentally tumbles to the rocks below and is rushed unconscious to the hospital. Unsure whether he will live or die, the guilty parents undertake a lonely vigil outside his hospital room.

Acting that vigil unnerved Jean. She brought to it her own vivid associations—the stark hospital room in Geneva, the two seemingly endless days during which Nina's life had hung in the balance, and the bludgeoning guilt she had felt when the child died. Once again she retreated into a bizarre fantasy world, imagining herself at the eye of complex conspiracies.

At the first available moment Dennis flew to Rome, where he learned that Jean and one of their mutual friends, a French actor named Marc Porel, were embroiled in a scheme to spirit Huey Newton out of the United States. The Panther leader had been accused of the murder of a seventeen-year-old Oakland prostitute, and his supporters believed that a fair trial was an impossibility and conviction a foregone conclusion.

"Jean said that Huey was the number-one enemy of the FBI and that she had to get him out of the States," says Berry. "I asked her if she'd talked to him, and she answered, 'Why, yes, of course.' She claimed that she and Marc had obtained false passports for him and had this whole underground organization lined up behind them. It just didn't seem to make any sense to me. When I got back to Paris I asked around and learned that Huey Newton had already been out of the U.S. for several months and, I think, was rumored to be in Cuba. Jean had made the whole thing up."

Newton confirms that Jean Seberg had nothing to do with his escape from the United States. In fact, he maintains he was totally unaware of her and her association with the Panthers until her death brought her name back into the headlines.

"Jean just couldn't stand the life she was leading," says Berry, "so she'd invented an imaginary one for herself. It was

317

my first real indication that she was not just emotionally distraught. She was mentally unstable. I knew that it would get worse and that there would be moments of pure delirium. A few days later she flipped out entirely."

Jean spent much of the end of 1974 in and out of clinics, heavily medicated with the barbiturates that were fast becoming an integral part of her regimen. (One of the poems she wrote in French that year, "Madame se promène," is a veritable shopping list of the drugs that propelled her through the day and put her to sleep at night. It ends with this confession to her doctor: "In spite of all your beautiful screwed-up science, you should know this—and why should I hide it—it's so good, so nice, just to talk with you.") During much of December she was in a haze, unable to dress herself on some days.

Life was turning into another kind of nightmare for Berry. Locked into a schedule that had him beginning his feature at the end of December, he no longer knew if Jean would be available to star in it. Or if she even wanted to. Replacing her could aggravate her feelings of abandonment. On the other hand, subjecting her to the rigors of filming could prove equally upsetting. It was hardly a propitious start for the young director, who had envisioned a close collaboration with his actors, free from the usual commercial bind.

Others noticed Jean's erratic behavior. Frédéric Mitterand came by her apartment on January 2 to wish her a happy New Year. In the Rue du Bac, just outside her door, Alain Delon was shooting scenes for a new movie, *Monsieur Klein*. "The entire subject of Jean's conversation that day was whether or not Alain Delon would come up to the apartment between shots and say hello to her," Mitterand recalls. "She couldn't talk about anything else. 'Will he?' 'Won't he?' And then, 'Why hasn't he?'"

Berry's intentions for *Le Grand Délire* were nothing if not ambitious. On one level it was to be an anarchic comedy that exploded all the bourgeois proprieties: Upon his father's death, the son (Yves Benneyton) of a prosperous family turns their mansion into a bordello—with the maid (Isabelle Huppert) functioning as the star attraction, his mother (Dennis' own mother, Gladys Berry) replacing the maid, and an American *femme fatale* (Jean) presiding over the unbridled fornication as an elegant madam. On another level, Berry intended to interweave a love-at-first-sight story, not unlike his own courtship of Jean, involving the *femme fatale* and a canny peasant (Pierre Blaise).

The two stories didn't always mesh, and hitting the proper tone—somewhere between cynical and zany—was the big challenge. "It was going to be a different film," says Benneyton, "but it wasn't the flowering we all hoped for. We found ourselves caught in the same old commercial mess—pressed for time, producers breathing down our backs. There was no special rapport among the actors. Dennis had moments when he just exploded. There was general tension everywhere."

To a television reporter who visited the set, Dennis admitted that he purposely kept Jean free from the writing and directing so that she would be "fresh for her role." Privately, he simply hoped that she would make it through the filming. Nervous, dissatisfied with her role, she was frequently so drugged that she would drift through her scenes, unconnected to anyone or anything around her. She had gained weight and insisted on having her hair whacked off in the *Breathless* style, as she did whenever she felt her artistic identity was imperiled. The style, so alluring when she was a gamine, was unflattering and only accentuated the puffiness of her face. There were days when Berry would have no choice but to film her looking spacy and adrift.

"Dennis lost control of the movie," says Mylene Demongeot, who with her husband, Marc Simenon, was one of its producers. "About halfway through the shooting, everyone began to suspect that it was going to be a total flop. One day Dennis barred Marc and myself from the set. That's when we thought we should stop the film altogether. But since Marc is also a director, he gave in and let Dennis carry on."

"I found it quite hard work," Jean confessed later. "Dennis was very rough on his mother and very demanding with us all. Isabelle Huppert and I, who both began with Preminger, nicknamed him 'Little Otto.'"

Remembering all the pressures on her son, Gladys Berry says simply, "I don't know how Dennis got through it all."

At the first public screening late in April 1975, Jean was sick with fright. "You'd have thought it was her first film," says an actress who accompanied her. "It got so bad she had to go to the ladies' room."

Berry admits that the film is flawed and that he never struck the proper balance between outrage and comedy. "There was a strained atmosphere on the set that didn't correspond to the mood I wanted," he says. While some of the left-wing critics would find things to like—mainly the depiction of society as a bordello and people as cattle to be bought and sold—*Le Grand Délire* did poorly at the box office. "An excessive first film," *Variety* chastised.

"Each time Jean made a film with one of her husbands, it was a disaster," says her agent Olga Horstig-Primuz. "*Le Grand Délire* did her career a lot of harm."

To Gladys Berry, it seemed that "Jean was really no longer interested in having a career. I think by then it had become painful for her to act. She just wanted to get away from the whole movie scene."

In the periods of lucidity that followed her breakdowns, Jean worried about her growing proclivity for madness and the apparent facility with which she could and did slip over the brink. "She knew she had a choice to make," says Berry. "Either she would live the rest of her life in a state of chemical dependency, a sort of half-mutilated state, or she could try through analysis to conquer her inadequacies."

Psychoanalysis, she knew, would open up painful vistas and reactivate old wounds. But perhaps it would answer some fundamental questions. Why did she, after all these years, still feel obliged to live up to the image of the good little girl from Marshalltown? Why could she only express her inner rage when she drank? Was she, as she sometimes feared, a true schizophrenic?

"Like most actresses when they start to grow old, Jean had a certain narcissistic image of herself that was no longer valid," Berry continues. "The doctors thought that the transition to middle age would be difficult for her, but they felt that she could handle analysis."

Still, it was a calculated risk. It meant taking her life apart and putting it back together again—possibly in a different shape altogether. Jean decided to take the risk. Berry supported her. Regularly throughout this period and up until six months before her death, she and a French-Canadian psychiatrist would dredge up the unsettled past in an attempt to master the uncertain future.

34

"I always felt that, even though there were these terrible crises, Jean was working her way through analysis to sanity. I made a terrible mistake."

—DENNIS BERRY

A fragile peace resumed in the summer of 1975. With *Le Grand Délire* behind her, Jean seemed more like her old self to her friends and her husband. She and Dennis escaped to Morocco in August and motored across the scenic country, soaking up the Arab culture Jean was growing to appreciate.

Dennis had an idea for a second film, about a young man who shields a female terrorist one night and then, two years later, unable to shake her image, goes looking for her in the Middle East, with tragic results. Jean came up with a title— *Sunkill.* They talked about it endlessly while in Morocco and casually scouted for possible locations. Although never realized, the project reveals the Berrys' mutual fascination with the myths and realities of terrorism.

From Morocco they flew to Greece and more lazy weeks in Jean's cottage on Mykonos. "Basically, we were just having a good time," says Berry. "Traveling was always a great adventure with Jean. She was so curious, and she loved to share everything she discovered. Wherever we went, she seemed to know people—a fisherman who had interesting stories to tell, a village tailor who was the greatest tailor in the world. When she wasn't ill, I had great communication with Jean. We'd discuss our lives, how we'd fucked up, where we wanted to go from there. On vacations like these, there was a romantic, almost poetic aura about her."

Dennis also tried to draw lessons from the failure of *Le Grand Délire*. There was something wrong, he felt, about the conditions under which films were made. Actors who hardly knew one another were summoned to a set and then expected, under stringent deadlines, to reveal their deepest emotions to one another. The hassles that had sabotaged his own film couldn't have been more different from the trusting atmosphere he had envisaged. Somehow, that trust had to be nurtured in other ways.

As his father had done in the 1950s, Dennis decided to start an acting workshop that fall in Paris. He invited a dozen or so of his friends to participate free of charge. Several times a week throughout the winter and spring, they would meet in an abandoned school on the Left Bank to work on improvisations. Out of their work and the discussions that followed—who knew?—maybe they could develop themes for another film.

Jean liked the idea initially. It was acting for acting's sake—free from the pressures of shooting, which made her clench up inside, and divorced from the threatening judgments of critics and audiences. One day she convulsed the members of the group with her impression of a clumsy actress auditioning for a job as a tap dancer. "It was one of the funniest things I've ever seen in my life," Berry recalls, laughing.

At a subsequent session, Berry had one actor play a madman while the others were instructed to create characters of their own and react to him. Jean pretended to be a Hare Krishna. "Most of the time we seemed to be improvising these violent, almost Sartrien situations, pushed to a state of paroxysm," one faintly disdainful actress recalls. "It was like a continuing psychodrama."

Another, who had studied with Lee Strasberg, found the sessions amateurish. "Jean was an intelligent and instinctive actress, but she had very little craft. I thought her efforts rather childish. It seemed to me that most of the improvisations dragged on too long and were awfully self-indulgent. But

Jean was adamant about not cutting them short. 'We're here to work, not criticize, so everyone should be allowed to do what he wants to do.' I sometimes felt she could be rather brusque with women. I don't think she liked them much, although maybe it was just me."

Yves Benneyton felt the life of the loosely organized group paralleled the state of the Berrys' marriage. When they were getting along, it went well. When they weren't, it didn't. And to some outsiders, the marriage was showing signs of wear. At times Dennis' inexhaustible energy overpowered Jean, who reacted by becoming more retiring and withdrawn. And there was the continuing financial problem: in the three and a half years they had been together, Dennis had earned virtually nothing.

"At first Jean didn't care," says Raymonde Waintraub. "But it came to bother her. If Dennis wanted to give her a gift, for example, he'd have to ask for the money. That bugged her. She'd thrown over so many of the traditional values, but in her eyes, the man of the house was still supposed to be the bread-winner."

Gladys Berry also perceived difficulties. "Dennis is very outgoing," she says. "He has a lot of drive and energy. He bounds out of bed in the morning. Jean didn't. She liked to get up slowly. There were always a lot of people around Dennis. On the one hand, Jean loved all that life, but on the other, she didn't. She wanted to be controlled, and she didn't. Dennis is a volatile person, and he has his bursts of anger. But I always believed that was why, subconsciously, Jean married him—to find someone who could express the aggressive qualities that she lacked except when she drank. Otherwise, Jean felt she had to be the loving little girl from Marshalltown."

"There was a bit of *Who's Afraid of Virginia Woolf?* in their marriage," says Benneyton. "They fought a lot that winter." Fought, broke up, reconciled, and fought all over again.

Jean expressed some of the difficulties in a letter to Barbara Nash early in 1976. During one of their separations, she admitted, "I decided I liked being independent. It didn't last long—just enough for me to become fairly shallowly involved with another guy and to follow all my astonishingly organized self-destructive patterns and then to run away for three days to the country with Denny and laugh and cry and decide it was time we got together again. So it's been a little rocky, but warm." Although Paris was a gracious and beautiful city, she confessed that "we have moments of feeling time slip by without really feeling a part of anything stimulating. It all seems to be happening in some other place."

For Dennis, that place was the United States. Compared to France, the money, resources and opportunities for a young film maker were greater there. Jean resisted. Living in the United States meant one of two places: Los Angeles, which she detested for its "caste and class system" and the specter of the stardom that had eluded her, or New York. And "New York panics me," she told a radio interviewer. "The crime. The drugs. After three days there, I'm completely paranoid."

She had also come to feel a revived sense of responsibility toward Diego. Eugenia, his nanny since birth and, as Jean admitted, "a grandmother, if not a second mother to him," was dying of cancer. Thirteen-year-old Diego was deeply affected by the old woman's illness and turned more and more to Dennis and Jean. But as one of the conditions of her divorce from Romain, she had agreed that their son would be raised and educated in France.

Drift and confusion seemed to be settling in all over again. At the beginning of 1976 Jean learned unexpectedly that she had been a target of the FBI's Cointelpro. For more than a year, the Senate Select Committee on Intelligence had been investigating the CIA and the FBI and had uncovered a raft of abuses. J. Edgar Hoover's forty-eight-year reign as head of the country's chief law enforcement agency was studded with violations of human rights and flagrant misuses of power. Reporter Narda Zacchino, who was covering the story for the Los Angeles *Times,* particularly as it related to the Panthers, was tipped off by a source in Washington that "one of the worst things the FBI did was aimed at Jean Seberg." There were said to be memos in the FBI files relating to a smear campaign directed against Seberg. If Zacchino could lay her hands on those memos, she would have a startling story.

That January, Zacchino telephoned Jean in Paris to explain

the situation and enlist her cooperation. "It was quite clear to me that she didn't know anything definite about the smear," says Zacchino. "She was shocked but not particularly surprised. She said she hadn't known it at the time, but later, as the revelations about the FBI had started to come out, it was something she had begun to suspect. She said it was all a lie and a vicious thing to do.

"I told her I wanted to expose their tactics, but that I couldn't do so without her help. 'I can't write the story without the actual documents,' I said. 'And I can't get the documents under the Freedom of Information Act without your permission.'"

Jean hesitated.

"She was talking very slowly," Zacchino recalls, "almost as if she didn't want to talk at all. She said the episode [the birth and death of the baby] had caused a great deal of turmoil in her life and had traumatized her whole relationship with Romain Gary. The child had meant a lot to her. 'The reporters will come after me,' she said. 'It's already caused me too much hurt and pain. I just don't want to bring it up all over again.'"

Zacchino could not convince her to change her mind.

The confirmation of FBI harassment lent credence to the acute paranoia Jean had experienced in the past. Her tendency to read menace into the world was not simply the working of a crazed mind. There was some basis in fact. She talked endlessly about it with Dennis and her analyst. While she was reluctant to have others chronicle the awful incident, perhaps she herself would write about it in the larger context of her life as a whole.

"Romain was not encouraging," says Berry. "Maybe he was afraid that Jean was going to reveal what their life together had really been like. Anyway, he was a bit condescending toward the idea. But I believed there was a greater book in her than there was in him. She wrote the first chapter, and it had a wonderful *Look Homeward, Angel*-y tone to it—you really got a sense of the moment—the smells, the temperature, what kind of light there was. I don't know if Jean had the discipline or structure to carry all the way through, but that first chapter was beautiful.

"What irks me is that there is no way of showing the kind of writing she was capable of. At the time of her death, most of her papers disappeared. No one knows what the guy she was living with did with them. All that remains is writing she did when she was under some form of mental stress. It's not of the same quality. But I always thought Jean had the potential for being a major author."

Writing, at any rate, gave her a hope for 1976. It would be a transition from the cinema, which extended only mediocre prospects—when it extended any at all. "I have to do something. I couldn't just be a housewife," Jean told an interviewer. "So I have entered my literary phase. I can write as easily in French as in English. Perhaps I'll give up the movies altogether someday. I've never programed my life. It's always been impulsive, instinctive. Things have happened to me—some good, some bad. Luck counts for so much, but I don't know if I believe in fate. What I find interesting now are the people who ask themselves questions. People who don't ask questions—the contented cows—don't interest me at all."

In April she made her last film, a transposition to the screen of Ibsen's *The Wild Duck*. "You're going to like me in this one," Jean told Ed Seberg. "I look just like G.G." ("G.G." or "Great-Grandmother" was the Sebergs' nickname for Frances Benson.) Jean was nearly fifty pounds overweight, but the period costumes masked her bulk. Her plump face, however, corresponded to the lower-class stolidity of her character, Gina, the wife of a deluded and shiftless photographer. And the hair style—braids worn on top of her head—brought out her Scandinavian features. Unfortunately, the part was small. Jean liked the director, a German named Hans Geissendörfer, but the film was static and talky—in essence, a filmed stage play. Most of the reviews would grant that Jean was "eye-pleasing" and leave it at that. Outside of academic circles, the film has not been widely seen.

Betty Desouches visited Jean and Dennis in Vienna during the shooting. Jean, she says, was full of the warmth and generosity she usually showered on her friends. But Desouches noticed that she also had cultivated a taste for Underberg, a popular alcoholic drink, blackish in color. Devotees claim its herb base gives it certain medicinal virtues, and Jean would announce, by way of excuse, "I don't feel very well today," before knocking back several in a row.

Sometimes she tried to make light of what her intimates suspected was a clear case of alcoholism. "I'm not an alcoholic," she would declare firmly. "I just have a drinking problem." And the engaging smile she flashed right afterward put a stop to any further discussion.

The final scene of *The Wild Duck* augured badly. Ibsen's play is an exploration of the disastrous effects that the truth has on a family living on lies and illusions. At the end Gina's illegitimate daughter climbs to the attic, intending to sacrifice her most precious possession, a wild duck. Instead the confused child shoots herself. In the play the action takes place off-stage. But Geissendörfer decided to show the parents discovering their child's lifeless body. The scene took its toll on Jean, although in this case the consequences did not show up for several months.

On her return to Paris, she received a letter from the United States Department of Justice, officially verifying what Zacchino had told her: she had been a Cointelpro target. Far from putting her fears to rest once and for all, the news actually seems to have reignited her paranoia.

The report issued by the Senate Select Committee on Intelligence that month detailed a record of FBI malfeasance going back to 1947: lying, wiretaps, surreptitious opening of private mail, the use of paid informants. The report also referred anonymously to Jean: "When the FBI learned that one well-known Hollywood actress had become pregnant during an affair with a BPP member, it reported this information to a famous Hollywood gossip columnist in the form of an anonymous letter. The story was used by the Hollywood columnist."

By late spring the Berrys' marriage was teetering badly. The bickering and misunderstanding had increased. While one friend concludes that "Dennis was just too young, too crazy for her," others, who had experienced her quixotic behavior, were slower to attribute all the blame to him.

"Jean would carp about Dennis and how he was trying to

manage her all the time," says one. "But I later came to believe all the wrongs were not his. Jean could be exploited so easily by people, and Dennis really helped her say 'no.' The trouble is, there were times when she resented it."

Dennis went to the Cannes Film Festival in May without Jean. Upon his return, they decided to separate. "Jean would have these moments," says Raymonde Waintraub, "when she'd just clear everyone out of her life."

There were also moments when Jean, usually demure and ladylike in public, could be tyrannical and unruly. Waintraub recalls dining with her at the Voltaire, one of Jean's favorite restaurants, about this time. "I picked her up in my car and immediately she started criticizing my driving. I was going too fast, too slow. 'Watch out for that car!' 'Turn here.' She made me stop several times along the way so she could get something to drink. We hadn't been at the restaurant for more than ten minutes when Jean started to complain loudly: the waiter wasn't efficient enough for her; the people around us were making too much noise. Before long the other customers were staring at her because she was, after all, Jean Seberg. That made her angrier than ever. It was an awful evening. Jean was nasty and insulting and made scene after scene. I dropped her off that night, and then phoned her the next morning to make sure she was all right. 'You certainly didn't rise to the occasion last night,' she snapped. And hung up the phone."

Ricardo Franco had come back into her life—indirectly at first. His film *The Family of Pascual Duarte* had been well received at the Cannes Film Festival and won that year's prize for best actor. Jean could not help comparing the acclaim to the sorry fate of *Le Grand Délire*. Dennis had not regenerated her career, as she had once expected. She wondered if she'd made a mistake and chosen the wrong man.

Married by then, Franco passed through Paris in the summer of 1976 and saw Jean. According to Fausto Canel, "Ricardo was really hurt by the way Jean had dropped him in order to marry Dennis. I think he wanted to get back at Dennis somehow. Anyway, Ricardo was about to return to Spain when he called me and asked me to come over to Jean's apartment. She was insisting on accompanying him, and he anticipated a crisis. I tried to tell Jean that there was no future to the relationship. Ricardo wasn't about to marry her. For one thing, there was no divorce in Spain. She was just feeling guilty about the past. At the train station, she wanted to climb on the train with him. She said she'd ride just as far as the border. But she had no cash with her, and they wouldn't let her pay for the ticket with a credit card."

Several days later Jean phoned Franco in Madrid and then abruptly flew to the Spanish capital. Afterward she told friends that Franco had invited her to come and talk about a picture with him.

Thinking his marriage was over, Dennis had rented a studio apartment, although he spent very little time there. Returning one night, he plugged in his phone and almost immediately received a call from Franco: Jean was in a hotel room in Madrid going out of her head. Dennis had better come get her. He, Franco, was washing his hands of the mess.

"Jean had made up her mind to take up with Ricardo once again. And it was becoming very obvious and embarrassing for him," says Canel. "This was not long after the death of [Generalissimo] Franco, and no one knew for certain whether the new regime in Spain would be liberal or not."

Finding herself alone in a Madrid hotel room and feeling abandoned, Jean had lost control. She had broken windows and shouted antifascist slogans in the streets. According to some reports, she had run through the lobby nude.

With producer Jean-Pierre Rassam, Dennis raced to Madrid. When they arrived at the hotel, they found Jean sitting patiently in the lobby like a little schoolgirl, quietly singing songs to herself. An elderly couple was keeping a watchful eye on her.

"She was in a strange state, worse than any time before," says Berry, "but she seemed to be happy to see us. I noticed that her body was covered with burns. When I asked her what happened, she said, 'They burned me with cigarettes.' It was obvious to me that she'd done it to herself."

Berry had brought along a bottle of Valium in 50-milligram tablets. "One of them puts me out for five days," he says. Jean took a handful and rode back to Paris in a stupor.

Canel saw her in the Rue du Bac apartment forty-eight hours

after her return. "She was in a terrible state psychologically," he says. "She was living in a complete fantasy world and insisted that the Spanish police had tortured her. When I asked her why, she said it was because on the flight to Madrid she had sat next to a girl who was a member of a Basque terrorist group. I told her I didn't believe her. The police didn't behave like that. So she lifted her blouse and showed me the burn marks on her stomach."

In addition to what Berry believes were self-inflicted injuries, her stomach still bore the faint scars from her burning at the stake in *St. Joan,* nineteen years before.

Alarmed by the gravity of her condition, Berry convinced Jean to check into a private sanitarium, the Villa Montsouris. This one was different from the others. The doors were locked. Only Dennis, as her husband, was accorded the right to visit her. Jean was put on lithium, which can flatten out the wild swings from euphoria to despair that characterize the manic-depressive state. Although she seemed to respond well to the drug, her doctors were hesitant to diagnose her as a true manic-depressive. Jean's condition baffled them. Lithium has many side effects of various severity; one of them is that it makes people put on weight. Jean ballooned. Before long she was an obese and swollen woman who bore no resemblance to the sylphlike innocent of the early sixties.

"I went to see Jean every day," Berry recalls. "I made it clear I was there as a friend who just wanted her to get better. Jean cried a lot and said that she had nobody else in the world. I felt tremendous responsibility toward her. One day I went to see her therapist and told him that I didn't envision Jean coming out of the clinic and going right back to her apartment. She still had a little money, so I said, 'Look, I'll take her to Corsica. We'll rent a small house there. She'll have time to come back to earth in a quiet atmosphere.' The doctors thought it was a good idea. After I told Jean about the plans, she really seemed to get better. It's strange. Whenever Jean was hostile to me or said she didn't want to live with me anymore, I chalked it up to the madness and convinced myself that it wasn't the real person."

Berry found a house near Bonifacio. Although it was late summer, the weather was still warm. Gnarled olive trees and weathered boulders gave the island a rugged beauty. Embarrassed about her girth, Jean would wear a voluminous Arab robe to the private beach, venture timidly to the water's edge, then quickly throw off the garment and plunge into the sea. One vacationer in a nearby cottage recalls that "sometimes Jean played for hours with the little children on the beach. Then suddenly, without warning, her mood would switch. She wouldn't have anything to do with them. They were bothering her by making too much noise."

Dennis, however, saw improvement. Some of the pressures seemed to have lifted. Now and again he sensed the dreamy, poetic aura that Jean projected when she was truly herself. One evening she started singing an Antillaise folk song to him: "Mon doudou, il est parti, mon capitain (My sweetheart has gone away, my captain)."

"It's a very moving song, and somehow it seemed to relate to our own situation," says Berry. "I was touched by it. Jean said to me, 'I'm still in love with you.' And I replied, 'I'm still in love with you too.' We decided to get back together again."

Dennis resumed his acting classes that fall. Jean attended them, less enthusiastically than before. In November the FBI mailed her a package of documents from her file, which gave her new impetus to write her autobiography. Jean entrusted the papers to Gary for safekeeping. Dennis says that when she later tried to get them back, Gary withheld them from her. Eventually, however, the writer would show the papers to a reporter on condition that no article about them appear without Jean's permission. Jean was not ready to take that step, but before friends she would often cite from memory the text of the letter that the FBI had drafted to use against her.

Jean had dropped out of the public eye completely. Even her contacts with Marshalltown were infrequent and noncommittal. However, she did respond at Christmastime to a letter from her old friend Dawn Murray Quinn, whom she hadn't seen in eighteen years:

> I was badly ill this year. I told my folks that I had viral hepatitis, so as not to worry them too much. The truth is I had a very bad nervous breakdown with persecution mania and the whole she-

bang. Don't ever let the folks know, dear Dawn, it will only frighten them, and they have had their worries with Kurt, who is apparently much better now. (He went into Lutheran State Hospital for a cure of disintoxication [detoxification].) As for myself, it took months and I am in psychotherapy, but the worst is behind me, and Dennis and Diego supported me wonderfully. I take lithium, which as a nurse I'm sure you know. It's an effective anti-depressant . . .

As for Dennis, he is active with a TV project and with his second long film. It's been hard for him, and it's also been painful that he has brought in practically no money since we were married, but it really hasn't been his fault. I'm sure things will pick up in 1977. They just have to.

When I hear you speak of your religious faith, I almost envy you. I lost mine somewhere along the line, and it saddens me as I know what consolation it can bring. But I still read from time to time the little white Bible you gave me so long ago and I think of you tenderly . . .

I love you, my friend. Be strong.

                                                                 Jeana

Quinn never heard from her again.

35

> *"I'm aware that there will come a time when Dennis may move on. Though it may be me, instead. That wouldn't be the end of the world."*
>
> —JEAN SEBERG

To Jean's closest friends, it was apparent that she was engaged in a process of self-destruction that steadily accelerated throughout 1977. They worried about the haunted look on her face; the killing quantities of liquor she consumed, always taking care to hide the bottles so Dennis wouldn't find them; the wild flashes of anger that would suddenly take hold of her, like a dybbuk, and then leave her spent and withdrawn. It was not the Jean they knew, loving and gentle, and they blamed her condition on the dubious company she kept. Dennis sometimes appeared to be the only barrier between her and a life of flagrant dissolution, and he, they thought, was too immature to contain the disorder.

At times Jean's embarrassment about her weight approached self-loathing. For more than a year she refused to see her agent, Olga Horstig-Primuz. They would talk on the telephone or exchange notes, but whenever Horstig-Primuz proposed a luncheon or a meeting, Jean would reply, "No, you can't see me now. I'm too fat. I'll see you when I get back into shape." But she made few efforts in that direction.

Bob Logan had a similar experience. Passing through Paris, he decided to look up his old bicycling companion and dropped by the Rue du Bac, where he and Jean had enjoyed many pleasant hours together. "The maid answered the bell, but Jean wouldn't come out of the bedroom to see me," he recalls. "Dennis was there, and he explained that she was ashamed to see her old friends when she was heavy. So Jean and I carried on a conversation through the closed door. It was terribly awkward. I could sense things were breaking up between her and Dennis. I just wanted to get out of there as fast as I could."

Acting classes now got on her nerves, and she complained that the improvisations made her tense. Sporadically she worked at her writing, and occasionally after dinner would recite her poems to her intimates or present them with handwritten copies. But she was hesitant to talk about them in public, almost as if she regarded them as closet scribblings. When a reporter from *Time* telephoned her to check out a rumor concerning their eventual publication, Jean replied tersely, "I have nothing to say, nor do I want to say anything about my poems."

In mid-April she made a quick trip to Marshalltown, accompanied by Dennis, Diego, who was almost fifteen, and Diego's French girl friend. Although it was her first time home in four years, Jean had little to tell the *Times-Republican*. "We had hoped to come home for a visit last summer," she explained vaguely, "but I've been ill with infectious hepatitis for nearly a year." She said that she had recently completed *The Wild Duck* and indicated that upon her return to Europe, she would begin an Italian picture, *Let's Laugh*. The latter, however, seems nothing more than one of the many nebulous projects floating around in her head—projects that would never come to pass.

Analysis had sharpened Jean's perspective on Marshalltown. She abhorred its small-mindedness and bigotry and blamed it for saddling her with impossible ideals. Sensing the trouble in their daughter, if not the extent of her illness, the Sebergs were helpless to do anything about it. For her part, Jean didn't want to burden them with additional concerns, thinking they had had trouble enough with her brother Kurt. Besides, she felt, they had never understood her, anyway.

Frances Benson was nearly ninety-six, and although she had been spunky enough the previous year to serve as the Grand

Marshal of the Bicentennial Parade, riding down Main Street in an open convertible, her health was frail. Jean relished the few moments she had with her grandmother, who resolutely continued to live alone. (Four months later Frances Benson suffered a stroke and had to be moved to a nursing home, where she died shortly afterward. Despite her strong attachment to the woman whose independence had always served as a model, Jean did not return for the funeral service.)

This was to be her last visit home. High-strung and jittery, she cut it short after three days, and she and Dennis took their young charges to New York City for some traditional sightseeing.

There were fewer and fewer possibilities for work when they got back to Paris. Commercially, her name meant nothing. If it came up, it was only in the nostalgic context of *Breathless*. Now and again a few venturesome directors or screenwriters would come to her with projects. While Jean was superficially excited about meeting and talking with them, she really had no intention of following through. And they, surprised by the huge woman they encountered, were generally happy to let matters drop.

"Jean found films too laborious and complicated to make," says Philippe Garrel. "She liked them only when they'd been made and were over with. She could never see the difference between worthwhile scripts and shit. She would listen to anyone—the first person off the street with an idea—and fall for it every time. Usually, the guy disappeared afterward, and Jean would despair. She wanted something to happen—anything."

To those who would listen, she complained constantly about her marriage, stating that she and Dennis no longer got along sexually, that he beat her, or that he had stopped loving her because she was fat and unattractive. Some of the stories came back to him, and he was pained to hear them. At the same time, she was progressively alienating her old friends, whom she accused, often to their faces, of being middle-class prigs. Dreading solitude, she replaced her friends with the down-and-out—sycophants she'd met in bars, and drug addicts off the street. She told herself it was her identification with the underdog that motivated her, and to a certain extent, it probably was. But also in their midst she enjoyed a recognition and status that the world at large had ceased to accord her. In the marginal kingdom of the drugged and the drifting, a bloated, alcoholic former cinema star can still be queen.

"Jean began taking risks," says Betty Desouches. "She'd leave Dennis for a passing fling, float into an affair whenever she felt like it, and put herself in danger time and again. Something just seemed to break in her. You could spot it in her eyes—they were unfocused and fuzzy."

"Jean was too quick to give her love and trust to people," says director Yves Boisset. Others, however, put it more bluntly and suspected her of nymphomania. "Jean needed desperately to feel desired and beautiful," says one of her doctors. "When she got fat or developed dark circles under her eyes or took on that haggard look, she was terribly bothered by it. It was very important for her to feel, well, excuse the term, 'fuckable.' In her depression, she'd turn to other men for reassurance. Jean could have sex on an elevator between the third and fourth floors."

Wanting to be supportive, a long-standing male friend had lunch with her one afternoon when Dennis was away. "Her hair was uncombed, and she was sloppily dressed," he recalls. "She had a lot of trouble just talking. The way she rambled on about her kid and the FBI scared the hell out of me. It was a very difficult lunch. Afterward she said that she was going to lie down, with the clear understanding that I was supposed to follow her into the bedroom. I said good-bye and left."

An American sculptor met her one night about this time at a private club. Jean was with Dennis and a lithe, hollow-eyed model strung out on heroin. "I sort of hit it off with the model," he relates. "When Jean got ready to leave, she said to me, 'Take good care of my girl friend. She has a tendency to get into trouble.' Several days later Jean showed up at the museum where I was working on a commission. 'You know,' she said, 'I was terribly jealous of that model the other night. She got to go home with you.'"

The sculptor says that he and Jean slipped away to a hotel that very afternoon and ended up having a fitful affair over the next few months. Her life was beginning to resemble *Birds in Peru,* but without the artistic pretensions.

An ever growing share of her acquaintances seemed to be addicts of one kind or another, even though Jean said she was violently opposed to drugs. Reports would circulate, especially after her death, that she herself indulged in them, but none of her close friends ever recalls her using anything stronger than marijuana—and that only infrequently. There were the mountains of pills, of course. But they were different. They were medicine. Prescribed. Official.

As Jean wrote Rabbi Serber: "Drugs injected into the Paris scene much later than in the United States wreak havoc around us . . . Pathetic phone calls in the middle of the night, begging for money and love, mostly money, perhaps as a demonstration of love. At times, we refer to our house as 'the clinic.' At times, weary, we just withdraw and turn off the phone and don't answer the doorbell."

Jean's horror of hard drugs went back many years. She claimed it stemmed from an experience she had shared with Jamal in 1969. One day in Compton they had gone to visit a nineteen-year-old girl. Entering the run-down house, they discovered her in the bedroom, dead from an overdose. The needle still dangled from her arm.

Jean was invariably moved to tears by the sight of young men and women whose minds had been destroyed by narcotics. Seized with a missionary zeal, she urged them to get help and pressed money into their hands, hoping that it wouldn't just go for the next fix.

To get away briefly from that depressing scene and to try to salvage their marriage, Jean and Dennis rented a cottage in Normandy that summer. Dennis invited his sister, Jan, to spend a weekend with them.

"That weekend was very marking," she says. "I was estranged from my brother, and we were making an effort to get closer. I think that's why he invited me. Jean was obviously at a very difficult stage in her life. She was very heavy, but at the same time she seemed incredibly fragile and withdrawn. She had hardly any contact with me, although I remember her dog Sandy died, and we all buried him in the garden. It was as if my brother and I had too much energy for her. Jean needed so much protection. By comparison, I felt loud and aggressive, which I'm not at all.

"At one point my brother and I had an argument about it. I tried to tell him that he was constantly invading Jean's space and that she wasn't strong enough to stand up for herself. Later, as I was leaving, Jean opened up a little and thanked me for taking her side. In a sense, though, that's why their marriage worked and why it was problematical. I think Jean really appreciated Dennis' warmth, his forward energy, his ability to generate things. But she also felt overwhelmed by him. I remember her saying that she loved him, but that she just couldn't live with him. It's funny. She was the one with the celebrity, and he was the one who was crushing her!"

Much of the stress in Jean's life was reflected, almost coincidentally, in a script she received that October. It was called *Je Parle d'Amour* (*I Speak of Love*) and revolved around a divorced middle-aged woman drawn to two men younger than herself—one whom she dominates, the other who dominates her. In psychoanalysis, she comes to realize that what we call love is often a not so subtle exercise of power.

The author, Madeleine Hartmann, envisioned Jean in the lead role from the start. "I had always found her an appealing and intelligent actress, which is rare in this profession," she says. "You could have a real dialogue with her. As soon as I met her, though, I sensed the extraordinary pain inside, ready to explode at any moment. The act of living seemed to have become too much for her."

Jean's working relationship with Hartmann was characteristic of a pattern that repeated itself over and over. Initially, she was thrilled by the opportunity to work. This would be her comeback. She would be surrounded by stars. In fact, she demanded nothing less.

"After we'd met several times, Jean came by my place one day and said, 'If we're going to work together, you have to know everything about me,'" Hartmann recalls. "Then she spilled out her entire life and told me all about the death of her baby. But it was such a disjointed account, I didn't understand much of it. It seemed to me that the whole episode with the

FBI was really incidental and that it was society as a whole that had mutilated her. Jean had this great compulsion to draw you into her personal life and involve you in it.

"She was seriously overweight, but she promised that she'd shape up for the film. She invited me to come over to her apartment every day and go through a program of exercises with her. I went one time, but I got the feeling that Jean was starved for affection, and that once you'd started taking care of her, there would be no end to it.

"It was very strange. As long as the plans for the film remained indeterminate, Jean was eager to make it. But when the project looked as if it was really going to happen, she started having all sorts of reservations. Or she'd fall sick.

"She arrived at my place one day, all out of breath, screaming, 'I can't do this film.' I asked her why. She said, 'The package! I have to know what's in the package.' At one point in the scenario, there was a reference to a package in the back seat of a car going through customs. It was nothing significant—a package of food. 'If there are drugs concealed in that package,' she said, 'I absolutely refuse to make this film.' She was irrational on the subject—like one who has drunk and drinks no more.

"By the time I finally had the money to make the film, Jean had dropped out altogether. 'Romain told me I shouldn't be in it' was her explanation. She still had a lot of respect for his authority, although I thought there was something perverse about that relationship. She was his creature. He'd molded her image as the lovely wife of a famous writer. Having lost her to another man, I think he wanted her back under his thumb."

Je Parle d'Amour was shot for French television the following spring. By then Jean pretended she knew nothing about it. "She was the most anguished person I've ever met," says Hartmann.

If nothing else, Jean could have used the money. In mid-October she wrote Rabbi Serber, informing him that her financial straits obliged her to sell the house she had purchased in Marshalltown for black students. "I would definitely like to get it on the market as soon as possible. It has been many a day since I filmed with a really good salary, so the house has become a weight on my shoulders," she explained. "I think of the house as a failure, which is sad."

Less than two weeks later she forwarded him the necessary legal authority along with a brief apology. "I do so wish I could say to you, Rabbi, take the house and use it as you feel best. But such is life—I'm just not in that position at the present."

Dealing with Jean on any level was delicate business. She would bristle at the hint of opposition. Any mention of her drinking or her weight stirred her to anger. She seemed to be in a state of psychological siege. "It was as if she were her own Manson," says producer Jean-Pierre Rassam. "I think she had so wanted the American dream to be true. And when she discovered that it wasn't, she revolted and began her descent into hell. She looked for persecution. There was tremendous violence in her attitudes—not her words so much, because she didn't always talk a great deal. But she wanted to push things to the very end and intentionally debase herself in reaction to her puritan upbringing. She would denounce her friends for their weakness or their hypocrisy, and in the process force them to abandon their pseudoliberalism, reveal their ugliest side or else bust her in the jaw. She was the last generation of the all-American girl, and she went further than any of the others."

Viewing the ravages, Dennis sometimes blamed analysis for opening up a Pandora's box of psychic ills, and he struggled to re-establish some direction in their life. One of his scenarios had elicited a certain interest in Hollywood, and his father was encouraging him to strike while the iron was, if not hot, at least warm. Dennis tried to convince Jean to go with him. Occasionally she entertained the notion. More often she rejected it outright and accused him of forsaking her like all the others—just as she'd known he would all along.

"Jean made a lot over the fact that Dennis was so much younger than she was," says Gladys Berry. "But what was it? Only a six-year difference."

After a particularly nasty squabble, Jean moved out of the Rue du Bac apartment and temporarily rented two rooms in the Hôtel de Suède just around the corner. There she held court, receiving at all hours the expanding cast of shadowy characters who fed on the remains of her money and fame. It was a parody of the Parisian salon. "Often, late at night, Jean would get the idea of inviting someone famous to come and see her. Once, I remember, it was Mick Jagger," says Raymonde Waintraub. "There was a long, impossible discussion about how to get in touch with Mick Jagger. 'Phone him.' 'Who has his number?' 'No one has his number.' 'Then call Information.' 'Information doesn't know.' 'Well, somebody should know. We've got to get Mick Jagger over here.' It was totally insane."

Unable to persuade Jean to move to the States, and yet torn about leaving her behind, Dennis vacillated for weeks. Returning home from the Hôtel de Suède, Jean finally ordered him to get out of the apartment. After the Christmas holidays Dennis flew to Los Angeles.

"I stopped living with Jean because that's what she wanted," Dennis says. "I didn't stop living with her just because she had mental problems. They were painful and destructive. But I would have lived it out to the end. Jean didn't want me to . . . She didn't want me to."

"I love Dennis very much," Jean told actress Michèle Moretti more than a year after his departure, "but we have to have an ocean between us."

36

Ciao, ciao, le mec
Je suis ravie que tu partes.
Pleure bien, le mec.
Il n'y a pas une larme chez moi.
Ta valise t'attend sur le paillasson.
Il n'y a pas une rose ni de violon.
Ciao, ciao, le mec, ciao, ciao,
salut, ciao, ciao.

(Ciao, ciao, pal
I'm delighted you're leaving.
Cry a lot, pal.
There are no tears in me.
Your suitcase is on the landing.
There's no rose and no violin.
So long, pal, so long,
farewell, so long.)

—FROM A SONG BY JEAN SEBERG

With Dennis gone, the floodgates burst open. The turbulent waters washed the drowning and the drowned into Jean's apartment and just as abruptly carried them away. It was a society of human flotsam to which she lent qualities and virtues visible to no one else. Some of the people she knew, others she didn't. No matter. She liked the activity, which staved off the emptiness of the early morning hours.

"The biggest asshole in the world could be Jesus Christ to her," says one friend who, appalled by the "vampirism" in her life, retreated in disgust. Addicts had the apartment marked for an easy handout, and petty crooks knew they could find refuge there if they convinced Jean they were being "persecuted" by the law, not merely pursued by it. Jean would invent fanciful biographies for the wrecks that landed on her doorstep, telling herself they were revolutionaries or artists when, more often than not, they were common bums.

A young Moroccan medical student named Mohammed became her more or less regular bedmate, even though he was married and the father of several children. She met him by chance one day on a foray to replenish her liquor supply. As Jean related the story, she had accidentally dropped a bottle of vodka in the street. While she surveyed the damage, he had come up alongside her and said, 'Allow me to buy you another bottle, and let's drink it together." They did. Jean nicknamed him "Gâteau" (Cookie).

"It was like a circus at her house, overrun with youth and fun," says Berthe Grandval, an artist whom Jean invited to share the apartment in the early months of 1978—until they quarreled and Jean kicked her out. More objective observers saw it as a sleazy sideshow. Jean had trouble keeping a maid, and the apartment often looked as though it had been bombed. Jean's two Persian cats delicately picked their way through the mess or viewed it disdainfully from atop the radiators. Romain prevailed upon an American friend to lend her Brazilian houseboy to Jean, but Jean found his services lacking and dismissed him without pay. Romain had to make good the man's wages.

Early in January Jean turned the apartment over to Philippe Garrel, who used it as the backdrop for several cryptic scenes in *Le Bleu des Origines (The Blue of the Beginning)*. It was another private exploration of his bottomless anguish, with one innovation: Garrel had rediscovered the hand-cranked camera from the days of silent films, and it allowed him to shoot anywhere, regardless of lighting conditions.

Raymonde Waintraub, one of the few friends from better days who did not abandon Jean, was there one evening when Garrel and his cast pulled in. "Most of them were completely out of it. Jean herself was in pretty bad shape. She was eating next to nothing but drinking a lot, and she wore this huge black robe to hide her bulk. She barked out orders left and right, and at one point slapped one of the actresses, who was missing half her teeth and who spent the rest of the evening slumped over the piano. Jean would talk about people behind their backs whenever they left the room, but as soon as they returned, she'd embrace them effusively. It was completely demented. Jean, who was normally so coherent, couldn't put together three rational words that night."

At the last moment Jean stepped into the film, replacing one of Garrel's performers who was too stoned to work. Garrel either filmed her from the back or else positioned her at such a distance that she was virtually unrecognizable. She received no mention in the credits.

While she was still living with Jean, Berthe Grandval redecorated part of the apartment. Operating on the theory that "Jean, as a star, had people around her all the time," Grandval designed a vast landscape of Monument Valley on marbled paper, which she cut out and then applied to the wall of Jean's bedroom. "This way," she told Jean, "you will have the impression of being alone now and again."

The Western motif also corresponded to Grandval's image of Jean. "She was . . . well, like a cowboy," the artist explains tentatively. "I mean, she loved the oldness of Europe, but she was out of place here. She wanted to plunge into the action, right all the wrongs she perceived, provoke a combat. She had her sentimental side—faded roses and valentines—but she was really a fighter. A fighter with fragile nerves. She got carried away easily. She wanted people to know her despair, to communicate it and force a showdown. I guess that's what I mean by cowboy." Jean liked the new decoration, but her favorite artwork hung in her exercise room. It was a sad, impressionistic vision of a woman all alone on a bridge, with a small dog beside her.

When she wasn't reigning over the tumult at the Rue du Bac, Jean would sally forth to the late-night bars and jazz clubs, often closing them at daybreak. She was especially fond of Les Chevaliers du Temple, a largely black club where the jam sessions were hot and heavy and the musicians came and went as if it were their second home. Jean found Sarah, the proprietor, "the coolest woman in Paris." Downing drink after drink, she would engage the patrons in endless debates about politics and jazz.

Some evenings she ended up at Le Boucanier, a Left Bank after-hours club that drew a mixed crowd of would-be intellectuals and expatriates, and, occasionally, the neighborhood plumber. "Jean always wanted to be the center of attention," says Jack Kennedy, the stocky American owner who looks more like a college professor than the night owl he is. "She was always standing up for the underdog—the revolutionaries, the artists, the blacks, the Indians. And in the final years of her life, it was the Algerians. Christ, any Algerian. She'd come into the bar with some pretty lowly types and get sloshed until dawn.

"She didn't seem to recognize reality after a while. Her megalomania swelled as she became less and less important. One night she took me aside and said, 'Jacky, I've got a MiG up in my apartment.' 'Oh yeah, Jean,' I said. 'How the hell did you get a MiG in your apartment?' 'In the elevator,' she replied. She was perfectly serious. And she launched into one of her long paranoid monologues, always with her at the center. It seemed to me that she was playing with dynamite."

If she didn't find sleeping partners in the bars she haunted, Jean would pick them up in front of the Hôtel Pont Royal at the foot of the Rue du Bac. "It became an absolute horror," says Michèle Moretti, who as a friend of Dennis' tried to keep an eye on Jean for his sake. "There was so much suppressed hostility and violence in her. It scared people. She had never been able to express it artistically. It got buried deeper and deeper. When it finally exploded, it exploded sexually.

"She'd often call me up at six A.M. to tell me that she'd just had great sex with some musician and that she was liberated at last. Her voice would take on this tone of superexcitement. It happened time and again. It was absolutely useless to talk morality with her. Jean wanted to throw off all the shackles."

Despite the frenzied activity, Jean was without real occupation. The movies were dead to her. "It's just as well," she told Gladys Berry; "I can't memorize lines anymore." To others, she would object indignantly that the only scripts she received were outright pornography. "And yet in life," says Betty Desouches, "here she was throwing herself into the very thing she said she hated."

Encouraged by the late-night company she kept, Jean hatched a passing ambition to be a songwriter. On and off during 1978, she would set her poems to the melodies of an ever changing parade of musicians—a black pianist who worked at a bar in the red-light district; a Ugandan percussionist whose instruments included the bicycle wheel; an Iranian chanteuse who had a small following in a Left Bank *cave;* and Sugar Blue, the American blues singer. Jean's songs were mostly bittersweet accounts of couples breaking up, but some of them had a political bite. In one she took Idi Amin to task, threatening to come settle the score with him. While Jean would talk enthusiastically about getting the songs published or having them recorded, outside her circle of friends they awoke little interest.

One of Jean's few writings actually to reach print appeared in the pages of *Libération* at the end of February. It was entitled "Love Letter to the Junkies" and is a revealing measure of her mind: the hypersensitive social consciousness, the sentimentalism, the aggressiveness and the would-be cool. Written in French laced with street talk and peppered with the names of the famous "cats" she knew or had once known, the article was a hopelessly rambling indictment the evils of addiction. It ended with this direct appeal—part plea, part threat —to the police:

> Don't beat up my pals, who are trying painfully to escape from their despair. Mind your manners, I beg of you. You know better than I where the smack is, who makes it, where it comes from and who profits by it. So don't break the fingers of some flaked-out musician. You also know better than I who protects whom, and why and where the money goes where it does. So stop the bad jokes. Be keepers of the peace: OF THE PEACE. That's noble . . .
> Just one last thing, but an important one. Be kind to the Arabs and the blacks in France. Treat the Portuguese and the Spaniards kindly. They don't have an easy row to hoe. Talk to them kindly. Man to man. Like equals. There was a time when France had a reputation for that. A magnificent reputation . . . And now, with a thousand excuses, I am obliged to be demanding. I beg you. Do all that, and people will look on you with esteem. Don't do it and—and I say this quietly (important), politely, as a woman who doesn't know how to defend herself—that there are two Mohammeds (snigger) in my life. (Oh, I know. All the Arabs are called Mohammed.) One of them is café au lait, American, famous, quick, but doesn't like to hurt people. The other is someplace else. Not far. Not close enough. But if I tell them softly that you are not being kind, they will come. They will get into planes. Be samurai, not

oppressors, of the sad Algerians or the victims of a cancerous society. In short, don't forget your catechism. (Even on welfare, you
learned it.) "Love your neighbor as yourself." So behave yourselves, be calm. Love one another. Each one of us sings the blues.
Thanks.

Jean Seberg

Former friends who read the article were embarrassed and
found it "not worthy of her." Romain, according to those who
knew him, was mortified. Publicly he liked to say that after
their divorce he had not lost a wife so much as gained a daughter. Given their difference in age, it was a natural enough evo-
lution. In fact, it was more like gaining a delinquent daughter.

Financially Jean was living on the edge, and most of the
merchants in the Rue du Bac refused her credit. Several of
Jean's friends say that Romain regularly supplied her with
6,000 francs a month (about $1,200), which she usually squan-
dered in a couple of days. Now that Dennis was in the
United States, people invariably came running to Gary whenever Jean got in trouble. His patience strained, he would listen
to the accounts of her latest outrage, pay some of the overdue
bills and try to shield Diego from his mother's excesses. "I
have *my* posterity to think about," he once told Raymonde
Waintraub. Preoccupied with his literary work, he appreciated
the intrusions less and less.

In the spring, however, Jean appears to have made an effort
to take control of herself. In the throes of another nervous
breakdown, she checked into a clinic in March for rest and
observation. Her doctors were able to convince her that she
was killing herself with the "bizarre cocktails" she concocted
out of liquor and pills. They strongly advised a program of
alcoholic detoxification, followed by a drastic reduction in
weight. If she could regain her figure, they felt, some of the
lacerating self-hatred might abate.

Dutifully, Jean reported to a weight-loss clinic in the town of
Mayenne, where she was put on a strict liquid protein diet. The
surroundings were cheerless and the daily regime draconian.
Jean received only rare visitors and found few sympathetic
companions among the wealthy, self-absorbed women who

patronized the establishment. Trying to look ahead, she wrote Rabbi Serber: "The time is long, but I'll be proud of the new, svelte me."

"Jean's body was like an accordion," says one of her doctors. "Fortunately, she could shape up fairly quickly."

The woman who checked out of the clinic six weeks later was model-thin. Her cheekbones had re-emerged, giving her face a flattering angularity. To celebrate the transformation, she had her hair cut in the *Breathless* style. Her friends complimented her on her looks. Some, however, were shocked. "Jean wasn't the ripe, mature woman she could have been," says journalist France Roche. "From a distance, she looked twenty-five. Up close, she was thin and drawn, like an old lady."

Gladys Berry believes that the shape-up program—taxing enough for a healthy woman, but brutal for one in a delicate mental condition—is what pushed Jean over the brink. At any rate, Jean was never the same to her afterward.

"She was like a zombie all that summer and fall," Gladys Berry recalls. "She seemed to be going through this period of intense self-discipline, and she was terribly drugged and toned down. She'd smoke cigarette after cigarette and drink pots and pots of coffee. She was eating sparingly and sipping only wine, but it was awfully hard on her. Nothing flowed. Nothing was free about her. Sometimes I'd call her up on the phone, and she'd reply, 'I can't talk now. I'm watching the news on television.' And she'd hang up. She'd never done that before."

Raymonde Waintraub met with a similar response whenever she telephoned. "Something always prevented her from talking to you. She was always busy. Either her hairdresser was coming by or she had an errand to run or there was a taxi waiting downstairs."

"She was certainly thin and beautiful again. She'd gotten back to the image people expected of her," says Jan Berry. "But she was broken. I felt there was nothing left of her when I saw her."

Jean made an attempt to go out in public, to renew old acquaintances and show the world that Jean Seberg was still alive and attractive. But crowds panicked her. At concerts or movie premieres, she would tighten up visibly and clutch the hand of her escort as if she were a timid young girl on her first date. "She made a huge effort, given what she was capable of," says Michèle Moretti, who accompanied her occasionally. "But she was petrified of people. Deep down, I think, she knew they no longer gave a damn."

Celebrities she had once known pretended they didn't recognize her, and friends from her days with Romain turned their backs. As if to compensate for their treatment, Jean would make up stories about people she *had* seen—boasting that she'd bumped into Jean-Paul Belmondo at the airport or had just signed Louis de Funès, France's top comic, to star in a film she herself would write and direct. "I have an important rendezvous with Fidel Castro tomorrow," she told her doctor one day. "The more her stature eroded, the wilder her imagination became," he says sadly.

Almost in defiance of the polite society that shunned her, Jean drew her companions from the ranks of the Algerians in Paris, a group that has traditionally suffered second-class citizenship in France. Politically, she identified with the Third World. The Black Power movement had played itself out in the United States, and to her, the only hope for revolution lay with the Arab bloc. In one of her rare letters home, she urged her parents to put up several Iranian exchange students; they could live and sleep in Marshalltown and commute by car to the University of Iowa at Ames. Although the Sebergs had once taken in a French foreign-exchange student, they told Jean they didn't think it would work out this time. She was annoyed.

"It actually became a kind of reverse racism with her," says Jean-Pierre Rassam. "Any Algerian automatically had a mystique for her. She would sleep with them just because they were Algerian—poor, misguided blokes—not because she loved them."

She let it be known that she was on close terms with Abdul Aziz Bouteflicka, the Algerian Minister of Foreign Affairs, who liked to frequent artistic circles in Paris. She would allude to the letters and bouquets of flowers she received from him, and sometimes, after hanging up the phone, would mention in passing, "That was Bouteflicka, you know." Her friends were never sure whether or not she was fantasizing and suspected her of sending the flowers herself. It seemed obvious to them that the Algerians she did consort with were of a distinctly lower class.

"The problem with Jean was trying to figure out exactly where the truth lay. Some of what she said corresponded to reality or at least a possible reality. But she had all these extraordinary illusions, and she believed them," says Jean-Claude Messager. Then a young cinema student, Messager called Jean one day early in September and asked her if he could drop by her house and show her a scenario he'd written. The two hit it off immediately. Jean liked the sensitive, bright lad, and he was impressed by her warmth and openness. "We didn't need to say a lot to communicate with each other," Messager recalls. "She sensed a lot of things about me intuitively, and I think I understood a lot about her." To Gladys Berry, it looked very much like a mother-son relationship, and Messager tends to agree. Only, in this case the surrogate son would be his mother's keeper. Messager's initial impression deepened over the months but never changed. It was that of a profoundly lonely woman, acting out the charade of a meaningful life.

"Jean could play the role of someone who was adjusted and caught up in her projects," he muses. "During the day she'd stay closed up in her apartment and say that she was working on her songs and poems. But what she actually put down on paper—well, that was always harder to know. There was a surface frenzy to her, but she had no follow-through and was incapable of viewing things on a long-term basis. I soon realized that her days were actually very monotonous, one quite similar to another. In many respects, she was like a child who needed constant reassurance and encouragement."

Her attempts to reconstitute a respectable social life seemed marked for failure. Vony Becker recalls inviting Jean to a party that fall. "Jean arrived with two gay friends who were late picking her up. She bitched about it a lot, saying, 'I'm Jean Seberg. Nobody makes me wait.' It was just the sort of remark she never would have allowed herself to make in the past. She was all dressed in black, and I thought she looked very lovely. But early in the evening she said she didn't feel well, retired to the bedroom and slept all through the party. The next day she sent me flowers and an apology."

It was typical behavior. If Jean forced herself to attend social functions, once there she would withdraw into her shell and scarcely utter a word. She became enthusiastic, however, when she learned that Sammy Davis Jr. would be playing the Olympia, Paris' celebrated music hall, early in December, and she invited Raymonde Waintraub to go to the opening-night gala with her. Davis was a link to a time when fame had been hers, and Jean was eager to renew ties with the past. "After the concert we went to a big reception at Maxim's," Waintraub recalls. "When Sammy Davis saw her coming in, he broke away from the crowd and ran over and greeted her. She sat next to him all evening and really appeared happy for a change. I drove her home afterward, and she told me not to bother coming up to her apartment. She said Sammy was stopping by later that evening and she was just going to wait up for him. When I called her the next morning, she said, 'I fell asleep on the couch. Sammy didn't make it last night.'"

Six days later Jean and Raymonde returned to the Olympia, this time to see Liza Minnelli. Although Jean appeared to be enjoying the evening, she was uncomfortably quiet. At intermission, she allowed herself one beer. Minnelli's performance dazzled the French, and as she strode out for her curtain call, a wildly enthusiastic audience leaped up en masse to give her a standing ovation. Jean also rose to her feet, then crumpled in a faint.

"When she came to, she didn't know where she was," says Waintraub. "Everyone was staring at her. I got her back into her seat and then tried to talk to her quietly, reassuring her that everything was all right and that I'd get her home right away. She looked me in the eye and snapped, 'You talk too much. Do you know that?'

"On our way out, her legs buckled again and she collapsed to the floor. The ushers came running, but Jean waved them away. Then she refused to go home. She had a dinner date with friends in a restaurant on the Left Bank, and there was no convincing her to break it. She simply had to see them. But once we got there, she hardly opened her mouth. She sat stiff and frozen, staring at the food on her plate. That was the beginning of the problems with her leg."

In the days that followed Jean would complain that she could barely walk and would shuffle about her apartment supporting herself with a cane. Some days even the cane didn't help, and she would not get out of bed. There were those miraculous days, however, when recovery seemed total and she walked without any apparent difficulty. Doctors would submit her to a rash of tests in an attempt to pinpoint the cause. They would find nothing. Jean's friends began to believe that the numbness in her leg was entirely psychosomatic.

37

*"Somehow, insanity seems a lot less sinister
to watch in a man than in a woman, doesn't it?"*

—KIM HUNTER TO WARREN BEATTY IN *Lilith*

By the end of the year, Jean had banished all but her most tenacious friends from her life and her Moroccan lover had left her. On January 3, 1979, she phoned for a taxi and checked herself into the Villa Montsouris for observation. "She said she needed rest," says Jean-Claude Messager. "She was walking badly and had trouble sleeping. She seemed more or less normal to me, but she told me that something was wrong with her head, and she wanted the doctors to find out what it was.

"She said that Romain was accusing her of trying to get attention, and that made her furious. As far as she was concerned, she was truly ill and the doctors had an obligation to treat her. And yet there was some of the Imaginary Invalid about her. She loved to dramatize her condition in front of other people, but once they'd left, she would laugh about it. Jean had her playful side, and it was often hard to understand just what was up."

Raymonde Waintraub spotted some disturbing signs. "Jean-Claude had done a pencil sketch of Jean at Montsouris," she says. "It was a lovely portrait that caught a lot of the sadness in her eyes. Jean had pinned it to the wall of her room. When I commented on it, she said, 'I can't leave it up there. They'll steal it. They steal everything.' It was a leitmotif with her. The old sense of persecution was coming back. She was talking a lot about the FBI again. That was never a good omen."

Although she was given sedatives to calm her, Jean found the care at Montsouris to be sorely lacking. She complained that the doctors weren't concerned and didn't take her ailments seriously enough. Brusquely, on January 13, without telling anyone, she had herself transferred to Bellevue, a posh sanitarium in Meudon, on the outskirts of Paris. The expenses there can easily mount up to more than $2,000 a week—money that Jean didn't have.

Her condition deteriorated badly over the next ten days. The paralysis in her left leg became more pronounced, and she would scuff down the halls like a mechanical doll, careening up against the walls or collapsing to the floor. Despite injections to put her to sleep at night, she slept fitfully, often waking up after two or three hours. If she slept five hours in a row, she considered it a good night's rest and was thrilled. Private nurses watched over her round the clock.

Although drugs kept her in a fuzzy mental state, during the days she wrote letters feverishly. On one of Gladys Berry's visits, Jean was busy composing a message to Ingmar Bergman. "She was on a huge high and she wanted to make a film with him," Gladys recalls. "Her letter said that she knew what it was like to be lonely because she ate alone, she slept alone, she drank alone."

On another occasion Jean dashed off an urgent appeal to Bouteflicka, requesting that he free Ben Bella, the former Algerian president who had been imprisoned after his overthrow.

"Whoever or whatever happened to be around inspired her," says Messager. "She had a Swedish nurse, and that was what gave her the idea to write to Bergman. Seeing one of the Algerian orderlies go by prompted the correspondence with Bouteflicka. Everything seemed to find its way into letters."

One of the most poignant, laboriously scrawled in pencil, was dispatched to Sugar Blue, the American singer with whom Jean had occasionally collaborated on songs.

Sweet, Sugar, Sugar, I miss you so much—I'm in a nicer clinic (the phone of the clinic is 027-9000 Meudon) but my leg is paralyzed (the left one)—I use a little cane. I try not to cry, but Sugar I've really got the blues man. I tell myself I have to be stoic and accept things—it ain't easy Sugar—I think I've written a blues you may like . . . Please Sugar; come Sunday if you can—bring a harmonica if you want to—it would cheer me up a lot. It's so lonely and blue. Don't turn your back on me—at least a call, OK?

Kisses—

Blue Jean

Marshalltown was not forgotten in the flurry. She wrote to the editor of the *Times-Republican* to inform him that she was deeply chagrined to learn of the continuing prejudice against her and the black causes she had always defended. Her pain, she said, was greatly accentuated by the loss of Nina. Consequently, she would never return to the United States again, except for brief visits to see her parents.

Jean even undertook a long letter to André Malraux. Malraux had been dead for three years.

Her other preoccupation centered on the movies she would make once she was out of the clinic. One day she informed Messager that she intended to do a screen adaptation of *The Wilder Shores of Love,* the novel that had brought fame to Lesley Blanch, Gary's first wife. Shortly after, Jean's ideas changed completely, and she wanted to make a film about Paris in the early 1960s, the era of her greatest celebrity.

To her visitors, Jean seemed to be regressing to childhood. However, one of her doctors diagnosed her state as nothing more than acute loneliness and assured Messager that once Jean had had enough of playing her little game, she'd get better and return home. Yet if they were incapable of pinning down the exact nature of her psychiatric problems, the doctors did acknowledge that she was in dreadful physical shape. Her liver was damaged from drink and pills, and her vision was weak. They recommended a complete physical checkup at St. Anne, a bleak public hospital in Paris.

There were other reasons for having her transferred. Jean was a difficult patient with a history of not paying her bills. She could be temperamental with the staff, while the entourage of dropouts who visited her often caused an unseemly commotion.

On January 24 Jean was moved to St. Anne. She loathed the place and felt that she had been put on public display. Several weeks of tests were scheduled, during which time, she was informed, it would be best not to have any visitors. Jean balked and after thirty-six hours packed up and fled to the Rue du Bac apartment.

No longer content with the rituals of illness, she threw herself into a frenzy of activity. Strewing bad checks behind her, she went on an erratic shopping spree and bought a completely new wardrobe from a dress shop in the Rue du Bac. Then she bought the dress shop itself and three neighboring boutiques. (Gladys Berry would have to call the owner of the dress shop, explain the situation and have him come reclaim the clothing.)

Once again, Jean believed that the FBI was tailing her. She would telephone her friends from unlikely locales where she had taken refuge. Raymonde Waintraub had to go fetch her one evening from the shabby two-room apartment of a black orderly Jean had met at one of the clinics. "She was ranting madly that night," Waintraub says. "She was bitching about how little money she had, and the bewildered orderly didn't see in a month what she spent in a day. Then she began raving that the Iranian situation was leading to World War III, and we'd all be dead in three weeks. The next minute, she was going to take a trip to Jamaica—Romain would pay for it—and she asked if I would go along. When I said no, she started screaming and threatening to commit suicide. 'Well, then,' I said to her, 'there isn't much point in worrying about World War III, is there? Not if you're going to commit suicide.' All of a sudden she stopped talking. She smiled and looked at me with this ironic glimmer in her eyes that indicated to me that she knew perfectly well what she was doing. That was the problem with Jean all during this period. Was she really sick? How sick? Where did the acting leave off and the truth take over?"

Others were confronted with the same questions. In a burst of candor, Jean took her stories to the *International Herald Tribune*. In an interview published February 8, 1979, she stated publicly for the first time that the FBI had tried to smear her and that she had the incriminating documents in her possession. Asserting that the United States government "got my daughter and they're going to pay for it," she told reporter Jane Friedman the details of her involvement with the Panthers and confessed that if a Panther had not been the father of Nina, neither had Gary. Friedman's article read, in part:

> Miss Seberg, who said she still has contacts with Black Panther and other militant groups, said she is followed constantly in Paris. She said she received two threatening phone calls recently in which the caller identified himself as a representative of the CIA and warned that she is being watched. She said she was "shot at" in December on a Paris street. She believes that the FBI or CIA is responsible for the alleged harassment. She talked about those incidents and the alleged 1970 FBI plot partly, she said, because she fears for her life.

Friends who knew Jean's history regretted that her remarks found their way into print. Unlike Gary, who attributed most of Jean's account to insanity, they conceded some elements of truth. Slipping back and forth between illusion and reality, Jean was now living out the elusive performance she had given in *Lilith*.

Jean-Claude Messager was at Jean's apartment early in February when she received what she claimed was a phone call from Bouteflicka, responding to her letter from Bellevue and inviting her to come to Algeria for meetings. Messager was skeptical, but the following morning, after hastily packing a few clothes, Jean flew to Algiers. She spent two days there before the authorities, finding her behavior puzzling, ordered her back to France.

The absurd goings-on appear to have been Jean's attempt to prove that she still counted, that she wasn't a minor player in a show that had actually closed a decade before. But the frenzy took its toll. Shortly after her return from Algeria, Jean was discovered on the floor of her apartment by her maid. Her eyes were rolled back, and she was foaming at the mouth.

This time Jean wound up at Vaucluse Hospital in Epinay-sur-Orge. The antithesis of all the private clinics where Jean had enjoyed her creature comforts and special status as a celebrity, Vaucluse is a cheerless state mental institution, built before the turn of the century and surrounded by a high wall.

One French psychiatrist describes it as "a real snake pit."

Its patients, often destitute, belong to the ranks of the seriously deranged. There is a large percentage of alcoholics who have proved dangerous to themselves or to society at large and have been committed by police orders. The less violent patients, who are allowed to stroll in the courtyards between the stone pavilions, are the sort who will approach the rare visitor, grab him by the lapels of his coat and insist that he listen to their most improbable obsessions.

At Romain Gary's request, Gladys Berry signed Jean into the institution in mid-February. When she returned the next day to see her, Jean—lethargic and unable to talk—nodded feebly by way of recognition.

Subsequent visitors were appalled by Jean's appearance and the sorry, broken-down characters who surrounded her. Vony Becker couldn't help bursting into tears. "Jean was so frightened and didn't want to leave her room," she recalls. "She just smoked and smoked and smoked. She'd attached herself to this pathetic girl who had tripped out on drugs. At dinnertime one of the staff came and tried to get Jean to go down to eat. Suddenly Jean couldn't walk."

The drug addict, a waif named Marianne, was just one of the friends Jean made among the derelicts who had landed in Vaucluse because they had no place else to go. "I'm not loved anymore," Jean told Philippe Garrel. "These are my only friends." Eventually Jean would arrange to bring some of them back to her apartment, baptizing them "my cook," "my valet de chambre," "my chauffeur."

"Jean seemed eighty years old," Garrel says. Supporting her, he took her walking in the courtyard until the orderlies, thinking Garrel was trying to sneak her away, sent her back to her room and ordered him to leave. For Garrel, "Vaucluse might as well have been Russia," and he viewed it as part of a conspiracy to force the irrational, creative people of the world into submission.

When Raymonde Waintraub came to visit, she found Jean sprawled on her bed, dressed in a filthy nightgown stained with food that she had spilled down her front. Her eyes were half closed, and the nightgown was hiked up to reveal her legs, discolored with black-and-blue marks that were the result of her many falls. Shocked by the sight, Waintraub called Romain Gary and urged him to do something. "He refused to go to Vaucluse," she says. "He was constantly getting calls from people asking him what to do about Jean. By then they'd been divorced nearly ten years. He'd paid and paid. Finally, he'd just had enough. 'I'm an old man,' he said to me. 'I have my work to do. I don't want my son to see any of that.'"

"Romain was one of those people who need to write in order to stay alive," says Gladys Berry. "And he couldn't write while Jean was at Vaucluse. Jean would call up Diego late at night, when she couldn't sleep, and scare him half to death. At that point Romain just disassociated himself from Jean and kept Diego from her. That made Jean feel even worse. She was so vulnerable and lonely by then."

Jean remained at Vaucluse for more than a month, and her behavior varied dramatically from day to day. She could be lifeless and self-absorbed. Then, forty-eight hours later, she would be imbued with energy and purpose. Sometimes she would pity herself and beg for sympathy, but just as easily, she could console her new-found friends and urge them to stop feeling sorry for themselves.

Raymonde Waintraub braced herself for the worst on her second visit. Instead, she found Jean totally transformed. Her hair was neatly combed, her face made up, and she radiated chic and confidence. She was also walking. The contrast with the bruised woman in the wretched nightgown was so complete that Waintraub asked herself afterward, "What was real? The filth and the paralysis? Or the recovery?

"I came to believe that Jean played the madwoman up to the point where she realized that she might get trapped in it," she says. "Once she had decided the experiment had gone far enough, she pulled back. There was so much theater in all of it. Ever since *Lilith,* Jean had been fascinated by madness. Months after she got out of Vaucluse, she talked about going back and making a film with the patients—which told me that she'd had a certain perspective on it all along."

"Oh, she called it the looney bin. She knew," Gladys Berry agrees. "When she started walking again, I asked Jean how she was able to do it. She looked at me and said, 'Will power. The doctors say I'm cured now.' She had just snapped out of it and had reverted to being in charge."

Reluctantly, hospital officials allowed Jean to leave Vaucluse in mid-March. A few attempts were made to locate a private clinic where she could continue her recovery. Knowing her history of unpaid bills, none would accept her. So Vony Becker drove her and several of her new companions from Vaucluse back to the Rue du Bac.

One of Jean's first acts upon returning home was to offer her services to "SOS Amitiés" (SOS Friendships). The organization maintains a telephone hotline in Paris. People who are in trouble or feeling suicidal can dial a given number at any hour and talk with a sympathetic listener. Jean volunteered to be one of those listeners.

"It was really an instance of the drowning trying to save the drowning," Waintraub comments.

38

"Nothing was protecting her—not even her own skin."

—A FRIEND

The destructive habits recommenced. During the day Jean shut herself up in the apartment and frequently stayed in bed until noon. Then, seized by a sudden necessity, she would bolt into the street and turn up on a friend's doorstep, spouting tales of wild chases. Sometimes she would take a taxi to the airport, saying she had important people to see off or welcome.

Evenings she usually went to a restaurant for a late dinner and then drifted on to a night club or a bar, where her stories seemed no more unlikely than those of the customer at the next table.

One of her haunts was La Medina, a Moroccan restaurant on the Avenue Trudaine, probably a favorite less for the quality of the food, which was mediocre, than for its owner, a swarthy Algerian named Kader Hamadi. She had met Kader on one of her solitary visits to the Keur Samba, a night club near the Champs Elysées named for its Senegalese proprietor. With an irony that was lost on him, she had bantered, "You are irritating me because you don't know who I am! I am Jean Seberg, the beautiful American actress." They had spent the evening drinking and dancing, and Jean had immediately given him a nickname, "Mes Yeux" (My Eyes). In a picture they had taken of themselves that night, Jean is hollow-cheeked and drawn—a veritable phantom.

Jean and Hamadi had a sporadic affair during the spring of 1979, although Jean appears to have done most of the pursuing. The restaurant owner has a handful of notes to show for the relationship. In them, Jean complains about being stood up once again or urges him to call her by a certain hour "without fail this time!" Workers in the restaurant say Jean would often burst into the kitchen, calling out, "Where is he? Where is Monsieur Godot?" and then tear out again, strewing messages behind her.

If Hamadi appreciated the publicity Jean brought to his struggling restaurant, he didn't always approve of her seedy entourage. "One night the cops came in looking for drugs," he recalls. "Jean was seated at a table in the back with six of her friends. One of them passed out and fell over backwards in his chair. In front of everybody, Jean got down on the floor and started giving him mouth-to-mouth resuscitation.

"Some evenings she would lie down on the floor herself and refuse to budge at closing time. She swore she wasn't drinking, but she cheated and snitched drinks behind your back. She'd go into the john, and when she returned, she'd be completely zonked. It was sad, because when she was sober she was very sweet. She had these dreams about us going to Algeria together. I don't know. Maybe, if she could have gotten back on her feet . . . I guess I wasn't tough enough with her . . . But, monsieur, I had a business to run. I finally had to kick her out of here."

The blond hostess at La Medina, who has heard all the stories, nods sadly and says, "Yes, but she was a good kid just the same."

If Kader Hamadi eventually wanted nothing to do with Jean, his nephew Ahmed Hasni was of another mind. In interviews he later gave to the French press, Hasni claimed to be twenty-nine years old and, alternately, a professional soccer player, an actor who had made six films (two of them in England) or the son of a family of rich Algerian mechants. On a plane going from Geneva to Paris, he said, Jean had tried to guess his nationality. It had been a case of love at first sight.

In fact, his background was considerably less romantic. One of six children whose mother manages a steambath in Oran,

Hasni had run away to France and kicked around Paris for a year before encountering Jean Seberg at La Medina in April of 1979. Although he liked to see himself as a potential movie idol, his features were massive and his high-pitched voice seemed incongruous coming from his hulking frame. According to his uncle, Hasni had altered the birth date on his passport, changing "1960" to "1950" and thereby adding ten years to his age. Whenever he found himself without a meal or a place to sleep, he would drop by La Medina and prevail upon his uncle's generosity. Hasni's mother disapproved of her son's Parisian life style. "Let him go hungry and he'll come home," she once told Hamadi.

Hasni had other visions for the future. Jean Seberg extended the promise of an easier life. Shortly after meeting her, he moved into the Rue du Bac apartment. Kader Hamadi was irate. "In my family, the men do not sleep with the same woman," he notes sternly.

Hasni was more than Jean's lover. He was her round-the-clock keeper and disciplinarian. "Jean suffered terribly from loneliness, and she needed someone twenty-four hours a day," says Jean-Claude Messager. "At least, Ahmed had that going for him. He was a real gorilla. He made all the decisions and screened her visitors. He was fascinated by Jean. He'd say that she was a big star and should be earning more money than Alain Delon. He was going to be her manager, although it seemed more like hustling to me.

"At first, though, he appeared to be a positive influence. Jean quit drinking and taking pills, except for her sleeping pills. She was a lot calmer, and she was no longer trying to get in touch with the first person who crossed her mind."

With her strong sympathies for the Arab world, Jean was eager to believe Hasni when he talked about his prominent political connections in Algeria. At home she called him "Sheriff," but she introduced him to others as "the cousin of Bouteflicka."

Yet it was obvious that he was without occupation. He lounged around the apartment all day in his pajamas, often not bothering to change when people dropped by. "Shhhhh! The desert is sleeping," Jean whispered to a friend who came by late one afternoon. Then she gestured toward the bedroom, where Hasni still dozed.

At the same time, she cast him as one of the unfortunate outsiders adrift, like herself, in a racist society. "We two—we no longer have any friends in life," Hasni wrote across Jean's favorite snapshot of them. They talked about leaving Paris altogether and starting anew in another country—Spain or Algeria.

In hopes of bringing in some money, Jean worked haphazardly on her memoirs, but they rambled from subject to subject, and her writing was heavy with clichés. She wrote that, during her childhood, a ray of sun had struck her while she sat under a weeping willow, convincing her of her unique destiny. Recounting the burial of Nina, she claimed that an elderly Indian woman from the Tama reservation had counseled gravely, "Jean, don't judge another man until you have walked twenty miles in his moccasins." In a curious lapse of memory, she credited John Maddox, her boyfriend from the Priscilla Beach Theater, with pulling her from the burning pyre during the filming of *St. Joan*.

Hasni kept what little money they had, doling out a small amount to Jean now and then. When angered, he would lock her out of the apartment, and Jean would have to retreat to the house of Aki Lehman, her long-ago friend who had recently moved next door.

"Sometimes he beats me," Jean confessed to Frédéric Mitterand. "I'm covered with black-and-blue marks. But I love him."

Despite her new liaison, she had not forsaken her companions at Vaucluse and made a point of visiting them periodically. Jean looked on it as "doing a little counseling."

An American artist went along with her one day in May. "Jean was wearing a ratty coat, her clothes were rumpled, and her hair was a strange reddish-orange color. For about an hour and a half she walked around the grounds, talking to these broken-down people. One of them thought he was Richard Nixon. You got the feeling that it was a home away from home for her. On the way back, she told me all about Nina and how the FBI had come after her. 'The agents came into my room at the hospital,' she said. 'They shook me and shook me until my baby fell out.'"

Money was a perpetual source of worry for her. On occasion she would actually call up friends and beg them to give her some food. One day she went out to the Studios de Billancourt, where Costa-Gavras was editing his latest film, *Clair de Femme*. Since the film was adopted from Romain Gary's novel of the same name and Costa-Gavras had been a friend in the past, Jean thought she would demonstrate her interest in the project. Over lunch, she casually informed the director that she was reduced to eating cat food. Costa-Gavras was dumbstruck.

Gladys Berry knew that Jean was on hard times and suggested, one night in May, that Jean throw a dinner party and ask each of her guests to bring a different dish. "I brought a chicken," Gladys recalls. "Jean snatched it from me and wanted to hide it behind the curtains. 'Ahmed steals everything,' she said. Then she told me that Fidel Castro and Daniel Cohn-Bendit (the radical leader of the 1968 student revolt) were coming for dinner. Also a cook from Maxim's, who turned out to be a fellow patient. Eventually she got around to cooking a pot of rice. She was giddy and gay all evening long. And completely mad."

A measure of Jean's fantasies is provided by a letter she wrote to Dean Reed at the end of May. Reed had been an actor with her in Paton Price's class at Columbia and had gone on to pursue his career in East Germany. He had plans to make a film with Yassir Arafat and the PLO and had been in contact with Jean about playing one of the roles.

> Don't hit me [Jean's letter began]. I'm getting married. It's a secret. You'll really like the man. His name is Hasni Ahmed Sheriff Bouteflicka, a professional football player from Oran, Algeria, cousin of my friend Abdul Aziz Bouteflicka, Minister of State. Sheriff is a husky Arab version of Montgomery Clift—sensitive, kind of heart, great charm . . .
>
> Lunched with Costa-Gavras yesterday at the studio. He's fine, but tired, "synching" his new film *Clair de Femme* (from a book by Romain Gary). It's a light love story—nice change for Costa.
>
> I'm leaving Paris—will come back for work. We plan to live in

Barcelona—it's Paris 20 years ago, whereas Paris is now aggression, rudeness, expense, and xenophobic racism. Plus drugs, drugs, drugs . . . They've all discovered cocaine. Sheriff has all the contacts we need in the Arab world to do the film for Arafat. He was with him at President Boumedienne's funeral.

Dig this—I was invited to Algeria by Abdul Aziz Bouteflicka and expelled two days later as a Black Panther! No way to make them understand that I left the Panthers in 1969 and have my letter of resignation to prove it. Oh well . . . !

Let's get this Palestinian film going!

On the last day of May, the Reverend Thomas E. Duggan, the roly-poly minister of the American Church in Paris, presided over a brief exchange of vows between Jean and Ahmed Hasni. Since Jean was still married to Dennis Berry, the ceremony carried no legal weight. Nonetheless, Jean considered Ahmed her husband and dreamed of having another child.

She had a doctor remove her birth-control device and began to redecorate one of the rooms in her apartment as a nursery, even though she was not sure she'd stay on in Paris. In one of the rare interviews she gave shortly before her death, she admitted, "Each time I get married, I'm very tempted to have a child. I would like to found a family. When I'm terribly depressed, I go down to the park and sit and watch the children. That's worth all the tranquilizers in the world. For a long time, because of the loss of my daughter, I ran away from life. Now I want to run toward it. With a little luck, I hope to be a grandmother before I'm fifty."

In the last week of June, Jean entered the Marignan Clinic because of what Hasni later told the press was a miscarriage. "He really wanted to believe that he had fathered a child by Jean," says Messager. But Jean confided to Raymonde Waintraub that it had been nothing more than a gynecological infection. Jean also informed Raymonde that she would be selling her apartment and moving to another country once she got out of the clinic.

"She showed me a letter she'd written—I don't know who it was for—but in it she said that she was leaving France forever. The country had let her down, just as America had let her down. All her friends had abandoned her. And she'd underlined that sentence. She had always been a woman in search of a man. But now, she seemed to be a woman in search of a country, too."

Although Jean had not made a motion picture in more than three years, Georges de Beauregard, the producer of *Breathless, The Road to Corinth* and *The Line of Demarcation,* still thought fondly of her and threw out what was the last lifeline. He offered her a role in *La Légion Saute sur Kolwezi (The Legion Parachutes into Kolwezi).* To be directed by Raoul Coutard, the cameraman on *Breathless,* the adventure film was based on an actual mission by the French Foreign Legion, which had been called upon to rescue the European population in the town of Kolwezi, Zaïre, after it was overrun by rebels in May 1978. The movie would be shot on location in Guyana that August and then finish up the following month in France. Jean was to play the courageous wife of a Belgian mining engineer.

Repeated warnings from his colleagues about Jean's mental fragility didn't discourage De Beauregard. "Jean had always been one of my friends," he says. "She had a lot of class."

Jean wavered. The film, which glorified the French military, was decidedly right-wing in its outlook. On the other hand, she would be working with people she knew, and the role was not difficult. Finally, she signed for nine days of filming at 10,000 francs (about $2,000) a day. Olga Horstig-Primuz disassociated herself from the project and refused to draw up the contract. "I knew Jean wouldn't finish the film," she says.

Jean asked to be paid in cash. After her shopping spree in February, her bank accounts had been closed and her check-writing privileges suspended.

Early in July, with Hasni's encouragement, Jean sold the apartment on the Rue du Bac, saying, "It has too many memories." In her haste, she accepted an offer for far less than it was worth. But Hasni had notions of starting a business, maybe a restaurant, in Barcelona, and she needed some quick funds. She also sold several of her oil paintings. The money went into a briefcase, which Hasni kept with him at all times. The rest of her possessions were rapidly packed away in boxes and stored with a Moroccan kitchen worker Jean knew from Bellevue.

To her friends, she announced that she and Hasni were taking a vacation in Spain and would scout out business properties there, but she would come back briefly for her new film. As they loaded up her car, they looked like any happy couple preparing for a holiday. Swallowing the misgivings that Hasni inspired in him, Jean-Claude Messager saw them off—Jean at the wheel, Hasni and his briefcase beside her. "Jean was calm and coherent," he says. "She had her script with her. For some reason, I thought it might work out all right. I told myself I didn't have to worry about her for a while."

Very quickly, the vacation turned bitter. Hasni subsequently claimed that they had eventually made their way to a hotel in Palma, Majorca. There, after a lover's spat, Jean had left him.

More ominous doings were suggested by one of Jean's friends in nearby Puerto Andraitx. The wife of a prominent architect, she later told *France-Soir* that one night Jean had shown up alone "as if she were running from some danger she didn't dare confide in me. She seemed terrorized. Safe at my place, she quickly reverted to the normal, warm, well-balanced woman I had always known. The menace that she seemed to feel hovering over her lessened. But all during her stay, the sadness and anguish never left her. When she departed to make her film, I had the impression I would never see her again."

A petrified Jean telephoned De Beauregard from Spain to inform him that she had run away from Hasni and needed a place to hide in Paris. "She said that Hasni had all her money," De Beauregard remembers. "She told me he was mistreating her and she could no longer reason with him."

De Beauregard put her up secretly at the Hôtel Régina on the Place des Pyramides, alerted the police to her whereabouts, but feigned ignorance with everyone else. Hasni arrived in Paris soon after and frantically started calling on all Jean's acquaintances, trying to locate her. Jan Berry was at her mother's house one Saturday when Hasni burst in.

"Where is she?" he blurted. "She's disappeared. There's eleven million francs in the car. The car has disappeared. What am I going to do? I can't stand it."

"I tried to talk to him because he was really in bad shape and

I felt sorry for him," says Berry. "He explained that all he had wanted to do was make love one night. Jean hadn't, and they'd quarreled. Jean had fled to a friend's house. Nobody would tell him anything now. He was an extremely young, immature man whose lover had left him. But his response was so extreme. He said that if he found Jean with someone else, he was going to burn her up. He'd burn them both up. He had that classic Arab macho mentality. He kept saying, 'Jean Seberg—she's my wife. My wife!' I realized after a while that anything I said in reply was totally lost on him. I can't tell you how nuts it was."

Gladys Berry tried to persuade Hasni that if Jean wanted to be free, maybe it was better to let her be free.

"No, she's done that to others. She's not going to do it to me," he objected.

Hasni also went to the police to signal Jean's disappearance and then telephoned Gladys Berry every day to complain that they weren't expending any effort to find her.

Jean stayed out of sight for several days. Early on the morning of August 3, De Beauregard picked her up in the bar of the hotel. She was impeccably groomed and handsomely dressed, and the producer noted that she looked like the movie star she had once been. He then drove her to Roissy Airport and put her on the eight-hour flight to Guyana.

Jean was scheduled for only one day of filming outside the compound that represented the living quarters of the Belgian population in Kolwezi. That weekend she telephoned De Beauregard long distance and repeated that she didn't want to live with Hasni on her return. Would the producer locate an apartment for her? De Beauregard found a small furnished apartment that rented by the week and once again apprised the police of the situation.

No longer capable of fending for herself, Jean came back to Paris the following Tuesday. She had no further work on the film until September 6. De Beauregard took her to the new lodgings and then called her the next morning to make sure she was all right. Jean assured him that she was.

"I could tell from the sound of her voice that he was there," De Beauregard says. "Hasni had found her."

"Jean was really scared silly of Ahmed," says Gladys

Berry, "and she was completely worn down. But when she returned from Guyana, she called him up to get her memoirs back. Despite all that had happened to her, she still had this faith in the goodness of people, and she agreed to see him one more time. By then, she was trapped. He wouldn't let her go. She told me later, 'If it hadn't been for the movie, I would have gone to Marshalltown.'"

The events of the last few weeks of Jean's life are cloudy. Hasni later painted a dismal picture for the press. He claimed that on three occasions after he moved back in with her, Jean had tried to throw herself from the window. "The first two times, I was away," he explained. "Jean confessed it to me when I came back. The third time, I was packing our suitcases to move to an apartment I had taken at 125 Rue de Longchamps. It was a temporary solution while we waited for Jean to finish her film. Afterward we were going to go to Algeria forever. While I was packing I heard a noise in the next room. I ran to her. She had already climbed up on the balustrade."

Each time, he said, he reprimanded her severely, and Jean hung her head like a naughty child. Sometimes she appeared to be so absorbed in her bleak thoughts that Hasni could see her temples throb, and he feared that her head would actually burst.

Then, on August 18, he said she had tried to throw herself before an oncoming subway train in the Montparnasse station. "Jean told me about it," he explained. In the absence of any official accounts of the suicide attempt, Jean's friends were dubious. "She might have gotten dizzy and fallen accidentally," says one. "But they were both full of stories."

Under Hasni's ever more watchful eyes, Jean spent her final days in the second-floor studio apartment on the Rue de Longchamps. A row of bushes and small trees just outside the window protected it from the noise of the street, although passers-by are few in August. Hasni was present at the last interview of her life, which Jean gave to sculptor-writer José Gerson. While Hasni sat quietly at her side, Jean reminisced about her career. Whenever she tried to light a cigarette, he took it from her mouth and broke it in two. "Every day, he is stricter and stricter with me," Jean said, laughing wearily.

It was a strange interview. Jean expressed her optimism for the future and her concern about the proliferation of nuclear weapons. "I personally know the man in France who will push the red button if it's necessary," she confided. "He's a friend of mine!"

And yet some of the old Jean Seberg, gentle and trusting, shone through. She advised women everywhere: "Live, emancipate yourselves, love your children. Don't think that being feminist means being aggressive, or hysterical, or masculine. Enjoy your femininity."

And then she cited a poem that she and Hasni had written together, a poem to the year 2000, when all would be peace and harmony.

The evening of August 29, Jean and Ahmed went out to the movies. "Just like ordinary people," Hasni said. "That's what Jean wanted—to live like everybody else."

39

"Between a successful career and the adventure of life, I chose the adventure of life."

—JEAN SEBERG

The movie they selected was *Clair de Femme,* Romain Gary's account of a middle-aged man whose wife is dying of cancer and who takes his first, tentative steps toward the future with another woman. Jean was despondent when she left the movie theater. "In a way, it was the story of Jean and Romain's life," said Ahmed Hasni. "The memories added to her depression."

Clair de Femme had turned out to be a big success for Gary (as *Birds in Peru* and *Kill* had not) and for director Costa-Gavras, who had once been Jean's close friend but had never cast her in a movie. In a role that Jean could have played—wanted to play, in fact—Romy Schneider had triumphed. Once again, Jean felt excluded.

"That film had to remind her of better times with Romain Gary," Betty Desouches speculates. "Then having to return to a studio apartment with an individual she had come to loathe—well, I'm sure Jean realized how far she'd fallen."

Jean's depression had not lifted by the time she went to bed. Usually she took several sleeping pills before retiring. This night, apparently, she passed them up.

Much later Hasni would recount a curious anecdote about his last evening with Jean. Just after he'd switched off the light and Jean had begun to drift off, a cat leaped into the apartment through an open window that faced the garden.

"It jumped onto a table," Hasni said. "I could only see its phosphorescent eyes in the dark. I turned the light back on and said to Jean, 'Did you see that black cat?' Jean didn't just get up. She lunged out of bed and ran to caress it. All of a sudden, the animal disappeared."

He then explained that "in my country, there are birds as black as crows. Whenever they perch on the roof of a house and caw seven times in a row, it is said that someone in that house has only seven days to live."

Jean had only a few hours. How they unfolded remains a mystery. Early on the morning of August 30, Hasni alerted the police that Jean was missing. They undertook a quick check of the area's clinics and hospitals, and when that proved fruitless, a country-wide alert was put out for her car.

Apparently Jean had got up sometime before six that morning. Wrapping herself only in a blanket, she collected her car keys, two months' worth of barbiturates that had recently been renewed by her pharmacist, and a bottle of mineral water. While Hasni slept on, she tiptoed out of the apartment, got in her Renault and drove it just around the corner to the Rue du Général Appert. She parked it and climbed into the back seat. Then, curling up on the floor, she swallowed the pills, pulled the blanket over her head and waited to die.

That was the story the Paris newspapers printed once the Renault was finally discovered ten days later at dusk on September 8. The suicide note, not to mention Jean's long history of psychiatric problems and suicide attempts, seemed to confirm it. So did the initial autopsy report, which concluded that death had resulted from an overdose of barbiturates and noted the absence of any bruises or contusions that might have indicated a violent struggle. And yet there was always more to Jean Seberg than seemed apparent.

On September 10 Romain Gary held a press conference in the offices of his publisher, Gallimard. His eyes were rimmed with red, and his hands trembled visibly. In a voice breaking with emotion, he declared to his audience, "It isn't *Clair de Femme,* a film that has nothing to do with the life of Jean Seberg, that is the indirect cause of the death of my son's mother. It is the FBI. Jean Seberg was destroyed by the FBI."

Producing documents from Jean's FBI file to support his accusation, he revealed the 1970 smear campaign. Not only had the FBI's lies been responsible for the death of Nina; just as surely, he said, they had killed Jean nine years later. "When an important American magazine published the rumor launched by the FBI, Jean became like a crazed woman. She never got over the calumny, and that's why she lost her child at birth," he explained. "She wanted the child to be buried in a glass coffin in order to prove that it was white. From then on, she went from one psychiatric clinic to another, from one suicide attempt to another. She tried to kill herself seven times, usually on the anniversary of her little girl's birth.

"From 1961 to 1969 I lived night and day with a perfectly normal woman—neurotic, perhaps—a movie star has fragile nerves—but healthy. After this incident, she became psychotic. . . . She was obsessed by this dead child."

Throughout the press conference, Diego sat silently at his father's side, occasionally brushing back his long dark hair.

Gary's accusations made bigger headlines than Jean's death. In newspapers across the world, a woman who had been forgotten as a movie star briefly re-emerged as a martyr— "St. Jean," burned at the stake for her ideals by J. Edgar Hoover's henchmen.

Some of Jean's friends agreed with Mylene Demongeot, who thought that Gary's press conference was "a gallant effort to rehabilitate the mother in the son's eyes." Others, however, judged it crass and exploitative. "It was a press conference to vindicate Romain Gary," says one. "Here he'd refused to let his son visit Jean at Vaucluse. Then he turned right around and had Diego sit at his side, before the TV cameras and all the newspaper reporters. Well, it wasn't right, that's all."

Without condoning the actions of the FBI, most of them dismissed Gary's charges. "The FBI was just the catchall explanation for Jean's problems," says an actress. "I really don't know how Gary could say those things. We all knew her. We saw where her life was heading."

"I owed it to Jean," Gary said later, defending himself. "She had asked me that if anything happened to her—she thought she might be killed—I was to produce these documents. Besides, my son asked for it, too. Now I'm bloody happy I did it. I am at peace with myself because I did manage to set the record straight and her image will forever remain very pure." Nonetheless, afterward Gary refused to grant any further interviews about Jean Seberg. "I have spent several years in hell and have no intention of getting back there even for a short visit," he told one reporter. "My commitment is first and last to my son. That means silence."

Jean would not be buried in "the fourth most beautiful cemetery in the world," as she had once predicted. Her final resting place was Montparnasse Cemetery in Paris, under an unadorned stone slab that reads simply JEAN SEBERG 1938–1979, in contrast to the elaborate monuments on either side.

About a hundred people gathered in the lingering summer sunlight on September 14 for the funeral service. Jean's three husbands were present, as was Ahmed Hasni. Standing discreetly in the back of the crowd was Jean-Paul Belmondo. Diego held a bouquet of flowers in his hands.

Before long, dozens of gawkers and curiosity seekers had swollen the ranks, turning the simple ceremony into what Yves Benneyton described as "pure Fellini." Photographers jostled the mourners aside to get exclusive shots, and the constant click of the cameras provided a surrealistic counterpoint to the murmured prayers. Some of Jean's friends complained audibly about the presence of Hasni in the front row, while others asked, "Who is he?" "Where does he come from?" At the end of the brief service, each of Jean's husbands laid a single rose on her mahogany coffin. Diego followed suit, and one photographer, in his eagerness to record the moment, crouched down on the edge of the grave.

The Seberg family attended a memorial service held the same day at Trinity Lutheran Church in Marshalltown. A large basket of chrysanthemums sat next to the lectern. Beside it stood a black-and-white photograph of Jean as St. Joan. The picture had been taken more than twenty years earlier by the local portrait photographer in the basement of his studio on Main Street. Prophetically, he had entitled the work "St. Joan in Despair."

The Reverend Warren Johnson, a tall, craggy minister, praised Jean's ideals and her boundless acts of generosity and tried to tell what he called "the other side of the story." Although his remarks were meant to be comforting, his strong, rolling delivery had the rigor of nineteenth-century church oratory.

In the weeks that followed, the Paris police would wrestle with doubts about Jean's suicide. The detailed autopsy report had revealed an alarmingly high percentage of alcohol in Jean's bloodstream—nearly 8 percent per liter of blood. Except in the most hardened drinkers, 6 percent usually induces coma. In such a state of intoxication, the police wondered, how had Jean been able to drive? No liquor bottles were discovered in the Renault, ruling out the possibility that she had consumed the alcohol once she'd parked the car. Had she gone elsewhere first? Draped in a blanket as she was, it seemed unlikely. The press speculated that possibly someone had driven her to the Rue du Général Appert and simply abandoned her. There was yet another disturbing detail. In a search of the apartment on the Rue de Longchamps, the police discovered a suitcase filled with money, Jean's driver's license, which she had reported lost several months before, and her eyeglasses. Without her glasses, all her friends confirmed, she was incapable of driving an automobile.

Nearly ten months after her disappearance, the inquest into the death of Jean Seberg was reopened by the Public Prosecutor's Office of the Paris Tribunal. On the orders of Judge Guy Joly, charges were drawn up in the name of Romain Gary and filed against "persons unknown" for failure to assist a person in danger. What the charges implied was that someone may actually have stood by and watched as Jean Seberg took her own life. Investigators requestioned many of her friends and acquaintances about her final days. After a long search Ahmed Hasni was located by the police, grilled and eventually released.

Some people believe that the absence of any hard answers about Jean's death came to haunt sixty-six-year-old Romain Gary. Neighbors said that he seemed to age visibly from one month to the next. His walk had lost its spring, and his hair had gone almost totally gray. For weeks on end he would closet himself in the Rue du Bac apartment, keeping the curtains drawn even on sunny days. He was said to be writing, but according to one acquaintance, writing no longer appeared to sustain him through his depressions, as it had in the past.

Occasionally he would dine at the Brasserie Lipp, his favorite restaurant. But if he entered "like a seigneur," according to one witness, he left "like a beggar," looking frail and distracted.

The mystery of Jean's death was still intact by December 1980, but with the passage of time, the actual details appeared less important to her friends. "If they are ever known, they will be messy and squalid," says Betty Desouches. "There was no high drama left in Jean's life." The real tragedy, Desouches thought, had occurred years before, when a fresh-faced girl from Iowa had set out to be a movie star.

Winter settled over Paris and the late afternoon light was milky-gray. On December 2, Romain Gary walked into his bedroom, lay down on his back, stuck a Smith & Wesson .38 in his mouth and pulled the trigger. A note was found at the foot of his bed, but lest it be overlooked, Gary had taken the precaution beforehand of sending a copy to his publisher.

"No connection with Jean Seberg," it read. "Lovers of broken hearts are kindly asked to look elsewhere." Recognizing that some would view his act as the result of a nervous breakdown, Gary wrote: "Then it must be added that [the breakdown] has been going on since I reached my manhood and has not prevented me from successfully carrying out my literary endeavors. Why then? Perhaps one should look for the answer in the title of my autobiography, *The Night Will Be Calm,* and in the last words of my last novel. . . . 'I have said all I have to say.'"

The *Times-Republican* carried an AP report of Gary's suicide. In Marshalltown, Gary was famous primarily because he was Jean's former husband. There, his death was seen as yet another awful extension of the Jean Seberg story, a story that had long since gone beyond the town's capacity to understand.

In some of Marshalltown's churches, God is hard, but in none of them is He malevolent. "Things," said one weather-beaten resident, stroking his chin, "just aren't supposed to turn out this way."

Epilogue

The Forequarter Restaurant is just one of many nondescript shingle-and-cinderblock buildings located south of Marshalltown on Highway 30, which runs east and west and bisects the state of Iowa into two almost equal portions. The banquet room at the back would be just as nondescript were it not for a few old farm implements suspended from the wall in a half-hearted attempt to relieve the tan-and-brown color scheme.

It is safe to say, however, that the twenty high school students who had gathered there at six o'clock on May 22, 1980, probably didn't notice the décor. Members of Masque and Dagger, Marshalltown High School's drama club, they were in the midst of their annual banquet, a $6.50 meal (25 cents for dues) that consisted of fried chicken, string beans, corn, baked potatoes, and all the milk they could drink.

Drama activities are still eclipsed in Marshalltown by athletics. The Bobcats basketball team remains the local pride. When the town put up a new high school a few years back, a fancy gym got built. But somehow no auditorium. So there was something almost incidental about the banquet that night, although it was hardly incidental in the lives of the twenty students.

In fact, Patty Tiffany, an eighteen-year-old graduating senior, had devoted most of the day to baking a chocolate cake for dessert. Her first try had fallen flat, but the second one had paid off. And the red, yellow and blue sour cream frosting commemorated the club's milestones that year—the two-day field trip to the Tyrone Guthrie Theater in Minneapolis, the variety show and the production of *The Rainmaker*.

The Rainmaker had turned out to be a big spring success and had pulled nearly three hundred spectators a night for three nights to the Martha Ellen Tye Playhouse in the community center. Patty had played the role of Lizzie, a love-starved Mid-

379

western spinster. Actually, she'd played it for one performance. Kris Hoelscher, the willowy redhead at the end of the banquet table, got to play it the other two.

Most of the drama students felt that either Patty or Kris would win the Jean Seberg Award that night. If Patty was the go-getter—she'd just thrown herself into the role—Kris had an otherworldliness that seemed to mark her as an actress. Maybe it was the way she tossed back her long red hair or the wry detachment in her eyes. Something about her presence suggested that she was passing through Marshalltown, not that she'd spent her lifetime there.

Few of the younger generation in the area know who Jean Seberg was. Sometimes her movies play on television. But not often. "I heard there was an actress from here," admitted Kris Hoelscher. "So I asked my mother about her once. She said, 'Oh, yes, Jean Seberg played Joan of Arc and some other things. But she never amounted to too much.' It was a pretty long time ago. I guess my mother read about her in the papers."

For all that, the Jean Seberg Award is still the major honor discerned by Masque and Dagger. "I feel it's sort of like an Academy Award" is the way one member put it. Earlier in the week the members of the club had met to decide by secret ballot which of the four graduating seniors would receive the memorial certificate. The original plaque has been missing for some years.

Lots of awards were distributed, so practically no one went home empty-handed, even if it was only with a harlequin mask or a pin or one of the poems that Patty Tiffany had composed while she was waiting for her cake to bake. The presentations were alternately earnest and silly, the way well-brought-up adolescents often are when they're trying to be adult. The Jean Seberg Award was saved for last.

Tom Owens, a serious-looking young man in a plaid sports jacket, was there to announce it. As the previous year's winner, he'd made a special effort to return for the banquet, although returning in this case meant driving the few miles from Marshalltown Junior College, where he was majoring in journalism. Gravely, he opened the envelope and said, "The winner is . . . Kris Hoelscher."

A collective shriek—not so much of surprise as of sheer relief—went up. Kris threw her hands to her face and then floated forward to receive her certificate. Because she is a tall girl, she had to bend over to hug Tom Owens, and that provoked a few giggles along with the applause.

"Jean Seberg was able to try to achieve her goals," she said, fumbling for the right words. "And, well, this award gives me confidence in myself to try too."

If Patty Tiffany was disappointed, there was no telling from the vigor of her applause or the shining look of belief—in her friends, in the club, maybe in the sheer bountifulness of the future—that lit up her round face.

Patty later confessed that she'd only seen one of Jean Seberg's movies when she was in the second grade and she couldn't remember which one. She thought that some of her relatives owned the Seberg drugstore over on 13th Street. But the Seberg Award—that was something else. She knew it mattered ever since her best friend had won it three years ago. Her best friend was just one of the most outstanding people she'd ever met.

"You see, the award is for someone who has worked very hard all through high school," she explained. "She has to be exceptional in drama and should want to go into the theater, like Kris does. But the most important thing of all, I guess, is that she's really got to be interested in people."

And before long, because this was graduation week in Marshalltown, the leather chairs had been pushed askew and the students had scattered to other activities. The banquet room was empty and a lot drabber without the silvery laughter. A few crumbs, flecked with yellow and red frosting, were all that was left of Patty Tiffany's cake.

Outside, the sun had set. But the countryside was still light, with that pure white light that emanates from halos and sometimes from neon signs. A truck or two rumbled down Highway 30. The fields on either side had budded green only a few days before. In that pure white light, they seemed to undulate like a soft green carpet.

Index

About the Author

DAVID RICHARDS has been the drama critic of the Washington *Star* since 1970. He holds degrees in French as well as speech and drama from Occidental College, Middlebury College, Catholic University and the Sorbonne. He has taught at Howard University, worked for the Voice of America, written for numerous publications and acted professionally. He served for two years in the Peace Corps in Africa.